AUGUSTINE'S
CITY OF GOD

A READER'S GUIDE

Gerard O'Daly

D0142541

CLARENDON PRESS · OXFORD
1999

Oxford University Press, Great Clarendon Street, Oxford OX2 6DP

Oxford New York

Athens Auckland Bangkok Bogotá Buenos Aires Calcutta
Cape Town Chennai Dar es Salaam Delhi Florence Hong Kong Istanbul
Karachi Kuala Lumpur Madrid Melbourne Mexico City Mumbai
Nairobi Paris São Paolo Singapore Taipei Tokyo Toronto Warsaw
and associated companies in
Berlin Ibadan

Oxford is a registered trade mark of Oxford University Press

Published in the United States
by Oxford University Press Inc., New York

© Gerard O'Daly 1999

British Library Cataloguing in Publication Data
Data available

Library of Congress Cataloging in Publication Data
Augustine's City of God: a reader's guide/Gerard O'Daly.
Includes bibliographical references and index.
1. Augustine, Saint, Bishop of Hippo. De civitate Dei.
2. Kingdom of God. 3. Apologetics. I. Title
BR65.A65O33   239'.3–dc21   98-30960
ISBN 0–19–826354–6

1 3 5 7 9 10 8 6 4 2

Typeset by J&L Composition Ltd, Filey, North Yorkshire
Printed in Great Britain on acid-free paper by
Biddles Ltd, Guildford and King's Lynn

Preface

The *City of God* is the most influential of Augustine's works, but there is no comprehensive modern guide to it in any language. My book provides a detailed yet accessible reading of Augustine's vast and complex masterpiece. I have written it bearing in mind that most of Augustine's readers are not specialists, but that he is consulted by students of late antiquity, historians, theologians, philosophers, medievalists, Renaissance scholars, interpreters of art and iconography, and many more. Therefore all the Latin cited is translated, and essential information about the principal features of Augustine's thought is given, with copious references to more detailed studies. The *City of God* has a wide-ranging scope, embracing cosmology, psychology, political thought, polemic, Christian apologetic, theory of history, biblical interpretation, and apocalyptic themes. To understand this work is to appreciate the ways in which Augustine's ideas are interrelated, and there is no clearer evidence of the formative role that he has played in the history of the Christian West.

Chapters 1–5 elucidate the early fifth-century political, social, literary, and religious background to the *City of God*, and the structure of the work. In Chapters 6–10 a running commentary on each part of the work considers both the principal themes of each section and the development of Augustine's argument. Chapters 11–12 are on influences and sources, and the place of the work in Augustine's writings. Translations are my own, unless otherwise indicated. In biblical citations from Augustine and other Patristic authors I translate their version of the text: where appropriate, I adopt the Revised Standard Version.

Many friends and colleagues have helped me in the writing of this book. It would be impossible to name them all, and invidious to name only some. I should, however, like to acknowledge the encouragement and criticism which I received at the start of the project from Reinhart Herzog: his incisive scholarship is sadly missed by all who knew him. The Alexander von Humboldt Foundation made a generous gift of books which greatly facilitated my work.

An earlier version of parts of Chapter 1 was delivered as an Inaugural Lecture at University College London in May 1994, by kind invitation of the Provost. A version of the last section of Chapter 1 formed part of the Leon and Thea Kœrner Lecture at the University of British Columbia in Vancouver in September 1997.

Grateful acknowledgement for permission to produce, in adapted form, copyright material is due to the publisher of the *Augustinus-Lexikon*, Schwabe & Co. of Basle, and to Levante Editori of Bari.

I owe a special debt to my wife Ursula, who gave moral and practical support from start to finish, buoyed by the assurance that this would be my last book on Augustine.

I should like to thank Hilary O'Shea at Oxford University Press for her interest in the book, and her advice at various stages during the writing of it; Georga Godwin, Enid Barker, and my copy-editor for the care which has gone into its production.

I have great pleasure in dedicating this book to my brothers Paul and Fergal and their families.

G.J.P.O'D.

University College London

Contents

Abbreviated Titles: General

ACW   Ancient Christian Writers (1946–).
AL   C. Mayer *et al.* (eds.), *Augustinus-Lexikon*, (1986–).
AM   *Augustinus Magister.* Congrès international augustinien,
            Paris, 21–4 Septembre 1954, 3 vols. (Paris, 1955).
ANRW   H. Temporini and W. Haase (eds.), *Aufstieg und*
            Niedergang der römischen Welt (1972–).
AugStud   *Augustinian Studies* (1970–).
BA   Bibliothèque Augustinienne (1936–).
BEFAR   Bibliothèque des Écoles françaises d'Athènes et de Rome.
CAH   *Cambridge Ancient History* (2nd edn; 1961–).
CIL   *Corpus Inscriptionum Latinarum* (1863–).
CCL   Corpus Christianorum. Series Latina (1953–).
CLA   *Codices Latini Antiquiores*, ed. E. A. Lowe (1934–66);
            Suppl. (1971); 2nd edn. of vol. i (1972).
CSEL   Corpus Scriptorum Ecclesiasticorum Latinorum (1866–).
CTh   *Codex Theodosianus.*
DB   *Dictionnaire de la Bible* (1895–1912), Suppl. (1928–).
DG   *Doxographi Graeci*, ed. H. Diels (1879).
EPRO   Études préliminaires aux religions orientales dans
            l'Empire romain (1961–).
FGrH   *Fragmente der griechischen Historiker*, ed. F. Jacoby
            (1923–).
FIRA   *Fontes Iuris Romani Antelustiniani*, ed. S. Riccobono
            (1941).
GCS   Die griechischen christlichen Schriftsteller der ersten
            (drei) Jahrhunderte (1897–).
GLL   A. Souter (ed.), *Glossary of Later Latin to 600 AD*,
            (1949, repr. 1996).
ILS   *Inscriptiones Latinae Selectae*, ed. H. Dessau (1892–
            1916).
JbAC   *Jahrbuch für Antike und Christentum* (1958–).
JECS   *Journal of Early Christian Studies* (1993–).
JTS   *Journal of Theological Studies*, New Series (1950–).

LCL	Loeb Classical Library (1911–).
LSJ	H. G. Liddell, R. Scott, H. S. Jones (eds.), *A Greek–English Lexicon*, 9th edn. (Oxford, 1940), with revised Supplement (1996).
MA	*Miscellanea Agostiniana* (1930–1).
MGH AA	*Monumenta Germaniae Historica. Auctores Antiquissimi* (1877–1919).
OCD³	S. Hornblower and A. Spawforth (eds.), *The Oxford Classical Dictionary* (3rd edn.; 1996).
ODCC³	F. L. Cross and E. A. Livingstone (eds.), *The Oxford Dictionary of the Christian Church* (3rd edn.; 1997).
OLD	P. G. W. Glare (ed.), *Oxford Latin Dictionary* (1968–82).
PL	*Patrologiae cursus completus. Series Latina*, ed. J. P. Migne (1844–64).
RAC	T. Klauser *et al.* (eds.), *Reallexikon für Antike und Christentum* (1950–).
RB	*Revue bénédictine* (1890–).
REAug	*Revue des études augustiniennes* (1955–).
RechAug	*Recherches augustiniennes* (1958–).
RSV	Revised Standard Version of the Bible.
StudPatr	*Studia Patristica* (1957–).
SVF	*Stoicorum Veterum Fragmenta*, ed. H. von Arnim (1903–24).
TLL	*Thesaurus Linguae Latinae* (1900–).
TRE	*Theologische Realenzyklopädie* (1977–).
TU	*Texte und Untersuchungen* (1882–).

Abbreviated Titles of Augustine's and Other Writings

The following list is confined to those works of Augustine cited in abbreviated form in the book. In addition, the *City of God* (*De Civitate Dei*) is referred to as *City*, and the correspondence (*Epistulae*) as *Letter(s)*. Letter numbers followed by an asterisk refer to the letters (1*–29*) discovered and edited by J. Divjak (CSEL 88, 1981; BA 46B, 1987). The abbreviations follow for the most part those of the *Augustinus-Lexikon*, i, pp. xxvi–xlii, to which the reader is referred for a conspectus of the variant titles and principal editions of Augustine's works. The chronological tables in Brown (1967) provide information on the location of the individual works in *PL* and English translations. For information on editions and translations of *City*, see Bibliography A. Bibliography B gives details of editions and translations of the other works of Augustine that are frequently cited in this book: for general information see the prefatory note there.

C. Acad.	*Contra Academicos*
Adn. Iob	*Adnotationes in Iob*
C. Adv. Leg.	*Contra Adversarium Legis et Prophetarum*
An. et Or.	*De Anima et eius Origine*
Beata V.	*De Beata Vita*
Bon. Vid.	*De Bono Viduitatis*
Cat. Rud.	*De Catechizandis Rudibus*
Conf.	*Confessions*
Cons. Ev.	*De Consensu Evangelistarum*
Corrept.	*De Correptione et Gratia*
Div. Qu.	*De Diversis Quaestionibus LXXXIII*
Divin. Daem.	*De Divinatione Daemonum*
Doctr. Chr.	*De Doctrina Christiana*
En. Ps.	*Enarrationes in Psalmos*
Ench.	*Enchiridion sive De Fide Spe et Caritate*

Exp. Prop. Rom.	*Expositio quarundam Propositionum ex Epistula ad Romanos*
Exc. Vrb.	*De Excidio Vrbis Romae*
C. Faust.	*Contra Faustum Manicheum*
F. et Symb.	*De Fide et Symbolo*
C. Gaud.	*Contra Gaudentium Donatistarum Episcopum*
Gen. ad Litt.	*De Genesi ad Litteram*
Gen. adv. Man.	*De Genesi aduersus Manicheos*
Haer.	*De Haeresibus*
Io. Ev. Tr.	*In Iohannis Evangelium Tractatus CXXIV*
C. Iul.	*Contra Iulianum*
C. Iul. imp.	*Contra Iulianum opus imperfectum*
Lib. Arb.	*De Libero Arbitrio*
Mag.	*De Magistro*
C. Max.	*Contra Maximinum Arrianum*
Mor.	*De Moribus Ecclesiae Catholicae et de Moribus Manicheorum*
Mus.	*De Musica*
Nat. Bon.	*De Natura Boni*
Nupt. et Conc.	*De Nuptiis et Concupiscentia*
Ord.	*De Ordine*
Pecc. Mer.	*De Peccatorum Meritis*
Persev.	*De Dono Perseverantiae*
C. Prisc.	*Contra Priscillianistas*
Qu. Hept.	*Quaestiones in Heptateuchum*
Qu. Ev.	*Quaestiones Evangeliorum*
Retr.	*Retractations*
Ser.	*Sermones*
Ser. Caillau	*Sermones ab A. B. Caillau et B. Saint-Yves editi*
Ser. Casin.	*Sermones in Bibliotheca Casinensi editi*
Ser. Denis	*Sermones a M. Denis editi*
Ser. Dolbeau	*Sermones a F. Dolbeau editi*
Ser. Dom. Mont.	*De Sermone Domini in Monte*
Simpl.	*Ad Simplicianum*
Sol.	*Soliloquia*
Spir. et Litt.	*De Spiritu et Littera*
Trin.	*De Trinitate*
Vera Rel.	*De Vera Religione*
Vtil. Cred.	*De Vtilitate Credendi*
Vtil. Ieiun.	*De Vtilitate Ieiunii*

Some names and works of other authors are cited in abbreviated form
in the book. These are:

Arnob.	Arnobius
Nat.	*Adversus Nationes*
Cic.	Cicero
Rep.	*Republic (De Re Publica)*
Acad. Post.	*Academica Posteriora*
Lactant.	Lactantius
Div. Inst.	*Divine Institutions (Divinae Institutiones)*
Min. Fel.	Minucius Felix
Octav.	*Octavius*
Prudent.	Prudentius
Symmach.	*Contra Orationem Symmachi*
Tert.	Tertullian
Apol.	*Apologeticum*

Other abbreviated titles of non-Augustinian works follow closely
upon citation of the full title in the text or notes, and should be
immediately intelligible. For editions and translations of the above
works see Bibliography C.

I

Cities Real and Desired

The other day a man here—an English—mistaking the statues of Charlemagne and Constantine—which are Equestrian—for those of Peter and Paul—asked another—which was Paul of these same horsemen?—to which the reply was—'I thought Sir that St Paul had never got on horseback since his accident!'

(George Gordon Byron[1])

1. *The Christianization of the Roman Empire*

When, in 412 or thereabouts, Augustine[2] began to write the *City of God*, the Christian religion had for a century enjoyed a privileged position in the Roman empire. It owed this position pre-eminently to one man: Constantine, the first Christian emperor, who gained control over the western part of the empire by his victory at the battle of the Milvian Bridge in 312, and favoured and patronized Christianity in the western provinces from that time. The transition from persecuted to privileged Church came rapidly for Christians. After a generation of official tolerance, during which the Church had expanded and developed as an institution, it had experienced what came to be known as the Great Persecution under the emperor Diocletian (and probably at the instigation of his colleague Galerius)

---

[1] Writing from Rome in May 1817 to his publisher John Murray (*Byron's Letters and Journals*, ed. L. A. Marchand, v (London, 1976), 221).

[2] The standard (and remarkable) biography of Augustine is Brown (1967). For introductions to his thought see Chadwick (1986), O'Donnell (1985), and Horn (1995). Bonner (1963), TeSelle (1970), and Rist (1994) are more advanced, but eminently accessible, general studies. J. J. O'Meara (1954) is an unsurpassed account of Augustine's early intellectual development. Burnaby (1938) is a classic account of his views on love, grace, sin, and punishment. Evans (1982) discusses his thinking on the themes of evil, freedom, and goodness. Kirwan (1989) reviews his principal arguments from the stance of an analytic philosopher. Deane (1963) is a wide-ranging study of his political and social thought. Van der Meer (1961) surveys in magisterial fashion the life of the Christian Church—especially cult, preaching, and popular piety—in Augustine's North Africa, using his writings extensively. For general histories of the period see n. 6 below. For a brief survey of introductory and general works on the *City of God* see below, Ch. 6 n. 1.

in 303–4.[3] Although the provisions of the edict of 23 February 303 (Lactantius, *De Mortibus Persecutorum* 12–13) and subsequent edicts were not always carried out, and not everywhere with the same severity, Christian churches were demolished, Bibles and liturgical books were surrendered and burned, Christians who refused to make acts of conformity to the state religion were deprived of official status and legal privileges, and their property was confiscated. The origins of the Donatist schism in Augustine's North Africa can be traced back to this persecution: it also left the Christian community in Rome in disarray.[4] The Church acquired martyrs, but its strength (particularly in Africa) was by this time such that its existence could not be undermined. In April 311 Galerius rescinded the persecuting edicts in some eastern provinces; the effects of this change of policy were perceptible by 313. Persecution of Christians had ended in Italy and Africa by the winter of 306–7, and it had also been ended in Gaul, Spain, and Britain by Constantine, newly proclaimed western emperor, in summer 306. Yet there were still Christians in Italy and Africa who, in 312, had not recovered property confiscated in 303–4.

Constantine, whose family had Christian sympathies, underwent a conversion experience, whose details remain puzzling, in 312. By 324 he was ruler of the whole Roman world.[5] From 312 on, in the western provinces, court ceremonial reflected the emperor's religion, Christians served without impediment in the army, confiscated property was returned to them, the imperial treasury provided funds for the building or extension of churches, the clergy enjoyed special legal privileges and exemptions. This massive consolidation of what was, in effect, a new established religion was replicated in the East after 324. Paganism was not yet persecuted: Constantine and his

[3] For discussions of the reasons for persecution of Christians see de Sainte-Croix (1954, 1963), Frend (1965), Liebeschuetz (1979: 245–52), Lane Fox (1986: 419–92, 592–608), T. D. Barnes (1981: 18–24, 148–63), Demandt (1989: 57–9), Creed (edn. of Lactant. *De Mort. Pers.* pp. xxi–xxv). For Roman attitudes to Christians from Pliny to Julian see Wilken (1984).

[4] Donatism: Frend (1952), here 315–32 on its rigorous non-conformism, Willis (1950), T. D. Barnes (1981: 53–61). Church at Rome: ibid. 38.

[5] On Constantine's dream-vision prior to the battle of the Milvian Bridge see Lactant. *De Mort. Pers.* 44. 5–6 (cf. ibid. 46) with Creed ad loc., Eusebius, *Life of Constantine* 1. 28–30 and *Ecclesiastical History* 9. 9. Cf. Liebeschuetz (1979: 277–91), T. D. Barnes (1981: 43), Lane Fox (1986: 613–27). For a succinct account of Constantine's reign see Jones (1948; 1966: 39–50); cf. Averil Cameron (1993a: 47–65), Fowden (1993: 80–99). For some of the details in this para. see T. D. Barnes (1981: 48–53, 208–12).

fellow-emperor Licinius declared universal religious toleration in the
so-called Edict of Milan in 313. Nevertheless, the restrictions placed
upon traditional state religion from 324 were considerable: consulta-
tion of oracles, divination, dedication of cult images, and sacrifice
were all prohibited. Pagans were allowed to retain their temples and
priesthoods: paganism as a form of belief was tolerated, but its
traditional cultic expression was threatened. Christians received pre-
ferential treatment in official appointments. Other books were now
burned: Porphyry's *Against the Christians* was proscribed, probably
in 324–5 (*CTh* 15. 5. 66). But edicts are not always indicators of
enforcement: the prohibition of sacrifice was not seriously implemented in the West, as it appears to have been in the East. A law of 392
(*CTh* 16. 10. 12) was still attempting to prohibit it. Nevertheless, the
language of the imperial documents of 324–5 is uncompromisingly
hostile to paganism, and after Constantine's death in 337 no pagan
became emperor, with the exception of his apostate nephew Julian,
whose reign (360–3) was brief.

   Although imperial policy and, in some cases, legislation reflected
the new status of Christianity under and after Constantine, there was
no change in the organization of imperial, provincial, and local
government.[6] If Christianity was a revolution in religious and cultural
terms, the revolution did not extend to institutions. This fact set the
pattern for relations between the emperor and the Church in the
Christianized empire. After the condemnation of Donatus and his
African followers by a Church council in Rome in 313, the Donatists
appealed to Constantine. His reaction showed him 'adopting a
procedural stance towards the Church already familiar in imperial
transactions with disgruntled provincials, or in individual disputes'
(Averil Cameron 1993*a*: 66). He established the mechanism for
attempting to resolve the dispute, without directly intervening in
the decision on the action to be taken. Constantine's approach on
this occasion set a precedent: he summoned a council of bishops from
all the western provinces at Arles in 314. This council merely

---

[6] General histories of the period include the standard and monumental work of
Jones (1964), abridged as Jones (1966); Demandt (1989); Averil Cameron (1993*a*,
1993*b*), two authoritative and accessible accounts, with extensive bibliographies; see
her remarks (1993*b*: 4–7) on Jones and other modern studies of the period. Lepelley
(1979, 1981) is an unmatched study of the municipal history and culture of late
antique Roman North Africa. Herrin (1987: 19–89) is an incisive discussion of
Christianization in late antiquity. Dihle (1994) surveys the Greek and Latin literature
of the imperial period generally: Döpp (1988) Latin literature from AD 350 to 450.

confirmed the resolutions of the Rome council. There was a further
appeal by the Donatists and further investigations were ordered by
Constantine in 314–16, but he saw it as his role to allow the bishops
to make decisions, and to see to it that their decisions were implemented. Thus, probably in 316, Constantine ordered the confiscation
of churches belonging to Donatists: in effect, he was treating Donatism
as a crime. There were violent scenes in Carthage and several Donatists
were killed. Only in 321 did Constantine reverse a policy that was
tantamount to Christian persecution of fellow Christians. In 324 he
legislated against heretics (Donatists were schismatics), but the law
was not enforced, and Marcionites, Valentinians, and others continued
to function. These steps might not always have immediate practical
consequences, but their implications were enormous. The theological
decisions of bishops might be translated into policy by the Christian
emperor. But Constantine's faith in episcopal expertise was ill-
founded. It gave bishops considerable, if indirect, power, which they
did not always use wisely. Above all, as at the Council of Nicaea in 325,
it gave an aura of authority and orthodoxy to theological views that
were not universally accepted, and thus it led directly to the growth of
party politics—Arian and orthodox—in church and state (T. D. Barnes
1981: 224–6). But, though Constantine and his successors influenced
Church thinking and policy, they did not control the Church, legally or
politically. Constantine gave prestige and authority to church councils,
building on the already existing structures within the Church. Yet the
Church had no single leader, although the holders of certain episcopal
posts—Alexandria, Antioch, Rome, Constantinople—enjoyed special
influence, which could also be exercised locally (Carthage in Africa) or
gained by dominant individual bishops (Ambrose at Milan).[7]

Support for Christianity of the kind given by Constantine continued
throughout the fourth century, and it was sometimes accompanied by
acts of overt hostility towards paganism, such as the anti-pagan
measures of Constantius II in 353–4 and his removal of the altar of
Victory from the Roman Senate house in 357 (it was subsequently
restored, probably in Julian's reign). Yet at the same time Constantius
replenished the priestly colleges in Rome. Moreover, the temples
remained open, sacrifice and other cult acts continued, and it was
not until late in the century that more sustained attempts to under-

---

[7] On Ambrose's authority see McLynn (1994); for a different account see Lizzi
(1990).

mine and suppress paganism were made. These are usually associated with the reign of the emperor Theodosius I (379–95), but Theodosius' policy had been anticipated in some important respects by Gratian (375–83), who ended a policy of toleration that his father Valentinian I (364–75) had maintained. Gratian was the first emperor to refuse, in 382, the honorific title of *pontifex maximus*. At about the same time he cut off the public subsidies to pagan cults in Rome, including those paid to the Vestal Virgins. He had the altar of Victory removed once more from the Senate. These actions are as much the symptoms of the gradual Christianization of the governing classes and the growth of Church influence as they are evidence for persecution of pagans. But there were more sinister events (Averil Cameron 1993*a*: 74–6). In 386 bishop Marcellus of Apamea in Syria used soldiers to destroy the great temple of Zeus in the city. In 391 or 392 bishop Theophilus of Alexandria organized the assault on the temple of Serapis that led to its destruction (Brown 1992: 113–14). It was in February 391 that Theodosius promulgated the law banning all pagan sacrifices, public as well as private, and prohibiting other use of temples (*CTh* 16. 10. 10–11), which was followed in 392 by a further decree banning pagan cult (*CTh* 16. 10. 12). There was pagan senatorial involvement in the attempt by Eugenius, a Christian rhetor, to seize power in Italy between 392 and 394, although restoration of paganism was not Eugenius' primary motive, and his promises to influential pagan backers were limited. They did not extend to a re-establishment of the old religion, and no state funds were promised in its support: Eugenius offered money from his own pocket to prominent pagans, who could then use it to fund pagan ceremonies (J. Matthews 1975: 240–1). While some pagan senators like the praetorian prefect Nicomachus Flavianus, consul in 394, rallied to Eugenius' cause, others like Quintus Aurelius Symmachus, who observed that Eugenius was not prepared to go so far as to restore the altar of Victory to the Senate house, were reticent. Eugenius' army was defeated by Theodosius' forces in 394 at the battle of the river Frigidus: Christian propagandists read the outcome as God's judgement on the pagans. Theodosius' death in January 395 prevented him from exploiting this victory. But, although further legislation against pagans is known from the reigns of Theodosius' sons, Arcadius and Honorius, pagan resilience, at least in Italy, was strong: by 399 Nicomachus Flavianus, on the losing side at the Frigidus, was sufficiently rehabilitated to become prefect of Rome,

and a leading figure like Symmachus enjoyed close contact with the
imperial court at Milan and with the *de facto* head of government
there, Stilicho, the protector of Theodosius' young sons (J. Matthews
1975: 257–70).

The Christian empire eventually brought about a significant
deterioration in the social position of Jews.[8] In the later fourth
century emperors legislated to prevent local Christian fanatics from
attacking synagogues, but in the later fourth and early fifth centuries
Jews were increasingly ostracized, and banned from the imperial
service and from positions of status (Averil Cameron 1993*a*: 76).
The virulent anti-Semitism of the preaching of John Chrysostom,
bishop of Constantinople from 398 to 404, provides evidence for
Christian interest in, and contacts with, Jews, against which John's
sermons react with an intolerance that is matched only by his
eloquence.[9] Similar anti-Semitism was promoted by Cyril, bishop
of Alexandria from 412: in his case it led to a Jewish backlash in
which Christians were killed. There was, however, a continuing,
prosperous, cultured Jewish presence in Palestine, which lasted
into the seventh century, and which, despite the promotion of
Jerusalem as a Christian holy city and place of pilgrimage, led to
contacts between Jews and Christians (Averil Cameron 1993*b*:
140–1). But the behaviour of Christianity in its dealings with other
religions (Manichaeism is a prime example) or with deviant versions
of its own religion was that of an exclusive religion, where intolerance
was the norm, even if, in practice, intolerant policy and legislation
were not always implemented. It often depended on the willingness of
local church or other leaders to countenance violent action, as some
of the events referred to above indicate. Some groups were readier
than others to take the law into their own hands. Monks, in particular, operating in an ill-defined ecclesiastical structure where they
were often under no official control, could get dangerous: some of
them were responsible for the lynching of the pagan Neoplatonist
woman philosopher Hypatia at Alexandria in 415, though bishop
Cyril was also affected by the scandal surrounding her murder
(Dzielska 1995).

---

[8] T. D. Barnes (1981: 252) argues that Constantine imposed legal disabilities on
Jews; cf. however Avi-Jonah (1984: 161–6), Fowden (1993: 87).
[9] Cf. Wilken (1983: 34–65). On Chrysostom's preaching and career see Kelly
(1995); on his preaching see also Liebeschuetz (1990: 166–88). Augustine on Jews:
Frederiksen (1995).

There is much evidence for continuity in Roman civic life after the Constantinian religious revolution. This evidence is particularly persuasive in the case of North Africa (Lepelley 1979). Whereas earlier scholarship painted a picture of an African urban civilization in decay in the fourth and fifth centuries, torn apart by social inequality and schism, recent archaeological and historical study has emphasized the prosperity and relative stability of African society and institutions in Augustine's day. The Donatist schism polarized society, but it was neither caused nor influenced by, nor did it cause, serious economic hardship, and where it was divisive, the divisions did not coincide with social rank or status. There were serious social inequalities, and visible extremes of wealth and poverty, but these did not undermine the fabric of urban life, which persisted until, and after, the Vandal invasion of 429. The institutions of municipal government continued unimpaired, and the prestige attached to them, and the scope which they gave for euergetism, were not lessened when the office-holders or the beneficiaries were Christian: a local pagan notable like Augustine's patron Romanianus at Thagaste could win praise from Christian citizens for putting on bear-fights and other lavish spectacles (*Contra Academicos* 1. 1. 2). Despite Christianization, pagan cult continued. Augustine, as a young schoolboy at Madauros between 365 and 369, witnessed the city elders and decurions 'ranting and raving' ('bacchantes et furentes') in a rite in honour of the Dea Virtus or Bellona (*Letter* 17. 4). As a student and teacher at Carthage (370–383) he saw the rites of Caelestis, which he later found obscene (*City of God* 2. 4, 26). Offerings were made at the temple of Saturn at Carthage until the end of the fourth century (Lepelley 1979: 350). Although there was destruction of temples in the aftermath of the defeat of Eugenius in 394 and the attendant anti-pagan legislation, an official brake was put on their demolition (cf. *City* 18. 54), as they were seen, then and subsequently, as civic monuments of value, and also used as municipal treasuries and meeting-places. The temple of Caelestis at Carthage was used as a church from 407 or 408 until 421, when, because of pagan protests against its use, it was demolished: evidently the pagans had to be appeased, if not favoured (Lepelley 1979: 356–7). When Augustine was a bishop, pagans were one social group that he singled out for treatment in his preaching: a recently discovered sermon informs us that on the occasion on which it was delivered, pagans were actually present, presumably by invitation, in the congregation.[10] The violent clashes between pagans and Christians at Sufes in 399 and Calama in 408 show the strength of pagan numbers and feeling.[11]

Such was the prestige attaching to traditional offices and titles that priestly titles such as *flamen perpetuus* and *sacerdotalis provinciae* were sought after by Christians of distinguished social status throughout the fourth to sixth centuries, and this practice was not denounced by Augustine or other polemicists against paganism.[12] The titles had probably lost their religious significance, and the principal function of the office-holders may have been to preside over acts of public loyalty and homage to the emperor, a form of successor-rite or imperial cult, shorn of explicit religious significance. The pagan religious institution survived, in secularized form. This was a typical development. The new established religion did not, generally speaking, create new civic forms of expression that were expressly Christian, whether in municipal buildings or ceremonies, civic calendars, or education.[13] Where bishops gained certain rights, such as that of acting as judges in civil suits ('audientia episcopalis', officially recognized by Constantine in 318 to remove the necessity for Christians to appear before potentially hostile pagan judges), their activity did not encroach seriously on municipal authority and institutions.

2. *Cities in the Mind*

The focus in this chapter so far has been on the realities of life in the Christianized empire. But the events surveyed received an ideological colouring in contemporary writings, which served in turn to mould the ways in which they were generally perceived. The process began in the reign of Constantine, in the works of his chief apologist Eusebius.

---

[10] The sermon is Mainz 61 (= *Ser. Dolbeau* 25 = *Ser.* 360B): for discussion and text see Dolbeau's edn. 243–67 (repr. from *REAug* 37 (1991), 53–77); here 244 n. 4 on speculation on the reasons for, and nature, of pagans' presence. Cf. Chadwick (1996: 85). For pagans at Ambrose's sermons see his *In Psalmos* 36. 61 (CSEL 64. 118): cf. Alan Cameron (1970: 219 with n. 5).

[11] Augustine, *Letters* 50, 90–1, 103–4. See further Sect. 3 below and Ch. 2.

[12] For further details of this and the following see Lepelley (1979: 362–76, 389–95).

[13] See Lepelley (1979: 371–6). On continuity in education and literary culture, and the role of the teacher (*grammaticus*) in late antiquity, see Kaster (1988) who (pp. 237–440) provides a prosopography of known grammarians from 250 to 565, including Augustine and his principal contemporaries.

In a panegyric written in 336 to celebrate the thirtieth anniversary of Constantine's accession, Eusebius puts forward an interpretation of the emperor's achievement that is usually considered typical of his understanding of the role of a Christian emperor. Throughout the panegyric, Constantine is compared to Christ. His earthly empire replicates the heavenly kingdom: the monotheism of the heavenly kingdom is reflected in the monarchical empire, and Constantine models himself on a divine exemplar. His reign reflects the rule of the eternal Logos, and his role is that of a saviour, to prepare humanity for the kingdom of God. This role includes persecution of error: Constantine fights paganism's demons as he did barbarians. Eusebius here uses ideas found in Hellenistic theories of kingship, giving them a distinctively Christian colouring (T. D. Barnes 1981: 253–5; Averil Cameron 1993a, 68–9). In the *City of God* Augustine would repudiate this kind of interpretation of the Christian emperor's role, but Eusebius' views were to become the basis of Byzantine political theory (and they had some influence on Prudentius: see below). There is no way of knowing whether Constantine appreciated or agreed with Eusebius. As we have seen, his Christian politics were more complex and pragmatic than their idealization in the panegyric suggests. But Constantine was not unaware of the symbolic significance of his reign, evoked particularly in his action of founding a new city as his capital and naming it 'New Rome', a place where a Christian court and Senate could function, away from the religious associations of old Rome. Later anecdote emphasized the symbolism of this new foundation, with the story that Constantine first intended, as Julius Caesar allegedly had, to rebuild Troy, and with details of the foundation myth that linked the establishment of what became known as Constantinople with the foundation myths of Rome (T. D. Barnes 1981: 212 with n. 18).

Constantine's new city linked the reality of Christianization with the Roman civic ideal. Later in the fourth century the theme of the city featured in the celebrated exchange between Symmachus, prefect of the city of Rome, and Ambrose, bishop of Milan. After the removal of the altar of Victory, at which sacrifices had inaugurated senatorial sessions since Augustus' day, from the Senate house by Gratian in 382, Symmachus addressed in 384 a so-called 'relatio' (*Relatio* 3)[14] on

---

[14] The term 'relatio' originally applies to a motion introduced before the Senate by a magistrate (*OLD* 1).

religious tolerance to the boy-emperor Valentinian II and his advisers.
Symmachus argues for the restoration of the altar and the renewal of
the discontinued state subsidies to traditional cults and their
ministers. The debate has been much studied.[15] Modern research
has shown that its importance does not lie in any practical influence
which it might have had on the Christianization of the Roman
aristocracy, or on any pagan revival or resistance to such a revival.
The Christianization of Italy's élite was a long and steady process
from the early fourth century, and the pagan revival of the later fourth
century may be a modern scholarly myth.[16] But on the ideological
level the debate inaugurated by Symmachus and taken up by Ambrose
is important for the attitudes which it reveals on both sides. It has
rightly been seen as 'an uncharacteristically lucid episode in the untidy
and unplanned process by which the Roman governing class
abandoned their patronage of the old forms of religion in favour of
the new' (J. Matthews 1975: 210–11). It also throws light on the
definition of Rome by pagans and Christians at this time. Though
Symmachus' plea for religious tolerance and diversity is celebrated,
and summed up in his famous phrase 'not by one route only may we
arrive at so tremendous a mystery' (*Rel*. 3. 9) as religious truth, his
essay is perhaps more interesting for the subtle manner in which it
elucidates contemporary relations between religion and Rome.

The key to Symmachus' argument lies in his appeal to justice. 'You
rule everything', he says, addressing 'good emperors'—and he means
Theodosius and Arcadius as well as Valentinian—'but you also
preserve for each his own possessions, and justice weighs more
with you than power' (*Rel*. 3. 18, tr. R. H. Barrow, adapted).
Symmachus is not denying that the emperor has absolute power.
But what he is appealing to is the sense of responsibility which, in
strict justice, an emperor has, irrespective of his power, to tradition,
established practice ('consuetudo'), and the rights consecrated by
usage (Dihle 1973). Established practice is a familiar concept in
Roman jurisprudence. It underlies the claims which Symmachus
makes on behalf of Roman state religious tradition and the subsidies

---

[15] See esp. Barrow's edn. of Symmachus, *Rel*. 3; Dihle (1973); J. Matthews (1975:
203–11), Fuhrmann (1994: 59–80); on 'providentialism' in the debate see Paschoud
(1983).
[16] For arguments against a pagan revival or reaction (not to be confused with
renewed scholarly interest in Greek and Latin literature) in the late 4th c. see Alan
Cameron (1977), Markus (1974), Averil Cameron (1993*a*: 157–9).

and privileges which time has consecrated. This argument reveals in turn a fundamental principle of Roman religion—its concept of the relations between gods and humans in terms of law ('ius divinum', 'ius sacrum'), agreements of a legal kind that bind humans to religious practices, and in turn bind gods to services to the community. To break with religious tradition, Symmachus suggests, is to break the law, no less.

Symmachus' argument for the maintenance of traditional religious practices is based on the concept of 'beneficium', of benefits conferred and received. It is about the right of benefactors, but also of those whose long-established receipt of benefits creates a legal entitlement to them. He can thus present the discontinuance of the subsidy to the Vestal Virgins, for example, as the infringement of a right, damaging the ethos of a state based on law: 'Let no one imagine that I am pleading the case only of religion' (*Rel.* 3. 15). Using the rhetorical device of prosopopeia, he introduces a personified Rome who argues the case of benefits received: the acquisition of empire, the invulnerability of the city of Rome itself. The assumption is that Roman religion has produced tangible historical results: 'This worship has brought the whole world under the rule of my laws' (*Rel.* 3. 9). In this personification Rome is presented as a woman of venerable old age whose length of years should command respect. Around this image of Rome cluster the legal defence of tradition and the sense of historical continuity in Symmachus' argument.

Symmachus is invoking traditional personifications of Rome, found on coins and other artistic depictions, including the consular diptychs of the period.[17] The personified city whose historical phases may be compared to the stages of human life from infancy to old age is a motif from earlier Latin literature. It has been merged with the late Republican and Augustan ideology of a city 'destined to endure as long as the human race survives' (Ammianus Marcellinus, 14. 6. 3), where valour and good fortune have conspired to achieve an empire.[18] Ammianus Marcellinus had

---

[17] See MacCormack (1981: 177–8, 210, 227–8, with pls. 56–7).

[18] On Rome eulogy, the idea of Rome, and personification of the city see Paschoud (1967), Alan Cameron (1970: 273–6, 349–89), Fuhrmann (1994: 78–80, 282–98), Edwards (1996), Zwierlein (1978: 46–58), Mellor (1981). Florus, *Epitome* 1. pref. 4–8 compares the stages of Rome's history from the early kingship period to his day (the 2nd c. AD) to the life of an individual from infancy to old age. Cf. Lactant. *Div. Inst.* 7. 15. 14, attributing to 'Seneca' a scheme of Rome's history in terms of the six ages of human life, possibly from the younger Seneca: see Ogilvie (1978: 74); Griffin

provided a memorable fourth-century adaptation of the personification, written some years before 384 (14. 6. 3–6).[19] A Greek from
Antioch, Ammianus' education had equipped him with an image of
Rome as the source and centre of the Roman imperial achievement:
his Latin studies had almost certainly begun at Antioch and were a
fashionable development that worried that city's most distinguished
contemporary teacher and orator, Libanius. When he came to Rome,
Ammianus confronted the historical ideal with the real present. He
did not like what he found in Rome. His descriptions of Rome are well
known and revealing. He found a city that was xenophobic and
violent, a cultural wilderness, with a frivolous and irresponsible élite
indulging its taste for extravagant living (14. 6, 28. 4).

Yet Ammianus cannot quite let this depressing experience of contemporary Rome overthrow the ideal in his mind. His personified
Rome in her maturity entrusted the administration of empire to the
Caesars, as one might make a will or bequest: Ammianus is thinking
of the end of the Roman Republic, a republic, so to speak, on the
verge of retirement (14. 6. 5). Like its senators, who are 'paid the
respect due to their grey hairs' (14. 6. 6), Rome's authority, the laws
and institutions which characterize it, depend upon its age and traditions, but also on the sentiment that it will survive. Ammianus'
account of the visit of Constantius II, son of Constantine, to Rome
in 357 reflects this ideology (16. 10). Although the city was no
longer an imperial residence in the fourth century—whereas Trier
and Milan (and later Ravenna) in the West were—the 'adventus' or
ceremonial entry of an emperor into the city was regularly celebrated,
sometimes in the form of a traditional triumph.[20] It could, for
example, mark ten or twenty years of an emperor's rule. Yet
Constantius was the first emperor for seven years to pay such a formal
visit, and he was to be the last for a further nineteen. Ammianus
stresses two aspects of the 'adventus' of Constantius. One is his
static, hieratic pose and undeviating gaze in the procession, so that
he became almost an image or statue, remote from his immediate

(1976: 194–201), who refers to uses of the same biological metaphor in Cic. *Rep.*
2. 3, 2. 21 (derived from Polybius, 6. 51) and Livy, 2. 1.

[19] On Ammianus and his history see J. Matthews (1989); for the Rome theme in
Ammianus, see ibid. 250, 279–80, 470 See below for further personification of Rome
in Claudian and Prudentius.

[20] On 'adventus' see MacCormack (1981); on Constantius II in Rome, see ibid. 40–5
and J. Matthews (1989: 231–5). Cf. Alan Cameron (1970: 382–6).

surroundings: the pose reflects, and is reflected in, artistic depictions of fourth-century emperors, making the living ruler into an icon (16. 10. 10).[21] It contrasts with the other aspect highlighted by Ammianus, the change in Constantius' conduct while sightseeing in Rome and mixing with the people in the Circus Maximus and elsewhere—his relaxed and friendly familiarity, his enjoyment of the traditional outspokenness ('dicacitas') of the Romans, making him a citizen among citizens (16. 10. 13). Theodosius was to behave in exactly the same way in 389 (Pacatus, *Panegyric to Theodosius* 47. 3). In Rome the emperor must be a citizen: it was long-established tradition, behaviour commended to Trajan by Pliny (*Panegyricus* 22–3). This informality was no less artificial than the formal 'adventus'. But it represented something that Roman emperors and Romans liked to believe about one another, a form of relationship that suggested that the emperor was really only a 'princeps', a first citizen, and not a 'dominus', a despot. The emperor on these visits is often represented paying compliments to some Roman building: in Ammianus, Constantius reserves most admiration for the Forum of Trajan (16. 10. 15–16). In such ceremonies imperial tribute is paid to the idea of Roman rule. Strikingly, there is nothing in the account of this visit to indicate that Constantius is a Christian emperor (although he had the altar of Victory removed from the Senate house, he also took steps to replenish the priestly colleges[22]). Indeed, Symmachus, recalling this visit in his 'relatio', mentions how the emperor, 'with no sign of disapproval in his face . . . saw its [Rome's] shrines . . . read the inscriptions giving the names of the gods on the pediments . . . put questions about the origins of the temples . . . showed his admiration for their founders' (*Rel.* 3. 7, tr. R. H. Barrow). It is not necessary to believe that this impression of an imperial visit is entirely due to the fact that both Ammianus and Symmachus are pagans: the Christian emperor's 'adventus' in 357 still preserved its traditional pre-Christian format, like other imperial institutions. Ammianus knows the symbolic value of the city of Rome. He wishes that his hero Julian were buried there: 'To perpetuate the memory of his exploits, they [his ashes] should have been laid where they might be lapped by the Tiber, which . . . skirts the monuments of earlier deified emperors' (25. 10. 5, tr. W. Hamilton). When Septimius Severus died

---

[21] Cf. MacCormack (1981: 43–4 with pl. 16). The motif of the intensity of the emperor's gaze in early 4th c. imperial portraits and panegyrics is discussed by R. R. R. Smith (1997: 194–201, with pl. 1 and 8. 4).

[22] Symmachus, *Rel.* 3. 6–7; Ambrose, *Letter* 18 (73). 32.

in Britain in 211 his urn was brought back to Rome for a civic funeral and burial. In the late fourth century, in changed circumstances, Ammianus understood the significance of such ceremony.[23]

The *Relatio* of Symmachus provoked a written reply from Ambrose in the form of two letters also addressed to the emperor Valentinian (Ambrose, *Letters* 17–18 (= 72–3 in CSEL)), the second of which deals with the details of Symmachus' argument. Ambrose realized that he had to break the mould of Symmachus' coherent account. His debating tone is subtle and respectful. He was Symmachus' kinsman and social equal, and a provincial governor before his appointment as bishop.[24] Ambrose knows that he must face the legal aspects of Symmachus' argument. His starting-point is formulated in terms reminiscent of a rule ('regula') in a legal textbook: 'No wrong is done to the one to whom the almighty God is preferred' (*Letter* 17 (72). 7). Relations with the Christian God cannot be subsumed under the traditional Roman 'sacred law' ('ius sacrum'), and disregard for another's 'right' ('ius') in the service of the Christian God is not an infringement. This assumption appears to be based on the absolute authority of the one God. For legal obligations Ambrose substitutes the conditions of military service, in which the emperor is under divine command, a 'soldier of God' ('miles dei'), and the imperial subjects are in the emperor's service. It is important not to underestimate the significance of this re-ordering of religious priorities. For 'fides' in the sense of the kind of binding guarantees that legal obligations involve, invoked by Symmachus, Ambrose substitutes 'fides' in the sense of the binding principles of religious belief: the ultimate appeal is to the emperor's faith. This radical change of perspective is reinforced by an appeal to the figure of Rome. What Ambrose does is take up the personification of Rome in Symmachus and exploit the opportunity that it offers to present a novel image of a Rome in the process of change and development. Rome speaks, but her message is different from that of the Rome of Symmachus:

[23] On Christians and Christianity in Ammianus see J. Matthews (1989: 420–51). The most celebrated episode which he narrates is the violence attending the accession of Damasus as bishop of Rome in 366 (27. 3. 11–15); cf. Brown (1992: 103) on the episode, and ibid. 80–1, 85–7 on violence in Rome at this time.

[24] On Ambrose see Homes Dudden (1935), here 2 n. 3 on the family connection with Symmachus; cf. T. D. Barnes (1992); McLynn (1994); Ramsey (1997), who provides an Eng. tr. of *Letters* 17 (72) and 18 (73).

I do not blush at being converted in my old age along with the whole world. For it is true that no age is too late to learn. Let old age blush that cannot correct itself. It is not the maturity of years which is worthy of praise, but that of character. There is no disgrace in proceeding to better things.   (*Letter* 18 (73). 7)

The notion of religious conversion is linked by Ambrose to the concept of historical progress, of new horizons rather than the maintenance of old traditions. He creates the positive image of a dynamic Rome. This image in turn depends upon a rationalization of Rome's historical achievement. It was not, Ambrose argues, because of religious observance, but on account of military prowess ('virtus'), that Rome acquired an empire: 'bravery has laid low those whom religious observance could not budge' (*Letter* 17 (72). 7). Ambrose extrapolates a recognizable Roman moral quality from its traditional civic religious context and secularizes it, while at the same time proposing the image of the emperor as soldier of the Christian God. The manipulation of traditional values and their re-arrangement in a new ideological order is conducted in the language of imperial panegyric, with praise of the ruler's qualities as benefactor of the state, and in particular as the agent of its renewal. In this process, Ambrose implies, the transformation of Rome and the growth of Christianity are parallel phenomena, expressible in related metaphors: to Rome's venerable old age corresponds the mature harvest or vintage of the late expansion of the Church. Both Church and Rome are in process of change, and both have a destiny commensurate with the known world.

It is the exposure of ideological assumptions, rather than the scoring of debating points, that makes the altar of Victory dispute so revealing. There was never any doubt that Ambrose and the Christian position would prevail. When in 387 Symmachus supported the usurper Maximus against Theodosius and Valentinian, it was on behalf of the Senate and not because Maximus offered any hopes for the pagan cause. After Maximus' defeat, Symmachus was rehabilitated by Theodosius and went on to become consul in 391, the very year in which Theodosius' edicts against paganism were promulgated. Symmachus did not become involved in the power bid of Eugenius, whose sympathies with paganism, though limited, were, as has been seen above, more obvious. The Christianization of Roman life did not depend on debates or on edicts, but on such factors as Theodosius' consolidation of power and his resultant

influence. What was important was the establishment of an unequivocal Christian atmosphere in public life, permeating every
sphere, and powerfully advanced by patronage. Theodosius visited
Rome in 389, bringing his 5-year old son Honorius with him to be
presented to the Senate.[25] In many respects it was like other official
visits. But there was an unmistakable new dimension, missing from
Constantius II's visit in 357 (see above). Visits to the Christian
churches of Rome and to martyrs' shrines were now part of the
programme. One of Theodosius' most prominent supporters, Flavius
Rufinus, acquired on this visit relics of Peter and Paul that he was
subsequently to install in a splendid new shrine in his palace at
Chalcedon on the Bosporus. Work was already in progress on the
magnificent new basilica of St Paul on the Ostia road: it would be
dedicated in 391. The architectural face of Rome was changing.[26] In
the church of Santa Pudenziana, built at the end of the century,
mosaics depict Christ and his apostles as emperor with his Roman
Senate, anticipating the portrayal of Mary in the regalia of an
empress in the mosaics of Santa Maria Maggiore, built in the
430s. Pope Damasus built a basilica on the Via Ardeatina where he
was buried in 384 with his mother and sister, in a Christian mauso-
leum that acknowledged the symbolic value of Roman family tombs
like that of the Scipios. 'Rome' and 'Roman' were quickly and irre-
sistibly coming to mean something new, but the striking feature was
the redeployment of the old idiom in a new context, not its total
replacement.

The theme of Rome was essentially, or at least had become, a
religiously neutral motif, a shell capable of being filled with various
kinds of content. This is certainly the case with the uses of the Rome
theme in the poetry of Claudian.[27] Claudian, who came from
Alexandria, and whose native language was Greek, arrived in Italy

[25] See Pacatus, *Panegyric* 45. 7–47 (= *Panegyr.* 2 in Mynors's edn.); cf. J. Matthews
(1975: 227–31), MacCormack (1981: 50–2). On Flavius Rufinus' acquisition and
installation of relics see Callinicus, *Vita Sancti Hypatii* 66b; cf. J. Matthews (1975:
134).

[26] Cf. on church building Averil Cameron (1993a: 103, 126; 1993b: 58–61).
Krautheimer (1980) is informative. Pietri (1976) is a remarkable study of every aspect
of Christian Rome in the 4th and early 5th c. General survey of Rome's development
from antiquity to the Renaissance: Rand (1943).

[27] Alan Cameron (1970) remains the most valuable study: on Claudian's panegyrics
see pp. 30–45, 253–304; on Claudian and Rome, 349–89; on the question of his
Christianity, 189–227. On the panegyric for Probinus and Olybrius see Taegert's
comm. Cf. on panegyric generally MacCormack (1976; 1981).

in 394 as a poet in his mid-twenties, brilliant and ambitious. He was probably not a Christian, but the patrons for whom he wrote his poetry were, and these included the great family of the Anicii, the young emperor Honorius, who had succeeded his father Theodosius in the West in 395 at the age of 10, and Stilicho, Honorius' regent, and the most powerful man in the western empire between 395 and 408, whose official propagandist Claudian was to become. In his panegyrics Claudian uses the Rome theme in a functional way, skilfully relating it to the occasion in question. Rome becomes a means to an end, and Claudian bears in mind the interests of his patrons and the audience of his recitations. In these poems Rome is no artificial decoration. Personification of the city reflects real situations. In his first great Latin poem, the panegyric on the consulship of the brothers Probinus and Olybrius in 395, the figure of Rome supplicates Theodosius on behalf of the two candidates (*Panegyricus Dictus Olybrio et Probino Consulibus* 75–7). Rome cannot, after all, appoint its own consuls: they have to be an emperor's nominees. But in a poem to glorify the family of the Anicii, from which the brothers came, and to embellish the prestigious office of consul, Rome cannot appear merely as a suppliant. She is described as a warrior-goddess, a Minerva, journeying in her chariot to the Alps to meet Theodosius (*Prob.* 73–104). This attractive and forceful Amazonian figure symbolizes many things. She represents the victory of Theodosius over Eugenius at the river Frigidus: Theodosius is still sweating from the toils of battle when he receives Rome (*Prob.* 117–18). His victory is evoked as a restoration of Rome's 'libertas' (*Prob.* 140). But that victory is chiefly the setting which enhances the praise of the new consuls and their father Probus. The consuls, not yet 20, can show no military achievements of their own, but Theodosius' success is refracted upon them from the warrior-image of Rome.

The Rome of this poem is thriving and in the prime of life. But in another memorable personification composed by Claudian a few years later we find resurrected the aged Rome of Ammianus and Symmachus. When the African prince Gildo was putting pressure on Italy and Stilicho by cutting off the vital corn-supply to Rome, and after Stilicho had suppressed the ensuing revolt and crushed Gildo in 398, Claudian presents a suffering Rome, weak from famine, feeble, grey-haired, with a rusting spear (*In Gildonem* 17–25). The image of Rome has become a cipher, reflecting shifting fortunes of the city and the imperial regime. When Stilicho becomes consul in 400, it is at the personal request of Rome, now fully restored to warrior-queen splendour, and Stilicho receives the consular toga from her hands. The toga bears images of Stilicho's life: the birth of a son to Maria, Stilicho's daughter, married to the emperor Honorius, and the growth of the child as emperor-in-waiting (*De Consulatu Stilichonis* 2. 269–361). The triumphal 'adventus' of Stilicho in Rome takes on surreal dimensions: it is Mars or Romulus entering the city, surrounded by Bellona, Fear, and Terror as lictors (*Stil*. 2. 367–76). A few lines later the scene has normalized and crowds of ordinary Romans throng the Via Flaminia, while Stilicho climbs the Pincian hill or enters the theatre of Pompey (*Stil*. 2. 397–405). The real Rome and the imaginary city are brilliantly blended.

The obligatory visit to Rome was made by Honorius in 403 or 404.[28] He was a reluctant 19–year-old visitor, consul already for the sixth time. He had not been to the city since 389, when he was taken there by his father Theodosius. Neither this visit nor the later one in 407–8 was a success. On the second visit Honorius was upset by the boisterous, outspoken Romans and retired sulkily to Ravenna (Alan Cameron 1970: 384). On the former occasion (Claudian, *Panegyricus Dictus Honorio Augusto Sextum Consuli* 543–660) his speech to the Senate seems to have been a failure. In Claudian's panegyric no such outcome can be admitted. But when the poet praises Honorius for the lack of rhetoric in his speech, we may feel that failure is being tactfully concealed (*VI Cons*. 592–4). Elsewhere in Claudian's account of the 'adventus' of Honorius one notes the familiar stress on the emperor as citizen (*VI Cons*. 55–64, 590–1). His predecessors, with the honourable exception of Theodosius, may have been 'domini', tyrants, but not he (*VI Cons*. 559). He enters Rome as a splendid youth, admired by all the women, a boy addressing his elders with wisdom and authority. But he remains a human figure. In Rome, Honorius is not the godlike ruler carried on a golden throne and dressed in brilliant golden vestments, as portrayed by Claudian in the poem on the emperor's fourth consulship, recited in Milan at the court

---

[28] On the date see most recently Dolbeau's edn. of new Augustine sermons, pp. 626, 640. Honorius' 'adventus' in Rome is a theme in the newly discovered Mainz sermons 61 (= *Ser. Dolbeau* 25 = *Ser.* 360B), here ll. 521 ff. (originally pub. *REAug* 37 (1991), 37–77), and 55 (= *Ser. Dolbeau* 22 = *Ser.* 341, augmented), here ll. 98 ff. (originally pub. *REAug* 40 (1994), 143–96). Augustine's preaching adds the Christian dimension that Claudian's genre precludes (see further next para.). For comment see Dolbeau's edn. 246, 627–8; cf. 325, 543.

(*Panegyricus Dictus Honorio Augusto Quartum Consuli* 565–610).
It would be a crude misrepresentation to say that the purpose of
Claudian's panegyric was to praise or flatter Honorius. The emperor's
Roman visit has to be presented as a success to a Roman audience, to
which the poem will be recited. It is Rome's self-image that is being
constructed here. Claudian is engaged in the manipulation of tradi-
tional themes with much diplomatic tact, so that senators, who have
great wealth and influence, may approve. Hence Honorius' love of
Rome, for which there is not a scrap of evidence, is stressed (*VI Cons.*
53–87). In his childhood games with brother Arcadius and father
Theodosius, he always opts for the city. 'Let me have my beloved
Rome', the petulant child cries (*VI Cons.* 77–87). He is an honorary
Roman.

It sometimes seems as if Claudian were writing as if nothing had
changed in the Roman world. The effective exclusion of Christianity
from his panegyric and propaganda is not surprising, given the epic
and civic idiom of such writings. He writes for Christian patrons, but
he knows the rules governing literary genres. They have a limited and
well-defined artistic function. More puzzling is the theme of the
barbarization of the empire in his writings. For this is the major
political and military problem of his day.[29] German auxiliaries in the
ranks of the Roman army, Goths fighting alongside the emperor at
the Frigidus, the menacing presence of Alaric and his armies in Italy
in 401–2 and 407–12: these are the great issues of the time. They
are, of course, reflected in Claudian's poetry. But the absorption of
barbarians into the Roman army is Stilicho's policy, and Claudian
must praise it. At the same time, he represents his and others' distrust
and dislike of barbarization by focusing on confrontations between
Goth and Roman. In this connection, hostilities with Alaric were a
godsend. Stilicho's confrontation with Alaric at Pollentia, south of
Turin, in 402, as presented by Claudian to a Roman audience, is seen
as a deadly obstacle placed in the way of what is alleged to be Alaric's
great ambition—to take Rome (*Bellum Geticum* 50–103, 267–313,
450–634).[30] Alaric was eventually to fulfil this Roman fear in 410,
but it was unlikely to have been on his agenda in 402, except as a
threat. Yet it is undoubtedly the case that the threat was taken

---

[29] See Heather (1991), esp. 193–224 on Alaric; Averil Cameron (1993*b*: 33–56).
[30] On the indecisive nature of the battle and Alaric's subsequent retreat to the
Balkans, which gave the Romans a pretext for claiming victory, see Heather (1991:
209).

seriously in Rome: Claudian is not engaging in fantasy. The city walls were repaired and reinforced, a detail that Claudian links to the panegyrical theme of the rejuvenation of the city in the consulship of Honorius: 'fear was the architect of beauty, and . . . war put an end to the old age that peace had brought on' (*VI Cons.* 531–6). It is appropriate that Claudian should stress the threat to Rome in poetry for a Roman audience. It puts Stilicho's success in a Roman context. It may distort Alaric's policy, but it does so in a way that is complimentary to Rome, and that is what matters.

Alaric, the Goths, Pollentia, and the symbolic role of Rome are all given a quite different interpretation in a Christian setting in a poem written by a contemporary of Claudian's, the *Contra Orationem Symmachi* of Prudentius. As its title indicates, we have come back to the 'relatio' of Symmachus and its repercussions. Prudentius too was a provincial, like many of the writers who represent the theme of Rome at this period. That theme was learnt, acquired, a cultural complex infused by adult experience of the city, developed by specific uses directed at audiences who were to be instructed, persuaded, flattered, and entertained. Like the emperor Theodosius who promoted his career, Prudentius came from Spain. Late in the fourth century, after provincial governorships in Spain or Gaul, he may have held office at the imperial court in Milan (Palmer 1989: 20–31). He visited Rome as a pious Christian pilgrim. His poetry contains some of the most far-reaching attempts of late antiquity to remodel the history and cultural traditions of Rome along Christian lines.

Prudentius' confrontation of the arguments of Symmachus' 'relatio' as late as 402 or 403 (Shanzer 1989) shows the symbolic value that the document and Ambrose's responses to it had acquired in the intervening two decades. But Prudentius is writing in a different world, marked by the Christianization programmes of Theodosius and his successors. What he presents, using Symmachus' arguments as a starting-point in the second book of the *Contra Orationem Symmachi*, is a radical extension of Ambrose's response. He adopts a theme that had been exploited in the third and early fourth centuries by Greek Christian writers: that the establishment of the principate by Augustus and the *pax Augusta* had been the providential setting for the coming of Christ (*Symmach.* 2. 602–22; cf. *Peristephanon* 2. 413–40).[31] Rome's single universal empire, enjoying concord and peace, is

[31] See further Ch. 6 n. 24, Ch. 9 n. 58.

like an individual in whom the discord of the passions has been subdued (*Symmach.* 2. 623–33). This notion of the 'praeparatio evangelica' is linked to a concept of progress and change as a universal law: even traditional Roman religion was constantly changing (*Symmach.* 2. 270–369). Rome, personified in the first book of the work as blushing, feeling shame for previous religious observances, repenting, atoning, and loving Christ (*Symmach.* 1. 507–23), is now shown not to have grown old and feeble. Her grey hairs blond again, Rome has become a warrior-queen once more: we sense that Prudentius is echoing Claudian and adapting him (*Symmach.* 2. 640–60). The claim that Rome is now invulnerable to the barbarians (*Symmach.* 2. 692–768) seems odd in the historical circumstances, until one realizes that the battle of Pollentia and the subsequent retreat of Alaric have been magnified to an irreversible success. The battle was fought under Christian auspices, but Prudentius hesitates to call it a divinely granted victory. Rather it was 'the fierce strength of men' ('vis cruda virum', *Symmach.* 2. 705) which triumphed. Ambrose's rationalization of Roman military success (*Letter* 17 (72). 7) has prevailed. A triumphal 'adventus' in Rome is imagined, in which Stilicho, the real hero of Pollentia, is named, but where the young emperor Honorius is the centre of the ceremony, with Christ as his ally (*Symmach.* 2. 727–68). 'Under his leadership', Rome says, 'you draw my kingdom to the heavens', for Christ is the 'saviour of palaces' (*Symmach.* 2. 759, 766). Prudentius rewrites Jupiter's pledge in Book 1 of the *Aeneid*—'I have granted an empire without end' ('imperium sine fine dedi', *Aen.* 1. 279)—as the legacy of the Christian Theodosius: 'he preaches an empire without end' ('imperium sine fine docet', *Symmach.* 1. 542). And this unending rule is very much of this world. Prudentius fuses Roman civic pride at a victory over barbarians with a Christian reading of that victory as part of the triumph of Christianity in the Roman world at large. And he does so in Roman terms, seeing it as an achievement of the family of Theodosius. At the same time, the Roman pagan past is de-sacralized. Alluding to edicts such as that of Honorius of the year 399 on the protection and preservation of pagan works of art, he makes a plea for their use as 'embellishments of our country' ('ornamenta . . . patriae', *Symmach.* 1. 501–5). Cleansed of blood, laundered of their religious significance, they will be beautiful—and harmless—objects of aesthetic appreciation rather than of worship (cf. *Peristephanon* 2. 481–4). They will become cultural artefacts.

Worship, for Prudentius, is concentrated elsewhere. His poetry reflects the contemporary growth and consolidation of martyr-cult in a Christianized empire where martyrdom was a thing of the past.[32] The significance of this bridging of the gap between the Christians of late antiquity and the persecuted Church, the ways in which space and time are sacralized by the creation of shrines as holy places and the proliferation of festivals in the calendar year, have recently been explored. Such tendencies gave a sense of self-identity to Christians. Prudentius' martyr-poems contribute to this movement, and some of them treat the theme of martyrdom in a Roman context, building upon the epigrams of Damasus and the hymns of Ambrose. Of these, the martyrdom of Lawrence (*Peristephanon* 2) is of particular interest for our theme. Prudentius rewrites the traditional account of the martyr's confrontation with authority to see Lawrence's death as a victory of Rome over itself, over polytheism, savage rites, idolatry, a crowning glory of the 'city of the toga' (*Peristeph.* 2. 10), destroying death in some homeopathic way by means of the martyr's death (*Peristeph.* 2. 1–20). Lawrence's fate is defined in civic terms. He becomes the citizen ('municeps') of heaven, a 'consul perennis' in an eternal 'curia' (*Peristeph.* 2. 553–6). Rome itself is presented as a city founded by Christ, who is evoked in terms associated with Romulus (ibid. 416). These are not merely empty formulas. While preserving the antithesis between pagan and Christian, and even barbarian and Roman, Prudentius sees martyrdom as the renewal of Rome's greatness (Buchheit 1966). Echoes and reworkings of Virgil present martyrs as transformations of heroism. The martyr-poems of Prudentius have been rightly compared with Ovid's poetic calendar of Roman festivals, the *Fasti*.[33] Their combination of myth, cult, festival, and building as themes of poetry contribute to the new articulation of Roman values. At times, as in the poem about Peter and Paul, it is the feast, with the Roman crowds flocking to the shrines, and the brilliant gold panelling and mosaics of St Paul's new basilica, that dominate, crowding out the martyrdom account itself, and focusing on the community and its environment (*Peristeph.* 12. 1–4, 31–64). And what is done at Rome should be imitated elsewhere, in Prudentius' native Spain, for example: 'It is enough for you to have learned all this at Rome: when you return

---

[32] Recent studies of martyrdom and martyr-cult: Markus (1990: 97–106, 139–55), esp. on the sacralization of space and time; Bowersock (1995); on Prudentius' martyr-poems (*Peristephanon*) see Palmer (1989), M. Roberts (1993).
[33] See Palmer (1989: 111–21), Charlet (1993: 158–60).

home, remember to keep this day of two festivals as you see it here'
(*Peristeph*. 12. 65–6). Once more Rome is providing norms of practice
and aspiration for the peoples of its empire. Rome, transformed, is re-
entering Christianized minds.

Yet the ideology promoted by Prudentius in *Contra Orationem
Symmachi* was fragile, for it depended on the assumed invulnerability
of the city of Rome and the sense of continuity in change which that
invulnerability provided. When Alaric besieged and occupied Rome in
410 the cultural shock outweighed the physical or political consequences of the event. It made Prudentius' image of Rome seem
suddenly outdated. Augustine's views on cities and kingdoms, real
or ideal, were to be quite different, partly in response to these
changed circumstances.

The preceding pages have shown that literary discourse about society
and religion in the fourth century often took the form of exploring
the theme of the city, and of Rome in particular. A historical sense of
the significance of the act of founding a city coloured Constantine's
establishment of his eastern capital on the site of Byzantium, the
'New Rome' that was to be known as Constantinople. Augustine's
choice of the theme of the two cities in history, his exploration of the
meaning of Christianity in terms of citizenship of the city of God,
bear traces of the influence of this focusing of discourse on the topos
of the 'civitas' or 'urbs'.[34] Other influences played a part, and several
of these are explored in Chapter 4: the apocalyptic tradition that
filtered through from Judaism to early Christianity, and the New
Testament Book of Revelation in particular; the typological use of
Jerusalem and Babylon in Christian writings from Paul to Ambrose;
antitheses in Donatist theology, especially in the writings of
Tyconius, who, though not an orthodox Donatist, held beliefs formed
by the views of that schismatic movement. To these one might add
Augustine's corresponding model of a church which should be unified but is divided against itself into Catholic and Donatist factions,
and the strong cultural tendency of his society to analyse phenomena,
and verbalize that analysis, in terms of polar opposites. But Augustine
was also attracted to discourse about humans in society in terms of
cities because it allowed him to engage with both pagan critics of
Christianity and those who, while attracted to or influenced by

---

[34] On the significance of 'civitas' in *City*'s title (*De Civitate Dei*) see App. A.

Christianity, were steeped in traditional Graeco-Roman culture. They
would understand the idealization of the city-theme that Ammianus,
Symmachus, Claudian, and Prudentius had exploited, and that was to
be further developed in a poem which some modern scholars have
understood as a pagan riposte to the early books of the *City of God*:
Rutilius Namatianus' *De Reditu*, written in 416 or 417.[35]

3. *Augustine and Nectarius*

In the aftermath of the violence involving Christians and pagans at
Calama in 408, a cultured pagan, Nectarius, wrote requesting
Augustine's intervention on behalf of fellow pagans charged with
holding an illegal procession and attacking the Christian church in
the town.[36] Nectarius' appeal is made on behalf of the civic loyalties
of those accused:

I pass over the importance of love of one's country, since you appreciate it. For
it is the only love which, by right, surpasses the affection felt for one's
parents. If there is any measure or limit to the care [for one's country] that
the good should have, we have on this occasion deserved to be excused from
its obligations. But since the love for, and attraction of, one's city grows day
by day, the closer one's life is to its end, the more one wants to leave one's
native place free from harm and flourishing.   (*Letter* 90)

Nectarius understands this civic ideal to have a transcendental, afterlife dimension, as a further letter to Augustine makes clear:

[this city] which the great god, and those souls who have deserved well of
him, inhabit, which all laws strive towards by different roads and ways, which
we cannot express in speech, but might perhaps discover by thought . . . of
which most learned men say that, for those who deserve it, a dwelling-place is
prepared in the heavens, so that a kind of advancement (*promotio quaedam*)
to the celestial world is proffered to those who have deserved well of their
native cities, and they live closer to God, who are shown to have brought
salvation to their country by their counsel or their deeds.   (*Letter* 103. 2)

Nectarius is clearly alluding to the celestial afterlife of deserving
Roman statesmen described in the finale of Cicero's *Republic*, the
so-called *Somnium Scipionis* (cf. especially *Rep.* 6. 13. 13). Even

[35] For Rutilius' eulogy of Rome see *De Reditu* 1. 47–164. On possible links between
City 1–3 and *De Reditu* see Ch. 2. 2 below, with n. 18.
[36] See further Ch. 2. 1. The correspondence between Augustine and Nectarius is
found in Augustine, *Letters* 90–1, 103–4.

before receiving *Letter* 103, Augustine had recognized the source of Nectarius' idealism, and his citation from Cicero ('if there is any measure . . . the good should have'; cf. *Letter* 91. 1), in *Letter* 90: it is 'those very books on the state, from which you have absorbed that affection of the most devoted citizen' (*Letter* 91. 3). This part of Cicero's *Republic* is lost, but it becomes clear from what Augustine says that in it, one of the interlocutors had asserted that there 'is no measure or limit to the care that the good should have for their country'.[37] It is an assertion of which Augustine approves (*Letter* 91. 1). He approves because he believes that it translates easily into Christian terms:

For which reason we would wish also to have one such as yourself as a citizen of a certain celestial country, for which, in devoted love, to the best of our ability, we run risks and labour among those for whom we take thought, that they may apprehend it: it would be our wish that you might conclude that there is no measure and limit to the care for even a small part of it that a man in exile (*peregrinanti*) on this earth should have. (*Letter* 91. 1)

The moral values advocated by Cicero are, Augustine argues, realized in the Christian Church, and prepare those who live by them to attain, with divine help, 'to a dwelling-place in the eternal and celestial city' (*Letter* 91. 3). In defending official opposition to pagan cult Augustine cites Cicero's critique of the immorality of the gods, in terms that anticipate the polemic of the *City of God* (*Letter* 91. 4–5), including its method of retortion (here using Cicero, a hero of the pagan traditionalists, against them).[38] Cicero's views on the afterlife are, Augustine argues, consistent with Christian beliefs (*Letter* 104. 3). Throughout this exchange, which antedates the writing of the *City of God* by a few years, Augustine defines the Christian concept of the society of the good in terms of 'city' ('civitas'), and 'native country' ('patria'), employing some of the language that characterizes *City*, such as 'country of the flesh' ('patria carnalis', *Letter* 91. 6, 104. 17), without adducing the two cities' model explicitly. The importance of the correspondence with Nectarius lies in the way in which Augustine engages in debate with a pagan on the basis of

[37] See *Rep.* 4. 7. 7. For the importance of this letter-sequence for the reconstruction of *Rep.* see Heck (1966: 142–7). Cicero in *City*: see below, Ch. 11. 1c. The Christian appropriation of Classical culture is studied by Gnilka (1984, 1993).

[38] Cf. Augustine's reference to Terence, *Eunuchus* 583 ff. in *Letter* 91. 4, and his citation of the same passage in *City* 2. 7: see further below, Ch. 11. 1a. On retortion see further Ch. 7 n. 5.

common assumptions about cities, real and ideal. The tone is civil rather than polemical, and this may be due as much to Augustine's sense of being at ease (and wishing to be seen, by Nectarius and other readers of his correspondence, to be at ease) with Cicero's views as to the delicate nature of the correspondence. The common assumptions allow Augustine to articulate his own vision of the city ('civitas').

2

The Making of the Book

In its fall, stones and timber fell; but in their lives all the
defences and embellishments, not of walls, but of morals,
came tumbling down.

(*City of God* 2. 2)

1. *Occasion and Time of Composition*

Augustine says that he was motivated to write the *City of God* by the
sack of Rome by Alaric and his Gothic army in August 410 and
subsequent pagan attempts to blame Christians for the event:

In the meantime, Rome was overwhelmed by an invasion of the Goths under
their king Alaric and by the force of a great disaster. The worshippers of the
many false gods, whom we call by the well-established name of 'pagans',
attempting to attribute Rome's troubles to the Christian religion, began more
sharply and bitterly than usual to blaspheme the true God. (*Retractations*
2. 43. 1)[1]

Alaric had been in Italy since 401, and Romans had long been
nervous about the Goths.[2] There is inscriptional evidence from 402
for the restoration of the Aurelian walls in anticipation of a siege.[3]
When Claudian celebrates Roman confrontation with Alaric at
Pollentia in 402 as a Roman victory, his panegyric presents the event
as saving Rome from attack (*Bellum Geticum* 50–62, 77–103, 546–9).
Claudian had to flatter the emperor Honorius and his general and
minister Stilicho, not to mention the Roman Senate, and he may have
distorted Alaric's aims in the process. But if Alaric did not have
designs on the city of Rome in 401–2, he was to fulfil Claudian's
aims by laying siege to the city in 408 and 409 in pursuit of his

---

[1] For the background to, and details of, Alaric's sieges of Rome see Heather (1991:
193–224), Courcelle (1964: 31–77), J. Matthews (1975: 273–300), Averil Cameron
(1993b: 43–9), Zwierlein (1978: 45–6).
[2] For the following see the general discussion in Ch. 1. 2 above, with nn. 29–30.
[3] *CIL* vi. 1189; *ILS* 797. See Zwierlein (1978: 45). On the survival of pagan rites
generally, and Christian adaptations of these, see Dihle (1996: 198, 201 n. 87).

claims for massive payments, first for withdrawing from Italy to Pannonia, then for military operations carried out in Epirus on behalf of the imperial government, and finally for releasing the corn supply, which he had seized, to the city. Alaric was showing Honorius' court at Ravenna, as well as the Romans, how vulnerable they were to a ruler who was also an ally. What attracted him to Rome was its wealth and its status as the visible symbol of the empire's historical identity. The Goths departed with rich plunder and with prisoners and hostages after three days of pillage and slaughter. Great buildings—above all the palace of the Sallustii—were destroyed, but not the basilicas of Saints Peter and Paul, where many, Christians and others, had sought sanctuary: for Alaric and his Goths were Christians, of the Arian variety.

There is evidence that Alaric's presence in Italy led to demands for the renewal of the pagan cult that had been suppressed, or at least threatened with suppression, since Theodosius' edicts of the 390s. At Rome the prohibition of pagan cult was apparently relaxed in an atmosphere of deep uncertainty.[4] The shock of the sack of Rome was as much psychological as it was material, and it affected Christians and others alike. Jerome compared Rome's fall with the Babylonian destruction of Jerusalem and—as Augustine was to do in Book 1 of the *City of God*—with the Greek sack of Troy (Jerome, *Letter* 123. 15–16, 127. 12; *Commentary on Ezekiel* 1. pref.).[5] He and others had absorbed the ideology of *Roma aeterna* to the extent that a threat to the Roman empire appeared to undermine the political and social basis upon which the Christian Church was presumed to be founded.

These events caused much ideological uncertainty in Rome and elsewhere. Confusion was caused by the latent or overt paganism of many Romans, not least among the governing class, and also by the adoption of ideas of divine protection taken over by Christians from their pagan forerunners.[6] Had Peter, Paul, and the other martyrs failed to protect their city where Rome's pagan gods had, in the past, succeeded? Augustine's sermons of 410 and 411 show that

[4] See Courcelle (1964: 32–4, 46–7), J. Matthews (1975: 290).
[5] See Zwierlein (1978: 49–55), Kelly (1975: 296–8), Palanque (1952), Paschoud (1967: 218–21), Doignon (1990).
[6] Cf. Paschoud (1967: 169–233), Thraede (1977: 91–9). Paganism's continued strength is shown by the severity of Honorius' decree of 407 (*CTh* 16. 5. 43, 16. 10. 19), and, in Africa, by the Calama riots of 408 (see further below).

these concerns were also those of his community at Hippo, a community that may have been swollen by refugees from Rome. In these sermons Augustine develops themes that are to become those of the *City of God*.[7] He stresses the presence of suffering (often divinely sent, to try us) as part of the human condition, and not merely a feature of the present 'tempora christiana' (*Ser.* 25. 3–5, 80. 8, 81. 8, 105. 8; *Ser. Casin.* 1. 133. 10–11; *Ser. Caillau* 2. 92. 2; *Ser. Denis* 23. 2–3, 24. 11; *Exc. Vrb.* 1. 9), and the impermanence of all human institutions, whether Christian or not (*Ser. Denis* 24. 13; *Ser.* 81. 9). Tribulations such as Rome's fall are foretold in Scripture (*Ser.* 81. 7–8, 105. 9; *Ser. Casin.* 1. 133. 10). Rome's vulnerability is not lessened by the presence there of martyrs' shrines (*Ser. Casin.* 1. 133. 6, 9, 12). Nor was Rome invulnerable in the pagan past (*Ser.* 105. 12; *Ser. Casin.* 1. 133. 9). Yet Rome has none the less survived the recent sack (*Exc. Vrb.* 2). Irrespective of whether this is a divinely ordained punishment or just a warning (cf. *Exc. Vrb.* 7, on the warning given to Constantinople and its consequences), the fact remains that the real city, its citizens ('civitas'), has been preserved (*Ser.* 81. 9; *Exc. Vrb.* 6; *Ser. Casin.* 1. 133. 7). The sack of Rome should focus men's minds on the superior worth and durability of spiritual values: we are aliens ('peregrini')[8] in this world (*Ser. Caillau* 2. 92; *Ser.* 81. 7, 105. 12), and our heavenly home or city is the goal where eternal peace will be achieved. The concept of the heavenly city is developed as a foil or contrast to the *Roma aeterna* concept (*Ser.* 105. 9–10, 12; *Ser. Denis* 23. 2; *Ser. Casin.* 1. 133. 7). Troy was not saved by its gods, who later became the gods of Rome (*Ser.* 81. 9), yet the pagan Ostrogoth Radagaisus was turned away from Christian Rome in 406, and Alaric was a Christian, if a heretic (*Ser.* 105. 13). It was all very bewildering. Pagan religion does not save cities, any more than Christianity causes their ruin: Constantinople has survived and flourished as a Christian city, but only so long as God wills (*Ser.* 105. 12). Augustine's overriding aim is to disassociate Rome's historical destiny from that of Christianity, or any religion. He attacks Christian as well as pagan versions of the Rome myth. In so doing he secularizes Roman history and institutions, reacting to

---

[7] See Courcelle (1964: 67–77), Hagendahl (1967: 415–17), Perler and Maier (1969: 397–405), Zwierlein (1978: 58–80), Doignon (1990: 134–45), Paschoud (1967: 239–45), Arbesmann (1954), O'Reilly's edn. of *Exc. Vrb.*
[8] See further Ch. 5 n. 4.

some extent against his own tendency to Christian triumphalism in the Theodosian 390s.[9]

Augustine is not attacking phantoms when he takes on pagan critics of Christianity in the aftermath of 410. Paganism had by no means died, even in heavily Christianized Roman North Africa. After the overturning of the statue of Hercules at Sufes in Byzacena, possibly in 399, a pagan mob killed sixty Christians and the local Senate, some of whose number had been involved in the riot, insisted that the church make good the damage (Augustine, *Letter* 50). At Calama in 408 pagans held an illegal religious procession which led to a riot and looting of Christian property: the church was stoned and its bishop Possidius, Augustine's future biographer, protested formally to the local council (Augustine, *Letter* 91. 8–10).[10] Church councils at Carthage in 407 and 408 sent protests to the imperial court at Ravenna concerning, among other things, the murder of bishops by pagans. We may suspect that these incidents were not isolated. But Augustine had more specific adversaries, Roman aristocrats driven out of Italy by Alaric's march on the Strait of Messina after his sack of Rome (Brown 1967: 290–4). Augustine presents these sophisticated critics of Christianity as subverting impressionable Christian minds, primarily at Carthage, by blaming recent disasters on the Christian religion (*Ser.* 81. 7–9). There is continuity between these views and those of the *City of God* (1. 1, 2. 3, 29, 3. 17).

Other themes of the sermons recur in the early part of the work. The polemical argument that Troy's gods, adopted by Rome, did not defend Troy is found in 1. 2–4. Augustine emphasizes that many non-Christians were saved by being allowed to take refuge in martyrs' shrines and basilicas (1. 1, 7), and that Rome's destruction was not total (1. 34). There are indications that Augustine has more information about events during the sack when he begins writing the *City of God* than he has in the sermons of 410–11. He knows about the rape and subsequent suicides of Christian women (1. 16–28). The events of August 410 are, furthermore, seen in a broader context. It is,

---

[9] For the stages of this development in Augustine's position from the 390s see Markus (1970: 22–71), Duchrow (1970: 291–8), Mommsen (1959: 265–98); all developing the pioneering approach of Kamlah (1951).

[10] On Sufes and Calama see Lepelley (1979: 293–5, 355–6), T. D. Barnes (1982), Perler and Maier (1969: 266–9), who also (p. 269) give references for violence against bishops and the Church's reaction; cf. on contemporary paganism in general van der Meer (1961: 29–45). On Augustine's correspondence after the Calama affair see above Ch. 1. 3.

Augustine argues, an inescapable feature of the human condition that the innocent suffer alongside the wicked (1. 8–9). Death is the human lot (1. 11), and lack of burial is immaterial to a Christian (1. 12–13). Augustine looks beyond the immediate polemical and apologetic purpose of his arguments to considerations of Roman history and *exempla* like Cato, Lucretia, and Regulus (1. 15, 19, 23–24, 30–31, 33). But it is undeniable that the aftermath of the sack of Rome has provided him with the impetus to begin the composition of the *City of God*.

That this is so becomes clearer if we consider the implications of Augustine's *Letter* 111 to the priest Victorianus, which he probably wrote at the end of 409. Victorianus had requested of Augustine that he deal 'in an extended work' ('prolixo opere': see Augustine, *Letter* 111. 1) with the suffering and uncertainty caused by barbarian invasions and depredations in Egypt, Spain, Gaul, and Italy. In his reply (that *Letter* 111 is intended as such is clear from 111. 9) Augustine points out that violence is found, even without barbarians, in Africa: in Hippo there are the crimes of Donatists and Circumcellions against Catholics (111. 1). Augustine sees in the suffering of Christians a fulfilment of divine prophecy and a punishment for neglect of the message of the Gospels (using the same imagery of pressing oil as in the sermons following the sack of Rome); he refers to those who say that before the 'tempora christiana' such evils had not afflicted the human race (111. 2).[11] Christianity does not promise protection from suffering or death (111. 5). Augustine quotes texts of the Old and New Testaments (Daniel 3: 26–37 and 9: 3–20; Proverbs 3: 12; Hebrews 12: 6; 1 Corinthians 11: 31–2) that focus on God's power to punish and the proper human response to this (111. 3–5). What difference does it make whether one dies by the barbarian's sword or of a fever? The important thing is one's moral and spiritual standing at death (111. 6). Augustine addresses the concerns of those who worry about the fate of holy women captured by the barbarians (111. 7–8). If they do not consent to whatever sexual violence they may suffer, they commit no sin: their purity is preserved (111. 9).

This letter shows that many of the concerns and themes of the

---

[11] For Augustine's mode of argument here and in *Ser. Casin.* 1. 133. 11 see Zwierlein (1978: 65–76). On Augustine's use at this time of the metaphor of pressing oil to express the paradoxically productive nature of some kinds of violence and suffering, see Brown (1967: 292–3) and, more generally, Poque (1984: i. 157–70).

sermons of 410–11 and the opening books of the *City of God* had already begun to preoccupy Augustine before the sack of Rome, just as had the theme of the two cities.[12] That should come as no surprise: such concerns and themes do not spring up spontaneously in response to a single military event. What is clear, however, is Augustine's belief, before the sack of Rome, that his answer to such problems can be concisely put, and that an essay of the scope of *Letter* 111 will suffice, particularly if it directs the reader to the richer consolation of the Scriptures (111. 9; cf. 111. 2).[13] He is not yet aware of the need for the 'extended work' which Victorianus requests.

It is unlikely that Augustine started composing the *City of God* before 412. Throughout the first half of 411 he was occupied with preparations for the Donatist Conference at Carthage. Then he quickly compiled two works directly related to the Conference, the *Breviculus* and the *Contra Donatistas*, as well as involving himself in the practical consequences of the proscription of Donatism. Moreover, a remarkable letter-sequence, most likely from late 411 and early 412, may provide further evidence of the gestation of the *City of God*.[14] In these years Augustine exchanged letters with the tribune and notary Flavius Marcellinus, appointed late in 410 as the imperial commissioner to supervise and preside over the Donatist Conference (*Letters* 136—from Marcellinus to Augustine—and 138–9), and to whom Augustine was later to dedicate Books 1–3 of the *City of God*. He also corresponded with Rufius Antonius Agrypinus Volusianus, sometime proconsul of Africa and future prefect of the city of Rome and prefect of Italy (*Letters* 132, 135—from Volusianus to Augustine—and 137). Marcellinus was a devout and theologically interested Christian of senatorial background, who also corresponded with Jerome on the question of the soul's origin (Jerome, *Letter* 126). Volusianus was loyal to the ancestral paganism of his family, the Caeonii, although several members of his family were pious, charitable, and active Christians. His sister Albina, his niece Melania the Younger, and Melania's husband Pinianus took up residence on their estates at Thagaste after fleeing Italy in the aftermath of the sack of Rome.[15] But Volusianus was curious about Christian

---

[12] See Ch. 4 below.

[13] On the consolation theme in *City* 1. 10–29 see Ch. 6 below.

[14] On these letters see Moreau (1973), and on their dates, ibid. 49–52; cf. Bardy, BA 33. 17–19. On Marcellinus see further below Sect. 2.

[15] For the movements of Melania and her relatives after the siege of Rome see *Life of Melania* 19–21. Events in Thagaste after their return: Augustine, *Letters* 124–6.

doctrines such as the Incarnation and the Virgin Birth (*Letter* 135. 2). Augustine replies to him at length, giving a careful account of the grounds for these central Christian beliefs (*Letter* 137. 2–18).[16] Marcellinus clearly acted as an intermediary between Augustine and Volusianus (*Letter* 136. 1), reporting to Augustine difficulties which Volusianus has in reconciling Roman political and legal practices with the Christian injunctions to turn the other cheek and not to return evil for evil or even resist theft (*Letter* 136. 2, citing Matthew 5: 39–41 and Romans 12: 17). Augustine replies directly but briefly to Volusianus on this point, suggesting that conventional Roman political practices are, in fact, condoned crimes, which God will not omit to punish, and arguing that the Christian's prize will be in the future life: 'they will receive an eternal reward in the celestial and divine city' ('in civitate superna atque divina') (*Letter* 137.20).

There are other signs in this correspondence that Augustine is thinking about political issues. He argues that trust or loyalty ('fides') and concord ('concordia') alone provide the security of the state (137. 17; cf. 138. 10). Moreover, in *Letter* 138, to Marcellinus, he deals in greater detail with the problems which Marcellinus had raised in *Letter* 136. 2. The cultivation of forgiveness of wrongs is something that Romans themselves traditionally appreciated as crucial to the interests of the state (138. 9–10). The Christian precepts are not incompatible with punitive measures, even with war, when they are undertaken for the good of offenders and the general welfare (138. 14–15). Sallust and Juvenal are cited as evidence that the decline of Rome began in the late Republic, long antedating its Christianization (138. 16). In these arguments elements of the apologia found in the *City of God* are adumbrated. The 'books' for which Marcellinus asks (136. 3) and which Augustine seems to promise (138. 20) may be that work which Augustine, in the dedicatory preface to the first book, presents as follows: 'having undertaken this work, owed because of my promise to you' (1. pref.; cf. 22. 30). The correspondence with Marcellinus and Volusianus also informs us about the kind of reader Augustine had in mind when he wrote the *City of God* (see below, Sect. 3).

---

[16] For an analysis of *Letter* 137. 12 see Gnilka (1993: 177–86).

2. Publication

Books 1–3 of the work were published when completed (5. 26). From letters between Augustine and Macedonius, *vicarius* of Africa, written in 413–14, we can see first reactions to them (*Letters* 154. 2—from Macedonius to Augustine—and 155. 2). Marcellinus was executed on 13 September 413, a victim (possibly framed by Donatists) of the purge following the suppression of Heraclian's rebellion. It is usually assumed that Augustine could not have persisted in his dedication of the work to Marcellinus (*City of God* 1. pref.), who is also addressed in 2. 1, after the latter's death, without in some way indicating that the dedication was posthumous. But it is possible that Augustine, having completed Book 1 before Marcellinus' death, left the dedication unchanged in commemoration of the friend whom he eulogized in a letter (*Letter* 151) written in late 413 or early 414, and who was quickly rehabilitated.[17] Books 1–3 could, therefore, have appeared in late 413 or in 414. After Book 2 no further book is addressed or dedicated to any person.

In 5. 26 Augustine refers to unnamed individuals who planned a riposte (presumably from the pagan point of view) to Books 1–3. Their identity is not known, nor is it known whether they wrote anything, though attempts have been made to link the poem *De Reditu Suo* by Rutilius Namatianus, which describes a journey made along the Italian coast in 416 or 417, with the riposte.[18]

Books 4 and 5 were begun in 415 and completed by late that year (*Letter* 169. 1). Books 6–10 were written by 417, the year in which Orosius completed his *Histories*, undertaken at Augustine's instigation. There Orosius refers to the first ten books of Augustine's work as 'ten rising beams which, as soon as they had issued forth from the height of the ecclesiastical brightness, shone over all the world', and informs us that he had begun Book 11 (Orosius, *Hist.* 1. prol. 11). The next secure dating depends on the reference to Book 14 in Augustine's *Contra Adversarium Legis* 1. 18, which was written no earlier than 420 (Raveaux 1986: 107). In *Letter* 184A. 5 Augustine

---

[17] For the whole episode see Perler and Maier (1969: 320–4); Brown (1967: 336–7); cf. Thraede (1977: 109). Augustine also dedicated two works written in 411–12, *Pecc. Mer.* and *Spir. et Litt.*, to Marcellinus.

[18] On the date of Rutilius' poem see Alan Cameron (1967) and Doblhofer's edn. i. 33–41; on Rutilius and Augustine see Dufourcq (1905), Courcelle (1964: 104–7), Bardy in BA 33. 23–5.

writes that he is working on Book 14: the letter may be dated to
about 418. Books 15–16 make frequent use of Augustine's work
Quaestiones in Heptateuchum, which was not begun before 419
(Zarb 1934: 70). A confusing passage, 18. 54, may be interpreted
to give the information that Augustine wrote it in 424 or 425 (see
Appendix D). By the time of composition of the *Retractations* 2. 43
(426–427) the work is fully complete. It had been written over at
least fourteen highly eventful years of Augustine's career. In his own
words, 'this work occupied me for several years because many other
matters intervened which I could not put off, and which kept me busy
sorting them out first' (*Retractations* 2. 43. 1).

The one piece of explicit evidence for separate publication of a
part of the *City of God* relates to the appearance of Books 1–3,
though it is evident from the reference to the work in Orosius that
associates of Augustine (and possibly others) were kept familiar
with the work as it progressed. It is only in 4. 1–2 that we find
an extensive summary of the preceding books, suggesting that
publication of instalments was not repeated after the appearance
of Books 1–3. *Letter* 2*. 3 refers to a reading of Book 18 over three
consecutive afternoons.[19] Such recitals for the benefit of Augustine's
circle will also have been a means of diffusion of the work. Whether
it was published in instalments or not, it is likely that so large a
work, written over such a extended period, was available only in
parts to some readers: *Letter* 1A*. 2 suggests that readers in
Carthage may have had incomplete copies. The same letter gives
valuable information about the proposed dissemination of the work.
Its twenty-two books are in individual notebooks ('quaterniones').
Augustine suggests that these be grouped in either two (Books 1–
10; 11–22) or five (Books 1–5; 6–10; 11–14; 15–18; 19–22)
'codices', following the main subdivisions of the work (*Letter*
1A*. 1). He advises Firmus, the recipient of the letter as well as
of a copy of the complete text of the work, to release the complete
text only to one or two individuals in Carthage: further copies can
be made from those done by them. Augustine may be intent on
cutting out the professional booksellers from the publishing process.
Alternatively, he may simply be concerned that the master copy of
the work remains securely in Firmus' possession: for he leaves him

---

[19] One of the recently discovered letters: see Chadwick (1983: 427–8), Braun in BA
46B. 427–9.

free to decide how he shall make it available to his own friends
(*Letter* 1A*. 2).[20]

3. *Readership*

It cannot be assumed that, because the *City of God* is an apologetic
work, it is primarily written for the non-Christian critics of Christianity to whom it so often refers. Augustine's correspondence with
Marcellinus and Volusianus demonstrates that there were potential
readers, both within the Christian Church and on its fringes (cultivated pagan aristocrats like Volusianus, whose family was largely
Christianized), whose interest in such a work would be considerable
(cf. *City* 2. 1). Writing to Firmus after its completion, Augustine
stresses its role in persuading potential converts, and strengthening
the perseverance of those already converted—a hortatory rather than
a catechetical function:[21]

> For their effect is not to delight the reader or make the ignorant learn lots of
> things, but to persuade [the reader] that he should enter the city of God
> without hesitation or persevere in living there.   (*Letter* 2*. 3)

In the letter to Firmus accompanying a copy of the work, Augustine
writes:

> You will find out yourself how you may distribute [the work] to your friends,
> whether they desire to be instructed in the Christian community, or are held
> in the grip of some superstition, from which they might conceivably be freed
> through God's grace by means of this labour of mine.   (*Letter* 1A*. 2)

Rather than seeing the *City of God* as refutation of pagan objections to Christianity, to be read directly by pagans, it is more in
keeping with what Augustine actually says about his aims to think
of the work's readers as Christians or others closely concerned with
Christianity, who require fluent and convincing rebuttal of pagan
views, both for their own satisfaction and as weapons to be used in
arguments with defenders of paganism. Firmus is a catechumen
(*Letter* 2*. 4), and it is to readers like Marcellinus and Volusianus

---

[20] Cf. Marrou (1976: 248); on Augustine's instructions in *Letter* 174 regarding *De
Trinitate* see ibid. 249–50. On *Letter* 1A* see also Madec in BA 46B. 424–6. On the
summary of *City* which accompanied the letter see App. C. On the codex in Augustine's
day see Petitmengin (1994); cf. in general C. H. Roberts and Skeat (1983).

[21] Yet in an important sense *City* is both apology and catechesis: see van Oort
(1991: 164–98) and Ch. 4 below; cf. TeSelle (1974*a*).

that Augustine refers when he writes that some readers were satisfied, and others most likely not, by the manner of his refutation: 'although it may be less than some eagerly wanted from us, still we have met the wishes of some by refuting the objections of the wicked' (*City of God* 10. 32). One must also reckon with the fact that in a time of crisis, such as obtained in a Roman world threatened by the Goths, the influence of traditional ideas, values, and beliefs, even among those who called themselves Christians, was pervasive and considerable. The language which Augustine uses about pagan critics is not calculated to persuade them of the folly of their views, but rather to denigrate such views among those who, openly or latently, are hostile to, or disturbed by, them. The preface to Book 6 of the *City of God* is a blatant instance. Augustine appeals there against the 'stupidity', 'obstinacy', 'incurable disease', and 'crazed wickedness' of his adversaries to reflective and judicious readers who are not excessively attached to paganism: 'those who understand what they read, and weigh it with due consideration, without any, or at least without grossly excessive obstinacy in clinging to their old delusion'. One must allow for the virulence of contemporary polemic (Loi 1977, Opelt 1980) and the rhetorical device of appeals to the reader's good sense. But the language used here and elsewhere about adversaries referred to in the third person, and the nature of the arguments advanced against their religious views and practices, suggest that ridicule, and the discrediting of such attitudes in others' eyes, rather than direct refutation, is the work's principal aim in its apologetic parts.

The same considerations apply to the exposition and defence of Christianity in the work. It is easier to appreciate its functions of exhortation and instruction than its polemical aspects. The extent and detail of its presentation of Christian views cannot be explained in apologetic terms alone. The importance of the *City of God* resides in the fact that its scope covers questions of cosmology, history, and eschatology, presupposing and utilizing the full range of Augustinian doctrines. A distinguished early reader of the first three books, Macedonius, *vicarius* of Africa, was impressed by their range, admiring 'the perfection of the priestly ministry, the philosophical doctrines, the full knowledge of history . . . the delights of eloquence', and seeing beyond the immediate occasion of the work ('the most powerful example of the recent calamity') to its wider significance (*Letter* 154. 2 in Augustine's correspondence).

4. *A Revised Text?*

Did Augustine revise the text of the *City of God*? In *Letter* 1A*. 1 Augustine writes: 'I have sent you, as I had promised, the books *On the City of God* which you asked me for with such insistence. I have even had them reread to me'. It has been suggested that this rereading amounted to a revision of the text, and even that some variant readings found in the manuscripts may derive from Augustine's successive editions of the work.[22] The latter suggestion must remain speculative. In favour of the former—revision by Augustine—is the fact that he considers his rereading worthy of mention, although it is possible that he is referring to no more than the review undertaken during the composition of the *Retractations*, with which *Letter* 1A* is contemporary.[23] In the *Retractations* itself Augustine is content to summarize the overall structure and general themes of the work. He explicitly corrects (*Retractations* 2. 43. 2) only two statements in the work: the assertion in 10. 8 that the divinely sent flame of Genesis 15: 17 was a miracle (it was, in fact, seen by Abraham in a vision), and the statement that Samuel 'was not one of the sons of Aaron' (17. 5), for which one should read that 'he was not the son of a priest' (he was, in fact, a descendant, and so, in one sense, a 'son', of Aaron: but his father was not a priest, and that is the point which Augustine wishes to make). The specific nature of these corrections might seem to suggest that Augustine reread the *City of God* thoroughly when working on the *Retractations*. On the other hand, these points may have been brought to his attention by other readers, and that might explain why he does not note more corrections in the *Retractations* chapter.[24]

---

[22] Dombart and Kalb's edn., vol. ii, p. xix, Lambot (1939: 116–17); cf. Divjak (1977), Gorman (1982: 409 n. 3).

[23] Cf. Madec in BA 46B. 426.

[24] The small number of revisions is not unusual in *Retr.*: see e.g. 2. 6 on *Conf.* On *Retr.* in general see Madec (1996).

3

The Apologetic Tradition

It is possible even for one who has grasped in the highest degree
the principles of rhetoric, and who uses them in the right way, to
do all in his power to persuade, and yet, because he fails to gain
the will of the one who ought to be persuaded, he seems to be
unconvincing.

(Origen[1])

The *City of God* is arguably the culmination of the Latin Christian
apologetic tradition in antiquity, and Augustine's work concludes a
series of writings that begins in the late second and early third
centuries with Tertullian and Minucius Felix.[2] Augustine's apologetic
addresses other questions and problems than Tertullian's. The post-
Constantinian Christianization of the Roman empire had altered the
context of apologetic. Rome had a new public religion, and the
question of its efficacy in protecting Rome called for new arguments.
Yet many elements of earlier apologetic could be, and were, exploited
by Augustine, and he may also be compared with near-contemporary
Christian writers like Ambrose and Prudentius, working, like him, in
the Theodosian and post-Theodosian periods. If Augustine is the last
of the Christian Latin apologists, he is also the culmination of an
African apologetic tradition: for Tertullian, Cyprian, Arnobius, and
Lactantius all have an African background.[3]

It is not easy to ascertain how much of earlier apologetic writings
Augustine knew and used. When citing Sibylline verses in 18. 23 he

---

[1] *Contra Celsum* 6. 57, tr. H. Chadwick (modified).

[2] Studies of Christian apologetic: Geffcken (1907), still fundamental; Grant (1988),
a useful introduction; Herzog (1989: 363–407), studies of Arnobius, Lactantius, and
others, by various scholars, with extensive bibliographies; Liebeschuetz (1979: 252–
77), on Arnobius and Lactantius; Chadwick (1966), on Justin, Clement, and Origen;
Dodds (1965: 102–38); Simmons (1995); T. D. Barnes (1981: 164–88); G. W.
Clarke's edn. of Minucius Felix, esp. 12–32 (bringing out the influence of Cicero's *De
Natura Deorum*): the notes of Clarke's edn. are a rich repertory of information on
apologetic. Pagan criticism of Christianity: Wilken (1979). Polemic in the Latin
Fathers: Opelt (1980). Augustine as apologist: TeSelle (1974a).

[3] For Minucius Felix see Clarke's edn. 5–8.

demonstrates that he knows Lactantius' *Divine Institutions*, quoting
a Latin prose translation of verses cited in the original Greek in that
work (*Div. Inst.* 4. 18. 15). But this passage does not prove extensive
use of Lactantius by Augustine: was he referred to Lactantius' use of
the Sibylline Oracles by the learned proconsul Flaccianus who showed
him the Sibylline Greek acrostic (partly quoted by Lactantius, *Div.
Inst.* 7. 16. 11 and 7. 20. 3) which he also cites, in Latin verse
translation, in 18. 23?[4] It is striking that the division of *Div. Inst.*
into negative (Books 1–3, on false religion and wisdom) and positive
(Books 4–7, on Christian religion and wisdom) parts anticipates a
similar division in the *City of God*, but this may be coincidental, with
both writers following the systematic progression of refutation
followed by positive doctrine.

Tertullian, *Ad Nationes* 2. 9 is cited at *City* 7. 1, and there may be
echoes of celebrated passages of his *Apologeticum* at 2. 3 (where
'There's no rain: it's the fault of the Christians' recalls *Apol.* 40. 2)
and 22. 7 (Christian beliefs as seed made more fertile by martyr's
blood, where *Apol.* 50. 13 may be recalled). But, although Tertullian
defines the scope of Latin Christian apologetic, and, like Augustine
and other apologists, uses Varro in his polemic, the piecemeal nature
of that polemic, particularly in the *Ad Nationes*, is different from
Augustine's, and suggests a distinctive approach to apologetic.[5]

Yet certain apologetic passages of the *City of God* are typical of the
tradition, and it is with the typical nature of apologetic themes,
rather than discernible specific influences on Augustine, that this
chapter is chiefly concerned. It will therefore consider a range of
themes in Tertullian and the *Octavius* of Minucius Felix, in Arnobius
and Tertullian, Ambrose and Prudentius, despite the fact that there is
no evidence that Augustine knew Minucius Felix, Arnobius, or
Prudentius. What is important is that Augustine was familiar with
the topics and arguments of a tradition (of which, in Latin, Lactantius

---

[4] See further Ch. 11. 2e, with nn. 65–6.
[5] Tertullian in *City*: see Bardy, BA 37. 823–4. Tertullian's theology: Osborn (1997).
The motif of martyrs' blood as seed is widespread in early Christian literature: there
are several instances in Augustine's *Enarrationes in Psalmos*, e.g. *En. Ps.* 58, *ser.* 1. 5;
for several references in Augustine and other writers see Mayor on Tert. *Apol.* 50. 13.
Uses of Varro in Christian polemic: Jocelyn (1982: 152), with references to older
studies; Ogilvie (1978: 50–5), on Lactantius, arguing, on balance, against direct use;
Simmons (1995: 55–62, 203–4), on Arnobius; Waszink (1948) on Varro in Tertullian's
De Spectaculis. On the piecemeal nature of Tertullian's polemic in *Ad Nationes* see
Waszink (1979).

is already conscious),[6] irrespective of how he absorbed it, and whether his absorption of it was exclusively literary or, as is more likely, due to a mixture of literary and oral influences. One cannot exclude the possibility of an available apologetic handbook or compendium, along the lines of known scriptural anthologies, such as Cyprian's *Ad Quirinum* (Ogilvie 1978: 95, 109). What follows, therefore, is chiefly a repertoire of apologetic themes, found in these other writers as well as in Augustine. This is a necessary prelude to an understanding of the import of Augustine's polemic, which was written in apparent ignorance of the two most powerful pagan critiques of Christianity, those of Celsus and Porphyry.[7]

One pagan line of attack on Christianity is to blame Christians for natural catastrophes, on account of their neglect of traditional cult of the gods. This is famously satirized in Tertullian:

If the Tiber reaches the walls, if the Nile does not rise to the fields, if the sky doesn't move or the earth does, if there is famine, if there is plague, the cry is at once: 'The Christians to the lion!' What, all of them to one lion? (*Apologeticum* 40. 2, tr. T. R. Glover)

Arnobius devotes the opening chapters of his *Adversus Nationes* to the charge, and both Ambrose and Prudentius counter it. Both Tertullian and Arnobius argue that the occurrence of such calamities antedates the advent of Christianity, and both suggest that they have decreased in the Christian era, but Prudentius (possibly developing a theme in Arnobius) argues rather that they are a constant fact of nature.[8] Other calamities, such as military defeats, were adduced by pagans in the same way, and dealt with similarly by the apologists. Augustine's encounter with such themes in the aftermath of Alaric's sack of Rome is nothing new. This line of attack is usually countered by Christians in the positive way just described, but the apologists

[6] Lactant. *Div. Inst.* 5. 1. 4 shows awareness of Cyprian, Minucius Felix, and Tertullian; cf. Ogilvie (1978: 88–95), who is cautious about Lactantius' direct use of Tertullian.

[7] On Augustine's knowledge of Porphyry see Ch. 11. 2b, with nn. 54, 61. But even if Augustine did not know Porphyry's *Against the Christians*, he will have encountered anti-Christian polemic in the *Philosophy from Oracles*, as *City* 19. 23 shows; cf. Simmons (1995: 222–42).

[8] Cf. Arnob. *Nat.* 1. 2–12, 2. 60; Ambrose, *Letter* 18. 4 ff.; Prudent. *Symmach.* 2. 568–77, 910–1063 (focusing on constant laws of nature rather than divine intervention; cf. Arnob. *Nat.* 1. 8–12). Calamities occurred before the Christian era: Tert. *Apol.* 40. 3–8; Arnob. *Nat.* 1. 2–5. Calamities less frequent since advent of Christianity: Tert. *Apol.* 40. 13–15; Arnob. *Nat.* 1. 6. See *City* 3. 17.

and Augustine, following an argument found in Seneca, could also claim that God does not distinguish between good and evil recipients of earthly punishments or rewards.[9]

The moral superiority of Christianity is often argued by the apologists. This argument frequently takes the form of an attack on the vulgarity and obscenity of pagan gods and of mystery rites, or on the immoral behaviour of gods in myths and poetic treatments of these. Minucius Felix, like Origen and Tertullian, cites with approval Plato's expulsion of poets from his ideal state: in the Latin tradition Cicero is important for the transmission of this theme.[10] Christian polemic (most spectacularly and brilliantly in Tertullian's *De Spectaculis*) often focuses on theatrical shows, the circus, games, and other public celebrations and entertainments, drawing on pagan satirists' attacks on their degrading and absurd nature. The theme forms the climactic conclusion of Prudentius' *Contra Orationem Symmachi*.[11]

Much space is given in apologetic to mockery of the pagan gods ('ludibria deorum'), their appearance, the existence of deities like Cloacina (the sewer-goddess), the vulnerability of gods, the perceived oddities and savagery of sacrificial ritual, the treatment of Vestal Virgins.[12] Absurdities of myth and iconography are frequently identified: by implication, aniconic worship is approved. There is

---

[9] Cf. Tert. *Apol.* 41. 3–4; Arnob. *Nat.* 1. 16. See Seneca, *De Beneficiis* 4. 28, *De Providentia* 1 ff. Cf. *City* 1. 8–9.

[10] Obscenity of mysteries, vulgar deities: Min. Fel. *Octav.* 25–8; Arnob. *Nat.* 5. Immorality of gods in myth and poetry: Min. Fel. *Octav.* 23 (here 23. 2 Plato's expulsion of poets; cf. Tert. *Ad Nat.* 2. 7. 11; Origen, *Contra Celsum* 4. 36); Tert. *Apol.* 14. 2–15. 8; Arnob. *Nat.* 4. 19–37 (here 32 ff. specific critique of poetry), 5. 32–45 (critique of allegorical interpretations); Lactant. *Div. Inst.* 1. 9–11; Prudent. *Symmach.* 1. 59–296. Origen, *C. Cels.* 4. 48: Stoic allegorization of obscene myths. Plato's expulsion of poets in Cicero: *De Natura Deorum* 1. 16. 42 (with Pease ad loc.); *Rep.* 4 (where *City* 2. 9–14 is important evidence: see Büchner's comm., esp. 370–87).

[11] Satirists' attacks on shows, games, etc.: see esp. Juvenal, *Sat.* 3. 93–100, 11. 162–70, 193–202; cf. Seneca, *Letter* 7, with Summers's comm. Polemic against 'spectacula': Min. Fel. *Octav.* 12. 5, 37. 11–12; Tert. *Apol.* 38. 4–5, *De Spectaculis* (cf. Waszink (1948)); Arnob. *Nat.* 4. 35 (cf. Geffcken (1907: 288 n. 3)); Lactant. *Div. Inst.* 6. 20 (see Ogilvie (1978: 88–9) for the possible influence of Cicero's *Republic* and Cyprian, *Ad Donatum* 8); Prudent. *Symmach.* 2. 1091–1129. Cf. Augustine, *Conf.* 6. 8. 13; *En. Ps.* 147. 7.

[12] 'Ludibria deorum': Min. Fel. *Octav.* 22. 5–8 (on Cloacina here cf. *City* 4. 8); Tert. *Apol.* 12. 2–7 (vulnerable gods), 25. 3; Arnob. *Nat.* 6–7 (e.g. 6. 7 on Capitol; 7. 24 on sacrificial ingredients; 7. 9 the sacrificial animal's plea to Jupiter); Lactant. *Div. Inst.* 1. 20; Prudent. *Symmach.* 1. 42–407, 2. 370–487 (against the 'genius' of the Roman people), 1. 379–407 (the savagery of sacrificial ritual, cf. 1. 578–9, 2. 1124), 2. 1064–1132 (Vestal Virgins).

an extensive polemic against statues, with a diverse background in Hellenistic Jewish apologetic, philosophical scepticism, Neoplatonism, and other areas: the mediating influence of Seneca's *De Superstitione*, to which Lactantius refers as well as Augustine, is important in the Latin tradition.[13] The multiplicity of paganism's local and special gods ('dei peculiares') is rich terrain for Christian satire: occasionally Rome's tolerance of 'dei peculiares' is used as an argument by Christians that their faith should be treated tolerantly.[14] Egyptian theriolatry is singled out for particular castigation, as it had been in Jewish apologetic and in sceptical attacks on traditional religious beliefs.[15] Pagan gods are frequently equated with demons: Arnobius, exceptionally, grants that there may be subordinate divine beings, but argues that they should not be worshipped by devotees of the High God.[16]

Use of the rationalistic explanation of worship of the gods given by Euhemerus of Messene (late fourth century BC) is widespread in Christian writers. The notion that gods had been great humans, and that honour for them had become cult was a convenient argument which had the advantages of deriving from a pagan source and of being systematic: Clement of Alexandria had used Euhemerus, and Lactantius may have had direct knowledge of Ennius' Latin translation of his *Sacred History*. Whether Euhemerus is cited or not, he lies behind similar arguments found, not just in Lactantius,

---

[13] Polemic against absurdities of myth and iconography, and praise of aniconic worship: Min. Fel. *Octav.* 22, 24. 5–10; Tert. *Apol.* 12. 2–7, 14. 2–6, Arnob. *Nat.* 6. 8–26; Lactant. *Div. Inst.* 2. 2, 6. 25 (both passages referring to Seneca's *De Superstitione*, cf. Augustine, *City* 6. 10); Prudent. *Symmach.* 2. 27–66, 245–69. On the background in Judaism and Greek philosophy see Geffcken (1907: pp. xx–xxxiii). Varro and aniconic worship: *City* 4. 9, 31; cf. Ch. 6 n. 34, Ch. 7 n. 6.

[14] Polemic against 'dei peculiares': Arnob. *Nat.* 4. 1–12 (cf. 3. 25); Min. Fel. *Octav.* 6. 1; Tert. *Apol.* 24. 7–8. Roman tolerance a reason for tolerance towards Christians: Tert. *Apol.* 24. 9–10; cf. Origen, *Contra Celsum* 5. 27.

[15] Jewish, philosophical, and Christian polemic against Egyptian theriolatry: Geffcken (1907: pp. xxvi–xxvii). Cf. Min. Fel. *Octav.* 28. 8 with Clarke's n. 466; Prudent. *Symmach.* 2. 869–72. See Augustine, *Conf.* 8. 2. 3 (citing Virgil, *Aeneid* 8. 698–700) and O'Donnell ad loc.

[16] Pagan gods equated with demons: Min. Fel. *Octav.* 26–7; Tert. *Apol.* 22–4; Lactant. *Div. Inst.* 4. 27 (cf. 2. 15–18); Prudent. *Symmach.* 1. 369–78 (cf. 1. 89–101). Contrast Arnob. *Nat.* 3. 2–3, on subordinate divine beings, whom Christians none the less do not worship. On Arnobius' concept of God and gods see Simmons (1995: 131–83). The equation of pagan gods with demons is pervasive in *City*: see esp. Ch. 7 below.

but in Minucius, Tertullian, Arnobius, and Prudentius, as well as Augustine himself.[17]

Some of the ways in which polytheism is attacked have been noted above. There are other forms of attack. Arnobius anticipates Augustine (*City* 6–7) in criticizing a superfluity of gods with overlapping functions, and in engaging in a reductionist argument against a multiplicity of gods (*Nat.* 3. 29–44). When they are not identified with demons, pagan gods may be equated with natural phenomena, a tendency already developed in Stoicism.[18] Other systematic pagan accounts of religious belief were also employed by Christians: one that is of great importance for Augustine, the so-called 'theologia tripertita' ('threefold discourse about gods'), is found also in Minucius Felix, where, differently from its use in Augustine, it is employed to argue that monotheism is a widespread popular belief.[19]

One charge which Christians had to face was that their religion undermined tradition, and so was an un-Roman activity. This charge was countered in various ways. One was to argue for the antiquity of the religious beliefs to which Christians subscribe. A variant of this is to suggest that Christian belief in the one true God is a reflection of what respected pagan philosophers of the past have maintained. Another approach was to appeal to Roman inclusiveness in religious observation. A third argument sought to demonstrate that Christians were good citizens.[20] Understandably, neither the second nor the

---

[17] Euhemerus: Min. Fel. *Octav.* 20–1, 23–4, with Clarke n. 276; Tert. *Apol.* 10. 3–12. 1; Arnob. *Nat.* 4 (cf. 3. 39); Lactant. *Div. Inst.* 1. 11, 14–15 (cf. Ogilvie (1978: 55–7)); Prudent. *Symmach.* 1. 102–63, 245–77. Augustine refers to Euhemerus by name in *City* 6. 7, 7. 27 and uses his theories extensively in Books 8–10; cf. Ch. 7 below, on 6. 7–8, with n. 5.

[18] Prudent. *Symmach.* 1. 297–353. Cf. *City* 6. 8, 7. 15 ff., 4. 12.

[19] Min. Fel. *Octav.* 18. 11–19. 14 with Clarke n. 228. For a survey of the tradition of 'theologia tripertita' with an appendix of texts see Lieberg (1973). The term is a modern coinage: Augustine talks of Varro's 'three kinds ("genera") of gods' (*City* 4. 27), or 'three kinds of discourse about gods' ('theologia', 6. 5; cf. 6. 12). Tertullian mentions a 'threefold classification ("triplex genus") of gods', *Ad Nat.* 2. 1. 10. The terminology does not necessarily presuppose a normative concept: see Beard (*CAH*² ix. 757) on the real and the fictional Scaevola; Rawson (1985: 299–300).

[20] Antiquity of Christian beliefs: Tert. *Apol.* 19. 2–8. Celsus argued that Christianity was a corruption of ancient religious traditions: see Chadwick's edn. of *C. Cels.*, pp. xx–xxi. Ancient philosophers anticipated Christianity: Min. Fel. *Octav.* 20. 1–2, replying to the pagan charge that adherence to Christianity entailed a divorce from ancestral traditions (ibid. 6. 1). Inclusiveness in Roman religious observation: Min. Fel. *Octav.* 6–7 (giving the pagan defence); cf. Origen, *C. Cels.* 8. 66. Possible allusion to the Roman practice of 'evocatio' in Min. Fel. *Octav.* 6. 2; cf. Livy, 5. 21–2 and Ogilvie ad loc. Christians are good citizens: Tert. *Apol.* 28. 2–37.

third of these arguments is found in post-Constantinian apologetic: they had become superfluous. But the notion that pagan philosophy anticipates Christianity is congenial to Augustine. Apologists often argue that there is support for Christian doctrines in philosophical arguments, whether these are about the nature of the human soul, or concepts of deity, or the attainability of truth, or the nature of authentic wisdom: 'it is open to anyone to suppose that either present-day Christians are philosophers or philosophers of the past were already Christians' (Minucius Felix, *Octavius* 20. 1, tr. G. W. Clarke).[21] Philosophical and rhetorical methods are appropriated in the defence of Christianity: the use of the dilemma is an obvious instance.[22] Despite the close affinities between rhetorical and philosophical forms of argument, this is not felt to be inconsistent with polemic against rhetoric.[23]

When Romans appealed to the help which their gods had given them, particularly in the acquisition of empire, Christians could point to the achievements of other peoples, without the assistance of Rome's gods.[24] But another related argument could be even more effective. Why was it maintained that certain gods helped the Romans, when they were worshipped by peoples defeated by the Romans?[25] A similar argument, arising out of Roman claims to be descended from Troy, ran: how could the Romans have confidence in their gods of Trojan origin, when Troy itself had been defeated? But the most subtle apologetic move of all was to account for past Roman

---

[21] Support for Christian doctrines in pagan philosophers: Arnob. *Nat.* 2. 14–30, 37–47, using Lucretius to argue for mortal nature of soul; cf. Hagendahl (1958. 12 47), Liebeschuetz (1979: 256–7). See also Lactant. *Div. Inst.* 1. 6, 7. 13, 18 (all using *Hermetica*; cf. use of oracles in relation to Christian doctrines: 1. 7, 4. 18, 7. 20, 23–4), 7. 7–9 (various philosophers on world, soul's immortality, etc.); cf. *Div. Inst.* 3 generally on truth and untruth in philosophy, and on the distinction between philosophy and 'wisdom', and Book 4 on 'true wisdom' in religion. A variant of the theme is found in Augustine, *Letter* 137. 5. 17: the two commandments of Matthew 22: 37–9 (love of God and of neighbour) contain the whole of philosophy, presented here by Augustine in the traditional tripartite scheme physics–ethics–logic (on the use of the scheme in *City* see below, Ch. 7 with n. 15). Amelius in Eusebius, *Praeparatio Evangelica* 11. 18. 26, reveals Platonist sympathy for the prologue of John's Gospel (cf. *City* 10. 2, 10. 29). Philosophers as critics of Greek religion, and of other philosophers' theologies: see Geffcken (1907: pp. xviii–xx). Christian apologetic uses of philosophers: Wolfson (1970: 7–14); Chadwick (1966: 1–22), on Justin.

[22] On Augustine's use of the dilemma in *City* see Ch. 6 on 1. 15 and 19, with n. 8.

[23] Cf. Prudent. *Symmach.* 1. 632–42, 2. 642–8.

[24] Min. Fel. *Octav.* 25. 12; Tert. *Apol.* 26. 2–3.

[25] Min. Fel. *Octav.* 25. 9; Tert. *Apol.* 25. 4–9; cf. Prudent. *Symmach.* 2. 347–70, 488–577.

success by assuming that it was a divine reward, providentially bestowed, for Roman piety and virtue. This argument adapted views found in Polybius and Cicero. It might be accompanied by a review of early Roman history that was, however, not always entirely laudatory: criticism of Rome's origins through concentration on the violent elements in the Romulus–Remus legend (itself a rhetorical topic) could temper praise of Rome.[26] But once the principle that genuine virtue is found among pagan Romans is accepted, Christians can cite traditional examples of virtue, such as Regulus, with approval: Arnobius compares Christ with both Regulus and Manius Aquilius.[27]

The argument that an ordered universe entails monotheism was exploited by the apologists, and is found in Arnobius and Lactantius. Prudentius argues that since the universe is one, Symmachus' appeal on behalf of religious pluralism is invalid: there is only one path to the truth.[28] But of the Latin apologists only Prudentius gives expression to a theme advanced by some Greek writers, especially Eusebius, that there is a correlation between monotheism and the Roman empire, unified under its Christian emperor: the theme is also found in Orosius.[29] In Eusebius the theme eulogizes Constantine, and Constantine is also the focus of Prudentius' panegyric: but Prudentius sets the Constantinian achievement in the context of Theodosius' 'tempora Christiana'.[30]

[26] Roman success a divine reward for Roman virtue: Tert. *Apol.* 25; Min. Fel. *Octav.* 25 (takes the form in 25. 2–5 of a selective review of early Roman history); Arnob. *Nat.* 7. 38–51; Prudent. *Symmach.* 1. 287–90; cf. Orosius, *Histories* 7. 1. 7–11. See *City* 1. 3, 3. 6, 12 ff., 5. 12–26, 15. 5, etc. For the argument see Polybius, 6. 56. 6, with Walbank ad loc.; Cicero, *De Nat. Deor.* 2. 8, 3. 5, with Pease ad loc.; cf. Min. Fel. *Octav.* 6. 3, with Clarke ad loc. Romulus–Remus legend as rhetorical topic: used by Christians e.g. Min. Fel. *Octav.* 25. 2; Tert. *De Spectaculis* 5. 5–6 (for its background in Latin literature, with examples, and further Christian instances, see Clarke's edn. of *Octav.* n. 382). See further below, Ch. 9 n. 6.   [27] See further Ch. 6 n. 10.
[28] Prudent. *Symmach.* 2. 769–909. Cf. Arnob. *Nat.* 3. 35 (tension between philosophical view of world as single rational being and polytheism); Lactant. *Div. Inst.* 1. 3–6, 4. 3, 29 (monotheism consistent with belief in Father and Son); Orosius, *Hist.* 6. 1. 1–3. In Min. Fel. *Octav.* 18. 11–19. 4 the 'theologia tripertita' (see n. 19 above) is used to argue that there is widespread belief in monotheism.
[29] Prudent. *Symmach.* 2. 578–768; Orosius, *Hist.* 6. 22–7. 1. 1. For texts in Eusebius and other writers see n. 30 below, Ch. 6 n. 24, Ch. 9 n. 58.
[30] Eusebius' eulogy of Constantine: *Panegyric to Constantine* 3. 3–6, 16. 3–8; *Life of Constantine* 1. 5, 24, 2. 19. Cf. Mommsen (1959: 282–4), T. D. Barnes (1981: 261–71), Fowden (1993: 86–90). 'Tempora Christiana' under Theodosius: Prudent. *Symmach.* 1. 408–642 (here 467–95 highlighting Constantine's achievement); cf. Augustine, *Cons. Ev.* 1. 14. 21, 1. 34. 52. For these and other texts of Augustine prior to *City* see Markus (1970: 30–1, 53–4), and for the topic generally, and Augustine's change of perspective, ibid. 22–71.

Augustine was attracted to the idea of a radically Christianized empire under Theodosius in the 390s, but had retreated from it by the time he came to write the *City of God*.

Apologetic did not merely attack paganism and defend Christianity. It also provided elements of positive Christian teaching. In this dual aspect it anticipates both the polemical and the doctrinal aspects of the *City of God*. Thus the apologists give details of beliefs about the afterlife, especially the resurrection of the body, the final judgement, and the eternal punishment of the damned, the themes of the last two books of Augustine's work.[31] They provide, as does Book 1 of the *City of God*, a synopsis of Christian attitudes to burial of the dead.[32] They expand on the theme of martyrdom and the metaphor of the Christian warrior.[33] They stress the belief in the freedom of the human will.[34] They contrast true religion with superstition.[35] Arnobius links conversion and the need to engage in apologetic (*Nat.* 1. 39). Lactantius, like Augustine, discourses on the nature and legitimacy of the passions.[36] Minucius Felix and Tertullian argue that bad Christians are no Christians at all.[37] Yet none of the pre-Augustinian apologists, with the exception of Lactantius, provides anything approaching a comprehensive overview of Christian beliefs. Furthermore, neither Arnobius nor Lactantius has much to say about the Church, and it is arguable that 'their silence is partly tactical' (Liebeschuetz 1979: 276). They do not wish to underplay what Christians and non-Christians have in common by placing too much

---

[31] Resurrection of body: Min. Fel. *Octav.* 34. 9–12; Tert. *Apol.* 48. 1–13; Lactant. *Div. Inst.* 7. 23. Final judgement: Tert. *Apol.* 47. 12–48. 15; Lactant. *Div. Inst.* 7. 19–27. Eternal punishment: Min. Fel. *Octav.* 11. 5, 34. 12–35. 6; Tert. *Apol.* 47. 12, 48. 12–15; Lactant. *Div. Inst.* 7. 21.

[32] Min. Fel. *Octav.* 11. 4, 12. 6, 34. 10, 38. 3–4; Lactant. *Div. Inst.* 6. 12.

[33] Metaphor of Christian warrior: Min. Fel. *Octav.* 37. 1–5 (also on martyrs), with Clarke, n. 622; Lactant. *Div. Inst.* 6. 4 (on war metaphors in Lactantius see Liebeschuetz (1979: 270 n. 2)); Prudent. *Symmach.* 1. 461–510 (using the examples of Constantine and Theodosius), 2. 1130–2. On the theme of 'militia Christi' and martyrdom see Palmer (1989: 140–54). Harnack (1981 (originally pub. 1905)) remains fundamental. Cf. M. Roberts (1993: 45–51).

[34] Min. Fel. *Octav.* 34. 12; Prudent. *Symmach.* 1. 335–40; cf. Orosius, *Hist.* 7. 1. 3–4.

[35] Min. Fel. *Octav.* 1. 5, 13. 5, 38. 7; Lactant. *Div. Inst.* 4. 28, 6. 1–2. Cf. Augustine, *City* 4. 30, 6. 9.

[36] Lactant. *Div. Inst.* 6. 14–19; see Hagendahl (1958: 338–41) on the influence of Cicero, *Tusculan Disputations* 4. 11–14 here; Liebeschuetz (1979: 273–4). Cf. Augustine, *City* 9. 4–6, 14. 5–19.

[37] Min. Fel. *Octav.* 35. 6; Tert. *Apol.* 44. 3, which clarifies the *Octav.* passage. Cf. Origen, *C. Cels.* 4. 25.

emphasis on what separates them. Yet there is greater emphasis in
Arnobius than in the earlier apologists on 'making paganism
intellectually disreputable' (Nock 1933: 259). But their reticence
may also reflect contemporary Christian individualism, especially
among converts from higher social classes (Liebeschuetz 1979:
276–7).

In this chapter the themes of apologetic have so far been considered
without reference to the literary form and style of the individual
works. It is beyond the scope of the present study to go into detail
on such matters, but the following remarks are intended to provide
the elements of the literary background to the apologetic aspects of
the *City of God*. I concentrate on the four prose works whose form
and scope make them the true predecessors of Augustine's apologetic:
Tertullian's *Apologeticum*, Minucius Felix's *Octavius*, Arnobius'
Adversus Nationes, and Lactantius' *Divine Institutions*.[38]

Tertullian's *Apologeticum*[39] is addressed to high Roman magistrates, the governors of provinces and their associates (1. 1, 2. 5, 50.
12, and elsewhere). Ostensibly, it has the form of a speech before a
legal tribunal, a 'defence' (1. 1) of Christians. But Tertullian stresses
at the outset that it is, in fact, a literary substitute for such a public
defence: 'If you . . . who, in the light of day, set on high, at the very
head of the state, preside to do justice,—if you are not allowed openly
to investigate, face to face to examine, the Christian issue . . . then let
truth be allowed to reach your ears at least by the hidden path of
silent literature' (*Apol.* 1. 1, tr. T. R. Glover). Because it is in the form
of a law-court speech, addressed to non-Christians and dealing with
charges made against Christians, Tertullian has no occasion to refer
to, or regularly cite, Scripture: an exception are the references to
Moses, but they are made to establish his early date by comparison
with figures like Inachus, Danaus, and Priam (19. 3–4, 45. 4), or to
make the point that different peoples have human religious

---

[38] On Tertullian's unrevised *Ad Nationes* see T. D. Barnes (1971: 104–6). On
Prudentius' *Symmach.* see Shanzer (1989). Cyprian is one of the predecessors named
by Lactant. *Div. Inst.* 5. 1, and his *Ad Demetrianum* is echoed in *Div. Inst.* 5. 4. 3: see
Ogilvie (1978: 88), who also (pp. 88–9) discusses the possible influence of Cyprian's
polemic against the theatre (*Ad Donatum* 8) in *Div. Inst.* 6. 20. There is no discernible
influence of Cyprian's polemic on *City*, despite Augustine's familiarity with, and use of,
Cyprian, esp. in the context of the Donatist controversy: Bonner (1963: 276–94).

[39] Tertullian's *Ad Nat.* and *Apol.* were written in or after 197: Budé edn. p. xxxviii,
Waltzing's comm. p. 232, T. D. Barnes (1971: 33–4).

innovators (21. 29). Tertullian does not expect his readers necessarily
to have heard of Moses (19. 3). The story of Christ is told in summary
form (21). Explicit biblical references are few (21. 16, 21. 22, 22. 3,
31. 3, 32. 1, 39. 9, 47. 9, 48. 13).

The *Octavius* of Minucius Felix[40] is written in dialogue form, with
obvious indebtedness to the philosophical dialogue, and especially
Cicero's *De Natura Deorum*.[41] General references to Scripture are
few and vague (33. 4, 34. 5, 35. 1). Verbal echoes of the New
Testament are uncertain and in any case minimal (31. 6, 32. 1, 4,
9). Christ is referred to only in oblique paraphrase (9. 4, 29. 2). As
with Tertullian, Minucius Felix may be influenced by his audience,
wishing to avoid giving a detailed insider account of Christianity.
Considerations of genre will also have played a role: the philosophical
dialogue form determines themes and their treatment.[42]

Both the *Apologeticum* and the *Octavius* are relatively short works.
The apologetic of Arnobius and Lactantius is of greater scope.
Arnobius' *Adversus Nationes*[43] is in seven books. It is influenced
by both Minucius Felix and Tertullian, and Arnobius may have
chosen the title and literary form of his work under the influence
of Tertullian's *Ad Nationes*. Both are treatises, and in both use is
made of devices like retortion (turning an opponent's argument back
on himself) and the introduced adversary whose views are refuted.[44]
At 3. 1 Arnobius refers, without naming any names, to apologetic
predecessors. His engagement with contemporary Platonism, which
he opposes as well as being under both its influence and that of
Hermeticism, is of particular interest (*Nat.* 2). He uses Latin classical
authors and antiquarian writing on Roman religion.[45] His knowledge

[40] The date of composition of the *Octav.* is unknown. Cyprian (martyred 258)
knows the work. The question of its date relative to Tertullian's *Ad. Nat.* and *Apol.*,
with which it has strong thematic affinities, is now generally answered by arguing that it
presupposes them: see Clarke's edn. 8–12, suggesting composition in the first third of
the 3rd c.: the classic discussion of the question is Axelson (1941).
[41] See Clarke's edn. 26–32.
[42] Cf. Augustine's remarks, *Conf.* 9. 4. 7, on the question of including Christian
elements in the Cassiciacum dialogues. O'Donnell ad loc. reads Alypius' objection
there to mention of the name of Christ in the dialogues as a biographical detail
(Alypius' conversion was limited at this stage), but the matter may rather be one of
genre.
[43] Date: Herzog (1989: 366–7) gives 303–11, Simmons (1995: 47–93) suggests
late 302 to mid-305.
[44] See McCracken's tr. i. 45; Simmons (1995: 243 ff.). See below, Ch. 7 n. 5.
[45] On Porphyry as Arnobius' opponent see Simmons (1995: 216–318). Hagendahl
(1958: 12–47) discusses Lucretian elements in *Nat.*

of Christianity is imperfect, and he has some odd views about its doctrines (Simmons 1995: 16–21). His acquaintance with Scripture is limited, and he does not appeal to its authority in his arguments. He appears not to realize the significance of the Jewish Bible for Christianity (3. 12), and his citations from the New Testament are minimal, and do not prove direct acquaintance with the texts (1. 6, 2. 6). But one should be careful about the conclusions to be drawn from this: Arnobius' apologetic, directed, like those of Minucius Felix and Tertullian, at non-Christians, does not necessarily call for detailed citation of Scripture.[46] But he does address the common jibe against the perceived crudity of Scripture's style with vigorous if misguided defence of some of its oddities (1. 58–9).

Although the evidence that Lactantius was Arnobius' pupil (Jerome, *De Viris Illustribus* 80; *Letter* 70. 5. 2) is sound, Lactantius appears not to have known the *Adversus Nationes* when composing his *Divine Institutions*.[47] Thus his critique of his apologetic predecessors (itself an indication of his awareness of being part of a tradition) in *Div. Inst.* 5. 1 and 4, though mentioning Minucius Felix, Tertullian, and Cyprian by name, does not refer to Arnobius (Ogilvie 1978: 88–95). Of Greek theological writers Lactantius refers by name only to Theophilus of Antioch (*Div. Inst.* 1. 23. 2; used ibid. 4. 5. 6–8 (Ogilvie 1978: 29)), whose apologetic work *Ad Autolycum* was widely read in the Latin West, and popular in North Africa (Ogilvie 1978: 92). The *Divine Institutions*, like Arnobius' work, is in seven books (in Lactantius' case, at least, probably on grounds of numerical symbolism). Lactantius employs the full resources of classical rhetoric and philosophical argument in his defence of Christianity. His work, written in Ciceronian style, appropriates and addresses itself to the classical literary and intellectual tradition. It also provides, from Book 4 on, a presentation of elements of Christian belief, in a Gnostic form heavily influenced by Hermetic writings.[48] Lactantius' aim is not merely to attack false religion and wisdom, but also to write a Christian protreptic. He has a positive attitude to literature and learning in general: classical authors are regularly cited. In the *Epitome* of the work which Lactantius himself made (some time after 314, when he became tutor

---

[46] For the whole question see McCracken's tr. i. 25–7.
[47] Cf. Ogilvie (1978: 89–90). Date of *Div. Inst.*: Herzog (1989: 377) gives 304–11.
[48] The standard account is Wlosok (1960); cf. Loi (1970).

to Constantine's son Crispus at Trier), some philosophical themes are further developed and documented (Herzog 1989: 392). As for the addressees of his work, Lactantius writes it to persuade not merely pagans hostile to Christianity, especially 'the wise and learned and rulers of this age' (*Div. Inst.* 5. 1. 15), but also wavering and uncertain Christians themselves (5. 1. 9). Lactantius' apologetic, begun in the time of the Great Persecution, was completed (with work on a revised edition of *Div. Inst.*, as well as on the *Epitome*) under the emperor Constantine, in whose honour he inserted two panegyrical passages in Books 1 and 7 of *Div. Inst.* (Heck 1972: 127–33). Thus, in certain respects it stands at the threshold of the new Christian empire. To Jerome Lactantius was, above all, a master of destructive argument ('if only he had been able to reinforce our beliefs as readily as he demolished those of others!', Jerome, *Letter* 58. 10. 2). His unorthodox dualism and rejection of Trinitarian views, and his millennialist tendencies, may have cost him readers in antiquity. His principle of not citing biblical texts is abandoned in *Div. Inst.* 4 (cf. 4. 5). It has been argued that a high proportion of his citations derives from Cyprian's collection of biblical testimonia. He also quotes from apocrypha (*Div. Inst.* 4. 12. 3).[49] His work ends, as does the *City of God*, with eschatological and millennialist themes: the end of the universe, the judgement of Christ, the eternal punishment of the damned, the resurrection of the dead. The influence of the Book of Revelation and the tendencies to which it gave rise are pervasive.

In a formal literary sense, only the extended treatises of Arnobius and Lactantius could serve as models for Augustine's apologetic. Tertullian might provide examples of polemical argument, but his method and the scope of his writings differ fundamentally from Augustine's. While there is no evidence that Augustine read and knew Arnobius, he had some acquaintance with Lactantius. Yet the spirit of Lactantius has left no profound traces in Augustine's work. This may have to do with Augustine's rejection of the Eusebian understanding of Christianity. Lactantius was not Eusebius, but his 'interpretatio Romana' of the Christian religion gave it a place in the Roman political and conceptual tradition that Augustine would have found unacceptable. Nor would Lactantius have been theologically

---

[49] On the question of Lactantius' use of Cyprian's collection of testimonia see Ogilvie (1978: 96–108); ibid. 105–8 on his use of apocryphal texts.

attractive to Augustine. Thus, while Augustine undoubtedly borrows
themes and arguments from the earlier apologists and related literature, no one of his precursors has either a dominant or a profound
influence on his apologetic concerns and strategies.

Common to all the principal apologists in the Latin tradition is the
use of classical authors, chiefly Varro and Cicero. Varro's antiquarian
writing on Roman religion is an important source for Tertullian and
Minucius Felix, as it will be for Augustine, and Varro's critical and
sceptical attitude may have been a stimulus to their polemic. But
only Augustine fully exploits the principles of the Varronian critique
of religion, and there is uncertainty over whether Arnobius and
Lactantius had direct access to the *Antiquitates*.[50] The philosophical critiques of traditional religion found in such works of
Cicero as *De Natura Deorum* and *De Divinatione* had considerable
influence on Minucius Felix, Arnobius, and Lactantius. Indeed, if
Arnobius is to be believed, pagan contemporaries of his could be
found to argue that those works of Cicero which criticized traditional religion should be destroyed by senatorial decree (*Nat.* 3. 7).
Seneca's *De Superstitione* (used by Minucius Felix, 25. 8[51]) plays a
similar role. It would be an exaggeration to claim that these classical
authors provided the primary impetus to Latin Christian apologetic,
but they undoubtedly serve to define some of its principal characteristics, just as confrontation of Lucretius and Epicureanism influences
the apologetic of Arnobius and Lactantius.[52] This is a different
intellectual world from that of Augustine. Yet Lactantius, to a limited
extent and probably through intermediaries, and Arnobius, more
extensively and directly, engage with Plato and the Platonist tradition,
and in that respect they, especially Arnobius, are forerunners of
Augustine.[53]

[50] Varro in Arnobius and Lactantius: for modern discussions see n. 5 above.
[51] Seneca, fr. 33 Haase, from *City* 6. 10, is regarded as also being the source of
Octav. 25. 8: see Clarke ad loc.
[52] Cf. Hagendahl (1958: 9–88) on the influence of Lucretius on Arnobius' polemic
and vocabulary. Cf. Schmid in *RAC* v. 681 ff. Simmons (1995: 131–42) takes issue
with those scholars who argue that Arnobius' concept of God is Epicurean.
[53] On Lactantius' knowledge of Plato (chiefly, it is argued, through Cicero, Seneca,
Minucius Felix, and anthologies) see Ogilvie (1978: 78–81). Lactantius knows something of more recent philosophical debate, as *Div. Inst.* 5. 2 (where Hierocles is named)
shows. For Arnobius' confrontation of Porphyry see Simmons (1995: 216–318).

4

The Theme of the Two Cities

O Jerusalem, Jerusalem, I have forsaken thy Courts,
Thy Pillars of ivory & gold, thy Curtains of silk & fine
Linen, thy Pavements of precious stones, thy Walls of pearl
And gold, thy Gates of Thanksgiving, thy Windows of Praise,
Thy Clouds of Blessing, thy Cherubims of Tender-mercy
Stretching their Wings sublime over the Little-ones of Albion!
O Human Imagination, O Divine Body I have Crucified,
I have turned my back upon thee into the Wastes of Moral Law.
There Babylon is builded in the Waste, founded in Human desolation.

(William Blake, *Jerusalem*)

1. *The Theme of the Two Cities, and Related Themes, before Augustine*

The theme of the two cities is implicit in Scripture.[1] In the apocalyptic Book of Revelation the new Jerusalem symbolizes the city of God:

and I will write on him the name of my God, and the name of the city of my God, the new Jerusalem, which comes down from my God out of heaven. (Rev. 3: 12)

And I saw the holy city, new Jerusalem, coming down out of heaven from God, prepared as a bride adorned for her husband. (Rev. 21: 2)

And in the spirit he carried me away to a great, high mountain, and showed me the holy city Jerusalem, coming down out of heaven from God. (Rev. 21: 10)

Earthly cities (including Jerusalem: Revelation 11) and rulers (17: 10) fall. Babylon symbolizes earthly evils and the vulnerability of power:

[1] In addition to the texts cited below, see Gen. 25: 23 (Esau and Jacob as two nations/peoples in Rebekah's womb), Eph. 2: 19–22 (themes: alien status ('then'); citizenship ('now'), together with the saints, of God's household, which is built on foundation of prophets and apostles). For the theme of the city of God in general see Thraede (1983). Cf. van Oort (1991, 1997); App. A below.

And the woman that you saw is the great city which has dominion over the kings of the earth.   (Rev. 17: 18)

Babylon the great is fallen, is fallen, and has become a dwelling place of demons.   (Rev. 18: 2)

The same kind of typological use of Jerusalem is found elsewhere in the New Testament:

But you have come to Mount Sion and to the city of the living God, the heavenly Jerusalem, and to an innumerable company of angels.   (Hebrews 12: 22)

Now this is an allegory: these women are two covenants. One is from Mount Sinai, bearing children for slavery; she is Hagar. Now Hagar is Mount Sinai in Arabia; she corresponds to the present Jerusalem, for she is in slavery with her children. But the Jerusalem above is free, and she is our mother.   (Galatians 4: 24–6)

And, without explicit reference to Jerusalem:

But our commonwealth (*politeuma*) is in heaven, and from it we await a Saviour, the Lord Jesus Christ.   (Philippians 3: 20)

The Book of Revelation, and possibly other New Testament texts, are influenced by elements in the Jewish apocalyptic traditions, in particular their dualism, and the antitheses between this world or age and the one to come.[2] These apocalyptic texts stress the demonization of the present world, and contrast it with a heavenly world or city. The antithesis Babylon–Jerusalem is used. It is also found in the so-called New Testament Apocrypha, which speak of the kingdom of God, Satan's reign, the city of Christ, and two 'mētropoleis'. The imagery of the two cities is found in the Coptic Nag Hammadi *Acts of Peter and the Twelve Apostles*. Similar imagery is found in a work of apocalyptic literature written in the first half of the second century, and which circulated widely in early Christian communities: the *Shepherd of Hermas*. The first Similitude of this work develops an antithesis between two cities, and the theme of the Christian's alien status. The two cities are not named, but they represent antithetical values, and the Christian Church is elsewhere in the *Shepherd* a

---

[2] e.g. among the Old Testament Apocrypha, Baruch and 4 Esdras. This para. and the next are indebted to van Oort (1991: 284–322), to which reference should be made for details. For a guide to the early Christian writings referred to in this Sect. see Koester (1982).

heavenly city, or a tower or mountain. The alienation of the Christian is a theme of the *Gospel of Thomas* and the *Pseudo-Clementines*, and in the latter it is related to the themes of the two kingdoms, of good and evil, of the future age and the present one.

In the apologists the metaphor of the city is used to evoke the sense of identity of the Christian community as a spiritual entity (*Letter to Diognetus* 5. 17). Tertullian famously develops the image of a Christian city:

But your orders and your magistracies and the very name of your senate-house (*curia*) is the Church of Christ. You are enrolled as his in the books of life. There your crimson robes are the Lord's blood . . . but you, an alien in this world and a citizen of the city on high, Jersualem—our community (*municipatus*), he said, is in heaven—you have your endowments (*census*), your religious rites (*fastos*); you have nothing to do with the delights of this world, rather, you are obliged not to rejoice in them.   (*De Corona* 13. 1–4)

These words[3] are to be read against a background cluster of themes in Tertullian: the negative way in which he talks of the 'world' ('saeculum', 'mundus'); the demonization of the Roman state, its politics and its cult; the soldier of Christ contrasted with the soldier of Caesar. Rome is sometimes identified with Babylon. Occasionally, the Church is called 'city' or 'kingdom' or 'house' of God ('civitas dei', 'regnum dei', 'domus dei'). But there is in Tertullian no extensive thematization of the antithesis of the two cities or kingdoms. Nor is there in Cyprian, although in his writings also pessimism about this world ('saeculum') and its values goes hand in hand with the themes of the Christian's alien and warrior ('militia Christi') status, in which the armies of God and the devil confront one another. Similar conclusions can be reached about Lactantius. There is no theme of antithetical cities or kingdoms, but there is much emphasis on contrasting powers, good and evil spirits created by God, symbolized by light and darkness, soul and body, the path to heaven and the path to hell.[4] The theme of the two ways, and the Jerusalem–Babylon contrast of Revelation 18 and 20–1, are also found in Commodian. In the *Commentary on the Apocalypse* of Victorinus of Pettau[5] the downfall of Rome is linked to that of Babylon in Revelation. There

[3] Note the play upon 'curia' ('Senate-house'), implicitly linked to Greek 'kurios' ('Lord'), the use of Phil. 3: 20, and of John 16: 20 as the sub-text of the last words quoted.
[4] The influence of Lactantius on Augustine's apologetic and polemic is another matter: see Ch. 3 above.   [5] Referred to by Augustine in *Doctr. Chr.* 2. 40. 61.

are elements of a theology of two opposing forces in Donatist literature, where the Roman state is readily equated with Babylon, and its
authority with the devil's warriors, against whom the alienated
soldiers of Christ fight.[6] The views of Tyconius will be dealt with
separately below.

Ambrose's influence on Augustine in several areas is well attested.
Did he influence the theme of the two cities? The antithesis of the
kingdoms of God and sin, and the equation of the 'saeculum' with
the kingdom of sin (the earthly domain of the devil), are frequent
themes in Ambrose. He equates the Church with the city of God (*In
Psalm. 118 Expos. ser.* 15. 35), and speaks of it as the 'heavenly city
of Jersualem': the motif is also found in Clement of Alexandria,
Origen, Hilary of Poitiers, and Jerome.[7] The earthly city and the
heavenly Jerusalem are contrasted:

consider, dearly beloved, that Jesus suffered outside the gates, and withdraw
from this earthly city; for your city is the Jerusalem on high. Live there, that
you may say, 'but our community is in heaven'. Jesus went out of the city, that
you, going out of this world, may be above the world.   (Ambrose, *Letter* 63.
104).

Ambrose also talks of two groups ('sectae'), symbolized by Cain and
Abel, in opposition (*De Cain et Abel* 1. 1. 4). The allegorical
antithesis of Jerusalem and Babylon in Ambrose more often than
not refers to an inner conflict in the individual, so that the soul can
be called a city, and the believer's soul Jerusalem (e.g. *De Isaac vel
Anima* 5. 39, 6. 54; van Oort 1991: 276–81).

Several of Ambrose's themes are anticipated in Origen, by whom
Ambrose was greatly influenced, especially in his exegetical method.
The theme of the soul as a city, as Jerusalem, as the city of God, and
the antithesis Jerusalem–Babylon as one in the individual soul, are
found in Origen. But for him the city can also be a metaphor for the
world, and the earthly Church can, together with the heavenly
Church, form one city (van Oort 1991: 281–3). The metaphor of
the earthly Church as a city within a city is developed by Origen in an
interesting way:

---

[6] Van Oort (1991: 301 n. 594) refers to the *Passio Maximiani et Isaaci*, which
speaks of the struggle 'inter militem Christi et milites diaboli' (*PL* 8. 769C).

[7] See Lamirande (1992–4: 958–9) for details.

if you compare the council of the Church of God with the council in each city, you will find that some councillors of the Church are worthy to hold office in a city which is God's, if there is such a city anywhere in the universe. (*Contra Celsum* 3. 30, tr. Chadwick; cf. ibid. 8. 74, on the heavenly city)

None of the texts so far adduced, and none of the writers hitherto referred to, puts forward the model of two cities as an interpretation of the course of history in the way in which Augustine does. Yet essential elements—theoretical and linguistic—of Augustine's theology of the two cities are present in them.

It is now time to consider a likely major source of Augustine's views, in the writings of the Donatist Tyconius. Tyconius met with critical opposition in his own church, from which he was excommunicated. He did not become a Catholic, but his influence on later Catholic thinking was considerable. We know of him chiefly thanks to Augustine, whose hermeneutics was influenced by Tyconius' extant *Liber Regularum*, cited and criticized extensively in *De Doctrina Christiana* 3. 42–56. The central idea of the *Liber Regularum* is that Old Testament prophecies refer either to Christ and the Church, or to the devil. The Church is the body of Christ, but it is a 'body in two parts' ('corpus bipertitum'), composed of true and false Christians. There is no such duality in the completely evil 'body of the devil' ('corpus diaboli'). Hermeneutics is the key, through its 'rules' ('regulae'), to finding the appropriate significance of prophecies. In another work, his *Commentary on Revelation*, which survives only in fragmentary (and possibly adapted[8]) form, Tyconius may have put forward a system of two cities. Much depends on the extent to which one can establish, or believe, that extracts from the Revelation commentary by the Carolingian presbyter Beatus of Liebana report Tyconius' views and vocabulary. In Beatus we find an unequivocal reference to the two 'civitates' in the exegesis of Revelation 14: 8 and 17: 18, where 21: 9–10 and 21: 24 are adduced.[9] But it is possible that Beatus and other later commentators superimposed ideas and language of Augustine's on Tyconian models: Beatus refers to, and quotes from, the *City of God* in his Revelation commentary. In his

---

[8] See Lo Bue's edn. 32–8 for a discussion. Augustine appears to have been familiar with Tyconius' commentary on Rev.: see *Doctr. Chr.* 3. 42; Steinhauser (1987).

[9] Beatus, *In Apocalypsin* 515 and 574–5 (in Sanders's edn.); cf. van Oort (1991: 270–1).

ecclesiology Tyconius develops ideas that anticipate Augustine's.[10] The concept of the Church as a 'corpus bipertitum' is similar to Augustine's views on it as a 'mixed body' ('corpus permixtum'), even if Augustine distances himself from Tyconius on this topic in *Doctr. Chr.* 3. 45. The view that the 'corpus diaboli' originates in the evil will rather than in an evil nature, and is thus not in absolute contrast to the 'Lord's body' ('corpus domini')—not least because it can be identified with the evil part of the 'corpus bipertitum'—is also a clear anticipation of Augustine's thinking.[11] Augustine often asserts the fundamental antithesis of the two cities, but he stresses no less often their intermingling in the 'saeculum'. It is true that he does not make his argument depend on texts from Revelation, but neither is it certain that Tyconius did so: the *Liber Regularum*, with its doctrine of two 'corpora', does not explicitly use Revelation. It is certainly the case that we do not find, in the evidence as we have it, any trace in Tyconius of a history of the world from creation as a history of two cities: Beatus speaks of the two 'civitates' in the present only. In this respect Augustine's model of history may be original, though the lack of any reference in Augustine to Tyconius as a source of this particular idea does not prove Augustine's originality, given his (and, in general, ancient writers') cavalier attitude to naming sources.

It is now generally assumed that Augustine's views on the two cities are not influenced in any detailed way by Manichaean or Greek philosophical writings. A recent examination (van Oort 1991:

[10] The contrast Jerusalem–Babylon was important to Tyconius: *Liber Regularum* 3 (p. 50 Burkitt); cf. Chadwick (1989: 50). Tyconius related this contrast to the 'civitas' theme: *Reg.* 5 (p. 63. 3 ff. on 'Hierusalem bipertita'; cf. p. 63. 10 'civitatis Hierusalem'). Jerusalem, as a 'body in two parts' ('corpus bipertitum'), includes Babylon: *Reg.* 3 (p. 50. 10—12); cf. van Oort (1991: 269) who refers (p. 269 n. 387) to further passages in *Reg.* But in commenting on Rev. 11: 8, where the word 'civitas' occurs in his Latin version, Tyconius does not relate it to his duality theme, but rather equates 'civitas' with Church ('ecclesia'): *In Apocalypsin* 375 Lo Bue. The Turin fragments extend only from Rev. 2: 20 (in part) to 4: 1, and from 7: 16 to 12: 6, thus providing no evidence for Tyconius' commentary on 'Babylon' in Rev. 14: 8. But he may not have said much of import there, if we consider *In Apoc.* 91 ff. on Rev. 3: 12 ('Hierusalem'), and ibid. 377 on Rev. 11: 8. Nor have we any evidence of what Tyconius said on the later parts of Rev., namely those parts where Beatus speaks of two 'civitates' in his exegesis of Rev. 14: 8 and 17: 18 (where 21: 9—10 and 21: 24 are adduced). But the Turin fragments stress the duality of the Church, which is Christ's body (*In Apoc.* 285): cf. ibid. 172 ('there are two peoples in the Church . . . God's party ["pars"] . . . and the devil's party'), 412 ('two . . . dwelling-places (*aedificia*) in the Church').

[11] In this and the following points I differ from the interpretation given by van Oort (1991: 269, 272—4). But his section on Tyconius (pp. 254–74) is none the less of considerable value.

199–234) discusses possible Manichaean influences in detail, and concludes that, despite some similarities (the two kingdoms' doctrine, the division of history into three periods), the differences between Manichaean and Augustinian dualism are fundamental. One might add that Augustine's anti-Manichaean polemic makes deliberate borrowings inherently implausible. It seems reasonable to conclude that any similarities between Manichaean principles and Augustine's views are part of their shared Jewish-Christian background.[12] Augustine will have been trained as a rhetor to express his ideas in terms of polar opposites, and the Manichees probably reinforced this tendency, but the opposites which his mature thought expounds are essentially distinct from those of Manichaeism.

What of the Greek philosophical tradition? Augustine is aware of the purport of Plato's *Republic*:

Or should the prize rather be awarded to Plato the Greek, who, when he was forming his ideal of what a state should be like, judged that poets should be expelled from the city as enemies of truth? (*City* 2. 14)

Like Plato, Augustine thinks of individuals and states as analogous (*City* 4. 3, 12. 28). But Augustine's model city is not, as Plato's is, a paradigm for actual political states, which might be its image (*Republic* 592b; cf. 500e). In Plotinus, the intelligible world is a 'homeland' (*Enneads* 1. 6. 8), and Augustine echoes Plotinus' words in *City* 9. 17 and *Confessions* 8. 8. 19. Moreover, Plotinus (in a rare instance of political analogy in the *Enneads*), compares harmony in the individual, when the mind rules the body and the passions, with harmony in the city, and he talks of an intelligible 'city above' and a 'city of the things below, ordered according to the things above' (*Enn.* 4. 4. 17). This kind of talk may reinforce Augustine's tendency to think in terms of contrasting cities, although, as with Plato, Plotinus' paradigm/image model is not at the heart of Augustine's thinking.

Stoic views on the cosmic city generate metaphors of dual citizenship, and also the idea of a community of gods and humans. This is given powerful expression in Seneca:

[12] Mani's background was first fully revealed by publication and elucidation between 1970 and 1982 (see Bibliog. C) of the papyrus Cologne Mani-Codex (*P. Colon. inv.* 4780), a biography in Greek (partly translated into English) which traces his early religious development: see Lieu (1985: 28–37, 54–5); Brown (1989: 197–201).

We have a notion of two republics: one great and truly 'public', which comprises gods and humans, in which we do not look to this corner or to that, but plot the extent of our state by the sun; the other, in which the circumstances of our birth have enrolled us . . . some people concern themselves with both republics, the greater and the lesser, some only with the greater, some only with the lesser. We can serve this greater republic even in retirement (*in otio*): in fact, we can somehow do so better in retirement, investigating what virtue is, whether it is one or manifold.   (*De Otio* 4. 1–2)

The Stoic notion of membership of a group that is defined in terms of an ethical ideal, a community of rational and morally good beings, has more in common with Augustine's concept of the city of God than is often recognized. Like Augustine's city of God, the Stoic cosmic city was conceived of as one coexisting with actual societies. Augustine's adoption of the Stoic natural law theory is the appropriation of a consequence of Stoic thinking, since Zeno, about the relation between community and virtue, even if Augustine was not aware that it is such a consequence.[13]

Stoic views blend with Platonic themes in Philo of Alexandria. The alien status of the soul in this life, the contrast between visible and intelligible worlds, the image of the immaterial world as a city or commonwealth: these are notions that seem to be echoed in Augustine. They may not derive from Philo (if they do, Ambrose is a possible intermediary), but rather from the philosophical and exegetical traditions that influence both Philo and Augustine.

Much of what Augustine knows of Stoic natural-law theory comes from Cicero's *Republic*. The same probably applies to his knowledge of Stoic, and indeed Platonic, political theory.[14] When Augustine thought about philosophical reflections on the relation between justice and the state, he will have thought above all of this topic as it is elaborated in Cicero: his references to the *Republic* throughout the *City of God* make this clear. It is no less clear that the preoccupations of the *Republic* are not identical, in scope or emphasis, with those of Augustine. Yet Cicero's themes of the universality of natural law, right reason, and the transcendental nature of true justice, his

---

[13] Cf. Schofield (1991: 57–103) on Stoic views, here 102–3 on the development towards natural law theory. Van Oort (1991: 235–54) discusses possible influences on Augustine's two cities' doctrine of the Platonic tradition, the Stoics, and Philo.

[14] On the Platonism of Cicero's *Rep.* see Zetzel's edn. 13–17, 25–9. On Cicero and Plato see Sedley (1997: 116–22). Augustine's uses of Cicero's *Rep.* in *City* are discussed below in Chs. 6 (on 2. 11–13, 2. 21), 10 (19. 21, 23–4; 22. 6), and 11. 1c.

critique of the failings of the Roman Republic, and his search for an account of the state that is consistent with human ethical aspirations, will all, *mutatis mutandis*, have contributed to the formation of Augustine's theory of the two cities.

Recently, the Jewish-Christian catechetical tradition has been investigated as a possible source of Augustine's two cities' theory.[15] The principal motive for this investigation is the fact that the two cities' theme is anticipated, several years before the composition of the *City of God*, in Augustine's *De Catechizandis Rudibus*.[16] In the Dead Sea Scrolls from Qumran there is a catechetical text, the *Manual of Discipline*, which includes a description of two opposing spirits (or angels), two antithetical ways (of light and darkness), and two societies of good and evil people. In early Christian texts like the *Didache* and the *Epistle of Barnabas* this Jewish doctrine of the two ways (in *Didache* 1. 1 the ways of life and death; cf. Matthew 7: 13–14) is linked to baptismal instruction, and developed in relation to the moral antithesis of the two societies. A similar cluster of themes is found in the *Pseudo-Clementines*, where the motif of two kingdoms (of those who now rule the earth, and whose rule will pass, and of the future king of heaven) is central. More-over, the Qumran texts, the *Apostolic Constitutions*, the *Pseudo-Clementines*, and Irenaeus' *Proof of the Apostolic Preaching* present, in the context of an introductory catechesis, a narrative of the history of salvation, as Augustine does in the *De Catechizandis Rudibus*, and, on a massive scale, in the *City of God*. In addition, the precepts and exhortation that are a feature of *Cat. Rud.* are found in a number of these earlier writings, such as the *Didache*. But in Augustine talk of the two ways is not explicitly related to the theme of the two cities or kingdoms.[17]

---

[15] See van Oort (1991: 322–51), to whom reference should be made for details of the texts and themes alluded to in this para.

[16] See further Sect. 2 of this Ch., and Ch. 12.

[17] References to the (right) way in *Cat. Rud.* 11 (with implicit reference to the wrong way), 17, 40, 48–9. References to the good way and the two ways: *En. Ps.* 48 *ser.* 2. 4; 106. 4, 9, 14; 125. 4; *Ser.* 224. 1. I owe these references to van Oort (1991: 344, 347–8). On links between *Cat. Rud.* and *City* see Ch. 12 below. There is no evidence that Augustine knew the *Didache* (or the work known as *Doctrina Apostolorum*, a Latin version of the doctrine of the two ways, on which see van Oort (1991: 328 n. 717)), but he was clearly familiar with the catechetical tradition of which the *Didache* is the outstanding example. Van Oort (1991: 348–51) surveys briefly some later sermons and tractates by Caesarius of Arles and others under Augustinian influence, where the theme of the two ways is linked to spirits, kingdoms, and cities, making explicit (unlike Augustine, but like the earlier catechetical writings in the Jewish and early Jewish-Christian traditions) the connection between the theme of the two ways and that of the two kingdoms or cities.

What, in conclusion, can be said about the influence of these various writings upon Augustine? In many cases his direct acquaintance with the texts discussed cannot be countenanced. In others, such as the writings of Cicero, Tyconius, and Ambrose, Augustine's knowledge is documented. The assumption of the influence of a widely defined, but none the less identifiable, catechetical tradition is plausible, and, even if specific antecedents cannot be determined, this influence should not be ruled out. But the sum total of possible influences does not equate with the scope of the theme of the two cities, and related themes, as we find them in the *City of God*. Augustine's synthesis is more than the ideas and texts that may have informed it. In particular, the application of the two cities' model to an account of the course of history seems novel. Interestingly, that application may be the aspect where Manichaean influence is greatest. For it was the Manichees, in common with other Gnostic groups, who understood history as the battleground of opposing principles or powers. Augustine does not present the two cities, or their conflict, in Manichaean terms, but he may have been inclined to see in the historicizing mythology of Manichaeism a scheme that could be adapted to the history of created beings, angelic and human, and the historiography, scriptural and other, that narrates this history.

2. The Theme of the Two Cities in Augustine's Other Writings

The theme of the city of God, with its scriptural origins, and the equation of the Church with a symbolic Jerusalem, are found in Augustine's early exegesis:[18]

He himself [the Lord] lives in Zion, which means 'Contemplation' (*Speculatio*), and contains the image of the Church which now is, just as Jerusalem contains the image of the Church which will be, that is, of the city of the saints already enjoying the angelic life; for Jerusalem means 'Vision of Peace'. Contemplation precedes vision, just as this Church precedes the one which is promised, the immortal and eternal city. (*En. Ps.* 9. 12)

[18] For the following see Lauras and Rondet (1953), Bardy in BA 33. 65–74. Tradition of city of God theme in general: Thraede (1983). *En. Ps.* 9 is usually dated to 392. For the biblical etymologies used by Augustine in this and some of the following texts, see Ch 9 below, on *City* 16. 4, with n. 25; Ch. 10 below, on *City* 19. 11, with n. 10. Jerome's *Onomasticon* is Augustine's source: see further Ch. 9 on *City* 15. 17 ff., with n. 16.

The *De Vera Religione*, written in 390–1, develops the notion of two classes ('genera') of people in history:

the entire human race, whose life, like that of a single person from Adam to the end of this world, is so governed by the laws of divine providence that it appears divided into two classes. In one of these is the crowd of the wicked, bearing the image of the earthly man from the beginning of the world until its end. In the other is the succession of people devoted to the one God, but from Adam until John the Baptist living the life of the earthly man under a kind of servile justice. Their history is called the Old Testament, which promises a kind of earthly kingdom, which, taken as a whole, is nothing other than the image of the new people and the New Testament that promises the kingdom of heaven. (*Vera Rel.* 27. 50)[19]

In *De Catechizandis Rudibus*, written about 400 or in 404–5,[20] Augustine develops the motif:

So two cities, one of the unrighteous, the other of the saints, persist from the beginning of the human race until the end of time; now they are mixed bodily, one with another, but separate in their wills; on the day of judgement, however, they are to be separated in body as well. (*Cat. Rud.* 31)[21]

Now, just as Jerusalem signifies the city and community of the saints, so Babylon signifies the city and community of the unrighteous, for it is said to mean 'Confusion'. We have just spoken about these two cities, whose course runs intermingled through the vicissitudes of time, from the beginning of the human race until the end of the world, and who will then be separated at the last judgement. (ibid. 37)

The symbolic contrast between Jerusalem and Babylon is a theme of a number of Augustine's sermons from the years 405–8, of which the most significant is one of the recently discovered Mainz sermons.[22]

---

[19] Links between *Vera Rel.*, *Cat. Rud.*, and *City* are explored in Ch. 12 below.
[20] On the chronology of *Cat. Rud.* see Steinmann and Wermelinger's edn. 101–2, van Oort (1991: 177 n. 72).
[21] On the links between 'body' ('corpus') and 'city' ('civitas') see further Augustine, *En. Ps.* 61. 6; 90 *ser.* 2. 1; 131. 3 (references from van Oort (1991: 272 n. 403)). The influence of the motif of the Church as Christ's body (Col. 1: 18, Eph. 5: 23–33), and Tyconius' image of the Church as 'corpus bipertitum' (see n. 10 above) is obvious. So may be the Greek and Roman analogy of the state and the human body, most famously used by Livy, 2. 32. 8 ff. in Menenius' reputed address to the seceding *plebs* on the Sacred Mount (see Ogilvie ad loc. and *OCD*³ s.v. 'Menenius Lanatus, Agrippa').
[22] The sermon is Mainz 9 (= *Ser. Dolbeau* 4 = *Ser.* 299A, augmented): for its text see Dolbeau's edn. 511–20 (repr. from *REAug* 39 (1993), 371–423, here 411–20). Dolbeau (edn. 506–7) dates it to 403–405/6. It thus becomes an early witness for Augustine's development of the two cities' theme, especially if *En. Ps.* 148. 4 (Jerusalem = life to come; Babylon = present life) is dated to 405–8 (so Dolbeau 509 n. 150,

There Augustine speaks of two cities ('civitates'), each given an allegorical name—Jerusalem and Babylon—in Scripture ('in scripturis mystice nominatur'). These cities are now intermingled, but will be separated at the end ('in fine'): one is the city of the holy, the other that of the impious. Then, commenting on Revelation 18: 6 ('render her double for her deeds'), he explains the double payment to 'Babylon', in somewhat sophistic terms, as payment for the death of paganism's Christian victims by, firstly, the real destruction of pagan shrines and idols, and, secondly, the symbolic death, to paganism, of those who have embraced the Christian faith. What is particularly interesting about this sermon is the fact that it relates the theme of the two cities to reflection on a text from the Book of Revelation.

In the *De Genesi ad Litteram*, completed by about 414–15, several cardinal themes of the *City of God* are developed. The two loves—of one's neighbour and oneself—are the origin of the two cities, in angels and humans:

Of these two loves, one is holy, the other unclean; one is social, the other selfish; one has regard to the common good for the sake of the community on high, the other goes so far as to bring the common interest under its own control through its arrogant dominance . . . [these loves] have been the distinguishing feature of the two cities which have been established in the human race, under the wondrous and inexpressible providence of God . . . one [city] of the just, the other of the wicked. The world pursues its course with these being in some way mixed until their separation at the last judgement, when the one, joined with the good angels, will gain eternal life in the presence of its king, whereas the other, joined with the bad angels, will be dispatched to eternal fire with its king. We shall perhaps, if the Lord wills, discourse more extensively on these two cities elsewhere. (*Gen. ad Litt.* 11. 15. 20)

The last sentence clearly refers to the *City of God*, especially Books 11–22, on which Augustine had begun work by 417. In the Genesis commentary another characteristic theme of the *City of God* is found: the city of God (angelic and human) exists in two forms,

following La Bonnardière) rather than 395 (less plausibly, van Oort (1991: 118), following Zarb). Cf. the Babylon–Zion antithesis in the contemporary *En. Ps.* 145. 20. For the exegesis of Rev. 18: 6 see also *En. Ps.* 149. 13. In assessing the importance of Mainz 9, Dolbeau (edn. 509) is perhaps too ready to find that it weakens van Oort's (1991: 315–17) conclusions, which are quite tentative, concerning the influence of Tyconius and exegesis of Revelation on Augustine's doctrine of the two cities.

that of earthly exile/wandering ('peregrinatio')[23] in the Church, and that of eternal repose (*Gen. ad Litt.* 12. 28. 56).

The contrast of Jerusalem and Babylon is developed in the following exegetical passage (preached sometime between 410 and 413, when the themes of the *City of God* were taking shape in Augustine's mind):

But, dearly beloved, reflect on the waters of Babylon. The waters of Babylon are all those things which are loved here below and are transient. Someone loves, for example, engaging in agriculture: he grows rich from it, becomes engrossed in it, gets pleasure out of it. Let him consider his end, and see that what he has loved is not the solid ground of Jerusalem but the river of Babylon. Another says, 'It's a great thing to a soldier! Every farmer fears the military, gives in to them, trembles at them: if I am a soldier, I shall be feared by the farmer.' Fool, you have thrown yourself into another stream of Babylon, a more turbulent and rapacious one . . . [then follow similar points made about the lawyer and the merchant]. So other citizens of Jerusalem the holy, realizing their captivity, observe that human wishes and various human desires carry them hither and thither, dragging and driving them towards the sea. They see this and do not throw themselves into the waters of Babylon, but they sit by the waters of Babylon and weep over the waters of Babylon . . . 'O holy Sion, where all is stationary and nothing flows! Who has cast us into this? Why have we abandoned your founder and your community?' See there: finding themselves among things that are in flux and slip away, scarcely anyone will escape the clutches of the river by holding on to the wood [of the cross]. (*En. Ps.* 136. 3–4)

Another *Enarratio*[24] develops related themes:

Jersualem had its beginning with Abel, Babylon with Cain. The actual buildings of the cities were erected later . . . two loves build these two cities. Love of God builds Jerusalem; love of the world builds Babylon. Let each of us, therefore, ask what he loves, and he will find of which one he is a citizen. And if he finds that he is a citizen of Babylon, let him root out desire and plant love. But if he finds that he is a citizen of Jerusalem, let him endure captivity and hope for freedom . . . Let us listen now, brothers, let us listen and sing and desire the city of which we are citizens. And of what joys do we sing? How may the love of our city, which we had forgotten in long exile, be reformed in us? Our father has sent us letters from there, God has provided the Scriptures for us, that by these letters a longing to return may be born in us. For, growing fond of our exile, we had turned our face towards the enemy, and our back on our homeland. (*En. Ps.* 64. 2)

[23] See Ch. 5 n. 4.
[24] For its date, probably between 412 and 415, see BA 33. 71 n. 2.

In the *Enchiridion*, written in the period 421–4, Augustine dwells on the eschatological state of the two cities, as he does in the closing books of the *City of God*:

But after the resurrection, once the general judgement has been brought to a conclusion, the two cities, that of Christ and that of the devil, will have their frontiers. One will be the city of the good, the other of the wicked, but both will consist of angels and humans. The one will have no will, the others no means, to sin any more. Neither shall be in a state of dying, for the one will live, truly and happily, in eternal life, the others will persist wretchedly in eternal death, without being able to die, both equally without end.   (*Ench.* III)

There is, therefore, in Augustine's writings from 390 onwards a series of elaborations of the two cities' theme and its attendant motifs. From the time when he begins to write the *City of God* (about 412) references to this thematic complex continue to be found, but they are infrequent: Augustine concentrates his exploration of these topics in the great work that will give them their fullest expression.

5

The Structure of the Work

His learning is too often borrowed, and his arguments are too
often his own; but the whole work claims the merit of a magnificent design, vigorously, and not unskilfully, executed.

(Edward Gibbon[1])

By the time of the completion of Books 1–3, which were separately
published (5. 26),[2] Augustine had already planned the overall
structure and scope of the work, although there is no clear indication
that he knew at that stage how long the work would be. The phrase
'magnum opus et arduum' (1. pref.) refers to the magnitude of the
task which he has undertaken, rather than to the length of the
proposed work. Augustine had used the same phrase at the start of
De Doctrina Christiana (1. 1; cf. prol. 1), and there as here in
conjunction with an appeal to, and acknowledgement of, divine
help. That 'opus' means 'task' rather than 'work' is clear, not merely
from the *De Doctrina Christiana* parallel, but also from the phrase's
source in Cicero, *Orator* 33 and 75 (Bauer 1965; Thraede 1977:
114–15).

But even if Augustine does not, at the outset, know how long the
work is going to be, the preface to Book 1 introduces fundamental
motifs and articulates important subdivisions of the work.[3] The long
opening period is rich in concentrated references to the themes to
come. (*a*) 'I have undertaken to defend the most glorious city of God
against those who prefer their gods to its founder': apart from the

---

[1] *The History of the Decline and Fall of the Roman Empire*, ed. J. B. Bury, iii. 211 n.
86 (London, 1897). Several recent writers on Augustine quote the first part of this
sentence on *City*, sometimes as if it were Gibbon's opinion of Augustine in general. The
laconic brilliance of the first part is irresistible, but it seems fairer, both to Gibbon and
to Augustine, to quote the sentence in its entirety. For further praise of Augustine by
Gibbon, mixed with eloquent criticism, see ibid. 406–7 (where Gibbon says that, of
Augustine's works, he knows only the *Confessions* and the *City of God*).
[2] See further Ch. 2. 2 above.
[3] On the structure of *City* see Guy (1961) and O'Donnell (1985), who provides a
helpful schematic summary of the work's contents. The analysis of Book 1, pref. which
follows owes much to Thraede (1977: 103–32).

allusion to the work's title, these words are a typical summary of the objectives of Books 1–10 in particular (cf. 10. 32, 11. 1, 18. 1). (b) 'the city of God either in the present course of time . . . or in the stability of its everlasting seat': the distinction implicit in these words between the city of God's historical or temporal and its eschato-logical or eternal functions anticipates the central theme of the second main part of the work, Books 11–22. (c) 'when it is an alien (*peregrinatur*) among the ungodly, living by faith': with these words an important motif—the Christian's 'outsider' status in human society—is introduced. The words 'peregrinari' and 'peregrinatio' usually refer in the work to the Roman legal term for an alien, rather than to the theme of pilgrimage.[4] (d) Words and phrases like 'patience', 'justice', and 'perfect peace' suggest and anticipate other cardinal themes of the work. This is the case with the preface as a whole. Its concluding sentence introduces the antithesis to the city of God of the earthly city with its 'lust to dominate' ('dominandi libido'), and also provides an explicit link to themes of Book 1, as the opening words of 1. 1 indicate: 'For it is from this [earthly city] that enemies arise, against whom the city of God has to be defended'. In addition, the theme of defence is here repeated from the opening period of the preface. Finally, other key terms of the preface have a proleptic function. The contrasting terms 'proud' ('superbi') and 'humble' ('humiles') point to the antithesis of the two cities by reference to characteristic moral positions; and the contrast is nicely pointed by the emblematic citations from Scripture and ideological Roman poetry.[5] In the scriptural quote ('God resists the proud, but gives grace to the humble', James 4: 6) both terms feature. When he cites Virgil, *Aeneid* 6. 853 (thereby introducing the Roman imperial theme, which will assume such importance in Book 5), although the word 'proud' occurs, it is the attitude of the imperial claim that Augustine stresses:

---

[4] For a discussion of Augustine's use of 'peregrinari' and 'peregrinatio' see Schmidt (1985: 84–8) and van Oort (1991: 131–42), whose analysis is more nuanced, bringing out differences in meaning; cf. Brown (1967: 323–4), Sherwin-White (1973: 461–4). Augustine exploited what he took to be the theme of 'peregrinatio' in 2 Cor. 5: 6 ('we know that while we are in the body we are away (*peregrinamur*) from the Lord'): see e.g. *En. Ps.* 37. 15, 41. 6.

[5] For further discussion of these citations in 1. pref. see Chapter 6 below. On pride see Ch. 8 below on 14. 13, with n. 43.

This prerogative [of resisting the proud, but giving grace to the humble] is God's, but the inflated spirit of a proud [human] soul arrogates it and delights hearing it said in its own praise: 'to spare the conquered and subdue the proud'.

A more detailed plan of the work is given only at the end of Book 1. In 1. 35 the themes of Books 11–22 are announced, with the tripartite division of that section of the work:

These two cities are indeed entangled (*perplexae*) and intermingled, one with the other, in this age (*in hoc saeculo*) until they will be separated in the final judgement. I shall set out, as far as I shall receive God's help, what I think has to be said about their origins [*de . . . exortu*, Books 11–14], course [*procursu*, Books 15–18], and appointed ends [*debitis finibus*, Books 19–22].[6]

That these words are not added later by Augustine (for example, when he was proceeding to plan Books 11 ff.) is clear from the next sentence (the beginning of 1. 36), and indeed from the rest of that chapter, which must now be examined in detail. In the course of this examination it will become clear that Augustine has no sense at the end of Book 1 of the space needed to treat these themes, or indeed those of Books 2 ff.

In 1. 36 the next sequence of topics is set out. The opening words of the chapter—'But there are still some things that I have to say'— refer to the themes specified in what immediately follows, as the subsequent structuring terms of the chapter ('next . . . finally' ('deinde . . . postremo')) indicate: they do not give any support to the assertion (in itself implausible) that Books 2–10 are, in any sense, a huge excursus, prior to the themes announced in 1. 35.[7] The

---

[6] The term 'procursus' does not necessarily denote 'progress', though Augustine may have been the first to use it in that sense, as well as in the sense of 'course' (*GLL*). In this connection Augustine also uses 'currere' (e.g. in 18. 1), and in *Letter* 1A*. 1 (cited at the end of this Ch.) he seems to distinguish between 'procursus' meaning 'progress' and 'excursus' meaning 'course'. For the triadic scheme origin–course–end applied to Augustine's life by his first biographer see Possidius, *Vita Augustini* pref. 3 ('de . . . viri et exortu et procursu et debito fine'). Possidius most likely modelled his scheme on the plan of *City* 11–22, and it is a somewhat forced adaptation, especially as Augustine's 'exortus' is scarcely described: see Bastiaensen ad loc. Studer (1991: 947) suggests that the scheme in Possidius and in *City* 11–22 reflects the structure of rhetorical 'laudatio' found e.g. in Quintilian 3. 7. 10–25, comparing *Doctr. Chr.* 3. 15, *Vera Rel.* 1, and *Trin.* 4. 21 (Studer loc. cit. incorrectly cites 6. 21).

[7] The idea that Books 2–10 are an excursus was advanced by Marrou (1958: 67), cited with approval by Bardy (BA 33. 43–4); cf. Guy (1961: 78). For a corrective analysis see Thraede (1977: 106–8), to whose discussion of 1. 36 I am much indebted in what follows.

themes indicated by 'some things that I have to say' in 1. 36 are (I) those of Books 2–3: the refutation of those who assert that Rome's calamities are exclusively due to Christian prohibition of pagan religion, especially of sacrifices. A second group (II) of three further themes is then announced: 'I must show [i] what their [the Romans'] moral qualities (*mores*) were and for what reason the true God, in whose power are all kingdoms, deigned to help them in extending their empire, [ii] and how those whom they consider to be gods helped them in no way, [iii] but rather, how much harm they did, by deceiving and tricking them' (1. 36). When, however, Augustine turns to the treatment of these themes in 4. 2, although he quotes the words of 1. 36 verbatim, he indicates a significant change of plan in relation to what follows. He claims to have dealt sufficiently with topic II (iii) in the foregoing part, especially in Book 2. Moreover, topic II (ii) is treated first, in Book 4, and with the important addition of the discussion of the possible role of fate in Rome's acquisition of empire in 5. 1–11. The justification for adding this last section to the previous books is given in 5. 12: once the alleged influence of fate is dismissed, the ground is cleared for exploration of other explanations of Rome's success. Topic II (i) then forms the subject-matter of the remainder of Book 5. At this stage of the work, in 4. 2, Augustine also formulates the overall theme of II (i)–(ii): it is 'about the growth of the Roman empire'. Evidently Augustine's views on the appropriate order of topics changed between the announcement of 1. 36 and the beginning of work on Book 4. After publication of Books 1–3 a change of plan was introduced, but in a way that does not compromise the contents of the scheme as initially announced, even if space for the section on fate has to be found, thereby disturbing the coincidence of themes and complete books hitherto maintained. Augustine shows his awareness of this in his concluding remarks to Book 4, where he says that the book has become over-long, and its themes will be continued in Book 5 (4. 34).

In 1. 36 Augustine also announces what becomes the theme of Books 6–10: (III) 'we shall argue against those who . . . try to claim that the gods are to be worshipped, not on account of any benefits in the present life, but because of those in the life that there will be after death.' It is possible that, when publishing Books 1–3, Augustine, having written two books on theme I, believed that theme II would require three books, one for each of its proposed sections (i)–(iii); but one cannot be certain of this. And no indication whatsoever is given of the estimated length of theme III.

Throughout the work Augustine articulates its subdivisions clearly. Chapter 26 of Book 5 looks back to the first five books as a completed whole, as does the preface to Book 6, using similar phrasing. At the beginning of 6. 1 the contents of the forthcoming books are described briefly in general terms, echoing the announcement of theme III in 1. 36. The wording of 1. 36, moreover, is quoted directly in 5. 26. Such verbal repetitions or echoes act as signposts throughout the work. At the end of Book 10 the first two pentads are summarized in now-familiar terms, and Augustine, referring explicitly back to the sub-division of 1. 35, announces the tripartite thematic sequence ('origin', 'course', 'appointed ends'[8]) of the work's second main part (10. 32). Acknowledgement and expectation of divine help is also a motif articulating the work's important divisions or their announcement (1. pref., 35, 10. 32, 11. 1, 17. 24).[9] In 11. 1 the tripartite sequence is repeated, and it is referred to at the beginning of the second part of the sequence (15. 1), at the end of that part (18. 54), and at the start of the third (19. 1). Likewise, the eschatological themes of Books 19–22 are gradually introduced at earlier junctions of the work. Thus at 15. 1 we read of 'one [society] which is predestined to reign with God for all eternity, the other to undergo eternal punishment with the devil'. At 18. 54 details are added:

Both [cities] alike either use temporal goods or are afflicted with temporal evils, but with a different faith, a different hope, a different love, until they are separated at the last judgement, and each assumes its own end, of which there is no end.

These details are then explicated in the following books. By such means Augustine maintains the reader's awareness of the direction of his work, amid the often distracting wealth of detail.

The first chapter of Book 18 is a special case. It begins with the standard summary of Books 1–10, and then gives the tripartite scheme of Books 11–22. But it also summarizes the three books (15–17) just completed on the history or 'course' of the two cities as far as the Flood (15), and from the end of the Flood until Abraham

---

[8] See above on 1. 35, with n. 6.

[9] This is probably a reflection of the convention in epic of invoking the help of a Muse or god before an important or complex part of the narrative, e.g. Virgil, *Aen.* 7. 37–45 and Fordyce ad loc.

(16. 1–11), followed by the history of the city of God only from Abraham to the coming of Christ (16. 12 to the end of Book 17). Thus the subject-matter of Book 18 is given. It is to be the history of the earthly city from Abraham's time. But the division is, in fact, not so clear-cut. In particular, the Jewish prophecies about Christ discussed in 17. 20–4 are extended and complemented by the discussion in 18. 27–36 (cf. 18. 38, 45–6, 48). It appears as if the extent of his material has, as at the end of Book 4, taken Augustine by surprise. In 17. 24 he apologizes for the length of the book, as he did in 4. 34; and in both chapters he announces the continuation of a theme in the next book. It may be that the parallel treatment of the history of the two cities was abandoned by Augustine at 16. 11, as he worked on the detail of his material, and the sheer mass of this material may have caught him unawares.[10] Neither 4 nor 17, the two books for whose length Augustine apologizes, is as long as Book 18, which is the longest of the work. Moreover, Books 17–18 are structurally confused and uncoordinated. In other words, the emphatic structural remarks of 18. 1—found otherwise only at the beginning of a new section of the work, but here introducing the last part of a section—indicate that Augustine feels the need to reorient his readers.[11] The work's structure is threatened by disparate, ill-synthesized, and copious material, and Augustine must force matters in order to complete his account of the two cities' 'course' in a fourth book.

That the symmetry of the tripartite division, four books per part, of Books 11–22 was important to Augustine is evident from his letter to Firmus, written after the work's completion. There we read:

For that part [Books 11–22] has been so divided by us that four books demonstrate the origins of that city and the same number its progress (*procursum*), or, as we prefer to say, its course (*excursum*), and the last four its appointed ends. (*Letter* 1A*. 1)

Such symmetry is not merely aesthetic, but also allows the work conveniently to be divided into five 'codices' (ibid.).[12] An organization of the latter part of the work on these lines may have occurred to

---

[10] Note that there is no clue at the end of Book 15 or in 16 that Augustine is going to deal separately with the history of the city of God, from Abraham onwards, in 16–17, and postpone treatment of the earthly city in the same period until 18. This division is only articulated retrospectively in 18. 1.

[11] See Bardy in BA 36. 17–19.   [12] See further Ch. 2. 2 above.

Augustine only when he knew the length of the treatment of the origins ('exortus') of the two cities (Books 11–14), even if it became increasingly likely as the work progressed that its latter part would have to balance the ten books of the first part. In *Letter* 184A, written while work on Book 14 was in progress, it appears as if Augustine is still uncertain about the overall length of the work:

The remaining [books] from the eleventh on, however many they may be (*quot esse potuerint*), of which I have already written three and have the fourth in hand, will contain what we hold and believe concerning the city of God. (*Letter* 184A. 5)

Such uncertainty is not incompatible with his sense of the work's general direction (ibid. 6; Lambot 1939: 118–19). But the descriptive account of the work's divisions found in retrospective summaries like *Letter* 1A*. 1 and *Retractations* 2. 43, while it reflects the sequence of themes enunciated at the end of Book 1 of the work itself (1. 35–6), presents a symmetry that was effected in the course of composition rather than one imposed upon the material in advance.

6

'Where Were the Gods?': Books 1–5

Although Augustine repeatedly refers to the first five books of the *City of God* as a distinct part of the work (5. 26, 6. pref.), dealing with the alleged benefits of Roman state religion, the first book stands apart from the others and from the rest of the work.[1] It is more closely related to the sack of Rome and the issues which the sack and its aftermath raise. In that respect, it has a specific apologetic purpose. Yet it is also a prelude or overture to the whole work, and contains several of the motifs to be developed in the later books. It is the clearest indication that by the time Books 1–3 were ready for publication Augustine had elaborated the overall plan of the *City of God*.

The polemical tone of the first book is struck in its preface. There, Augustine stresses the antithesis humility–pride—broadly equatable, for him, with Christian–pagan—by juxtaposing Scripture and Virgil:[2]

---

[1] Theiler (1966: 246) calls it a 'Sonderapologie'. On Book 1 see Orlandi (1965). The introductions by Bardy to each section of the work in the BA edn. are valuable: for Books 1–5 see BA 33. 175–83; Pollmann (1997). There is no adequate modern commentary on *City* in any language: the notes in the BA edn. are the closest approximation to one, but they were compiled in the 1950s. The older general books, like Burleigh (1949) and Versfeld (1958), are superficial and outdated: J. J. O'Meara (1961), by contrast, has worn well and remains an excellent short introduction to the work. Scholz (1911), inevitably outdated in many respects, is nevertheless still of considerable value. Barrow's edn. (see Bibliog. A) is a perceptive guide to Book 19 and related themes in the work as a whole. Among studies of particular topics, embracing *City* as well as other writings of Augustine, Deane (1963) and Markus (1970) are important: Markus, in particular, has had considerable influence on the modern debate about Augustine's views on secular society and history. The collections of essays edited by Donnelly (1995) and Horn (1997) contain much of value: Donnelly reprints, with some abridgement, several standard articles. Among introductory essays Baynes (1955: 288–306 (first pub. 1936)) is outstanding; cf. O'Donnell (1979). For bibliographies of studies of *City* and Augustine's writings generally see Bibliog. D. Studies of Roman religion (the dominant topic of Books 1–7 of *City*): Wissowa (1912), Latte (1960), Warde Fowler (1911), and Liebeschuetz (1979), who is particularly illuminating on the late imperial period. M. Beard, J. North, and S. R. F. Price, *Religions of Rome*, 2 vols. (Cambridge, 1998) will transform our access to, and understanding of, the evidence. Augustine and Roman religion: Fortin (1980).

[2] For Augustine's uses of Virgil in *City* see further below, Ch. 11.1e. On pride see below, Ch. 8, on 14. 13, with n. 43.

God resists the proud, but gives grace to the humble.   (James 4: 6)

To spare the conquered and subdue the proud.

(*Aeneid* 6. 853)

Although the reference to the 'proud' ('superbi') links both these texts, Augustine highlights the pride implicit in the Roman imperial claim of Virgil's words. The human claim of a mission to 'subdue the proud' is contrasted with the divine prerogative of 'resisting the proud'. Human pride, it is implied, is, as often in Augustine, a perverse imitation of God. And, since Virgil's line conjures up an avowed purpose of the Roman state, it is appropriate for Augustine to refer to God here as 'king and founder' of the divine city (cf. 10. 18). Mission statements apart, Virgil's words anticipate the polemical use of the *Aeneid* by Augustine in Book 1 of the *City of God*. The revelation by Anchises to his son Aeneas of Rome's future destiny and greatness (*Aen.* 6. 756–853) is linked by Virgil (and, for Augustine, fatally linked) with the myth of Troy and the Trojan origins of Rome. The book will go on to exploit that fatal link.

What links Troy and Rome in chapters 2–4, however, is the fact that both were victims of a siege. The fall of Troy is described in Book 2 of the *Aeneid*, and that book provides Augustine with a key phrase of his polemic: 'conquered gods' (*Aen.* 2. 320, quoted *City* 1. 3). The gods conquered at Troy are no less vulnerable when adopted by Rome. Augustine discerns what he understands to be, not the fiction of the *Aeneid*, but its truth: 'truth compelled them, as men of good sense, to admit the facts' (1. 3). A principal theme of *Aeneid* 2, the entrusting to Aeneas of the *penates* of Troy, thus becomes an exposé of Rome's flawed religion. The inability of Minerva and Juno to protect the Trojans is contrasted with the successful use of Roman basilicas as places of asylum respected by the Goths (1. 2, 4). But these themes are not all immediately developed. The Troy–Rome parallelism, and the attendant theme of vulnerable and ineffective gods, is expanded in 3. 2–8. It is a theme that excited Jerome, who, in a letter written in 413, compares Rome's fall with the Babylonian destruction of Jerusalem as well as with the sack of Troy (*Letter* 127. 12).[3] The allusion to the truth-content of Virgil's poem echoes a remarkable passage in one of Augustine's sermons of 410, where Virgil is

---

[3] For this and other texts in Jerome on the sack of Rome see Zwierlein (1978: 49–55), Kelly (1975: 296–308).

introduced and made to claim that, whereas he attributes Rome's eternity—'I have granted rule without end' (*Aen.* 1. 279)—to the 'false god' Jupiter, when he speaks 'in my own name' ('ex persona mea') he speaks the truth; as when he talks, in connection with Roman rule, of 'kingdoms that will perish' in *Georgics* 2. 498 (*Ser.* 105. 7. 10).[4] The notion that there is a core of truth in Virgil will recur in the *City of God*.

Alaric's clement Goths, on the other hand, provide Augustine with a theme for immediate exploitation. Augustine has no interest in whitewashing the Goths. For him, they are savage barbarians (1. 7). Whatever violence they perpetrate in Rome is only to be expected. Indeed, it reflects traditional Roman practice: Augustine comments on the lack of evidence for Roman respect for the sanctuaries and asylum-seekers of peoples defeated by them (1. 5–6). So Gothic clemency is a break with custom, and Augustine attributes it to the civilizing power of Christianity, and more specifically to the effectiveness of divine grace (1. 7). This partial lightening of a dark world by instances of goodness is often as far as Augustine is prepared to go in his praise of the material benefits of Christianity. The darkness of the world of violence and war is emphasized, as so often, by a detail from a Roman writer, here Sallust, describing what (as Augustine stresses) is Roman civil conflict (1. 5). The purpose of the emphasis is polemical: if this is what Romans fear from their own fellow citizens, how much more likely are they to fear it from external enemies. The particular perversity of civil war is suggested, rather than made explicit.

The theme of violence and suffering introduces a typically Augustinian view of the world in which we live, the *saeculum*. The apparently indiscriminate suffering of good and bad, innocent and guilty alike is a symptom of the inherent imperfections of life. Yet even in this bleak account Augustine finds meanings: elements of a theodicy are apparent. Misfortune affects the good and the bad in different ways; vulnerability emphasizes the relative lack of value of material and physical things; afflictions test and purify the virtuous; suffering can be seen as part of the moral development of the good (1. 8–10). An appropriate attitude to suffering and death, and also to burial, is advocated. The important thing is to perpetrate no evil. Bodily destruction is not an evil: funeral rites are for survivors, not for the dead themselves (1. 12), although the care given to burial is a

---

[4] See further Zwierlein (1978: 77).

sign of faith in the bodily resurrection in which Christians believe
(1. 13). But Christians, like philosophers and soldiers fighting for
their country, should not care about burial in itself (1. 12).[5]
    This is no merely theoretical discourse, however. Augustine must
deal with acute human problems caused by the sack of Rome. Some
Christian women took their own lives rather than submit to rape: was
this a sin? Augustine's treatment of this dilemma is partly pastoral,
partly ethical. Those who killed themselves deserve sympathy, even
pardon (1. 17). But suicide is none the less a crime. The crucial
feature of the moral act is mental assent. Mere vulnerability to
another's will, as when one is harmed physically, cannot be a moral
wrong. It is no crime to be a victim of rape (1. 18). Purity ('pudicitia')
is a mental state, and not a matter of physical integrity. Augustine
allows the theoretical possibility that women who killed themselves
might have been acting under a direct divine command: in that case,
their action would have been one of obedience rather than a crime, like
Samson's self-sacrifice, or Abraham's readiness to sacrifice his son
(1. 26; cf. 1. 21). This reservation on Augustine's part is, again, for
pastoral reasons. He does not wish to seem to condemn without
further evidence an apparent tendency to regard these women as
martyrs (1. 26). His detailed discussion of the wrongs of suicide
(in effect, chapters 16–29) has a dual purpose, which is also that of
much of the argument of the work as a whole. He is replying to critics
of Christianity who have pointed out that religion has not protected
its adherents: his reply takes the form that faith is not expected to
provide a buttress against suffering in this life, in which we are aliens
('peregrini', 1. 15). But he is at the same time answering Christian
questionings, and arguing that suicide is not an exception to the
command 'Thou shalt not kill', unlike, for example, the soldier's
act of killing in war in obedience to authority (1. 20–1, 26).[6]

---

[5] In *Conf.* 9. 11. 27–8 Augustine dramatizes this attitude to burial in the dying
words of his mother Monnica. The theme that burial and even funeral rites are
inessential has a long philosophical and rhetorical tradition: see e.g. Lucretius 3.
870–93; Cic., *Tusculan Disputations* 1. 43. 102–45. 109; Seneca the Elder, *Contro-
versiae* 8. 4. 1; Seneca, *Letter* 92. 34–5 (for further references see Clarke on Min. Fel.
11. 4). For Christian attitudes to death and burial contemporary with Augustine see
Scourfield (1992). Bingham (1708–22: Book 23) provides a survey of early Christian
attitudes to death and burial that remains unsurpassed; cf. Clarke on Min. Fel. 11. 4,
12. 6, 34. 10, 38. 3–4.
[6] Swift (1973) gives a perceptive analysis of 1. 21 and related Augustinian texts on
killing in war. On Augustine's views on the 'just war' see J. Barnes (1982), Markus
(1983); cf. n. 15 below. Suicide in antiquity: van Hooff (1990).

Sharpness is given to his argument by the use of *exempla*. Cato and Theombrotus pose problems, for both are men of moral integrity. But Theombrotus acts on the basis of a flawed reading of Plato's *Phaedo*, which argues against suicide (1. 22),[7] and Cato does not prescribe for his son the death which he chooses for himself, and so incurs the charge of being a victim of his own envy of Caesar's success (1. 23). Lucretia is a closer parallel than either Cato or Theombrotus to the Roman Christian suicides. Augustine uses her example as a polemical weapon to counter pagan critics of the Christian women: by their standards, they should admire these women. But, as with the examples of Cato and Theombrotus, he cannot overplay this card, for it would amount to condoning suicide. What he must do is find the flaw in Lucretia's position. His argument is based on the device of the dilemma, from whose two premises incompatible, and, for the adversary, unacceptable, conclusions can be drawn.[8] Either Lucretia's suicide is a consequence of her guilt at assenting to sexual pleasure in the rape, and so she cannot be praised. Or, on the contrary, she is innocent, and so does not merit death, as the Roman sources themselves conclude. To this Augustine adds the further argument that Lucretia is, if innocent, a victim of Roman concepts of guilt and shame: she felt that she had to die in order to rescue her reputation in society's eyes. Augustine's Christian women, who suffered and did not harm themselves, considered God's judgement, and not that of men (1. 19).

This detailed account reveals features of Augustine's method which are frequently found in the work. The use of *exempla* promotes the comparative method, and that method can, as here, be used in a two-edged way. Pagan ideals can weaken pagan critiques of Christianity, and at the same time be susceptible to close criticism, or undermined by counter-ideals, themselves drawn from the pagan repertoire.[9] Hence the use here of the counter-example of Regulus (1. 15, 1. 24), for long a standard example of virtue in pagan and Christian

---

[7] The Theombrotus anecdote is known to Augustine from Cic. *Tusculan Disputations* 1. 34. 84 (cf. Cic., *Pro Scauro* 4), and was also familiar to Lactantius (*Div. Inst.* 3. 18. 9). On the name ('Kleombrotos' in the Callimachus epigram (23 Pfeiffer) alluded to by Cicero) see Hagendahl (1967: 145 n. 3).
[8] Use of the dilemma ('complexio', 'conclusio duplex') as part of the technique of proof is advocated in ancient handbooks of rhetoric: see Cic., *De Inventione* 1. 29. 45; *Auctor ad Herennium* 2. 24. 38 with Caplan ad loc.; cf. J. Martin (1974: 127 with n. 28). Donaldson (1982) discusses the tradition of the Lucretia myth, Trout (1994) its use by Augustine here.   [9] On this method of 'retortion' in polemic see Ch. 7 n. 5.

contexts alike.[10] Once again, as with the case of Lucretia in 1. 19, Augustine uses the dilemma. Either Regulus believed that religious worship brought benefits in this life (the point that advocates of pagan religion stress), and so he was clearly mistaken. Or, on the other hand, he believed that worship brought benefits in the afterlife: then why is this belief among Christians the object of so much abuse (1. 15)? But in fact Regulus is a more powerful counter-example. For he exemplifies the man of principle who keeps his word and trust, without expecting any material rewards: he is an example that Christians can admire (1. 15), and ultimately an argument, in Roman terms, against the attractions of suicide (1. 24). This identification of Regulus' virtues anticipates the arguments of Book 5, where the virtues that gave Rome the means of acquiring an empire (and for which empire was a reward) are discussed.

The whole section so far surveyed (chapters 10–29) has a number of distinct, if complementary, aims. Its polemical purpose has been discussed. That polemic reveals a fundamental theme of the work. An individual's true moral status consists in his inner disposition, and not in any external standing or in others' judgement. It is ultimately a mental state, or a condition of the will. It cannot be violated physically. When Augustine comes later in the work to talk of membership of the city of God, he will refer to the same criterion of inner disposition, rather than external adherence to the Church. Furthermore, the apologetic purpose of these chapters contains a consolatory element. In the face of suffering, degradation, and death, principles of Christian faith are affirmed, and the purpose of suffering as a test or a punishment is asserted (1. 24). This multidimensional aspect of the work is typical.

The later chapters of Book 1 foreshadow themes of Books 2, 3, and 5. In particular, chapters 30 and 31 introduce briefly the theme of Rome's moral decline upon its acquisition of an empire, and Augustine, without quoting Sallust here, uses the Sallustian moral terminology ('extravagance', 'greed', 'the desire to dominate') to pinpoint the reasons for decline after the defeat of Carthage.[11] One instance of

[10] Regulus as example: Cic. *De Natura Deorum* 3. 32. 80 (see Pease ad loc. for other Ciceronian references), *De Officiis* 3. 26. 99–32. 115; Horace, *Odes* 3. 5; Min. Fel. *Octav.* 26. 3, 37. 5 (see Clarke's edn., nn. 412, 626); Tert. *Apol.* 50. 6 (see Mayor ad loc. for further references); Arnob. *Nat.* 1. 40 (comparing Regulus with Christ). The story of Regulus' principled self-sacrifice appears to have been an invention: see Walbank on Polybius 1. 82 ff. On Roman use of *exempla* see Litchfield (1914).
[11] For Augustine's use of Sallust in *City* see further below, Ch. 11. 1d.

such alleged decline is the growth in popularity of games and theatrical spectacles, a craze which, Augustine observes, has persisted to the present day, as evidenced by the theatrical mania of refugees from the sack of Rome in Carthage (1. 32). What is under attack here is not merely the immorality of stage performances, but their alleged religious origin and purpose: however, Augustine, at this stage of the work, merely alludes to this, and to the demons whom, he believes, Romans worshipped or placated in their theatrical festivals (1. 31–2). These are themes to be unfolded subsequently.

In chapter 34 Augustine returns to the theme of asylum. Just as Regulus can be an example which Christians may exploit, so also the establishment of asylum by Romulus and Remus can be seen as the forerunner of the successful use of Christian sanctuaries as places of refuge in the recent sack of the city.[12] Paradoxically, the would-be destroyers of the city have imitated its founders. Augustine is particularly sensitive to the implications of such transfers of Roman tradition to Christian contexts.

Finally, chapter 35 emphasizes the impossibility of distinguishing, in our temporal condition, between present and future members of the two cities, between those who will permanently adhere to the city of God, and those who only appear to do so for a while: 'For these two cities are intertwined and mixed, each with the other, in this life (*in hoc saeculo*), until they will be separated at the last judgement.' Thus a central theme of the work, and the related theme of the city of God as an alien city (van Oort 1991: 131–42), forms a climax to the first book: it will be particularly developed in Book 19.

Books 2, 3, and 5 are parallel historical surveys, broadly based and highly selective, with a limited polemical purpose. That purpose is, to illustrate the moral bankruptcy of Roman religion (Book 2), and to show that material and, in particular, military success and failure are not dependent upon the observance or neglect of Roman religious practices (Books 3 and 5). If Roman religion is morally bankrupt, alternative explanations must be given both of Roman virtue and its decline in political affairs (Books 3 and 5). In these books Augustine juxtaposes, as do his historical sources, quasi-mythical and historical personages and events, for example, Romulus, the rape of the Sabine women, Numa Pompilius, the Punic wars, the Gracchi, Sulla,

---

[12] On asylum in Christian churches in Augustine's day see Gaudemet (1990).

Mithridates (to name some instances from Books 2 and 3). This juxtaposition encourages and facilitates a typological reading of history, in which recent and contemporary events can be interpreted by comparison and contrast with those of the past; it also provides a means of exploring pagan–Christian contrasts and comparisons.

Book 2 opens with a plea for selectivity in polemic. Augustine suggests that there is a mean between the unvarnished presentation of the truth to receptive minds, and a tedious response to each and every adversarial point. Rhetoric has to come to terms with the relative lack of receptivity of some adversaries (2. 1). This points the way forward to what follows. It will not be an exhaustive, so much as a representative, treatment of the themes in question.

These themes are all related to the moral deficiencies of Roman religion. The ostensible starting-point is the alleged misfortunes that have hit the Roman world since the advent of Christianity: Augustine's reply is going to be that the history of the Roman people was full of calamities long before the Christian era (2. 3). But the argument actually begins with considerations about the lack of moral teaching in Roman religion, and not only about this lack, but about the ways in which Roman cults and myths apparently encourage immorality. Augustine's illustration of obscene and immoral cults comes from the specifically Carthaginian cult of Caelestis (Tanit), which was assimilated to the worship of Cybele, the Mother of the Gods.[13] The choice is made because the rite lends itself to vivid description, but also in order to introduce Augustine's own experience and to provide an example of a local cult which, though suppressed (probably in the 390s), was one that he and many of his readers had witnessed. It is one of many signs that Augustine has in mind primarily a North African audience (2. 4–5, 26). The absence of moral precepts from the gods contrasts with what satire (Persius is cited), with its basis in philosophical and popular ethics, perceives to be a need for moral guidance (2. 6). Augustine admits that Plato has more claim to be revered as divine or semi-divine than any god (2. 7; cf. 2. 14–15).

The example of the Caelestis rite (or that of the castrated Galli, 2. 7) is from cult, but it is relatively isolated, whereas immoral divine behaviour is common in myth and literature. Augustine must confront the claim that this is merely fiction (2. 8). Thus he lays

[13] On the cult of Caelestis see Toutain (1917–18: 29–47), Rives (1995: 65–72, 163–9).

considerable emphasis on the tradition that dramatic performances are not merely in honour of the gods but were introduced under explicit divine command (2. 8; cf. 1. 32). These gods are malicious and subversive demons: there is a purpose to their advocacy or tolerance of depictions of their own immoral behaviour. This is so, even if such depictions are not true (2. 10). As Augustine's principal target is Roman practices, it is to his advantage to see inconsistencies in those practices when they are compared to Greek ones. The Greeks allowed degrading depictions of gods in comedy, and vitriolic abuse of human politicians, and they respected actors. Using Book 4 of Cicero's *Republic (De Re Publica)*,[14] Augustine argues that Roman practice in the Republican period was, by comparison, inconsistent: the Romans placed no restraints on depictions of divine behaviour, yet they censored attacks on individuals in the Twelve Tables, and deprived actors of the right to vote or hold political office (2. 11–13). This polemical point made, Augustine can use a pagan critic of his own society and its religion and art, Plato, as an advocate against both Greek and Roman practices, but not against Roman law, which places upon poetry and the theatre some of the restrictions that Plato advocates (2. 14). Ironically, Roman law is stricter than Roman religion.

Augustine argues polemically that there is a sense in which Roman religion panders to, and reflects, the worst vices: lust (2. 14), and grovelling flattery (2. 15), exemplified in the deification and honours held worthy of a man, Romulus. That its religion generates no moral precepts or laws is evident from the tradition that has Rome deriving its laws from Solon's legislation, or establishing them in indisputably human fashion, as through Numa Pompilius (2. 16).

This preamble leads into the main argument of the book, the constant presence of evils and misfortunes in Roman history, from which gods did not, or would not, save Rome. Augustine attacks the implicit Golden Age assumption of Sallust, that early Romans were virtuous as much by nature as by law, by adducing the rape of the Sabine women,[15] the treatment of the innocent husband of the raped

---

[14] Cic. *Rep.* 4. 10. 10–11. 13 is mainly reconstructed from *City* 2. 9–13. See further below, Ch. 11. 1c. On the Roman theatre in general, see Beare (1964); on actors' status, ibid. 166–8, 237–40. On Augustine's attitude to theatrical shows see Weismann (1972: 123–95); cf. van der Meer (1961: 47–56), Markus (1990a: 110–23).

[15] Augustine's polemical critique of the Sabine rape reflects Livy's comments (1. 9. 13–15): for this, and the way in which Augustine relates the episode to the 'just war' theory, see Pollmann (1997: 28–30).

Lucretia, Lucius Tarquinius Collatinus, by Junius Brutus, and the fate of Camillus. Even in his depiction of the early Republic, his Golden Age, Sallust stresses the presence of fear and injustice in Roman society (2. 17–18). Augustine draws a double conclusion from this. On the one hand, he can adduce Sallust, like Plato, as a pagan critic of his own society (and one who, by implication, makes no claims—positive or negative—about the moral role of the gods). On the other hand, he can argue against pagan critics that, if the evils of Rome's history are never imputed by pagans to their gods, it is unreasonable to claim that Christianity is responsible for Rome's more recent misfortunes. As it is, there is a moral vacuum in Roman political life, and Christians are forced to live in a state that does not meet their standards (2. 19). This last point is a significant comment on Augustine's perception that even the Roman society of his day, though Christianized, is not one where Christian values prevail: there is a stark contrast between the realities of political life and the vision of life 'in that most sacred and venerable senate (*curia*) . . . and in the heavenly state (*res publica*), where God's will is law' (2. 19).

From chapter 20 on, Augustine turns to consider the form and function of the state. His discussion anticipates that of Book 19, and is one of the few sections of the work which can be said to deal with political theory, in the strict sense. His first point, made in an elaborate prosopopeia spoken by devotees of the pagan gods, is that the Roman state[16] proffers no definition of social justice. Its wealth, peace, and military success are desired goals, but in practice it is a vehicle for greed and exploitation, extravagance and immorality. Yet it encourages religious worship as an alleged means of preserving the *status quo*. This is a concept of the state as a pleasure machine. A discussion in Cicero's *Republic* is now adduced: once again, a pagan critic of paganism is a witness on Augustine's behalf. The definition of *res publica* given in Cicero's work (*Rep.* 1. 25. 39)[17] is based on the concepts of 'common sense of what is right' ('iuris consensus') and 'shared utility' ('utilitatis communio'). The *res publica* is a *res populi*, an 'organization of the people', but not every such organization: 'he

[16] It is convenient shorthand, though potentially misleading, to translate 'res publica' as 'state': see Schofield (1995: 66–9), who uses earlier studies, in particular Stark (1967) and Suerbaum (1977). Rudd's tr. of *Rep.* renders 'res publica' variously, according to context, as 'state', 'country', 'form of government', 'constitution', and 'nation' (cf. ibid. p. xxxiv).

[17] Schofield (1995) is a masterly study of the definition of 'res publica' in *Rep.* 1. 25. 39; cf. Zetzel ad loc. See n. 16.

[Scipio, the protagonist in Cicero's dialogue] defines a people as not every association of a large number, but an association brought together by a common sense of what is right and by shared utility' (2. 21). Scipio, Augustine reports, later argues in Book 3 of the *Republic* that the existence of the *res publica* does not depend upon the type of government, although when either a single ruler or the governing élite is unjust (presumably when the elements of 'iuris consensus' and 'utilitas' are missing), then the state's existence is undermined. To his summary of Book 3 of the *Republic* Augustine appends Cicero's critique, in the proem of Book 5 of the work (= *Rep.* 5. 1. 1–2), of the morally debased republic, a *res publica* in name only, of his day, a painting whose colours have faded (2. 21).[18]

Augustine, in his reaction to this Ciceronian account, proposes an easing of the strict definition of the state, anticipating a similar but more extended development in Book 19. There was a Roman *res publica* of a sort, he says, and it was better run by the early Romans than by their successors. But true justice exists only in the Christian city of God. Note that Augustine does not say 'in a Christian *state*' (2. 21). He is not concerned to make a point about actual political societies here.

Chapter 22 returns to the theme of the lack of moral guidance given by the gods. They cannot, these gods, have fled the city because of its moral degeneration: where were they when Rome was attacked by the Gauls and the Capitol only saved by the geese? That was long before the moral decline to which Sallust refers. What is more serious is that there is no evidence, then or later, that the gods ever provided moral rules. In fact, the gods were indifferent to good and evil, and to the success or downfall of the virtuous or bad among Rome's leaders. Augustine contrasts typical good *exempla* (Regulus, the Scipios) with bad (Sulla, Marius) (2. 23–4). He proposes a demonic reading of Roman history. The prodigy of malevolent spirits fighting among themselves is a symbol of the demonic destructiveness in Roman affairs (2. 25).[19] Civil war, in particular, is the concentration of such destructiveness: now Augustine can exploit its horrors—brother

[18] Cf. Plato, *Republic* 501, where the metaphor of the philosopher constructing a 'painting' of the ideal city is elaborated: the passage is likely to have influenced Cicero's image of the state as a faded painting.

[19] The anecdote is found in Julius Obsequens, *Prodigies* 118, as LCL i. 242 n. 1 notes: but whether Augustine uses Julius or his likely source, Livy, here cannot be ascertained.

killing brother—as he had not done in Book 1. Myths about theomachies are reinforced by real fights between gods on real battle-fields: as in Book 1 in relation to Virgil, the truth-element in poetic fictions is stressed. Far from providing precepts and laws to govern human behaviour, the gods have continually subverted morals. The gods did not quit Rome during the civil wars of the late Republic: they were present in divination, but also in adding to the violence of those wars (2. 25). Nor is there any evidence that those initiated into mystery cults were granted any esoteric moral doctrines (2. 26). Augustine fails to understand the significance of obscene rites (2. 27), contrasting them with the ceremonies of the Christian Church, which include moral instruction (2. 28). The book concludes with an appeal to all that is best in the Roman character to embrace Christianity, couched in positive political terminology—'patria', 'cives', 'asylum', 'libertas', 'victoria', 'dignitas', 'societas'—that is both familiar and at the same time covers the scope of the first two books of the work.

Book 3 turns from the theme of the moral bankruptcy of Roman religion to consideration of such evils as war, massacres, and famines. At the outset, Augustine stresses that, though confining himself to Rome, he is treating it as typical of all nations: the scope is thus universal, even if the method is selective (3. 1). Early chapters of the book return to themes of the beginning of Book 1: the fall of Troy, and the gods common to Troy and Rome. Augustine searches out apparent inconsistencies in Roman attitudes. Thus Troy is said to have fallen because Laomedon did not pay Apollo and Neptune for building the city, or because of Paris's adultery (3. 2–3). Were Neptune and Apollo unaware of what would happen in the future, that Laomedon would not pay? Could gods become hired labourers of men? Why did Apollo take sides with the Trojans later, in the great Trojan war? Why do gods not condemn adultery where one of them is a party—Venus (with Anchises) or Mars (when begetting Romulus)? These last two examples are aptly chosen in view of their importance in the foundation myth of Rome (3. 2–3).

   Augustine stresses that he does not believe these myths, emphasizing the falsehood in fiction, whereas he has often stressed the truth-element in it in the two previous books, and adducing Varro (mentioned here for the first time in the work) as a Roman non-believer who yet felt such fictions to be expedient, as a stimulus to

greater deeds on behalf of the state (3. 4).²⁰ Augustine has not yet
fully detached himself from the themes of Book 2, and perhaps he
does not wish to do so, for the links between the theme of gods as
punishers and the evils of history are close. What Augustine wants to
show is that moral wrongs (the adultery of Mars with Romulus'
mother, the killing of Remus) which led to the establishment and
early development of Rome (Remus is treated in 3. 6 as co-founder of
the city, so that his killing seems all the worse) were neither prevented
nor punished by the gods. He carefully avoids suggesting that the
course of Roman history²¹ might be read as a punishment for such
infringements. His sole aim is to drive home the point that the gods
are no reliable defenders of the city—neither of Troy when it first fell,
nor of the Troy loyal to Sulla that was sacked by Fimbria, Marius'
partisan, in 85 BC (3. 7), at a time when Rome's Trojan gods might
have been expected to protect their city of origin. Augustine makes
much of Livy's remark that the statue of Minerva survived this second
sack: the presence of the gods, it is insinuated, rather than their
absence, has much to do with the city's fall (3. 7).

In the selective account of Roman history which follows, Augustine
must minimize the peaceful periods, such as the reign of Numa
Pompilius. His arguments are various. Peace may be due to non-
aggression by others, or to a successful non-belligerent policy
(3. 10). It seems strange that peace was achieved at a time—Numa's
reign—when religious practices were only being established, and not
after their establishment, for that seems to imply that there is no
connection between peace and worship (3. 9). Demonic forces can
manipulate humans, but they do not appear always to have control
over events that lead to peace or war: an example of Apollo's help-
lessness in the Achaean war is given (3. 10–11). Grieving deities in
epic are a fiction that, once again, contains truth: these gods are often
helpless (3. 11). The 'more hidden and higher power' of 3. 10 which
frequently thwarts demons is probably the true God of 3. 11 who is
the genuine protector of cities. Many gods do not increase the protection of the city (3. 12).

In chapter 13 the violent catalogue of Roman history begins.
Augustine concentrates throughout on specific horrors, vividly
evoked, especially 'wars . . . worse than civil' (Lucan, *Civil War* 1.

---

²⁰ For Varro in *City* see below, Ch. 11. 1b.
²¹ For Augustine's sources for Roman history see below, Ch. 11. 1b, d, f.

1–2 is quoted)[22] where relatives by blood or marriage destroy one another. Thus the Sabine (3. 13) and Alban (3. 14) wars are seen from the viewpoint of the women sufferers—wives who see husbands killing their fathers and brothers, a girl whose betrothed is killed by her brother, who then kills her when she grieves. Wars between cities related in the same way as Alba and Rome (Augustine adopts the Virgilian sequence Troy–Lavinium–Alba–Rome, *Aeneid* 1. 267–77) are particularly terrible (3. 14). Where was the divine protection? Romulus may have been assassinated, not taken up to heaven: Augustine adduces sceptical evidence casting doubt on this myth, and places more credence on Cicero's unvarnished account in the *Hortensius* than on his rhetorically embellished one in the *Catilinarians*. Other Roman kings died violently. And what puny dominions this violence achieved (3. 15)!

Roman historians themselves provide the evidence for the violence of early Roman history. Even a period praised by Sallust as a time when 'life was lived under a system of fair and mild law' (*Histories* 1. 11), after the establishment of the consulship, was fraught with violence involving Collatinus and Brutus, and others (3. 16). Sallust's judgement on the period up to the Second Punic War is evidence from historiography of the violence endemic in the Roman Republic (3. 17). A series of disasters from the fifth to the third centuries BC is sketched (3. 17): Augustine's repeated, insistent question is, 'Where were the gods?' In the First Punic War Regulus was a victim (3. 18). In the Second Punic War loyal Saguntum was destroyed for keeping faith with Rome (3. 20), not to mention the horrors of Cannae (3. 19). If only the Romans had regarded their gods, not as material protectors, but as symbols of eternal good (3. 18). Even in an era admired by Sallust for its morality and concord, from the end of the Second Punic War to the destruction of Carthage, Rome turned on its human protector and conqueror of Hannibal, the great Scipio (3. 21). And that period, although praised by Sallust as one when morality was at a high, was also the time when fondness for luxury took root in Rome.

Augustine's catalogue of Roman disasters (itself a likely model for similar catalogues in Orosius)[23] culminates in the civil wars of the

---

[22] See further below, Ch. 11. 1h.
[23] For Orosius' *Histories* see Mommsen (1959: 325–48); see further below, Ch. 11. 3f. Orosius' work was probably written in 416–17, some years after the completion of *City* 1–3 (see Ch. 2 above). Cf. Bardy in BA 33. 792–3.

late Republic, and the horrific details are piled on: the massacre of
Roman citizens in Asian cities by Mithridates (3. 22); prodigies at the
time of the Social War (3. 23); violence in the time of the Gracchi
(3. 24); the slave revolts (3. 26); the civil strife between Marius and
Sulla; and Sulla's reign of terror (3. 27–8). By comparison with these,
the limited damage caused by the recent sack of Rome pales into
relative insignificance (3. 29), quite apart from the clemency shown
by the Goths. Even the Augustan settlement is loss of freedom
('libertas') and the imposition of kingly rule (3. 21): Augustus'
own path to power was brutal and violent, and he permitted the
killing of Cicero, the defender of the Republic's 'libertas' and his
own supporter (3. 30).

The book concludes with a crescendo of violence: prodigies, natural
disasters, erupting volcanoes, floods, swarms of locusts, terrible
battles fought on African soil with huge loss of life. Once more, the
contrast with contemporary, lesser calamities, and with the clemency
extended even to pagans who took or were given asylum in the
Christian sanctuaries in Rome, is stressed (3. 31). Augustine hopes
that by assembling a mass of catastrophic evidence, the claim that
Rome's gods ever protected it will ring hollow. It is significant that
he does not attempt to exploit the theme of the 'pax Augusta' or
the tradition linking it to the birth of Christ, although he makes
that chronological link in 3. 30.[24] The reasons lie in his polemical
purpose. He cannot give attention to the peaceful exceptions to
violence, as they would undermine his thesis. The reasons for
Rome's success, empire, and periods of peace will emerge later, in
Book 5, when other themes are in the forefront.

The two opening chapters of Book 4 are introductory. But for the first
time in the work Augustine suggests that the real adversary is not just
pagan, but pagan and educated (4. 1). The educated stir up the
feelings of the masses, who assume that contemporary events are
unique, and that recent misfortunes have no parallels in history.
The learned know better. Thus Augustine introduces a distinction
that will be important in this and later books, between those who
have a philosophical understanding of religion, and the broad mass of

[24] On the linking of 'pax Augusta' and Christ's birth in Christian apologetic see
Melito of Sardis, quoted in Eusebius, *Ecclesiastical History* 4. 26. 7–8, and Origen,
Contra Celsum 2. 30; cf. Mommsen (1959: 278–9). Cf. Ch. 9 n. 58.

people, who are prey to superstition. As yet, however, this distinction is not elaborated.

After a brief recapitulation of the themes of Books 2 and 3, dealing respectively with moral, and physical and external, evils, Augustine anticipates the topic of this book: it will be about the growth of Roman imperial rule (4. 2). In fact, most of the book will deal with the preliminaries of that theme, and it will not be fully treated until Book 5. Augustine emphasizes how selective his approach has been in Books 2–3, and he introduces a leitmotif of the present book, the theme of the one true God who granted Rome, and all empires, their rule (4. 2).

He first considers what constitutes greatness in imperial rule. It does not make sense to assume that what is achieved and maintained by war and violence either causes happiness or deserves praise. Augustine wants to demythologize the imperial ideology. He argues that one should not be led astray by the terminology of empire— peoples, provinces, kingdoms. Societies are collections of individuals: he compares the individual with the single letter ('littera', 'elementum') in a word ('sermo').[25] It is easier to discern goodness and happiness in individuals (what he is arguing appears to be the opposite of Plato's procedure in the *Republic*) than in societies.[26] Good rulers are good individuals, and their rule is for the benefit of their society: we should note that Augustine does not consider an alternative to some kind of monarchical or oligarchic rule. But evil rulers harm only themselves (this echoes an argument which goes back to Plato's *Gorgias*). This firm grounding of the quality of society in the moral standing of individuals is crucial in the development of what is, perhaps inaccurately, called Augustine's political theory (4. 3).

Good rule promotes and secures justice, and justice characterizes the good state. Continuing his demythologizing process, Augustine equates states without justice as 'large bands of robbers', and 'bands

---

[25] 'Sermo' can mean 'phrase' or 'word' from the late 2nd c. onwards (*GLL*; cf. *OLD*, 8a).

[26] In fact, like Plato, Augustine is arguing in 4. 3 that justice in the individual mirrors justice in the state, and vice versa. The influence of Cicero's *Republic* is discernible here. Both Cicero and Augustine maintain that the moral quality of individuals is a more important formative influence on the quality of government than any kind of constitution (cf. *Rep*. 1. 23. 42; *City* 2. 21). Cicero, quoted with approval by Augustine in *City* 2. 21 (= *Rep*. 5. 1. 1), argues that there is interaction, and mutual interdependence, between social traditions and good citizens. Individuals are the product of, and conserve, institutions; cf. Zetzel (edn. of *Rep*., pp. 24–5).

of robbers' as 'small kingdoms' (4. 4).[27] The mere fact of social organization confers no moral quality on a group. There is no value in the state *per se*. In fact, Augustine's paradigm state in 4. 4 is such a state without justice, developed over time from a criminal gang. The elements of organization in a gang—a leader's command, a compact of association, and agreed division of plunder—form the first part of a condensed account of society's structuring that is expressed in negative terms, but is none the less comprehensive enough to be a working definition.[28] The account is supplemented in 4. 4 by three further elements that mark the transformation of the gang into society: a larger number of people ('recruits'), acquisition of territory, and attainment of impunity without renunciation of aggression. The colouring of this account suits Augustine's polemic against the violence of actual societies in these books of the *City of God*.

Augustine is concerned to relativize imperial 'greatness'. The revolt of Spartacus created a 'kingdom' (= 'band of robbers') in the Roman state: was that divinely assisted? Yet its power, and the rule of other individuals, was short-lived (4. 5). In the following chapters Augustine implies that the rise and fall of empires earlier than Rome's drives home history's lesson that power is unstable and divine protection apparently fickle or vulnerable. When pagan Romans accuse Christians of responsibility for Rome's troubles, they fail to address the question of the causes, religious or otherwise, of the far greater catastrophes of earlier kingdoms' falls (4. 6–7). Consideration of other and earlier kingdoms also relativizes Rome's 'greatness'. Mention of the assumed duration—1,240 years—of the Assyrian kingdom suggests the scope of universal history, and also puts Rome in its place.[29]

Augustine's extended polemic against the plurality of minor deities listed by Varro as 'certain gods' ('di certi', cf. 7. 17) begins in 4. 8.

---

[27] The equation 'robber band' = 'kingdom' in 4. 4 is enriched by the anecdote from Cic. *Rep*. 3. 14. 24, of the pirate's riposte to Alexander the Great.

[28] See Höffe (1997: 266–74).

[29] Augustine derives the information from the *Chronicle* of Eusebius(-Jerome), p. 83 a. 9–10 (ed. Helm); cf. below, Ch. 11. 3e. Augustine's argument in *City* 4. 6–7 is one of many indications in the work that his polemic is not so much directed at Rome as such, as against Rome as representative of the earthly city. For the scholarly controversy on Augustine's attitude to Rome see Paschoud (1967: 263–75), who summarizes and discusses earlier pessimistic (Kamlah 1951, Maier 1955) and optimistic (Combès 1927, Straub 1954) interpretations. See further Thraede (1977: 100–2), Duchrow (1970: 247–98), and esp. Markus (1970: 45–71), who provides a balanced and judicious analysis.

These specialist minor gods, each preoccupied with a single function, could not care for the Roman empire. If three gods are concerned with the door (whereas one human doorkeeper is enough), how can they, or similar deities, have Rome's greatness in mind (4. 8)? It must be Jupiter who is responsible; Jupiter, whom Varro considers to be identical with the one God of monotheists, even when worshipped aniconically (4. 9).[30] Throughout the argument which follows the underlying assumption is that monotheism is the rational norm, and that contradictions between their rational monotheism and poly-theism in Roman thinkers and believers expose a fatal weakness in Roman religion. Augustine combines this with repeated references to the 'true God'—the leitmotif—often given at the end of chapters (15, 16, 22, 23, 25, 28, 29, 33, 34; cf. 17 and 20, where it is not at the end of the chapter). So the question becomes: what is Jupiter? Giving Jupiter a consort, Juno, and linking him with a specific part of the universe, the ether, undermines his singular authority and universality (4. 9). And such views are not confined to the fictions of myth: they are found in philosophically influenced poetry, like Virgil's *Georgics*.[31] The plurality of gods with similar functions fragments religious power (4. 10). The distinction later formally introduced (4. 27) is here assumed: poets and the mass of the people (and civic religion) are incurably polytheistic: philosophy embraces monotheism, and makes of Jupiter the world-soul (4. 11). If that is so, then Jupiter can be considered to be all gods, or they can be considered to be his parts or powers. But it would be more economical, and more rational, to worship one God, to accept the implications of making Jupiter the world-soul, the immanent deity of *Georgics* 4. 221–2 (4. 11).

In chapters 12 and 13 Augustine exploits the absurd possibilities of a pantheistic position, as he does in the early chapters of *Confessions* 7. If God is the world-soul and the universe his body, then every animal, including slaughtered ones, is God, and God can be beaten, or be immoral. And, given the plurality of gods in the Roman pantheon, why should not Victory, rather than Jupiter, be the god who establishes and extends the Roman empire (4. 14)? And is empire a good thing? In a rare glimpse of his political preferences,

---

[30] Cf. 4. 31 with n. 34 below, and Ch. 7 n. 6.
[31] *Georg.* 2. 325–7 is cited. The lines can only be said to be 'philosophically influenced' in that they are susceptible, and were subjected, to philosophical-allegorical and metaphorical interpretation. Their background is poetic and traditional: see Mynors on *Georg.* 2. 323–45.

Augustine suggests that a plurality of small kingdoms living in harmony with one another is preferable to, and safer than, dominant powers (4. 15).[32] In any case, aggression and victory are what drive empire-building: what role is there for Jupiter here, unless as giver of victory? Augustine seems to be back at playing polemics against polytheism. Why should there be a goddess Victory? And what are the distinct functions of Victory, Felicitas, and Fortuna (4. 17–18)? Why are some virtues, like Fides (and Virtus itself), deified, and not others (4. 20)? Indeed, why not confine oneself to having Virtus and Felicitas as gods, as between them they should be capable of conferring all good things (4. 21)? Or Felicitas on its own (4. 23)? Polytheism seems to confuse divine gifts with gods themselves (4. 23–5). Varro's claim that knowledge of the particular functions of each god in particular circumstances is essential to successful religious practice, just as one cannot live properly if one does not know the functions of doctors, bakers, plasterers, or blacksmiths (4. 22) is, Augustine feels, controverted by his counter-claim that polytheism simply confuses divine functions. Augustine finds it inconsistent to claim (*a*) that some functions are shared by some deities, and (*b*) that some moral functions are deified and their religious functions defined, whereas other moral qualities whose functions are no less suitable are not.

When Augustine reports a distinction between three kinds of gods (which he evidently found attributed to Q. Mucius Scaevola[33] in Varro's *Logistoricus* entitled *De Cultu Deorum*)—of the poets, of the philosophers, and of the political leaders—he finds it ironical that the one set of views that Scaevola finds true (the philosophical) is felt to be both superfluous and harmful in political contexts, and that the views of the poets are dismissed as nugatory, when they form the substantial content of theatrical performances, which have a religious function (4. 27; cf. 4. 26). This distinction will be exploited more fully later in the work.

---

[32] See Troeltsch (1915: 36–40).

[33] Quintus Mucius Scaevola, called 'Pontifex' (to distinguish him from Q. Mucius Scaevola 'Augur', consul in 117 BC and a character in a number of Cicero's dialogues, including the *De Re Publica*), was one of the most outstanding lawyers of the late Roman Republic, author of a legal treatise, consul in 95 BC, pontifex maximus from 89. He was evidently (*City* 3. 28, 4. 27) a character in Varro's *De Cultu Deorum*. His murder in 82 by the party of Marius is described by Augustine in 3. 28 in terms of sacrilege (he was killed despite taking sanctuary at the altar of Vesta), as an individualized detail of the terror of the civil war between the factions of Marius and Sulla. Cf. above, Ch. 3 n. 19.

Naïve explanations of Roman myths, such as the refusal of Mars, Terminus, and Iuventas to yield their places to Jupiter (4. 23), are ridiculed by Augustine (his source for the explanation is presumably Varro). If this myth signifies that Rome's empire and its boundaries are unshakeable, then the facts of history disprove it: this is one of the rare occasions in the work when Augustine refers to the history of the later Empire (Hadrian, Julian, Jovian: 4. 29). Philosophical attempts to distinguish between religion and superstition, and to claim that, not merely philosophical doctrines, but some early religious practices, are religious rather than superstitious, do not save civic religion (4. 30, where Balbus, in Cicero's *De Natura Deorum*, is quoted). Cicero, himself an augur, mocks augury. Varro claims that

if he were founding that state (*civitatem*) [Rome] afresh, he would dedicate shrines, and give names, to gods more in accordance with the exemplar of nature (*ex naturae potius formula*).   (4. 31)

Augustine reads this as a death-blow to traditional religion, which Varro wishes to preserve merely as something for ordinary, unphilosophical people, something politically expedient. Varro's own view is that God is the universal soul, governing through reason, and he approves aniconic worship (4. 31).[34] Varro is a monotheist *manqué*. Augustine allows his own familiar view to obtrude briefly. God is an unchanging being: not soul, which is mutable, but soul's creator (4. 31). This God it is who grants earthly kingdoms to good and evil alike, thus indicating that they are not the most important of possessions (4. 33). The many gods of Rome are deceiving demons (4. 32). The Jews believed in the one true God, and prospered without polytheism until they fell foul of the fault of curiosity, turning to idolatry (4. 34). Their history demonstrates that the source of earthly power lies in the true God: Augustine, here as elsewhere, is reflecting the teaching of Paul in Romans 13: 1–7. Thus far, then, Augustine has

[34] See Ch. 7 n. 6. The length of the period of aniconic worship at Rome given, according to *City* 4. 31, by Varro—170 years—is found also in Plutarch, *Numa* 8, which is most likely derived from Varro. The period represents the time-span from the foundation of the city until the end of the reign of Tarquinius Priscus (traditionally 579 BC), who is said to have begun the construction of the temple of Jupiter on the Capitoline. On the alleged aniconic phase in early Roman religion see Wissowa (1912: 32–8), Warde Fowler (1911: 114–68), Latte (1960: 150 n. 1): critical and sceptical discussion in Cornell (1995: 161–3). One of the newly discovered Mainz sermons (62 = *Ser. Dolbeau* 26 = *Ser.* 198, augmented), possibly preached by Augustine in 404, talks enigmatically (10–12, 16) of a contemporary African Christian cult of church pillars; see Dolbeau's edn. 360–1.

argued that Rome's empire must be granted, or at least tolerated, by the God whom Christians worship, and of whom the philosophers, and the monotheistic tendency in Roman thought, had an inkling.

Some books of the *City of God* have prefaces. This appears to reflect Augustine's authorial decision that they should contain material of import, to be emphasized by formal separation from the detail of the book itself.[35] At the beginning of Book 5, the preface summarizes the chief conclusions of the previous book, and turns to the question raised there, namely, what caused the greatness and survival of the Roman empire? Augustine has given his answer already: it is the one true God, not the Felicitas which is a gift of God (5. pref.); but he needs to argue the detail of this answer, and the preface draws attention to this, and hence to the principal theme of Book 5.

Chapters 1–11 of Book 5 form a short treatise on fate, free will, and providence.[36] The argument is relatively self-contained. Political themes are not broached, but the point is stressed that there are no fatalistic influences on any aspect of human lives. Augustine appears to reject out of hand the view that chance can be a cause of Rome's greatness, for that would make it irrational (5. 1). He spends more time speculating that it may be the result of fate, in the sense of some pattern of necessity, and he immediately assumes that a fatalistic interpretation is in some way related to astrological determination, whether independently of divine will or not (5. 1). Three possibilities are enumerated:

(*a*) the stars determine human actions;
(*b*) God determines human actions by means of the stars;
(*c*) the stars predict, but do not cause, human actions.

Augustine gives short shrift to (*a*): it undermines all belief in gods or God (he does not consider that the stars themselves might be held to be gods). (*b*) compromises divine sovereignty, and seems to impose compulsion on humans, and to make evil astrally determined: thus it shares a defect (compulsion) with (*a*), as well as having others. (*c*) is not, in fact, what astrologers say, although it is a view of some

---

[35] On chapter divisions in Augustine's books see App. C with n. 3.
[36] See Kirwan (1989: 82–128) for a discussion of Augustine's position in *City* and other writings; cf. O'Daly (1989*a*). Hagendahl (1967: 525–35) and Sharples (edn. of Cicero, *De Fato*, pp. 25, 162–3) discuss Augustine's use of Cicero in *City* 5.

philosophers. But it involves accepting the reliability of horoscopes as predictors, and to that question Augustine next turns.

Chapters 2–7 deal with horoscopes and related matters. The case of twin brothers is discussed. If they fall sick together, is this due to their being born or conceived under the same constellation, as Posidonius appears to believe? Or is the view of Hippocrates, that this is due to an inherited bodily constitution, more acceptable?[37] Augustine inclines to believe that constitution, diet, and other living conditions could lead them to contract the same illness simultaneously. He points out that twins often have quite different lives, including different medical histories. The astrologers' explanation, that during the time-lapse between the birth of twins the ascendant has changed, seems unable to account satisfactorily for substantial (e.g. character) differences between twins (because the difference in the ascendant is too little), or for similarities such as social rank (because there is none the less a difference in the ascendant). Nor do identical horoscopes lead to identical lives, which are never found (5. 2).

In chapter 3 Augustine reports the argument based on Nigidius Figulus' potter's wheel analogy. The comparison between the potter's wheel and celestial configurations is a false one: 'it is not the magnification of distance involved in transferring it to a circle of larger radius that would effect a change in the interpretation of a horoscope' (Pingree 1990: 484). But Augustine's argument accepts the astrological analogy at face value, and observes that if this explains astrological misreadings, then how can a precise determination be given at any birth, whether of twins or of individuals? Or are horoscopes only accurate about major matters, and not about small details? If so, would they be more reliable in the case of those who are not twins? How then to explain substantial differences between twins? The case of Jacob and Esau is adduced.

---

[37] This part of 5. 2 is printed as fr. 4 of Cicero's *De Fato* in most modern editions (see n. 36): see Sharples ad loc. For Posidonius' critique see Edelstein and Kidd on fr. 111 (= this passage from 5. 2). See further 5. 5; cf. Theiler (1982: ii. 311–13). If Hippocrates, *On Remedies* 1. 20 is, as is likely, being reported here, the report is inaccurate in a number of details: above all, the brothers in Hippocrates' account are not twins. Theiler (loc. cit.) assumes adaptation of Hippocrates by Posidonius and of the latter by Augustine (with emphasis placed on the astrological aspect). Cf. the anecdote about Firminus, born in privileged circumstances at the same time as the child of one of his father's slaves, *Conf.* 7. 6. 8–10: there also reference to the standard example of twins, and to Jacob and Esau (see O'Donnell ad loc.); cf. *Doctr. Chr.* 2. 21. 32–23. 35.

They are born at an interval of seconds only: one is born clutching the other's heel (Genesis 25: 26). Their radically different lives cannot be expressed in their horoscopes (5. 4).

Augustine returns to the sick twins in chapter 5. In the course of the chapter he distinguishes between birth horoscopes and conception horoscopes. He makes several points. If the small change in the ascendant accounts for differences other than health, why is the similarity between the twins limited to health? Why is there not difference there also? Their health cannot be determined astrologically at birth, because they cannot be born at the same time. If health is determined astrologically at conception, then why do twins not have identical lives? If the same conception horoscope produces different lives, it is not surprising if the same birth horoscope does so. Yet conception horoscopes are used by astrologers to determine a time for intercourse, in order to produce a wonder-child. How can destinies then be altered by birth (5. 5)? Even gender differences do not seem to be astrologically determined, for there can be twins of different sex (5. 6).

In chapter 7 Augustine turns to the theory of selections or catarchic astrology—choosing a particular moment for beginning something to ensure a desirable end, based on the horoscope of the beginning (Pingree 1990: 485). Augustine pinpoints problems in this theory. How can my fate, determined by my conception or birth horoscope, be changed by such elections? How can animals and plants born at different times be uniquely determined by a subsequent choice of planting or mating times by humans? Plants sown at the same time have different individual fates. Augustine concludes that success in astrology is due to demonic manipulation of a malicious kind (5. 7).

Augustine turns in chapters 8–11 to Cicero's attempt in *De Fato* (and possibly also in *De Divinatione*, which Augustine names in 5. 9) to argue against the Stoic concept of fate as a continuous sequence or chain of causes determining everything (5. 8).[38] Cicero's argument is based on a refutation of the idea of divination, or of

---

[38] Theiler (1982: ii. 311) surmises that Augustine confuses *De Divinatione* with *De Fato*, but it is arguable that there are echoes of some passages of *Div.* 2 in *City* 5. 9: see Hagendahl (1967: 70 nn. 2–4). Augustine appears to use *Div.* elsewhere in *City*: cf. 2. 16, 4. 30, 10. 13; see Hagendahl (1967: 71) for details. On the theme of divine foreknowledge and free will in Augustine see further *City* 11. 21, *Simpl.* 2. 2. 2. Boethius' discussion (*Consolation of Philosophy* 5. 3–6) resolves some of the difficulties with which Augustine engages: see Sorabji (1983: 253–67), Sharples edn. of Cicero, *Fat.* and Boethius, *Cons. Phil.*, pp. 25–9, 218–29.

any knowledge of the future, whether by God or humans. To save free will Cicero sacrifices foreknowledge, for he understood foreknowledge to determine future events, to corroborate, in effect, the Stoic causal chain. Augustine wishes to save both free will and foreknowledge. He wants to argue that there is something 'in our power' which may none the less be foreknown. His argument is based on the premiss that human wills are part of the sequence of causes known by divine foreknowledge (5. 9). The efficient causes of things are voluntary causes (Augustine argues this speciously, including natural causes, for instance, among voluntary causes, because God wills them, and even seeming to argue that animals can have wills). God gives powers to creatures: one such power is will, in the sense of good will (note that Augustine is not here arguing that will is a morally neutral faculty). Thus human minds, for example, both are caused (by God) and cause (because free will is present). God's foreknowledge is knowledge that I will use my power to act in a certain way in that particular way. In a sense, God is simply the observer of the exercise of that power (5. 9). This does not entail necessity. God's nature (immortal, infallible) is necessarily what it is, but it does not restrict God's omnipotence, both to do whatever he wills, and not to allow what he does not will. Restrictions on our wills can be the effect of other human wills: human willing is not omnipotent. And we do not fail to sin because of divine foreknowledge (5. 10). But there is also divine providence, a structuring force in nature and in human lives, creating and ordering all things. Its role in political affairs must now be examined (5. 11).

Sallust is again the source of the terminology and the parameters of the discussion of Roman imperial achievement which follows. Sallust's assertions that the early Romans were 'eager for praise' ('laudis avidi') and had a 'desire for glory' ('cupido gloriae') are assumed to be an adequate explanation of the driving force behind that achievement. It led to the maintenance of *libertas*, and the growth of power and rule. War often became the theatre in which praise and glory might be won. Power over others ('dominatio') was celebrated by Virgil as a characteristically Roman quality. Thus the rugged virtues of hard work, self-denial, and moderation in wealth all fired the imperial achievement. The Sallustian triad glory–honour–power ('gloria'–'honos'–'imperium'), epitomizing Roman political ambition, is cited: the true path of virtue led to power (5. 12). In chapter 13 Augustine deals with this ideological complex.

Love of praise, he argues, is in fact a vice rather than a virtue, as even
Roman moralists aver (Horace is cited). From chapter 13 the eschatological dimension, and from chapter 14 talk of the two cities (earthly
and heavenly) supervene. Thus the Roman virtues are immediately
assessed against the background of Christian values. Desire for
human praise is seen to militate against human spiritual progress.
Desire for justice is preferable to desire for glory. If the fear or the love
of God is overcast by the passion for glory, then the glory due to and
coming from God is jeopardized. The criterion of 'true religion'
('vera pietas') becomes ever more dominant (5. 14).[39] Membership
of the city of God is dependent upon true devotion ('pietas') towards
the true God (5. 15). The human and temporal is contrasted with the
divine and eternal. The Roman empire has a role for citizens of the
eternal city: they can derive benefit from it while they are aliens here
(5. 16). They can also consider Roman *exempla* as stimuli to excellence. This point is then developed massively in chapter 18. But
before that, Augustine has a number of other points to make. Chapter
17 is one of the few chapters where elements of a political theory are
adumbrated. One principle is that, if the same results can be obtained
by consensus as by war, then the peaceful option should be pursued.
The fellowship achieved by universal granting of citizenship (by
Caracalla in 212: cf. 4. 15) was something that should have been
aimed at earlier. Further, if glory entails that some are to be victors
and others defeated, then glory is insubstantial (5. 17). Chapter 17
concludes with a resounding series of antitheses to characterize the
two cities: heaven–earth, eternal life–temporal joys, true glory–empty
praise, angels–mortals, divine light–human and earthly lights. The
asylum of Romulus is a kind of prophetic 'shadow' of the divine city,
where sins are forgiven.[40]

   Having evoked the heavenly city in such desirable terms, Augustine
introduces a series of Roman *exempla* of valour, self-sacrifice, and
other glorious deeds with the formula: 'Is it such a great thing, if. . . ?'
('quid magnum est, si . . . ?').[41] What is so great about sacrificing

---

[39] For further allusions to 'true religion' ('vera religio', 'vera pietas') in *City* see 1.
36, 4. 1, 5. 19–20, 7. pref., 7. 33, 35, 8. 17, 10. 3. For the contrast with 'superstition'
see Ch. 7 below, on 6. 9. Christianity is the 'one true philosophy' (*C. Iul.* 4. 72); for the
term 'Christian philosophy' see also *C. Iul. imp.* 2. 166. The theme links Augustine's
earlier *De Vera Religione* to *City*; for further thematic links between the two works see
Madec (1991) and Ch. 12 below. Cf. Ch. 9 n. 56. The concept of 'Christian philosophy' is discussed critically by Stead (1994).
[40] Cf. 1. 34 with n. 12 above.   [41] Cf. n. 10 above.

everything for the heavenly city, if so many Romans have made sacrifices for their earthly city? Thus the *exempla* have the effect of inspiring Christians, but they are kept firmly in context. Yet the virtues which they exhibit are those which they who serve the city of God should practise (5. 18). And even if the Roman virtues are put into a temporal, historical context, their possession is not a matter of indifference: it is better, and more beneficial, that the citizens of the earthly city possess those virtues than that they do not (5. 19). Yet even the beginnings of Christian holiness are superior to Roman glory (5. 19). Desire for glory in the political arena can, however, check the worst excesses of the desire to dominate, just as love of praise is a vice that may prevent worse vices (5. 19; cf. 5. 13). The virtues should no more be slaves to pleasure than they should be subordinated to love of glory (5. 20).

Yet human empires are god-given, though the gift does not make the recipients just or good (5. 21). Contrast Constantine and Julian: the latter was a man of great natural ability, destroyed by curiosity (5. 21).[42] God may even manipulate the length and ferocity of wars, to punish or to give relief (5. 22). The ignorant who overestimate present disasters (cf. 4. 1) need reminding about the wars and violence of early Roman history (5. 21). The defeat of Radagaisus in 406 is an example of how in recent history God acts mercifully, sparing Rome, an event conveniently forgotten by pagan critics of Alaric, the milder and more clement leader (5. 23). God certainly intervenes in history. History is not neutrally 'secular'.

Chapter 24 develops a 'mirror for princes' (P. Hadot 1972: 618) which, although it is for Christian rulers, is full of characteristic Roman wisdom and values: good rulers should practise justice, be without pride, remember that they are human, be servants of God, god-fearing, clement, merciful, and self-disciplined. The specifically Christian values are also present, especially humility and the desire for eternal happiness. But much of what is said is traditional.

Because emperors are temporal rulers, even when they are Christian they are not guaranteed success and a long reign. Constantine ruled long, but not Jovian. Gratian died violently (5. 25). At the same time, Christian rulers behave very like their pagan counterparts.

---

[42] Augustine attributes similar 'curiosity' to the Jews in 4. 34. For the theme of 'curiosity' in Augustine see O'Donnell on *Conf.* 3. 2. 2, 10. 35. 54; cf. Labhardt (1960), who also deals with the pre-Augustinian history of the theme; Blumenberg (1983: 309–23); Rist (1994: 140–5).

Theodosius[43] avenged Gratian, and put the disturbed Roman world to rights by means of war and his authority. He was also a pursuer of pagans and heretics. He was fallible, yet repentant after the Thessalonica massacre (5. 26). Theodosius knew what Augustine has set out to demonstrate, that pagan gods (= demons) are not the givers of power: his edicts against paganism show this. The power of the true God—the theme of so many chapters of the past few books—is vindicated, but by a ruler who bows to Church discipline.

[43] For the possible sources of Augustine's comments on Theodosius see below, Ch. 11. 3e.

7
Varro, Platonists, and Demons:
Books 6–10

The true philosopher is the lover of God.
(*City* 8. 1)

The declared aim of Books 6 and 7 is to show that Roman religious beliefs and practices are ineffectual in relation to the afterlife (6. 1). But Augustine's argument seeks to expose general inadequacies and contradictions in Varro's philosophical explanations of religious phenomena.[1] Even if mention is made in Book 6 of the Mother of the gods and the Eleusinian mysteries (6. 7–8), and in Book 8 (23–4) of Hermes Trismegistus, Augustine does not enter into any discussion of the claims about the afterlife made by these rites. His general polemic is intended to make specific arguments superfluous. This gives the polemic against Varro a certain independence within the work, just as the work as a whole, after Book 1, moves away from the immediate implications of the sack of Rome, although returning to it from time to time when specific points are being made.

Why is Varro of such importance to Augustine? One reason is that Varro was appealed to by educated pagan contemporaries as a religious authority: this is the implication of a passage in 7. 22. Varro may not have intended to provide an apologia for Roman traditional religion, but Augustine certainly takes him to have done so, and it is reasonable to assume that Augustine's pagan contemporaries did. They were readers who, in a time of crisis and an atmosphere of uncertainty, 'had once again become extremely conscious of the historical roots of their culture' (Liebeschuetz 1979: 307). Such historical and cultural consciousness is evident in a work like Macrobius' *Saturnalia*, written probably about 431, a year or so after Augustine's death and about five years after the completion of the *City*

---

[1] For Varro see further Ch. 6 above, on *City* 4, and below, Ch. 11. 1b. On the themes and structure of Books 6–10 in general see Bardy, BA 34. 9–36; Fuhrer (1997) deals with the treatment of Platonism in Books 8–10.

of God (Alan Cameron 1967). Augustine knows that he is dealing
with readers possessing 'livelier and better minds' (7. pref.).

Augustine acknowledges the systematic nature of Varro's account
of Roman religion:

> Who has investigated these matters more attentively than Marcus Varro?
> Who has been more scholarly in his findings? Who has considered the
> questions more assiduously? Who has made finer distinctions? Who has
> written more carefully and more fully on the subject?   (6. 2)

These words echo those of Cicero in the *Academici Libri*, cited by
Augustine in the same chapter, and known only from there (*Acad.
Post.* 1. 3. 9). It is not, therefore, surprising that Augustine goes on to
summarize the structure of Varro's *Antiquitates* in 6. 3. Augustine
reacts systematically to Varro, and this reaction contrasts, for
example, with Tertullian's piecemeal polemic against details of
Varro's work in the *Ad Nationes* (Waszink 1976).

Varro's work had systematic tendencies. As its title (*Antiquitates
Rerum Divinarum*) suggests, it was a history of Roman religious
institutions, with encyclopaedic ambitions (Jocelyn 1982: 183–91).
It had no pretensions to be a work of religious reform, although
it argued, in a manner familiar also from Cicero and Seneca, for the
social utility of religious belief and practices. It seems evident that
Varro himself did not believe that sacrifice and prayer could be
efficacious (Arnobius, *Adversus Nationes* 7. 1). His attitude may
have been that of Seneca, as reported by Augustine later in Book 6
of *City*: 'The wise person will observe all these rites as being com-
manded by law, but not as pleasing to the gods' (6. 10). This attitude
has somehow to be reconciled with Varro's assertions (reported 4.
22) that knowledge of the functions of individual deities is essential
to successful religious practice. Those assertions should not be taken
as the programmatic utterance that they are often assumed to be. It is
more likely that they are 'defensive, justifying Varro's scholarship
against charges of pedantry and superstition, perhaps humorously'
(Jocelyn 1982: 181–2).

Belief in the social utility of popular religious beliefs is not
inconsistent with philosophical interpretations of those beliefs
that ultimately undermine them for the philosopher (Brunt 1989:
190–8). But that does not appear to have been Varro's aim in the
Antiquitates either. Varro stresses that his account is historical, and
that he is not writing 'about the whole of the nature of the gods'

(6. 4): we recall that Augustine had reported him as saying that, if he were writing a fully systematic account of the nature of the divine he would have developed it 'in accordance with the exemplar of nature' (4. 31; cf. 6. 4 end). Augustine senses that Varro's disbelief in the gods shows through, but that Varro had his reasons for leaving this implicit: 'The conclusion remains that he is to be understood to have not written about the divine nature at all, but that he did not wish to admit this openly, and left it to be assumed by judicious readers' (6. 4). Augustine feels that he can justifiably criticize Varro because, by his own admission, Varro's attitude to Roman religion is itself critical and reserved, and the criticism is based on a philosophical point of view. Varro's admission that there could be another form of discourse makes the *Antiquitates* into 'beliefs about unrealities' (6. 4).

Reference to 'beliefs' or opinions recalls another feature of Varro's account of religious practices. Varro stressed that his account could not be dogmatic. He reveals here his Academic allegiance (his allegiance to Antiochus of Ascalon must also be borne in mind: Cicero, *Acad. Post.* 1. 2. 7). In religious matters 'a human being has opinions, a god knowledge'. His views are 'uncertain opinions about the gods' (7. 17). Yet at the same time Varro propounds a *theologia naturalis*. Although he understands religion as a function of the state, a civic creation (6. 4; cf. 4. 31), and 'follows the institutions that the Roman state set up' (4. 31), he sees civic religion as embracing only one kind of discourse about gods (*theologia*). He appears to have adopted a variant of the formula of the three kinds ('tria genera') of theology (6. 5).[2] The 'genus mythicon' is found in myth and especially in literature. It is anthropomorphic in tendency. The 'genus civile' has to do with worship, rites, and sacrifices: it enshrines the beliefs to which Varro does not subscribe, but whose utility he commends. The 'genus physicon' is philosophical, and deals with the origins, identity, and nature of the gods in a speculative and often controversial way: but it is more appropriate to a school than to the public arena (6. 5). Yet Varro approves of this third kind of discourse, and Augustine allows us glimpses of how he applied it to Roman religion. Religious phenomena can be

---

[2] Cf. Lieberg (1973), Pépin (1958: 276–314). Dihle (1996) offers an explanation for the attractiveness of the formula for Augustine: it granted independent status, *qua* religious model, to civic cult, which was still relatively robust in the early 4th c. For use of 'vera theologia' with reference to Christianity see *City* 6. 8 (p. 261. 11 Dombart and Kalb).

interpreted 'physiologically', in terms of natural science. Thus the images, attributes, and ornaments of the gods are visible emblems of their true nature, that is, of the natural world and its parts, which they represent (7. 5). The anthropomorphic images suggest that the divine mind has similarities with human minds and rationality (7. 5). In fact, God is the soul of the universe, or rather the soul of the universe and its body together are God, but the universe's soul or mind makes it divine (7. 6). Thus Varro is—strictly speaking—a monotheist. Augustine will use this concession polemically against Varro, as we shall see. But it is Varro's monotheism and belief in divine providence that he stresses when he attempts to summarize what Varro really believed in:

> He knew that the universe existed, the sky and the earth, the sky bright with stars, the earth fertile with seeds . . . he believed with unshakeable assurance that this whole mass of nature is ruled and controlled by some invisible force. (7. 17)

That Varro subscribed to belief in the cosmic (possibly fiery) soul of the tradition of natural philosophy seems evident, and he seems to have identified the many deities of polytheism with this cosmic soul, as its attributes or powers, or as parts of the universe (7. 9). It would be wrong to label this theology Stoic, although it has elements to which Stoics would subscribe. For there is nothing in it that Varro could not maintain as an Academic thinker (Jocelyn 1982: 201–2). Varro offered an interpretation of statuary associated with the Samothracian mysteries in Platonist terms that may owe something to Antiochus. One statue, representing the sky, is that of Jupiter, and to be identified with the efficient ('a quo') cause; one, of Juno, represents the earth, and the material ('de qua') cause; the third, of Minerva, represents the Forms/Ideas ('ideae') or formal ('secundum quod') cause (7. 28). The identification of Juno = earth with secondary causes seems to be part of the same theory (7. 16), and a similar theory about Jupiter appears to be reflected in 7. 9.[3] So there is an ostensible systematic tendency of a theological kind in Varro's work. But the prominence given to it by Augustine reflects Augustine's need to confront a pagan theology with Christian theology. It is a need that may have caused him to magnify the systematic intent of Varro's work.

[3] Cf. Sharples (1995: 79–82), Dillon (1977: 95, 138–9; 1993: 93–100) for the philosophical background of these formulations.

It is now time to turn to the details of Augustine's polemic against Varro in Books 6 and 7. When he discusses the other two kinds of discourse about gods, the mythical/poetic and the state-religious, Augustine's strategy is a reductionist one. He wants to equate them, or at least show that they are inextricably linked. He builds on Varro's own admission of the links between mythical and civic theology in order to undermine the distinction between the two. The thrust of Augustine's argument is that myth and state religion are interactive, that divine imagery is influenced by myth and poetry and affects our perceptions of the gods, and that stage plays (Augustine is thinking chiefly of mime and pantomime), in particular, are part of, and shape the tone of, state religion (6. 5–7; cf. 4. 26).[4] Myth-making and festivals are linked: Augustine adduces Varro's account of the foundation myth of the festival of the Larentalia as an example of the way in which a fiction and a rite feed on each other (6. 7). This is a serious argument, and Augustine has found an aspect of Varro's approach—the attempt to drive a wedge between the myths which he finds embarrassing and religious cult—that is susceptible to criticism, especially by the criterion of Varro's historical approach. But much of his polemic in this context is tendentious. Augustine concentrates on rites where obscene and perverted elements can be isolated: Attis and Cybele, the Galli, Bacchic rites, elements of the Roman marriage ceremony (6. 8–9). Or he adduces obscene, frivolous, and degrading episodes involving gods in myths and theatrical productions (6. 5–7).

Augustine has another reason for wishing to link myths about the gods with civic religion. The anthropomorphic aspects of myths give support to an alternative theory with which Augustine, like other Christian apologists, finds himself in sympathy, that of Euhemerus (6. 7–8, 7. 18). He thus engages in his favourite ploy of playing off one pagan view (Varro's cosmic-soul theory) against another (Euhemerus).[5] In Books 8–10 the Euhemeristic theory will be

---

[4] See Wiseman (1995: 131–2) on the correctness of Augustine's insistence on the public and civic nature of theatrical festivals ('ludi scaenici'). See further above, Ch. 6 n. 14. Augustine and the theatre of his day: Weismann (1972); cf. *OCD*[3] s.v. 'ludi', 'mime', 'pantomime'. Augustine's point about the interactive nature of myth and state religion is perceptive: for an illuminating discussion of interaction between Roman religious ritual, divine representation, myth, and literature, chiefly in the Augustan period, see Feeney (1998); see ibid. 28–38 for a model analysis of the 'ludi saeculares' of 17 BC.

[5] This is a variant of the polemical method of literary retortion, which Augustine may have derived from Porphyry, as Arnobius probably did: see Simmons (1995:

applied to demonology. Euhemerus' *Sacred History* was translated, in whole or in part, by Ennius, and was much used by Christian writers, above all, Lactantius, in anti-pagan polemic: the view that the gods were deified great men was grist to the Christian mill (Ogilvie 1978: 55–7).

One motive that Varro identified for traditional religious beliefs was fear. He equates fear with 'superstitio', contrasting it with 'religio': 'The gods are feared by the superstitious person, but . . . revered by the religious person like parents, not feared as enemies' (6. 9). 'Superstitio' is contrasted with 'pietas', as it is by Cicero, for example, in *De Natura Deorum* 2. 71–2, quoted by Augustine elsewhere in the work (4. 30). Augustine adopts this distinction for himself, contrasting pagan religion ('superstitio') with the 'true religion' of Christianity in 7. 35. But although he can only praise this distinction, Augustine finds it vitiated by the hidden agenda which he imputes to Varro. It is bad enough that Varro commends the utility of civic religious practices that he knows to be fabrications (4. 9, 27). But he is also to be accused of suggesting that the human edifice of state religion can be seen for what it is by the discerning, so that his work— properly decoded—can be read as a demolition of the two theologies of which, intellectually, he disapproves, in order to clear the way for the third (6. 4). Augustine suggests that he was led into contradictions by wanting too much. He wanted to describe Roman religion as it was, and at the same time attribute natural explanations to religious phenomena (7. 23, 28). The contradictions which Augustine finds here and elsewhere in Varro are, of course, a consequence of his own polemical strategy and use of the *Antiquitates* (Jocelyn 1982: 202 n. 339). One such case is Varro's praise for the alleged aniconic phase in early Roman religion (4. 31),[6] and his justification for the

---

243 ff.). It is also related to the (*per se* non-polemical) interpretative principle of 'Homerum ex Homero', on which see Schäublin (1977), and which Augustine will have found in Tyconius: cf. Pollmann (1996: 209). For use of Euhemerus in apologetic contexts see further above, Ch. 3 with n. 17.

[6] Varro praised aniconic cult because he believed that it led to purer ('castius') religious observations at Rome, instancing also the Jews (*City* 4. 31). Cf. on the Jews Tacitus, *Histories* 5. 5. 4, which may, like Varro's comments, be related to views of Posidonius: for a discussion see Theiler (1982: ii. 283). For related considerations see Theophrastus 584A (= Porphyry, *De Abstinentia* 2. 26). For speculation that the late 4th-c. BC ethnographer Hecataeus of Abdera (*FGrH* 264 F 6; cf. Strabo 16. 2. 35) is the source of these views on Jewish religion see Henrichs (1982: 213); cf. Geffcken (1907: p. xi). See further Ch. 6 n. 34.

use of images and emblems of the gods as a way of making mysteries accessible by visible means (7. 5), whereas elsewhere he finds that such images diminish reverence and induce erroneous beliefs (4. 9, 31). Augustine seizes on the inconsistency. Yet he himself elsewhere repeatedly asserts the value and legitimacy of attempting to understand the invisible by means of the created and visible.[7] However, he is determined to give Varro no quarter here, merely conceding that he had a 'learned and clever mind' (7. 5), prevented by paganism from finding the true God.

The principal focus of Book 6 has been discourse about civic religion, or 'theologia civilis'. In Book 7 Augustine turns to Varro's 'select gods' ('di selecti'), the twenty most important gods enumerated by him and including the major gods of the Roman pantheon (7. 1–2). The context is still, therefore, chiefly civic religion, but Augustine now focuses attention upon the manner in which Varro attempts to provide a naturalistic explanation of beliefs and practices. There has been some discussion of this earlier in this chapter. Augustine's polemic is reminiscent of Book 4. Some of the 'di selecti' have no evident natural role. This is so with Mercury and Mars, unlike Liber and Ceres, whose functions are clear (7. 14, 16). And if planets like Mars, Saturn, and Venus are deified and if some of them have rites and temples, why are there no cults or shrines for the signs of the Zodiac (7. 15)? Another contradiction that Augustine purports to find in Varro is that singular divine functions are inappropriately divided between deities: Janus and Terminus (7. 7), Janus and Jupiter (7. 9–10), Jupiter and other gods (7. 11–13), and Juno, Ceres, and the Great Mother (7. 16).[8] But the chief criticism that Augustine makes of Varro's explanations of religious tradition and practice is that they confuse the creator god and his attributes

---

[7] See esp. *Conf.* 7. 17. 23, 7. 20. 26, here and elsewhere citing Rom. 1: 20 in support. On the role of the educational disciplines ('disciplinae liberales') in this connection see Augustine, *Retr.* 1. 6. The poem by Augustine's pupil Licentius (attached to Augustine, *Letter* 26 (CSEL 34: 89–95)) speaks of the disciplines constituting an ascending path, which he refers to as 'Varro's secret path' ('arcanum Varronis iter', 1). I. Hadot (1984: 176–87) argues unconvincingly that another Varro, the late Republican poet from Atax, may be referred to in the poem. Shanzer (1991) counters Hadot's argument, and provides a critical text, English tr., and full discussion of the poem.

[8] Cf. Arnobius' argument (*Adv. Nat.* 4. 14–15) against a plurality of Jupiters, Mercuries, etc. Simmons (1995: 292) suggests that Arnobius is here using Porphyrian methods of argument, seeking out contradictions and inconsistencies in the adversary's assertions. Augustine may be similarly influenced by Porphyry.

with the created universe and its ordered phenomena (7. 27–31).
This is strikingly put in 7. 30, where Augustine transfers the functions attributed to the 'di selecti' by Varro to the Christian God in his
role as creator and providential ruler of the universe (Jocelyn 1982:
195). In Book 7 Augustine simply asserts the superiority of the idea of
a transcendent God to any form of pantheism. The concept of God
that he opposes to Varro's is one based on Middle Platonist principles,
as Book 8 goes on to demonstrate. Essentially then, Augustine is here
appealing, without proof, to the assumed preferability of the monotheistic elements in Platonism. Book 8. 6–10 will show that this
assumed preferability is dependent upon the Platonist concept of
immaterial, eternal, unchanging, timeless being.

What Augustine finds odd is that Varro, despite his monotheistic
tendencies, none the less admits a plurality of elemental gods of the
ether and air, hyperlunary and sublunary deities. Despite his monotheistic claim, Varro constructs a polytheism (7. 6). But Varro—like
many of his contemporaries, and like any thinkers influenced by
Pythagoreanism (such as Ennius)—would not have seen any problem
in accepting state polytheism as well as the monotheism of the
philosophers. That monotheism was speculative and private: Varro
could identify the god of the Jews with the Roman Jupiter and the
cosmic soul (4. 31).[9]

Although, as has been seen, Augustine's favoured explanation of
polytheism is Euhemeristic, he allows for the malignant manipulation of beliefs by demons, a manipulation that, he suggests, was
revealed in the lost books of the legendary second king of Rome,
Numa Pompilius (7. 34–5). Varro's naturalistic explanation was an
attempt to make the demonic, especially in its obscene form,
respectable (7. 33).[10]

Varro is overwhelmingly the source of Augustine's knowledge of
symbolic interpretations of Roman religion in Books 6 and 7.[11] But
he is aware of other attempts to explain religious phenomena in
allegorical terms, such as Porphyry's account of the Attis myth and
cult and the self-castration of the Galli (7. 25).

---

[9] Cf. Augustine, *Cons. Ev.* 1. 22. 30–23. 31, 1. 27. 42; see Jocelyn (1982: 164).
[10] See 'Pompilius, Numa' in *OCD*³; cf. Ennius, *Annales* 113–19 Skutsch; Cic. *Rep.*
2. 25–30; Livy, 1. 18–21.
[11] In *City* 7. 20 he refers to Varro's interpretation of the Eleusinian mysteries, using
an etymology (from Latin 'proserpere', 'to creep forth') of Proserpina's name (cf. *City*
4. 8, 7. 24: a different etymology is proposed by Varro, *De Lingua Latina* 5. 68).

Nor is Varro the only critic of Roman religion adduced. In 6. 10 Seneca's *De Superstitione* is famously used. Augustine finds that Seneca is more freely critical than Varro. But Augustine betrays no awareness that the two works belong to different literary genres. Varro's is a historical, antiquarian, and scholarly account. Seneca's is a treatise on the gods in a long philosophical-critical tradition (Jocelyn 1982: 198 with n. 318). It is only to be expected that Seneca will be more forthright in his critique of traditional religious beliefs. Augustine finds much to approve in Seneca's view of divine nature: immortal, inviolable, not anthropomorphic, not requiring violent worship, sane and rational. Augustine sees Seneca demolishing, not only the respectability of myth and poetry about gods, but also civic religion. But Seneca's approval of the public utility of worship, like Varro's, seems to him dishonest (6. 10).

Since Book 2 Augustine has been engaged in a critique of popular polytheism. That critique is on a number of different registers. It can be philosophically sophisticated, as in the discussion in 5. 2–10 on astral determinism and fate. It can be tendentiously polemical, as in the attempts to trap Varro in inconsistencies. It can leave principles unanswered and undemonstrated, as in the preference shown for transcendent monotheism over other concepts of deity. And, although the focus of the polemic changes, there is an overriding use of certain techniques and arguments. The similarities between Books 4, 6, and 7 in the polemic against Varro are evident. Despite the fact that Augustine signals that Books 6 and 7 start the theme of religion and the afterlife, there is, as we have seen, nothing specifically about the afterlife in these books. The thrust of Augustine's argument is that if the polytheists (and a crypto-polytheist like Varro) hold contradictory views about the gods, these gods and the religious practices which they assume can have no beneficial effects in this life, and by implication in the next.

At the start of Book 8, Augustine is still under Varro's spell, although his echo of Varro's view that 'theologia naturalis' should not be discussed with ordinary people (*their* theology is mythical or civic) may carry a trace of irony (8. 1). What he now proposes is a discussion ('conlatio') with philosophers. He begins this discussion in formal manner, with a definition of philosophy (Regen 1983: 209–10) that owes something to the *erōs* theme in Platonism, something to the wisdom tradition in biblical texts (Proverbs, Wisdom of

Solomon), and much to Cicero (e.g. *De Legibus* 1. 58): 'If God is wisdom . . . the true philosopher is a lover of God.'

He immediately delimits the scope of his enquiry. He will confine it to *theologia*, which he defines as 'an account or discussion of the nature of the divine'. And, although he does not name them immediately, he will concentrate on the Platonists, who, even if they believe in divine providence, are polytheists. The ostensible theme of this part of the work—the afterlife—is mentioned here as the focus of Platonist worship of gods, but the theme will only be alluded to from time to time in Books 8–10, which concentrate on select aspects of Platonist theology—chiefly demonology—as tenable beliefs in themselves, rather than on their explicit ramifications for the afterlife. What distinguishes the Platonists from Varro is their belief in a transcendent deity who is unchangeable and incorporeal, and in whose nature the rational human soul somehow participates (8. 1).

The doxography of 8. 2 concentrates on those philosophers who can be shown to be precursors of Plato. Augustine has either adapted it to his own purpose, possibly from several sources, or he has had access to a Platonizing doxography.[12] At all events, treating the Italian before the Ionian philosophers, as he does, deviates from the normal doxographical order. Augustine confines his treatment of the Italian branch to Pythagoras, and to Pythagoras' contribution to the definition of philosophy: the probable source is Cicero, *Tusculan Disputations* 5. 8–10. But Pythagoras is also named because in 8. 4 he will represent the origin of the theoretical element in Platonism. The Atomists, whom Augustine knows, are not mentioned, as they do not fit into his perception of the influences on Platonism. The individual philosophers of the Ionian branch are familiar in doxographical contexts, and it is a familiar kind of presentation, concentrating on teacher–pupil tradition (Dillon 1977: p. xv), real or invented. The absence of the concept of a divine mind in Thales, Anaximander, and Anaximenes is deplored, but elements of their accounts of physical principles influence later thinkers (Anaxagoras, Diogenes of Apollonia, Archelaus), who provide differing accounts of the relation between a divine mind and matter. The source of some of this material is difficult to deter-

---

[12] For Augustine's use of doxographies see Solignac (1958), TeSelle (1970: 47–9); for *City* 8. 2 in particular see P. Hadot (1979), Regen (1983), Piccolomini (1971). See further n. 13 below.

mine (the doctrine of Archelaus, for example: the tradition that he taught Socrates is found in Cicero, *Tusc. Disp.* 5. 10), and some details are wrong (Anaxagoras as a pupil of Anaximenes). There is no overwhelming reason to suppose that Augustine's source must be late (or single), although Celsinus of Castabala, in a translation by Manlius Theodorus, has been suggested, as has Cornelius Celsus, whose *Opiniones Omnium Philosophorum* may be alluded to in 8. 1.[13]

Socrates is traditionally presented (Cicero, *Tusc. Disp.* 5. 10) as diverting the focus of philosophy from physics to ethics (8. 3). But the chapter has other details which are difficult to reconcile with one another. It is curiously disjointed. Socrates' concentration on ethics is first presented as susceptible to two interpretations. He may have believed that physical questions could not be readily answered, and concentrated on finding something certain about the conduct of our moral lives: in other words, he may have been a sceptic where physics is concerned. Alternatively, Augustine suggests, he may have held a kind of esoteric doctrine about physics, to which the morally unpurified should not be given access, for natural science deals with the first and highest causes, with eternal and divine things. The sceptical Socrates may derive from Antiochus, via Varro's *De Philosophia*, for example, or via Cicero,[14] in combination with the theory of a secret teaching. In the second part of 8. 3 a sceptical Socrates, whose chief activity is argumentational dexterity, is presented, without any hint of an ulterior dogmatic motive: Augustine is clearly hedging his bets. He does not want to have the great influence on Plato presented as a mere sceptic; yet he cannot define the contents of an alleged Socratic dogmatism, especially as his disciples (the master–pupil relationship again) adopted such widely different positions (Aristippus and Antisthenes are named, and then there is Plato). It is interesting to observe that Augustine reflects the position of those, especially

[13] Courcelle (1969: 192–4) argued for use of Celsinus in *City* 8. 1–4. For Augustine's possible use of him and Cornelius see below, Ch. 11.2c; cf. Hagendahl (1967: 675). Alan Cameron (1970: 323–6) argues against Courcelle's view that the brief references to philosophical doctrines in Claudian, *Panegyricus Dictus Mallio Theodoro Consuli* 70–83 suggest that Manlius Theodorus wrote a doxography, of which these lines are the source, and that this work was used by Augustine. There is no evidence that Theodorus translated Celsinus, although he did write a Latin work on Greek philosophy, to which Claudian, *Panegyricus* 84 ff. refers. For similar doxographical catalogues see Sidonius Apollinaris, *Carmina* 2. 164–81, 15. 51–125 (of which 87 ff. is most likely derived from Augustine, *City* 8. 2: see Diels, *DG*, 173–4), 23. 111–19.

[14] See Cic. *Acad. Post.* 1. 16; *Acad. Prior.* 2. 60, etc.; cf. Regen (1983: 221 n. 60); J. Barnes (1989: 81–2).

Antiochus, who revived Academic dogmatism in the first century BC, rather than, for example, the views of later Platonists like Apuleius, who in *De Platone* 1. 2 sees no problem in Plato simply expounding Socratic wisdom, and does not allude to Socrates' scepticism (Regen 1983: 221).

The beginning of Augustine's account of Plato in 8. 4 contains, apart from biographical commonplaces, elements of Cicero's version (*Republic* 1. 16) of Plato's travels to Egypt and Magna Graecia. But the picture of Plato's achievement presented here is not obviously indebted to any one source. Plato united the two branches of philosophy (the division is Aristotelian), the practical (Socrates) and the theoretical (Pythagoras: now we can understand why he was named in 8. 2, even if his contribution to theory was not referred to there). And Plato is made responsible for the tripartite division of philosophy that tradition ascribes to Xenocrates: ethics–physics–logic.[15] But Plato's own views are difficult to decipher, given that he introduced into his writings Socrates' habit of concealing or dissimulating his opinions. Augustine suggests, without saying so explicitly in 8. 4, that one has to turn to Platonist interpreters of Plato in order to derive a theology from him: perhaps, he says, they have a concept of God as 'the cause of existence, the ground of intellection, the ordering principle of life',[16] which humans can know, imitate, and love (or seek, see, and love: 8. 4 with the beginning of 8. 5). The implicit appeal to the Platonists' interpretation of Plato prepares for the ultimate focus of these books on Platonists, especially Apuleius and Porphyry.

Chapter 5 marks a return to the themes of 8. 1, and so to the preceding books. The claims of Platonist theologians put paid to belief in the gods of myth, even when, as with Varro (named here and in 8. 1), myths are allegorically interpreted, or rites (civic theology) symbolically explained. Augustine supposes that Numa's writings,[17] like Alexander's letter to Olympias, gave a Euhemerist interpretation of the origins of gods. Other philosophies also—Epicureanism and Stoicism, as well as the Presocratic believers in single-material first

---

[15] Xenocrates, fr. 1 Heinze (Sextus Empiricus, *Adversus Mathematicos* 7. 16); see Dillon (1977: 23). Cf. *C. Acad.* 3. 10. 23–13. 29 and Fuhrer ad loc.

[16] The intelligible triad 'esse'–'vivere'–'intellegere' is invoked here, as in 8. 6. On its history in the ancient Platonist tradition (deriving ultimately from exegesis of Plato, *Sophist* 248e) see P. Hadot (1960a; 1968: i. 213–46).

[17] See above on 7. 34 with n. 10.

principles, Thales and Anaximenes—are discredited by comparison with Platonism (Epicureans, because they believe that living things can be produced by lifeless entities; the Stoics, because living and lifeless objects alike are caused—they believe—by a living but material principle). But sense-perception demonstrates that the human mind deals with incorporeal bodily likenesses, and this entails that what creates the incorporeal mind (Augustine assumes that it is created) is itself an immaterial mind. But against the Platonists, who hold this view of sense-perception adopted by Augustine, Augustine himself stresses the mutability of the human mind, its difference from God (8. 5), who is a substance distinct from our minds.[18]

In chapters 6–8 Platonist teachings are surveyed under the tripartite headings, in the order physics–logic–ethics (P. Hadot 1979). In physics (8. 6) the following points are listed: God is not a body of any kind; nothing that changes can be God; every form in a changeable thing must be dependent on God's unchangeable nature or being; the whole material universe and its parts must likewise derive 'from him who, without qualification, exists'; in God being, life, intellect or thinking, and happiness are inseparable; life is superior to body, and the form of life is intelligible, that of body perceptible; the intelligible form is the higher form; the mind judges the beauty of bodily things, and can do so because it contains the ideal form within itself in a manner that is immaterial but nevertheless variable (for human judgements differ); there is a 'principle of things' ('rerum principium') which is the *locus* of the invariable form, uncreated, a first necessary principle of all else. Visible things are a means to the understanding of the invisible attributes of God (here as so often Augustine cites Romans 1: 19–20).[19]

In 8. 7 logic is ostensibly surveyed, but the emphasis is on theory of knowledge, and on the difference between the material, sensible criterion of truth in Epicureanism and Stoicism—derived from sense-perception—and Platonist idealism and illumination theory.

In 8. 8 the focus is on ethics, and on the highest good, attainment of which brings happiness. What characterizes the non-Platonist philosophers is the search for a human good, whether of body or mind or a combination of both (excluding external goods). The Platonists, by contrast, make 'enjoying God' ('frui deo') their highest

---

[18] Regen (1983: 225–6) discerns here Porphyrian rather than Plotinian emphasis. On the mutability of the human soul and mind in Augustine see O'Daly (1987: 34–7, 178–89).   [19] See n. 7 above.

good.[20] Augustine elucidates this concept by means of an optical analogy:

enjoying God, not as the mind enjoys the body or itself, or as friend enjoys friend, but as the eye enjoys the light . . . whence it follows that the one who is keen on wisdom—for that is the meaning of 'philosopher'—will be happy when he begins to enjoy God.

Thus themes of chapter 1—the definition of philosophy and the philosopher—are reiterated at the end of this schematic account of Platonism. Augustine stresses that Platonist beliefs about divine nature and substance, as well as about the relation of humans to God, are superior to other known theologies. But it is not the label 'Platonist' that is important. Any philosophers who held these views should receive the same accolade. It is the content of philosophy which counts (Regen 1983: 227). Doxography is thus a means to an end (8. 9).

Even non-philosophical Christians hold beliefs that are tantamount to a philosophical position, and will not be impressed by systems that confine themselves to the material universe. There are sufficient scriptural texts to give guidance, and Christians who do not know Platonism or even any other system will still know that God is the cause of our existence, that we are created in the divine image, that knowledge of God and self-knowledge are intimately related, and that God is the source of our happiness. Augustine is implying that there is a natural link between Christian beliefs and Platonist principles. Other philosophers may have come to accept these principles or work them out independently. But the Platonists are accessible, their writings well known, and even translated into Latin (8. 10).[21]

Book 8. 11 speculates about Plato's access to Jewish scriptures in Egypt, echoing a tradition that is found in Justin, Origen, and Eusebius, as well as Clement and Cyril, both of Alexandria.[22] Correspondences between the *Timaeus* and Genesis are established, but the possibility of contacts with Jeremiah or access to the

---

[20] On the theme of 'use' and 'enjoyment' ('uti', 'frui'), which lies behind this argument, see Bourke (1979: 29–65), O'Donovan (1980: 24–9), O'Connor (1985), O'Daly (1987: 38–9).   [21] Cf. below, Ch. 11. 2a–b.

[22] Cf. the view of Aristobulus and Philo of Alexandria that Moses is the source of Greek philosophical doctrines: for some of its consequences see Mansfeld (1988). Augustine regularly interprets Exod. 3: 14 to refer to God's pure, timeless being or substance: *En. Ps.* 38. 7, 121. 5; *Io. Ev. Tr.* 99. 5; *Ser.* 7. 7; *Ser. Caillau* 1. 57. 2; *Ser. Denis* 2. 5; *Trin.* 5. 3.

Septuagint is denied, on chronological grounds. Perhaps Plato found
an interpreter. Exodus 3: 14 ('And God said to Moses, I AM WHO I AM.
And he said, Say this to the people of Israel, I AM has sent me to you')
seems to reflect Platonic talk about that which really exists.

It is only in 8. 12 that Augustine relates Plato to the post-Platonic
tradition, and takes this up as far as Iamblichus, from its beginnings
with Speusippus and his 'beloved disciple' Xenocrates. It is interesting to observe that Augustine's insistence on the master–pupil
relationship makes of Aristotle a Platonist: for both Academics and
Peripatetics can be seen as followers of Plato, even if the modern
followers have chosen to call themselves 'Platonici' rather than adopt
either of the two other names. The named 'Platonici' are Apuleius,
Plotinus, Porphyry, and Iamblichus (8. 12).[23] All of these were polytheists, as was Plato, but the Platonists believe that gods are necessarily good. So no Platonist will believe that the gods of myth and ritual
are true representatives of divine power. But what is their status then?
Augustine will not accept that they do not exist, because they clearly
have power, and they are evidently evil powers. What has Platonism to
offer in explanation of this (8. 13)?

Augustine answers this question by referring to a Platonist
explanation which says that it is demons, not gods, who take pleasure
in myths and stage-plays and demand them as part of their worship.
These demons are clearly those of Apuleius' *De Deo Socratis*, which
Augustine goes on to use extensively in the following chapters of
Book 8 and in the subsequent two books.[24] Demons are part of a
hierarchy:

sky	gods	immortal, unchangeable, impassive
air	demons	immortal, with passions
earth	humans	mortal (bodily), with passions

Augustine spots an initial problem in the apparent contradiction
which makes Socrates' 'daimonion' a demon with guardian functions
of a benevolent kind, and yet makes of demons beings with evil
passions. Augustine speculates whether Apuleius avoided using the

[23] See further below, Ch. 11. 2b–c.
[24] For Apuleius' life and philosophical writings see Dillon (1977: 306–38, here
317–20 on *De Deo Socr.*); for Apuleius in *City* see further below, Ch. 11. 1k. On
demons and the devil in *City* see Evans (1982: 98–111). Augustine's demonology in
City 8–10 is his most extensive treatment of the topic: but see also his *Divin. Daem.*
(written 406–8); O'Daly (1987: 122–4).

word 'daemon' in the title of his book *De Deo Socratis*, because of embarrassment at the pejorative sense of the word. Yet in the details of his account of demons, Apuleius has discreditable things to say about them. So the problem remains (8. 14).

One characteristic of demons, according to Apuleius, is that their bodies have a stability and subtlety surpassing those of humans (8. 14). But these physical qualities, Augustine argues, do not make them superior to humans, for various animals surpass us in certain attributes, like speed, strength, and sight. Nor does their alleged dwelling-place, the air, make them our superiors: what about birds? Degrees of soul need not correspond accurately and consistently to the order of the elements (fire–air–water–earth: but human terres-trials are superior to aquatic creatures), and better souls may be in inferior bodies (8. 15). Thus doubts are cast on the validity of the hierarchy that places demons above humans.

For Apuleius the demons are subject to the same passions as humans, and so affected by worship or lack of it. None of their characteristics makes them unequivocally superior to humans: their eternal existence is of little use if they are unhappy. An aerial body is inferior to any kind of soul (8. 16). Augustine thus continues to hack away at the status of demons. Anything that is said about demonic emotions seems to equate them with humans. Augustine establishes a series of contrasts between demon-worship and the true religion (demons are angry, seduced by gifts, mollified by honours, they hate as well as love, are restless beings). We should not worship what we would not want to imitate (8. 17). Augustine reiterates the point that God is the being most worthy of imitation by humans.

Demons are presented as intermediaries between men and gods: this, Augustine suggests, is an encouragement to humans to dabble in degrading magical practices, as well as taking obscene theatrical performances seriously (8. 18). Magic is condemned by laws: Apuleius was arraigned on a charge of magical practices, and attempted in his *Apologia* to defend himself against the accusation. So pagans themselves condemn the magical arts that demons allegedly promote. What standing as intermediaries could such beings have (8. 19)? Contrast Apuleius' denial of magical involvement with the willing profession of faith of Christian martyrs (8. 19: the first of several allusions to martyrs in these books).

Augustine finds it paradoxical that gods, according to the Platonic dictum, have no dealings with humans (*Symposium* 203a), but would have dealings with dubious demons. No dealings with Plato, who was so concerned that poets defamed the gods—but dealings with demons who seem to demand obscene theatre? No dealings with legislators who punish magic, but with demons who encourage it (8. 20)? Augustine stresses that the human capacity for goodness makes humans potentially superior to demons, and so inherently more likely to gain divine attention. It would be absurd if demons, mendacious and deceitful as they are, were a barrier between gods and humans (8. 21). Augustine considers implications of demonic manipulation of gods, using ridicule as a polemical tool. Perhaps they reported Plato's critique of poetic fictions, but failed to reveal that they themselves approved of these fictions; or they did not even report the critique; or they revealed their approval; or they failed to report Plato's critique, while telling the gods of their approval of the fictions. In all of these cases Augustine finds divine impotence in the face of demonic manipulation unacceptable, and the inability of the gods to know directly about their human defender Plato an absurdity. This makes of the hierarchy a confining chain (8. 21). Better to accept that demons are malicious spirits, perhaps fallen from the sky-region to the air, inventors of their own divinity in order to entrap humans (8. 22).

From chapter 23 on Augustine turns to another work, the *Asclepius*, a Hermetic treatise[25] found among Apuleius' works in the manuscripts, but unlikely to be by Apuleius, and not explicitly identified here as Apuleian by Augustine. The work interests Augustine because it offers a different account of demons, with elements of which he can sympathize. In this account the inhabiting of statues by divine powers is a result of human techniques which can be called 'making gods' ('deos facere'), an aspect of theurgy, even if Augustine appears not to recognize that it is. Augustine understands the work to say that this making of gods is a consequence of human unbelief and religious degeneration, but he bases this interpretation on a causal reading of 'quoniam' in *Asclep.* 37,[26] a statement that Augustine finds puzzling in the context of the treatise's demonology, and for which he must find an ingenious explanation (Hermes is inspired by an evil spirit: 8. 24). The apocalyptic visions of future

[25] Edn. of the *Asclepius*: Nock and Festugière, *Corpus Hermeticum* ii. 257–355. For Lactantius' and Augustine's contrasting attitudes to Hermetism see Fowden (1986: 205–11).
[26] Cf. Scott's edn. of the *Hermetica* (Bibliog. C), iv. 183 n. 2, Loeb edn. of *City*, iii. 114–15 n. 2.

cataclysm, a feature of this kind of literature, and without any necessary historical reference, are understood by Augustine polemically to refer to the coming of Christianity and the downfall of paganism in Egypt (8. 23, on *Asclep.* 24). No less tendentious is Augustine's linking of the apocalyptic vision of tombs and dead people in *Asclep.* 24 with martyr-cult (8. 26). Augustine points out that this treatise does not make the demons intermediaries, as Apuleius does (8. 24). So in general the *Asclepius* gives Augustine polemical material to use against Platonist demonology. Demons are influential because of human degeneration, and the time of their influence is limited, as Hermes' prophecies indicate. Augustine contrasts those 'good gods', the angels, with demons. Much of what is wrongly said about human and demonic relations could, with appropriate modifications, be said about the relation between angels and humans (8. 25). Augustine finds the theurgic theory of the *Asclepius* yet another vindication of Euhemerism (8. 26). The deification of Asclepius as described in the treatise is further indication of the belief that gods were once men (8. 26). The difference between demon-cults and martyr-cults is stressed. The martyrs are not worshipped, nor is sacrifice made to them. Their cult is a mixture of thanksgiving service, victory celebration, and morale-boosting. Martyr-cult has no priests, and certainly no obscene rites. Socrates' 'daimonion' was perhaps foisted on Socrates (presumably Augustine means the Socratic tradition) by demon-worshippers. At the end of this chapter (8. 27) and of the book Augustine makes the point—again, rather perfunctorily—that there is no doubt, even among those with moderate sense, that worship of demons is not necessary for an afterlife of blessedness. But further examination of the claim that there are good demons is reserved for the next book.

The opening chapter of Book 9 is a *mise au point* of the discussion about demons so far achieved, and an anticipation of what is to follow. The position that a god can only be and do good, and that therefore malevolent supernatural powers are demonic, is reiterated, but so is the point that gods have no direct dealings with humans and that demons are thus necessary intermediaries between gods and humans. Against this Platonist view Augustine reminds the reader of his objections to a hierarchy with such a disreputable middle term. But the next question is: can there be distinctions between demons, and are they to be classified as good and bad (9. 1–2)?

Augustine seizes upon Apuleius' words in *De Deo Socratis* 12 (p. 20 Thomas), that seem to imply that demons' minds are prey to emotions (an unfair inference from Apuleius' vague psychological terminology), like the minds of 'fools' (the contrast is with the philosophically 'wise'): in other words, he concludes that Apuleius is saying that the demons cannot resist impulses, that they are morally incorrigible (9. 3). In 9. 4 the views of the schools on the passions are rehearsed, with the two principal positions being (*a*) the Stoic, that passions do not affect the sage, and (*b*) the Platonic-Peripatetic, that the sage's reason masters the passions, from which he is not exempt.[27] Augustine, following Cicero (*De Finibus* 3–4) and using the anecdote about the Stoic philosopher in the sea-storm from Aulus Gellius (*Noctes Atticae* 19. 1), argues that the Stoic view is based on a verbal quibble, and that it is in substance the same as the Platonic-Peripatetic one. In the Aulus Gellius story and its interpretation by the Stoic it is argued that some sensations ('visa' = 'phantasiae') are beyond reason's control, and occur spontaneously, like fear and grief. Only reason's consent to these sensations is within our power. The sage will not give way to the sensations, for that would be a morally faulty judgement: but he feels them none the less. The sage in the shipwreck feels terror, and believes that it is more 'advantageous' (a non-moral term) to be saved than drowned, but will also judge that his survival is not a 'good' like justice and has no moral implications. Thus the Christian—for Augustine subscribes to this analysis of the relation between mind and emotions—may apply emotions rightly, 'adapting them to the service of justice' (9. 5). Everything depends on the concept of assent: is reason the master or the slave (9. 4)? Augustine supports his view with a reference to parts of the soul, in Platonist manner. The passions affect only the lower parts (9. 4). If emotions like fear and anger can be controlled only with difficulty, it is a question of what makes the religious person angry or afraid, not whether he should ever be so. There are good and bad emotions (9. 5), and pity is a good emotion when it is consistent with behaving justly. God and angels can, by analogy, be said to be angry, when the nature or consequences of their actions are meant (9. 5). Augustine's views here, in what amounts to a digression on the emotions, can be paralleled by

---

[27] For the following see further O'Daly (1987: 46–50).

other Christian writers—Lactantius (*Divinae Institutiones* 6. 17) and Ambrose (*De Officiis* 2. 19), for instance.

In chapter 6 it is once again the reference to 'mind' ('mens') in Apuleius, *Socr.* 12, that is exploited polemically by Augustine. Demons seem neither to possess wisdom nor to have the ability to be a moral model to humans: how can they find favour for humans with the gods? Apuleius' definition and classification of demons seems to apply to all demons indifferently: he does not seem to take account of the good–bad distinction. The myths concerning the gods are poetic fictions, argues Apuleius, but there is an element of truth in the fiction, inasmuch as demons support some humans against others—like partisan spectators in the circus, says Augustine—and this support and enmity are falsely attributed to gods. In other words, the supernatural support is there, and so is the hostility, but it is demonic, not divine (9. 7).

The Apuleian definition of demons in *Socr.* 12 ('of genus animate, of soul passional, of mind rational, of body aery, of duration perpetual') is a morally indifferent one (9. 8). It also makes demons like gods merely because of their corporeal immortality, a bodily rather than a mental condition (9. 8). Moreover, they share with humans only a defective condition of the mind, its susceptibility to passions. Augustine finds this a flawed median position (contrasting the gods–humans–beasts sequence, where humans have mind in common with gods and body in common with beasts, alluded to in Sallust, *Catiline* 1): demons are 'bound and suspended upside down', and their bodies are not so much a vehicle ('vehiculum') as a chain ('vinculum') fettering a morally debased mind (9. 9). That kind of body becomes an eternal hindrance to moral betterment. Augustine contrasts it with the human condition, where the body is not an eternal prison ('vinculum'), thanks, according to Plotinus (*Enneads* 4. 3. 12), to the Father's mercy: apparently, no such mercy is shown to demons. Once again the argument is based on the perception that demons are not higher beings than humans (9. 10), and may indeed be no more than formerly living humans, and bad ones at that (9. 11).

Much of the argument of the next chapters continues to centre on the point that the demons do not constitute an acceptable mean between the extremes of divine and human existence. If, according to Apuleius, gods have three characteristic attributes—'a lofty location, perpetuity, blessedness'—and the humans have as attributes their opposites—'a low location, mortality, wretchedness'—then

Apuleius' demons are not poised between these extremes. They share perpetuity with the gods, and live in an intermediate place (the air), but they must also share human wretchedness. However, this seems inconsistent with their fivefold definition, which gives them three qualities in common with humans, and one with gods: that is, they tend more towards the human end of the scale. If, on the other hand, one were to argue that they are blessed ('eudaimones'), they are closer to gods than humans. Either way, Augustine sees their intermediate position compromised. A true hierarchy, and true intermediaries, are based on the mean category sharing an attribute each with the two extremes, not holding both in common with either extreme. Thus humans share reason with angels and mortality with beasts (9. 12–13). The Stoic or Epicurean sage would be a more appropriate intermediary between gods and humans, blessed but mortal (9. 14).

All this prepares the way for the suggestion that Christ, the Word, is a true intermediate being, for he is mortal but blessed.[28] Good angels cannot be mediators between gods and humans, for they are both blessed and immortal. But bad angels can be intermediaries, for they are immortal yet wretched. Thus Augustine establishes his good mediator and evil mediators, who work against human happiness and its attainment. Christ as mediator is so because he is human (so no need of demonic and supernatural mediators), and he enables humans, through fulfilment, to participate in his divinity (so no need of angels as intermediaries). So the human–divine mediator bridges the gulf between the divine and the human, and enables human deification to occur (9. 15).

Augustine is inclined to approve the Platonist view that the divine cannot be contaminated by human contact involving any of the five senses. And he uses this as an argument against the need for demons: demons are not required to keep gods free from human contamination. Again, the dilemma is employed: if demons are not contaminated, why should the gods be? The stars are not contaminated by being seen, or by casting light-rays on the earth: neither active nor passive contamination seems appropriate for a divine being (9. 16).

Augustine does not deny the need for a mediator, in order that humans may become godlike, purified, and freed from desire. Christ, uncontaminated by his human nature, also indicates that there is no

[28] Augustine's Christology: TeSelle (1970: 146–56), Miles (1979: 79–97), O'Connell (1968: 258–78). For the 4th- and early 5th-c. background see Kelly (1977: 280–343).

need to posit an aerial body in a supernatural being, in order to make
that being superior to humans (9. 17). Augustine rejects demons
contaminated by humans, and gods liable to contamination in favour
of a God who cannot be contaminated, any more than good angels
can, but through whom humans can be cleansed (9. 18).

After comments on the contemporary negative connotations of the
word 'demon' (9. 19), and a traditional linking of the word with
knowledge (9. 20), Augustine argues that, if demons have knowledge,
it is a kind of arrogant knowledge without love, appropriating the
worship due to God to themselves, in contrast with Christ's humility
(9. 20). That humility is not, however, incompatible with Christ's
confrontation with demons (9. 21). Their knowledge is of temporal
and material things, and this gives them a certain limited prophetic
power, but unlike angelic knowledge it does not discern the transcendent causes of things temporal and material; that is, it does not have
knowledge of the 'eternal and immutable laws of God' (9. 22).

As in 9. 19, Augustine does not wish to give the impression that he
is quibbling over words when he concedes that Platonists may wish to
call angels 'gods'. Such usage is even found in Scripture. The important distinction is between the creator and created being: created
angels are not God. Even humans can be called 'gods' in Scripture
(most famously in Psalm 82: 6, 'I have said, You are gods, and all of
you are sons of the Most High'). The term serves to highlight the
immortal and blessed nature, both of angels, and of the saints of God
(9. 23).

Augustine, at the end of Book 9, summarizes some of its main
points. Good angels do not meet the requirements of being intermediaries; bad angels do. But good angels do not seek worship, which
they want directed towards the one God, 'by participation in whom
they are blessed'. And bad angels, though intermediate beings, are no
mediators: their flawed moral standing, their wickedness, stands in
the way. They cannot secure for humans a blessed afterlife: once
again, Augustine only refers to the ostensible theme of these books
in passing, at the end (9. 23).

Book 9 has argued that there are good demons: the angels. In 10. 1
Augustine says that he must now focus on the question of whether
these angels require worship. In a sense, he has answered this
question already in the previous book. But he now wishes to concentrate more closely and in greater detail on the theme of worship. In

the rest of 10. 1 he reviews a number of terms for 'religion' ('cultus', 'religio', 'pietas'), none of which yields an exclusive meaning of 'worship of God alone': a Greek term like 'theosebeia' is more appropriate, better than 'eusebeia', which has some of the vaguer, wider range of meaning of the Latin terms just reviewed. What is the point of all this? Perhaps it is part of the flight from semantic distinctions, of which Augustine spoke in the previous book (9. 19, 23), although he does not refer explicitly to that here. Perhaps it is also a distancing technique for distinguishing between pagan and Christian attitudes: the inherited Latin pagan terminology is inadequate for monotheistic Christianity, even if individual terms have Christian meanings. Augustine's review of etymologies in this and later chapters of Book 10 (here 'religio', 'curia' in 10. 7, and 'heros' in 10. 21) utilizes a feature of his rhetorical training (and a method to which Varro was particularly prone) in elucidating his argument (den Boeft 1979).

Augustine believes (but cf. 10. 11) that a Platonist like Plotinus holds views that are similar to those held by Christians about the single source of human happiness for humans and for subordinate supernatural beings. For Plotinus the source is the 'intelligible light', a transcendent divine source and cause. This illumination concept is linked by Augustine with the light of John 1 (10. 2). This would seem to require that Platonists believe in a single object of human worship, this light or god. That they did not do so may have been due to fear of distancing themselves from religious conventions that are, in fact, erroneous; or because they generated errors of their own (10. 3).

The Christian dimension has been coming gradually to the fore in the most recent books of the work. It now moves, for the time being, centre stage. Augustine, with rich scriptural allusions, develops a theology of worship, in which its traditional forms—sacrifice, incense offerings, vows, dedications—are made into metaphors for the individual's spiritual devotion, in which love in the heart and the generation of virtues in the intellectual soul are the focus. This is Christian worship that would be palatable, he hopes, to a Platonist. Self-love, love of neighbour, and love of God are linked here to a Platonist context (10. 3). Partly this is because Augustine wishes to explain why certain forms of Jewish worship have not survived in Christianity. He invokes a sign ('signum', 'significare') theory to account for Jewish foreshadowings—in animal sacrifice, for

example—of present worship (10. 5).[29] The sacrifice of a contrite
heart is what God wants, but God has no need of animal sacrifice.
The true sacrifice, prefigured in all others, is the sacrifice of the self,
or the virtue of mercy. It is a form of dedication to God as our final
good, the establishment of a 'fellowship' ('societas') with God. These
two aspects—fellowship with God and 'clinging to God' ('adhaerere
deo')[30]—are the foundations of the city of God, which is another
symbolic sacrifice, whose meaning is evident in the mediator's
(Christ's) sacrifice, that of the head of which we are members, in
the 'one body' of the Church. Thus the themes of the renovation of
the heart, of mercy, and of worship are powerfully linked (10. 6). And
the Platonist language is maintained: the human soul is moulded in
conformity with the divine model, and derives its beauty through
virtue (abandonment of concupiscence) from divine beauty (10. 6).

Building on this notion of fellowship, Augustine next stresses that
the angels form, with us, one city of God, in worship of the one God.
We are one part of that city, the part which is in an alien place
('peregrinatur'), and they are the other part: this is the first mention
of a cardinal theme of the work. References to 'law' and 'Senate'
('curia') reinforce the political metaphor of the city or state ('civitas',
10. 7).

Miracles performed in support of God's promises to his chosen
people and recorded in Scripture are recounted: angels were often the
ministers or agents of God in these events. Augustine establishes his
alternative to demonology (10. 8). Miracles are not magic, but in 10.
9 the chief difference seems be between the paraphernalia of magic
(incantations, charms) and wonders that are the result of faith and
trust in God. Once again, as with demonology, Augustine is aware of a
Platonist distinction between good and bad magic. Good magic, for
Porphyry, is theurgy.[31] It is, of course, closely linked with demonology.
Porphyry's view is reported, that theurgy cannot provide a way of
return ('reversio') to God, but can only purify the 'spiritual part' of

[29] The literature on Augustine's sign theory grows apace. In addition to the older
works by Markus (1957) and Mayer (1969, 1974), see Rist (1994: 23–40), Stock
(1996), Pollmann (1996: 147–96), Markus (1996).
[30] The source of the phrase is Ps. 73: 28, 'But it is good for me to cling to God'.
[31] For Porphyry in City see further below, Ch. 11. 2b. On theurgy (magical techniques for establishing contact with the divine by use of words and symbols, such as
statues) among Hermetists, Chaldaeans, and Neoplatonists see Lewy (1978), Dodds
(1951: 283–311), A. Smith (1974: 81–144), G. Shaw (1985), and Fowden (1986:
116–53).

soul, the part which apprehends the images of corporeal things: it does not purify the 'intellectual part', which apprehends the truth of intelligible things, and which can 'escape' into its own sphere without the aid of rites of theurgy ('teletae'). Augustine reports a Porphyrian distinction between angels and demons: the latter can help the soul to rise after death a little above the earth, but worship of demons is something that the soul will abhor, with the insight gained as it expiates its guilt after death. In fact, Augustine's account in 10. 9–10, 26–7 distinguishes between three Porphyrian categories of angel or demon, which are related to the cosmic levels of ether, air, and earth. The three categories are:

(a) Angels in the ether who do not descend, and who reveal metaphysical truths: more specifically, they 'make . . . known the truth about the Father, his height and depth', they 'declare the will of the Father' (10. 26). They are also called 'gods' and 'divine', because of their dwelling-place in the ether (10. 9), though they are to be imitated rather than worshipped (10. 26). They are in the visible, and not in the intelligible world (10. 9). Although it is not explicitly said so, they correspond to the level of intellectual soul, which does not require theurgy and whose ignorance is purified by the 'Mind of the Father' ('patrikos nous', 10. 28).

(b) Angels in the ether who descend, who, though they are 'gods', can be malevolent, biddable (10. 9), and so subject to passions (10. 27). They are almost certainly the 'gods' who are 'seen' by the spiritual soul in 10. 9, but who are described there as not 'the true realities' ('ea quae vere sunt'). They illustrate the principle that theurgy can achieve good or evil (ibid.). They make pronouncements to theurgists, reveal 'divine prophecies', presumably like the Chaldaean oracles (10. 26; cf. 10. 27). They appear to be placed on the same level as the planetary deities (10. 26 end), if not actually equated with them. Augustine wants to equate then with malignant demons. Although it is not explicitly said so, they correspond to the spiritual soul, which can be purified by theurgic rites, which do not, however, ensure its attainment of immortality and eternity, or its 'return to God' (10. 9), for the soul purified by theurgy remains in the visible, if ethereal, world.

(c) Demons in the air, whose friendship is to be cultivated, for they can help the soul to rise after death above the earth, although it will subsequently spurn them as a result of the 'expiation' ('luendo poenas') which follows death (10. 9).[32]

Porphyry is ambivalent on the subject of theurgy, recognizing that there are malevolent supernatural powers that seek to harm or frustrate the soul in its efforts to seek purification. These 'divine' beings (category (*b*) above) can be influenced by human agents to block an individual's purification (10. 9). The fact that they can be intimidated and made to harm somebody is for Augustine another sign that these demons are diabolical powers (10. 10). Porphyry's 'gods' are subject to the passions, which only demons and humans experience in Apuleius (10. 9).

Augustine is apparently using here the work of Porphyry's that he calls *De Regressu Animae* in 10. 29. In 10. 11 he turns to another work of Porphyry's, the *Letter to Anebo*, where he seems to have been writing as a critic of popular religion: Augustine treats his views on demons there as one of a kind with those of the discussion of theurgy in the *De Regressu*, using the critical stance of the one work to corroborate his interpretation of the other.[33] The *Letter to Anebo* seems to have floated various theories about magic: is it a spiritual power, or is it caused by an outside agency? Porphyry finds evidence for the belief of others that the latter is the case. The use of certain stones and herbs seems to point towards external agents, but Porphyry is not, apparently, reporting his own views. He is, however, puzzled by the concept of divine powers subject to human wills (through sacrifice, for example), and by the notion that spiritual powers can inhabit material bodies and yet be variously good and evil, divine and demonic. The idea that gods, even the heavenly bodies, can be subject to human threats and menaces he finds odd. For Augustine it is important that Porphyry raises objections and is puzzled. He cannot decide what Porphyry's position is (genuine puzzlement? the pose of an enquirer in dialogue with a revered Egyptian priest? a writer of a polemic?), but he argues that the outcome is clear: Porphyry's questions undermine the popular beliefs that he is investigating. These demons who can be manipulated

---

[32] For the hierarchical sequence of elements behind this threefold scheme, which was apparently elaborated in the Old Academy after Plato's death (cf. Pseudo-Plato, *Epinomis* 981b–984d, where it is already related to gods and demons) see O'Daly (1989b: 46, 1991a: 146–7). For the location of category (*a*) angels in the visible world, see A. Smith (1974: 132 n. 18). For the 'Mind of the Father', see below on 10. 23.

[33] On the method of retortion used here see n. 5 above.

cannot deliver views on happiness: they are either deceivers or mere fantasy. This last observation is presented as Porphyry's concluding view (10. 11), in which a concept of happiness that is not mere material prosperity is suggested.

Augustine is not too happy with the notion that these demons might be mere fantasy. Once again, the dismissive concept of total fiction disturbs him. Supernatural events—or paranormal ones—seem to demand a superhuman cause: malevolent spirits are preferable. Augustine needs demons to explain certain observable, but otherwise inexplicable, phenomena. They become the counterparts of God and his miracles, which are distinguished from magic because they underpin the worship of God. For God can surely perform miracles when he is capable of the greatest wonders of all in the regular phenomena of his created universe; and in any case these miracles are also part of an unchangeable plan, and part of his fore-known temporal arrangement ('dispositio temporalis', 10. 12).[34] Among such plans were divine epiphanies to Moses and others. Divine interventions in human affairs, directly or through the ministry of angels, or by means of miraculous signs, are part of the workings of divine providence, the means whereby the law is delivered to the chosen people and its validity guaranteed (10. 13). Augustine compares this to the education of an individual, progressing by stages (10. 14). The historical dimension is subtly introduced, and linked to an ascent from the temporal to the eternal.[35] Plotinus understood that providence extended throughout all of nature. Turning to the one God even to obtain temporal things is good: it is, after all, true worship and a prelude to the later stage of contempt for, and aversion from, the temporal. The historical dimension is further explored in 10. 15. The God whose 'language' is spiritual, eternal, without end and beginning, may use temporal words. The law is delivered in a temporal succession, and its temporal components, in turn, are signs of things eternal (10. 15). In these pages central themes of the second half of the work are initially explored: God's timeless knowledge of things temporal; the importance of history; the miraculous nature of the ordered universe, in which paranormal miracles are, in a sense,

---

[34] Cf. below, Ch. 12 n. 10.

[35] See further n. 7 above. In *City* 18. 11 the progression scheme (earthly to spiritual) is related to the old and new covenants, and to the individual's development, with citation of 1 Cor. 15: 46–7. Horn (1997: 183–4) stresses the importance of such progression schemes in Augustine's account of history.

continuous with the normal; divine providence and its comprehensive nature; the special significance of Jewish history. Confrontation with the Platonists leads Augustine to define the elements of his Christian world-view. Those elements are formulated in terms that Platonists use and understand: the temporal as a sign of the eternal, inner and outer, the forming cause and the formed.

Worship which is focused upon the one true God, a contemplation of God such as Plotinus approves (10. 16), is clearly preferable to worship of supernatural beings lower than God: but demons often support their claim to be worshipped with miracles that distract men from rational and pious considerations. Augustine considers portents and prodigies, such as self-moving Penates and Tarquin cutting a whetstone with a razor, and argues that they are based on optical and other illusions, and are inherently inferior to, and less impressive than, the miracles recounted in Scripture. But he feels the need to bolster his argument by adding that pagan prodigies also serve inferior ends, that is, they do not promote the worship of the one God, whereas angels who direct us beyond themselves to worship of God have our interests at heart. The argument is weak (10. 16).

Chapter 17 recounts several scriptural miracles. Prodigies and signs accompanied the Ark of the Covenant on the desert wanderings of the Jews: the Ark itself is an emblem of the law and of wondrous manifestations of divine will. Other miracles associated with the Ark are mentioned. Augustine sees this as an instance of the Platonist belief in all-pervasive providence. The themes of law and progress are again combined: Old Testament sacrifices are a limited historical phenomenon, and point symbolically ('significare') towards later Christian ritual (10. 17).[36]

These scriptural miracles are well attested. It would be unreasonable for pagan critics, who themselves accept theurgy's aims, not to credit the miracles in which Christians believe. Augustine does not wish to enter into debate with any philosophers who deny the existence of gods or of divine providence. But by implication he feels he is on common ground with the Platonists when he defines the ultimate or highest Good in the language of Psalm 73: 28: 'But it is good for me to cling to God' (10. 18). Monotheism does not permit a division of sacrifice, such as making visible sacrifices to other divine beings, while offering a pure mind and a good will—an invisible,

---

[36] See 10. 5 and n. 29 above.

spiritual sacrifice—to the supreme God: visible sacrifices are not different from, but rather symbols of, the invisible sacrifice. Paul and Barnabas were on the right track (Acts 14) when they rejected the attempts of the Lycaonians to worship them as gods, and directed them towards the one God (10. 19). Christ the mediator is at once victim, sacrifice, and priest, and, as God, recipient of sacrifice. The eucharistic sacrifice symbolizes this act, in which the offering and he who offers are the same. It is the self-offering of the Church as a body of which Christ is the head (10. 20).

Martyrs are a kind of sacrificial victim. They might be called the 'heroes' of Christianity, if church usage allowed it. But their victory was over demons, and does not equate them with the demons.[37] This leads again to a brief consideration of a detail of demonology, the view attributed to Porphyry here (and supported by references to Juno in Virgil) that evil spirits have to be appeased if good spirits are to prevail. Augustine finds that this is equivalent to admitting that the evil demons are more powerful than the good, and only cease their actions when they are prevailed upon to do so voluntarily. Martyrs do not appease demons in this way (10. 21). Their victory is due to divine grace, as is their virtue, and it is due to the mediator Christ:

By this grace of God, by which he showed his great mercy towards us, we are ruled in this life by faith, and after this life we will be brought to the height of perfection by the actual sight of unchanging truth.   (10. 22)

Augustine now returns to Porphyry, and to his assertion that oracles once testified that lunar or solar mysteries ('teletae') do not purify us, but that the divine principles ('principia', 'archai') do. For Porphyry these principles are God the Father, God the Son = the Intellect of the Father or the Mind of the Father ('patrikos nous', cf. 10. 28), and a third midway between the two (which Augustine

---

[37] Augustine's etymology of 'hero' in 10. 21 is via Heros, son of Hera (a relationship that I have not found attested elsewhere, though scholars generally accept that the name 'Hera' is the feminine equivalent of 'heros'), and Hera is equated with the air (traditional Stoic etymological symbolism: Diogenes Laertius, 7. 147, etc.), which is the demonic medium. See den Boeft (1979: 250–2), reporting the view of A. B. Cook and others, who speculate that Augustine may be reflecting a tradition that Hercules is a son of Hera: but Augustine elsewhere knows of Juno's hatred of Hercules (*Ser.* 71. 2. 4), and is aware that he is her 'stepson' (*Vtil. Ieiun.* 7. 9). Den Boeft's comments on Augustine's use of a traditional function of etymology as a rhetorical topos (Aristotle, *Rhetoric* 2. 23. 1400[b]17–25) are valuable. Isidore of Seville reproduces Augustine's etymology of 'heros' (*Etymologiae* 8. 11. 98).

assumes is not the 'soul-faculty' referred to elsewhere by Porphyry and Plotinus, as it cannot be described as a middle term between the first two principles). Augustine is anxious here to include Porphyry in a Trinitarian context, and explains Porphyrian looseness of language as the way philosophers talk, whereas theologians must use more precise and regulated language, in accordance with the 'fixed rule' of faith (cf. 15. 7), in order not to generate an 'impious belief' (10. 23).[38]

Talk of principles, or indeed of gods, is not apt in a Christian context, however, even if Porphyry is right to insist that it is only by a principle that one can be purified. Porphyry did not recognize that Christ is such a principle (or rather *the* principle). Christ's incarnation and death demonstrate various things: that the body *per se* is not evil, but only sin is; that death is not to be avoided at all costs, especially when the cost is sinful, and that it should even be sought 'for justice's sake' (10. 24). In chapter 25 Augustine offers an exegesis of Psalm 73 that stresses its belief in and loyalty to the one true God. It can even be read to hint at higher spiritual things, and is not confined to the search for temporal benefits from God. The Psalmist speaks of hope, and Augustine interprets this hope eschatologically, seeing those who proclaim it as one with the angels of God, admitted to the fellowship of the city of God with them, who are our benefactors, and who will our happiness (10. 25).

Porphyry is accused of being soft on polytheistic worship. He had the critical weapons in his hands, but did not use them. Augustine attacks his distinction between two kinds of 'angel', those who proclaim on earth (without descending) the truths of metaphysics, and those who descend to make pronouncements to theurgists.[39] The former are to be imitated rather than worshipped. Porphyry should have stressed that this view of 'angels' excludes their worship, excludes even their will to be worshipped. That at least holds good for the first kind. As for the second kind (those who descend), Augustine suggests that they are malevolent demons, and criticizes Porphyry for placing them on the same level as planetary deities, and suggesting that they can be manipulated by theurgic arts (10. 26). Augustine argues that Porphyry's view about these descending angels

[38] Cf. below, Ch. 9 n. 7.
[39] Porphyry's distinction between kinds of angel, as reported by Augustine in these chapters, is described above in the discussion of 10. 9 with n. 32.

is inconsistent with his admission that the spiritual soul can be purified by moral self-control, without need of theurgy, and that theurgic rites do not necessarily elevate the soul after death; and also that it is only the Mind of the Father ('patrikos nous') that purifies the soul. It appears as if Augustine attributes to Porphyry a rejection of Christ as the 'patrikos nous' because of Christ's human birth and his death. For Augustine, this is proof of the limitations of wisdom, as it is understood by the philosophers, and he cites scriptural texts on the folly of Christ's death (1 Corinthians. 1: 20–5), and the real wisdom of God (10. 28). Yet despite having reservations about theurgy, Porphyry recommends it. Augustine sees this as a pupil paying his debt to his Chaldaean masters, even against Plato (the Platonist Apuleius was more of a true Platonist on the matter of higher and lower gods).[40] Porphyry is deaf to the Christian message of Christ's purifying, liberating incarnation. This need not have been so. Virgil's Fourth Eclogue, albeit symbolically, and although it is ostensibly about someone else, says things that could be spoken of Christ: Augustine believes it to contain the actual words of a Sibylline prophecy (10. 27).[41]

Chapter 29 returns to the three principles of Porphyrian metaphysics, again with the identification with the Trinity by Augustine. In a metaphor reminiscent of the conclusion of *Confessions* 7, Porphyry's insights are said to be a glimpse of a homeland through dark clouds, but not the road leading to it. Yet Porphyry has, Augustine argues, intimations of divine grace, as shown by his use of language like 'it has been granted (*esse concessum*) to a few to attain to God by the power of their understanding' (Augustine goes on to suggest that Porphyry speaks of God's 'providence and grace'). Why, then, did Porphyry balk at the notion of Christ incarnate in a human body, if the intellectual soul can be embodied? And that intellectual soul can, according to Porphyry, be made consubstantial with the second principle, the Mind of the Father. Yet imagine one such intellectual soul assumed by God for human salvation. It would be an instance of the union of two incorporeals, surely easier to conceive of than the incorporeal-corporeal union that is the human being. Perhaps it is the notion of a virgin birth that Porphyry finds difficult to accept? But that is an instance of a wonder-birth. Or perhaps it is the resurrection

---

[40] Yet, as Augustine remarks elsewhere (*City* 19. 23), Porphyry attacks Christians for deviating from the truth about Christ's nature.
[41] Cf. below, Ch. 11. 1e, 2e; S. Benko, *ANRW* ii. 31. 1 (1980) 646–705.

and transformation of Christ's body, especially if Porphyry applies to Christ the principle that 'one must escape from every kind of body' ('omne corpus fugiendum') found in his *De Regressu Animae*?[42] Yet Porphyry as a Platonist accepts an eternally embodied world-soul, and ensouled parts of the universe, like the heavenly bodies. Ultimately, it may be that Porphyry is simply too proud to accept the Christian message, simple and humble, yet containing, in John 1, principles of Platonism, words that, according to Simplicianus, 'a certain Platonist used to say should be written in letters of gold and displayed in the most prominent place in every church' (10. 29).[43]

When Porphyry wanted to, he could modify Platonic principles. This is evident from his views on transmigration of souls.[44] He limits metensomatosis of human souls to human bodies. Augustine finds this 'to a great extent' correct as a belief. The phrase is surprising, for Augustine rejects transmigration and reincarnation. The reason for its use here is the polemical context. Augustine is engaging in polemic when he speculates that Porphyry's rejection of the Platonic theory was because 'he was evidently ashamed to believe in it, for fear that a mother, returning as a mule, might carry her son on her back' (10. 30). Augustine prefers Porphyry's view that talk of metempsychosis is figurative, implying moral transformation (*De Genesi ad Litteram* 7. 10. 15). In fact, Augustine misrepresents Porphyry, as does the indirect tradition in general. For Porphyry, the soul in its primary choice can opt for human or animal existence, and it is only the secondary choice that is limited in the sense described by Augustine.

Another example of Porphyry's rejection of a Platonic doctrine is his claim that the soul can be permanently liberated from the body, if it is purified of all evil. The Platonic view is echoed in Virgil (*Aeneid* 6. 750–1). Augustine argues that Porphyry's position is necessary if the soul is to be really and perfectly happy. A perfectly happy condition cannot be troubled by longing for, or anxiety about, previous imperfect forms of existence (10. 30). So Porphyry is correct 'to a great extent', not because Augustine can accept his views, but because they seem to him to be a vast improvement on Plato's. Elsewhere, he

---

[42] A. Smith (1974: 20–39) puts Porphyry's views on separation of soul from body into their philosophical context.

[43] This Platonist is often identified with Marius Victorinus; see Courcelle (1968: 171), P. Hadot (1971: 237).

[44] For the following see Deuse (1983: 129–67), O'Daly (1987: 72–3).

implies that they are preferable because they safeguard the essentially rational nature of the human soul (O'Daly 1987: 74–5).

In chapter 31 Augustine remains on philosophical territory, and the theme of the eternity of the human soul and the universe. He criticizes the Platonist view that whatever is eternal must always have existed. He does so by appealing to the literal interpretation of the *Timaeus*, but also to divine authority. Yet Augustine does offer two arguments against the necessity of assuming eternal existence in the sense of pre-existence. Has the soul's wretchedness also always existed? If not, what is the reason for a condition of the soul coming into being, and at one instant rather than another? And why should this not be asked of the soul itself as well? Secondly, the soul's happiness after the trials of embodied existence will begin at moment *T*, and, according to Porphyry, exist for ever. So here is a case of something eternal coming into being. Augustine believes that he has found a contrary instance that undermines the thesis that what is without an end in time cannot have a beginning in time. But he is also determined to stress the divine authority behind the view that the soul is created (10. 31).

Augustine proffers Christianity as the 'universal way' ('via universalis') of which Porphyry wrote and whose absence he deplores in the philosophies, including the Chaldaean oracles, and Indian wisdom literature, which he had studied (10. 32).[45] What is sought is the liberation of the soul. Augustine infers that Porphyry believes that there is such a universal way.[46] He did not recognize it in Christianity,

[45] Augustine's report in 10. 32 has Porphyry referring to his study as 'historialis cognitio' (pp. 455, 9, 459. 10 Dombart and Kalb). What does the phrase mean? Augustine understands it in the sense of 'study of history', as 10. 32 (p. 459. 11 ff.), with its reference to biblical history, makes clear, and this is how modern interpreters also generally understand it. Studer (1996) goes so far as to suggest that there is a Porphyrian view of history, to which Augustine reacts: see also Horn (1997: 192–3). While Studer is right to insist that Porphyry's scholarly method in several areas, including his biblical and Homeric criticism, has a historical dimension, it does not follow that he has a distinctive concept of 'historical knowledge'. Nor need 'historialis cognitio' mean 'study of history'. The late Latin coinage 'historialis' usually means 'historical'. But it is not immediately intelligible why Porphyry should refer to his study of philosophy and wisdom literature as 'historical', and he can hardly be referring to historical, as opposed to philosophical, study. It is, therefore, possible that the phrase, which is likely to be a direct translation of a Greek phrase in Porphyry, might be using 'historialis' in a meaning which Greek *historikos* (LSJ, I) and Latin 'historicus' (*OLD*, 1) both have, to convey the sense 'study/investigation of (scholarly) evidence'.

[46] On the qualified sense in which Porphyry appears to have understood 'universal way' see A. Smith (1974: 136–9). See further Fowden (1986: 116–41, here 129–40 on Porphyry), Simmons (1995: 264–303). Augustine's idea of 'universal' includes, as 10. 32 makes clear, the notion, which is emphatically not that of Porphyry, that the whole person is saved.

despite being a contemporary of the martyrdom of Christians. In fact, Augustine implies that Porphyry believed that persecution of Christians would annihilate the religion (Simmons 1995: 281). Augustine cites scriptural texts with a universalist tone. Christianity, the true universal way, is historically and providentially prepared in the Jewish people 'whose actual state (*res publica*) was to a certain extent consecrated to be a prophecy and precursor of the city of God, which was to be assembled from all peoples' (10. 32). It is more openly revealed by Christ and the apostles, supported by miracles. It proffers purification of the whole man, not merely parts of the soul (purified differently, according to Porphyry). It has acquired a kind of universal authority. Its prophecies are not to be equated with the divination of which Porphyry and other Platonists are rightly critical. Even when the prophets foretold earthly and temporal events, it was with an ulterior, spiritual motive: to make more credible what they above all wanted to predict, namely, the history of Christ and his message, judgement and resurrection, the reign of the city of God, the end of idolatry. In other words, the test of true prophecy is its fulfilment, and so much has hitherto been fulfilled that belief in the rest is compelling. And this is unlike prediction of temporal events that is based on observation of secondary causes, and resultant forecasting of what may be expected to happen.

For the Christian, vision of, and union with, God remains: aspirations that Platonists share with Christians. Christianity is the path looked for by Porphyry. With this resounding claim Augustine concludes both his survey of Platonism, and the first half of his work. Much in the last book of this first half anticipates themes of the second part.

8

Creation, the Fall, and the Regime of the Passions: Books 11–14

The end of Book 10 marks the conclusion of what Augustine often refers to as the part of the work devoted to refutation ('we have replied to the enemies of this holy city in the previous ten books', 11. 1). According to his plan, he can now, in Books 11–14, proceed to discuss the origin of the two cities.[1] In fact, the continuity between this new section of the work and what went before is greater than Augustine's scheme suggests. A number of themes of Books 8–10 in particular (such as the nature of God and the role of Christ as mediator) are reiterated here. Moreover, there is further refutation of philosophical or theological positions, Christian or otherwise, of which Augustine disapproves. Indeed, he often defines his own position, which he takes to be the appropriate Christian one, by contrast with other views. None the less, the reader, who has been hearing more about the concept of the city of God in the preceding book, is made repeatedly aware of the links between Augustine's carefully articulated divisions of the work, even if these divisions do not always deliver what they ostensibly promise. Beneath the structural edifice, more subtle connections are discernible.

The principal themes of Books 11–14 are the creation of the universe, the nature of the angels and the rebellion of some angels, and the fall of Adam and Eve. This marks another shift in the work's themes. In Books 1–10 Augustine has been dealing with topics that had either not been treated elsewhere in his writings, or treated only in passing or briefly. But in this and subsequent sections of the work he will discuss topics that are both frequent and central in his writings.[2] The ostensible unifying thread is the theme of the two

---

[1] On the themes of Books 11–14 see Bardy, BA 35. 9–21.

[2] Creation of the universe: Sorabji (1983: 193–283) discusses Augustinian and other theories; cf. TeSelle (1970: 197–223), Pelland (1972), Kirwan (1989: 151–66). Angels: Madec (1986). Adam and Eve: Bonner (1986), E. A. Clark (1986: 353–85), G. Clark (1993: 120–6); Pagels (1988: 98–150) and Brown (1989: 387–427) discuss Adam and Eve and the Fall in the context of Augustine's views on sexuality.

cities, but essentially Augustine is providing a review of fundamental theological issues, to instruct and inform Christian or potentially Christian readers.

Chapter 1 of Book 11 retains the locutions of the preceding book, referring to angels as 'gods', partly in exegesis of the scriptural phrase 'God of gods' ('deus deorum'), partly to contrast angels, who focus their own and human worship on the one God, with the self-seeking demons of polytheism. These demons have an 'impoverished power', and what they offer to their devotees is contrasted with the divine light of the true God, in which all share. Chapter 2 explicates this. What all humans share is reason, and it is in this respect that they are made in God's image. But Augustine does not wish to stress the achievements of rational enquiry here. Reason may arrive at the concept of an unchangeable divine substance, but Augustine draws our attention to other ways of learning. Because, he says, our minds are weakened by 'certain dark and ancient faults' (a reference to original sin, perhaps not more specific because it would make sense, in this form, to non-Christians), we depend on belief or faith ('fides'), which in turn depends upon authority. Augustine makes the concepts of belief and authority accessible by appealing to the trust that we place in reliable witnesses when we believe in things that are not present to our senses (11. 3). The pre-eminent authority, for Christians, is, however, Scripture (11. 3). Presumably it is to Scripture that Augustine refers when he stresses in 11. 2 that, although reason may arrive at a concept of divine substance, we learn 'from God himself' that he is the maker of 'all nature'. The description of God speaking, not in ordinary language, but 'with truth itself' ('ipsa veritate') in a kind of mental meta-language (11. 2), is related to the account of divine wisdom 'soundlessly and inwardly' dictating the contents of the book of Genesis to the inspired spokesman (11. 4).[3] The Scriptures are one means whereby the invisible world is made

---

[3] For the ancient philosophical and Patristic background of the motif of a divine spiritual language see Theiler (1966: 302–12). Meijering (1979: 28–37) discusses the theme in *Conf.* 11 and other writings of Augustine. The notion of God's inner language may be influenced by Augustine's talk of 'inner man/light/truth' in the epistemological context of *De Magistro* and of 'inner word' elsewhere: on *Mag.* and related writings see Markus (1957), G. Matthews (1967), O'Daly (1987: 175–6), Watson (1988), Rist (1994: 23–40), Stock (1996: 145–62). Augustine, in common with biblical interpreters prior to the 18th c., assumes that Genesis is a single coherent narrative composed by Moses, and shows no awareness that its opening chapters contain two distinct creation stories: cf. Lane Fox (1991: 15–27).

accessible (11. 4). The incarnation of God's son—'truth itself' ('ipsa veritas')—is another (11. 2). Augustine emphasizes again the theme of the mediator, but in a scriptural context: the phenomenon of Christ defines (by means of the prophets, as well as through his own words and those of the apostles) the canonical Scriptures (11. 3).[4] We are thus being subtly led towards exegesis, and in particular towards exegesis of Genesis 1: 1: 'In the beginning God created the heaven and the earth.'

Genesis excludes an eternal universe, unless we are to conclude that its opening words refer, not to a beginning of time, but to the universe's eternal causal dependence upon God. Augustine will reject this view presently. But first he indicates that the universe itself manifests its created nature. Presumably he means that, considered in itself, the universe exhibits its changeable nature (and so it is secondary, and so caused in some way), and it also exhibits its greatness and order and beauty (and so points towards a maker whose qualities it reflects). We note that, once again, Augustine uses the concept of a meta-language, this time of the universe (11. 4).

It is therefore true to say that, even without Scripture, we could draw certain conclusions about the universe. But we could not conclude that it is not created. Could we, however, suppose that, though created in the sense of being a secondary nature, it exists eternally?[5] Augustine argues that the reasons adduced by philosophers (he clearly means Platonists) for an eternally existent universe of secondary status are not cogent. A principal reason given is that the assumption of a universe with a temporal beginning entails a random impulse or a new act of will on God's part. Augustine's strategy for refuting this argument here is to appeal to the phenomenon of change in the soul. The Platonists he is criticizing believe that the soul is co-eternal with God. But the soul notoriously changes, experiencing new forms of wretchedness or, it may be, happiness (O'Daly 1987: 34–8). Augustine rejects as absurd the notion that

---

[4] The idea that Christ is the principle of unity of Scripture is Origen's: see Chadwick (1966: 157). Macleod (1971: 371), in a page of characteristic lucidity, explains the Christocentric nature of Origen's allegorical exegesis: both Scripture and Christ are Logos, and Christ is incarnate in Scripture. So the biblical exegete renews, in intellectual form, the revelation of God in Christ, as well as participating in the search for God's truth. On Augustine's exegesis see further n. 12 below.

[5] Cf. esp. the account of creation, time and beginnings in City 11. 4 ff. with Conf. 11. 3. 5–13. 16. Sorabji (1983: 232–52) has a brilliant discussion of this topic in Augustine and others.

the soul might, so to speak, be programmed to alternate eternally between misery and happiness: in other words, that it might be God's unchanging plan that the soul changes eternally. That would involve the Platonists having to accept that the soul's happiness is never secure. He assumes, therefore, that they will agree with him that it is reasonable to expect that the soul undergoes the kinds of change that we perceive, and that it may change to a state of permanent happiness. Are such changes part of God's plan? If not, God is not the cause of human happiness, an absurd conclusion. If they are, then God might arguably undergo a change of purpose. If this is tenable in the case of the soul, then why object to it in the case of the universe? But if the Platonists maintain that the soul is created in time but lives eternally, and can be released from its unhappiness and become blessed for ever, without this final change involving a change in God's plan, why can they not maintain the same of God's relation to a universe created in time (11. 4)?

This answer is the first which Augustine gives to the Platonists on the question of the universe's beginning in time. Before pursuing the question further, he considers the related problem of the universe's location in space. He does not envisage his specific philosophical adversaries treating the question of why the universe is located in one particular place in infinite space, but he feels that they should. In order to protect God from inactivity in the space outside the universe, they would, he argues, be compelled to posit, with the Epicureans, countless universes. This is unacceptable to the Platonists, who are imagined by Augustine to answer his argument by saying that the notion of infinite tracts of space outside the universe is unnecessary, as the universe occupies all the space that there is. This imaginary dialogue with the Platonists is introduced to allow Augustine to argue the analogy between space and time. Just as there is no space outside the universe, there is no time before the existence of the universe (11. 5). In God's eternity there is no change, no before and after (Gunnersdorf von Jess 1975; O'Daly 1986). But time depends on change, and so on beings or bodies that change. With the creation of the universe time is created. There is no time before the creation of the universe in which God was inactive (11. 6).

In the Genesis account the sun is created on the fourth day.[6]

---

[6] For Augustine's exegesis of the days of creation in his other writings see Pelland (1972) and Solignac's notes (on *Gen. ad Litt.*) in BA 48–9.

Furthermore, God is said to rest on the seventh day. Augustine uses these aspects of the biblical account of creation to stress the necessity of understanding it symbolically (11. 6). What do the 'days' of creation mean, if time is measured by perceived solar movement? Augustine builds on the observation that in the scriptural account of the first days there is no reference to night, but only to evening and morning. He proffers a symbolic understanding of this, in terms of knowledge and its objects. If knowledge (and it is clear from 11. 29 that he means the knowledge possessed by a created being, angelic or human) is focused on God, in praise and love, it is 'daylight' knowledge (the associations with divine light, and the illumination theory of knowledge, are obvious). If knowledge is focused on created things, it is 'evening' knowledge: Augustine alludes to the notion that a clearer understanding of things is possessed when they are seen in the context of divine wisdom (11. 7). What this means becomes clearer in 11. 29. It is knowledge of created things 'in God's word, where they have their causes and the rational principles, immutably stable, in accordance with which they were made'. That is to say, it is knowledge of the Forms (in the Platonic sense) of things, as opposed to things themselves. In 11. 29 this daylight knowledge is said to be the angels' prerogative. As for God's resting on the seventh day, that symbolizes the rest of those who rest in God, and is part of the prophetic message of Genesis (11. 8).

God, in creating the universe, founds the city of God (11. 1): angels are a large and important part of that city (11. 9).[7] In talking of the origins of the city of God, Augustine must therefore talk of angels. They are not mentioned in the Genesis account, but, as creation is represented as complete in that account, they must be included in it, and several other Scriptural texts refer to them as created beings. Furthermore, because of Job 38: 7 ('When the stars were made, all my angels praised me with a great voice'),[8] Augustine concludes that they must have been created before the creation of the stars on the fourth day. As the specific creations of the second and third days are mentioned in the Genesis text, Augustine argues that the text of Genesis 1: 1–5 (which deals with 'day one', 'dies unus')[9] must

[7] On angels in Augustine see Madec (1986); on angels in the creation account see Solignac, BA 48. 645–53.

[8] The Latin version of Job 38: 7 used by Augustine renders the Septuagint translation of the verse.

[9] The Latin version of the verse is again based on the Septuagint translation (see n. 8 above). Cf. Philo's exegesis of Gen. 1: 5 in *De Opificio Mundi* 26–35.

contain a reference to angels. He finds this in the 'light' of Genesis 1: 3 (11. 9), just as the separation of light from darkness represents the distinction between good and bad angels. The angels were created as blessed beings, and even those who were to rebel and fall were created equal in happiness with the good angels (11. 11, 13). This involves assuming that it was only after the fall of some angels that the others gained that certainty of their own everlasting blessedness which is a prerequisite of true happiness: for to be truly happy one has to be certain that happiness will be continuous and permanent, and one must be unaffected by fear and uncertainty about its permanence (11. 11, 13). It is Augustine's overriding concern to reject the idea that the devil's nature is created defective in some way. He regards this as a Manichaean pitfall (11. 13), as attributing a substantial reality to evil, whereas evil is simply the loss of good (11. 9), and a consequence of free choice of the will (11. 13).[10] If the devil is said to sin from the beginning (1 John 3: 8), that must mean that he sins from the beginning of his sin of pride (11. 15).

Throughout these chapters Augustine is concerned to establish certain hierarchies which, he believes, are the key to an understanding of the created order. In 11. 10 he begins with the primal good, God the creator. Divine substance is simple; in it, quality and substance are the same, for it does not have anything which it can lose, and it is not different from what it has. The Trinity does not jeopardize this simplicity. In created beings substance and qualities are distinguishable: the body, in its resurrected form, acquires a quality which it did not have, incorruptibility; the souls of the blessed participate in unchanging wisdom, a quality distinguishable from the substance of the soul. There are also degrees of happiness. The happiness of humans is different from that of angels. But human happiness is in turn different when we speak of the happiness of the first human beings in paradise before their sin, the happiness of those who live a just and pious life, and the happiness of the saints in heaven (11. 12). In 11. 16 a hierarchy of created beings is established: immortal-rational (angels), mortal-rational (humans), sentient (animals), living (plants), non-living. This is the order of nature. But there is also a sequence based on utility and value. This might lead us to prefer bread to mice, or money to fleas. This sequence may be determined by

---

[10] On Augustine's exposure to, and critique of, Manichaeism see Bonner (1963: 157–236), Lieu (1985: 117–53).

need or pleasure (O'Donovan 1980: 14–16; O'Daly 1991*a*: 153–4). But it is also true to say that good humans rank above bad angels: the moral hierarchy need not coincide with the natural hierarchy that reason discerns.

Furthermore, the ordered universe contains evil, in the sense of evil wills. Thus God, without creating the devil as evil, makes providential use of the devil for the testing of the good (11. 17).[11] And just as there are antitheses in literary works, so there can be contraries in nature, which in some way enhance the whole (11. 18): 'through the opposition of contraries, a kind of rhetoric (*eloquentia*) of events, the beauty of the course of history (*saeculum*) is put together'.

Chapter 19 returns to biblical exegesis. There has already been some talk in previous chapters, with examples, of symbolic interpretation. Augustine now sets out some principles of hermeneutics.[12] Obscure scriptural passages may provoke more than one interpretation (interestingly, he compares this to different readings of any text). The possible interpretations of texts are controlled by evident facts and the meaning of other relevant passages that are not themselves obscure. Augustine thinks that his exegesis of Genesis 1: 4–6 is one such possible interpretation: in 11. 33 he points out that this interpretation is not certain. A by-product of such exegesis can be other truthful insights (11. 19). Chapter 20 provides a new instance. The phrase 'and God saw that it was good' and its variants recur in the creation account. Its presence after the creation of light contrasts with its absence after the separation of light from darkness (Genesis

---

[11] Kirwan (1989: 60–81) analyses Augustine's views on God and evil; cf. Evans (1982). On the 'aesthetic theodicy' of *City* 11. 18 and other texts, and on Augustine's theodicy and views on divine justice in general, see Burnaby (1938: 192–200); cf. Rist (1994: 261–2).

[12] Augustine's biblical exegesis here follows Origen's principles, for which, and the development of early Christian allegorizing in general, see de Lubac (1950, 1959–64: vol. i), Daniélou (1950), Grant (1957), Pépin (1958), Hanson (1959), Barr (1966), Ackroyd and Evans (1970: 412–563); cf. Chadwick (1966: 157), and Herzog (1966: 1–8), a brilliant short discussion, emphasizing Pauline influence. Simonetti (1994) provides a helpful historical introduction to biblical interpretation in the Fathers. Wolfson (1970: 24–72) discusses the background of Christian allegorical interpretation in Midrash and Philo of Alexandria; Dawson (1992) the Alexandrian background. For Augustine's exegesis as a preacher see Pontet (1944); for his allegorizing in general see Mayer (1986*b*). Ries (1961–4) shows how Augustine's biblical exegesis, especially of Genesis, develops against the background of his critique of Manichaeism (see n. 10 above). On the anti-Manichaean *Vtil. Cred.* see Hoffmann (1991), Stock (1996: 162–73). On the hermeneutics of Tyconius and Augustine's *Doctr. Chr.* see Pollmann (1996). Young (1997) is a vigorous critique of received opinion on early biblical exegesis.

1: 3–5). The reason which Augustine gives for this is that the fallen angels (= darkness) cannot be described as good. But when natural darkness, as opposed to moral darkness, is referred to, as in Genesis 1: 18, the phrase 'God saw that it was good' recurs. Moreover, the phrase does not entail any acquisition of knowledge or understanding by God: 'he does not discover, but teaches, that it is good' (11. 21). In fact, God's knowledge is atemporal: he knows everything that he knows simultaneously and always. His knowledge of things in time is timeless (11. 21; cf. 5. 9).

Why does God create? Augustine deliberately echoes Plato's reason (*Timaeus* 29e): 'that good things might be made by a good God' (11. 21). He maintains this position against the Manichees (the 'heretics' of 11. 22), stressing the view, derived from the Stoics, that the universe, including its harmful components, is a beautiful and ordered whole, which he describes as a kind of state ('res publica'). Harm and its absence have nothing to do with natural good, or even with moral or physical benefit: there are poisons with medicinal powers. Manichaean theories are based on a misunderstanding of the true nature of divine substance, which cannot be harmed by, and does not have to engage in a cosmic struggle with, the forces of evil. The Manichees also misunderstand the nature of the soul, which is not a fragment of the divine substance (11. 22).

But it is not just Manichees who have a negative view of the universe. In 11. 23 Augustine discusses Origen's theory that souls are embodied as a punishment for a pre-natal sin, and hence that the universe is a place of correction.[13] What Augustine objects to in this theory is the way in which it seems to contradict the unequivocal scriptural insistence on the goodness of the created universe. This goodness is not vitiated by the presence of sinful souls. He also finds fault with the attempt by Origen to relate kinds of body and kinds of sin (the wrong kind of hierarchy): why are demons given bodies of air and humans bodies of earth, when the former are evidently more

---

[13] Cf. Origen, *De Principiis* 1. 3. 8, 1. 4. 1, 1. 5. 5, 1. 6. 3. See Theiler (1970: 544–6). Augustine's polemical work *C. Prisc.* dates from 415: *City* 11 was not written before 417 (see Ch. 2 above). The extent of Augustine's direct knowledge of Origen is difficult to assess: see below, Ch. 11. 3c. On Rufinus' Latin translation, and distortion, of *De Principiis*, and Jerome's literal version, see Bardy (1923); on the consequences for the reception of Origen's doctrines in the Latin West see Kelly (1975: 227–58); E. A. Clark (1992: 159–244).

wicked than the latter? How can it be that there is only one sinner whose sin entails embodiment in the sun? Augustine attempts to reduce Origen's views to absurdity.

In chapters 24–8 Augustine identifies a series of Trinitarian analogies in created things, and especially in humans. The act of creation itself has Trinitarian aspects: the Father creates, the Word (the words of the creation account) is that through which the Father creates, the goodness of creation is the Spirit (11. 24). Philosophy has a tripartite division into physics, logic, and ethics,[14] and to these divisions corresponds the subject-matter of philosophy. The following tabulation displays Augustine's argument:

physics	logic	ethics
('pars physica')	('p. logica')	('p. ethica')
natural philosophy	rational p.	moral p.
('disciplina naturalis')	('d. rationalis')	('d. moralis')

Augustine next relates this division to the three things looked for in any artist:

natural ability	training	practice
('natura')	('doctrina')	('usus')

These divisions are then further related by Augustine, not terribly satisfactorily (perhaps he merely means to accumulate triads), to the criteria by which natural ability, training, and practice are judged in artistic contexts:

talent	knowledge	enjoyment
('ingenium')	('scientia')	('fructus')

Triadic structures are also identified in human thought processes: I exist, I know that I exist, I love my existence and my knowledge of it (11. 26). This is incontrovertible knowledge, about which I can be certain. Augustine is rehearsing his arguments against scepticism, drawing the following conclusions in 11. 26:

[14] See Augustine's use of the tripartite scheme in *City* 8. 4 ff. Cf. above, Ch. 7 n. 15.

If I am mistaken, I exist;

I know that I know;

I am not mistaken about the fact that I love, even if I love an illusion.[15]

The will to exist ('se esse velle') is a natural instinct in all animals, as is the will to 'know' or to perceive, or, in the case of plants, to experience something analogous to perception. This will is the 'love' that completes the triad (existing–knowing–loving), 11. 27. The importance of love in a human moral context is stressed in chapter 28. The good person is not merely the one who knows what the good is, but who also loves it. This love is a kind of weight of the soul: 'for a body is carried by its weight, just as a soul is by love, in the direction in which it is carried'.[16] By means of the concepts of love and weight Augustine links the tendencies of rational beings with those of animal, organic, and inorganic creation. Divine realities are imaged in human lives and the natural world; the triune God, 'who is supremely existent, supremely wise, supremely good', leaves triadic traces in creation.

Chapters 30 and 31 deal with the numerological symbolism of six (the days of creation) and seven (the day of rest).[17] The numerological perfection of six is based on the observation that it is the sum of its factors or aliquot parts: $1 \left(\frac{1}{6}\right) + 2 \left(\frac{1}{3}\right) + 3 \left(\frac{1}{2}\right)$. The perfection of seven is that it is the sum of the first odd integer (3) and the first even integer (4). Augustine gives examples of the use of seven in biblical texts to indicate completeness or universality.

[15] For this line of argument in Augustine see O'Daly (1987: 162–71, here 171 nn. 23–5 bibliog. on Augustine and Descartes), G. Matthews (1972). Matthews's later discussion (1992: 11–38) develops his analysis of Augustine's argument and relates it to Descartes' Cogito: cf. Horn (1997: 109–29), Menn (1998).

[16] On love as weight cf. *De Musica* 6. 11. 29; *Conf.* 13. 9. 10 and O'Donnell ad loc. The metaphor is derived from the principle of ancient physics that the weight of bodies determines their appropriate place in the universe: Bochet (1983: 105–7). O'Brien (1985) links the idea to Iamblichus (*apud* Simplicius, *In Cat.* 128. 32–5). See also Rist (1994: 174–5). On this and other triadic schemes in *City* see Du Roy (1966: 447–50). The 'will to exist' or self-love which Augustine identifies in animals in 11. 27 is an adaptation of the stoic concept of 'oikeiosis': cf. Ch. 10 n. 6.

[17] For a useful collection of texts where Augustine engages in numerological speculation see Horn (1994). Pontet (1944: 278–303) assembles instances of number symbolism, chiefly from Augustine's preaching. D. J. O'Meara (1989) describes the numerology of the neo-Pythagorean revival of late antiquity. O'Daly (1987: 88, 179–83, 191) discusses some uses of number analysis in Augustine. But much work on this topic still has to be done: we need a major study of Augustine on numbers.

Chapter 32 returns to the polyvalency of scriptural texts. The opening verses of Genesis induce a number of different interpretations. Apart from a reference to the creation of the angels, they allude to the Trinity. Augustine stresses that different interpretations need not be inconsistent with the rule of faith. In chapter 33 the theme of the two 'communities' of angels is developed, with a cluster of scriptural references to them. Augustine stresses that his interpretation of Genesis in relation to angels may not be correct, and may not represent the writer's intention ('voluntas'), but, as it does not lead to an unorthodox view, it is a legitimate interpretation. Chapter 34 gives a number of other interpretations of these verses, apparently Origen's. One interpretation makes the firmament separate good from bad angels. Augustine does not reject this view here, but he argues against its tenability, in that it depends on too rigid an application of the principle of the relative weight and position of elements.[18] Phlegm in the human head is an indication that the principle is not absolute.

Here Book 11 ends, somewhat abruptly. In its concluding lines Augustine points out that the two communities of angels are a kind of prologue ('quaedam exordia') to the two human cities (11. 34). This has been a rich and apparently diffuse book. It is above all important for the spectrum of themes which it introduces and develops. They establish the framework for what is to follow. Foremost among the themes is hierarchy, and the ways in which it is not mechanistically understood. But the use of polar opposites is also important. The contrasts visible–invisible, truth–belief, eternity–time, creator–creation, unchangeable–mutable, good–evil underpin the book, and are an indication of what is to come. So are the distinctions between language and meta-language, and the hermeneutical principles that justify polyvalency. It is not an easy book. Changes of theme are abrupt. One needs to remind oneself of the underlying links. And in his account of creation Augustine offers only a partial interpretation of the opening verses of Genesis, adapted to the requirements of the book, just like the account of *Confessions* 11–13. The reader who wants to know more must turn to the *De Genesi ad Litteram*, on which Augustine was working from about 401.[19]

---

[18] Cf. Ch. 7 n. 32.   [19] Cf. nn. 2, 6 above.

Although, at the end of Book 11, Augustine suggests that he will
go on to discuss human creation, the following Book 12 continues
to talk about angels (12. 1–9, 25–7). But the theme of humanity
and its history supervenes (12. 10–28). Once again, the interlock-
ing of themes is apparent. There is both continuity and development in the sub-themes of the will (12. 3–9), hierarchy (12. 4–5),
divine knowledge (12. 19, 23), and interpretation of Genesis (12.
15–18).

What distinguishes good from bad angels is a difference in their
wills. The good angels focus on the good, cling to God, whereas the
bad angels are deflected from God by pride and self-absorption. The
two groups thus exemplify the modes of happiness and unhappiness
of created rational beings (12. 1). The possibility of unhappiness is
exclusive to rational beings, and unhappiness is a defect which
highlights the status of the being thus affected, just as the possibility of experiencing pain distinguishes a sentient from a non-sentient
being. Nor do these defects ('vitia'), when present, harm the nature
of the being in whom they are present. Rather, they point towards
the goodness of that nature (12. 1; cf. 19. 13). These principles are
developed in the following chapters. God is the supreme being, and
the hierarchy of his creation exhibits different degrees ('gradus') of
being. But there is no being that is contrary to his being, for the
contrary of being is non-being. Bad angels cannot have natures
contrary to divine nature (or to other angelic natures, for that
matter), 12. 2. But a fault ('vitium') could be said to be contrary
to God as evil is to good, just as it is contrary to a good nature that
is vitiated by its presence. The presence of a fault, however, entails a
good that is vitiated. In rational created beings the presence of
faults is harmful and is justly punished, but it does not undermine
the natural goodness of the beings concerned, although it corrupts
it (12. 3). The goodness and beauty of creation extend to the whole
universe. Only an objective view of the total cosmic order, and not a
view that is based on notions of what is convenient or inconvenient
for humans, reveals its beauty. In that objective view, fire and
locusts, despite their harmful aspects, contribute to the excellence
of the whole (12. 4), and things have their place and inherent form
and harmony ('modus', 'species', 'pax'), 12. 5.[20]

[20] Cf. *Gen. ad Litt.* 4. 3. 7, with 'quies' for 'pax'; the triad 'modus', 'species', ordo'
in *City* 5. 11, 11. 28, *Nat. Bon.* 3 and *passim*; with 'pulchritudo' instead of 'ordo',

If the fault of a rational being is the consequence of an evil will, what is the cause of that evil will?[21] It cannot be the being's nature, for that, as has been established, is good, and good cannot be the efficient cause of evil. An evil will comes to existence in a being who is good yet subject to change. Augustine is inclined to argue that there is no efficient cause of an evil will, but that evil wills have to do with the fact that the beings in whom they are found are created from nothing (12. 6). The cause is deficient rather than efficient ('non . . . efficiens sed deficiens'), as Augustine rather sophistically puts it (12. 7).[22] Discerning the cause of the will is analogous to perceiving darkness or silence. Both the latter are discerned negatively, because of the absence of something. It is a case of 'knowing by not knowing' (12. 7). Moreover, an evil will is bad, even when its object is not. Gold, beautiful bodies, and glory are not bad things, but greed, lust, and boasting are. Power is not bad, but pride is, for it perversely loves its own power (12. 8).

Can one speak of an efficient cause of a good will? Augustine argues that the good will is caused by God, just as the beings who possess it are. The good will is in some sense directed by divine grace. A good will is by its nature informed with the love of God. It was by divine grace that the good angels did not fall (12. 9). There is thus no symmetry of good and evil wills. Nor is there any suggestion that the will is neutral, a faculty to be directed to good or evil ends. Wills are always already determined by the ends to which they are directed (O'Daly 1989a).

Augustine now turns specifically to humans. Some of the topics which he introduces raise issues already treated in relation to the universe itself and the angels. The question of the human race's eternity is one. Augustine refers to Apuleius' assertion (*De Deo Socr.* 4) that humans exist for ever as a species. The tradition of inventions and discoveries reflects periodic near-destruction of the

---

C. Faust. 21. 6. *Conf.* 1. 7. 12 has a similar formulation: O'Donnell ad loc. discusses the permutations of the triad, giving further examples. There is a Trinitarian dimension to Augustine's use of this and the related triad ('mensura', 'numerus', 'pondus') from Wisd. 11: 21 ('thou hast arranged all things by measure and number and weight'): see O'Donnell on *Conf.* 5. 4. 7, Du Roy (1966: 421–4), TeSelle (1970: 118–9).

[21] Studies of Augustine's concept of the will are legion: see esp. Dihle (1982: 123–32, 231–8), Rist (1969; 1994: 129–35, 148–202), O'Daly (1989a), M. T. Clark (1958), Kirwan (1989: 82–128), Wetzel (1992).

[22] On Augustine's use of the concept of 'deficient cause' or 'declinatio' see Rist (1994: 106–7), Babcock (1988).

human race, but not its entire destruction (12. 10). Against this, Augustine sets the biblical chronology that makes it less than 6,000 years since the creation of humans, and he makes it clear that he uses this biblical chronology to accept or reject secular chronologies (in this instance, those of the letter to Olympias, cf. 8. 5, 27). He believes that the fulfilment of biblical prophecies authenticates the Bible's historical information (12. 11). Arguments against the apparent lateness of the creation of human beings plough a familiar furrow. Irrespective of the length of human history, it is incommensurate with divine eternity. The beginning of temporal things is the beginning of time: the 'why not sooner?' question is as irrelevant as it is when the beginnings of the universe are being discussed (12. 13).[23]

In 12. 12 Augustine rehearses further theories of the universe's and humanity's history. In addition to the version alluded to in 12. 10, he identifies two others. One is the theory of countless worlds; the other is that of successive world-cycles.[24] In both these cases, Augustine argues, it has to be accepted that the human race is repeatedly generated out of the universe's materials. The discussion of periodic cycles is continued in 12. 14. Augustine's chief argument against it is that it undermines the concept of human happiness, which cannot, under this disposition, be permanent, as an endless series of reincarnations is assumed (cf. 11. 4). The same argument is developed in 12. 21, where Augustine points out that Porphyry dissented from the view that reincarnations might be endless. There is no Scriptural support for eternal recurrence, as Origen and others have supposed. Against this notion Augustine sets the historical uniqueness of Christ's redeeming death. In this context the text of Psalm 12: 8 ('the ungodly will walk in a circle')[25] is cleverly cited (12. 14). Augustine presents the theory of cycles as, by implication, a response to the perceived difficulty of positing a change in the divine will that led to a beginning of the universe. In 12. 15 he recalls earlier arguments briefly. There is no need to suppose that an eternally existing God creates anything other than by an eternal and unchangeable plan. It is the same with the question of divine sovereignty

---

[23] For modern discussions of Augustine's views on beginnings see n. 2 above.

[24] See further below, Ch. 11. 3c; cf. Theiler (1970: 546–53), Sorabji (1983: 182–90). On cyclical theories of history and Augustine's reaction to them see Mommsen (1959: 265–98).

[25] Augustine's version, which is that of the Latin Psalter (where is it Ps. 11: 9), is based on the Septuagint translation (cf. nn. 8–9 above).

(12. 16). There is no need to suppose a creation co-eternal with God, for the priority of eternity over temporality is, from the divine perspective, itself eternal. Angels are certainly not co-eternal with God, for they have a beginning in time, and they undergo change. It is true to say, in a trivial sense, that any immortal created being exists for all the time that it exists, and that, as angels are the first created beings, they exist for all the time that there is: thus God is sovereign throughout all time. But Augustine's other argument—the priority of eternity over time—is clearly the stronger one, even if it occupies less space in 12. 16.

Another reason reported by Augustine for the occurrence of world-cycles is the assumption that the infinite cannot be known, even by a divine mind (12. 18).[26] A continual recurrence of events and things can, however, be known by an omniscient deity in finite terms. Against this, Augustine argues that divine omniscience must be able to comprehend the infinite, an infinite series of numbers, for example: 'every infinity is, in some inexpressible way, finite to God, because it is not beyond the grasp of his knowledge' (12. 19).

Why did God propagate the human race from one man? Augustine suggests that it was to stress the desired unity of the human race, its harmony ('concordia'), 12. 23. Man's nature, midway between the angelic and animal orders, can lead to the unity of peace or to a violence that is unmatched in the animal world (12. 22–3; cf. 12. 28). Chapter 12. 24 suggests that the story of man's and woman's creation is to be understood in symbolic terms: God's fashioning hand is his power, achieving visible results by invisible means. The creation of the first humans is not subject to the laws of natural physical causation. Yet the myth of creation in Genesis is not pure fiction. Furthermore, that account makes it clear that angels have no part in the creation of humans, unlike the lesser gods of Plato's *Timaeus* (12. 25). They are not even to be imagined, with some Platonists, as makers of human bodies (12. 27). God creates human beings, using efficient immanent causal forms, a 'hidden' power within him (12. 26). These forms are in the mind of God (12. 27).[27] Augustine distinguishes them from the forms given externally to material substances by craftsmen (12. 26).

---

[26] For the arguments of Origen and Augustine see Sorabji (1983: 186–7).

[27] Augustine and the Platonic theory of Forms: O'Daly (1987: 189–99). For the Middle Platonic background of Augustine's version see Dillon (1977: 91–6, 159–60, 254–6; 1993: 93–100); cf. Sharples (1995).

In 12. 28 Augustine pulls the threads of his account of human creation together. Although the goodness of the created human being is stressed, Augustine also insists upon the human potential for evil. In God's foreknowledge, with the creation of Adam, the beginnings of the two cities in their human form are included. It is but a short step from creation to the Fall.

Book 13 focuses principally upon two themes, the Fall and death (13. 1–16), and the resurrected, spiritual body (13. 17–24). Augustine's method is once again to highlight certain themes and concentrate on their significance.

Death is a consequence of Adam's sin. But Augustine introduces the notion of a second kind of death (based on references to 'the second death' in Revelation 2: 11, 20: 6, etc.), that of the soul.[28] This is the irrevocable damnation of a soul, its total abandonment by God (13. 1–2). Death in the usual sense occurred as a change in human nature after Adam's sin, so that, like mental and physical weakness in infants, it became somehow a natural consequence for humans (13. 3), although it cannot be said to be a law of human nature (13. 15). Even after baptism it remains, as a means of strengthening faith. Martyrdom is a pre-eminent instance of the way in which fear of death is overcome. Thus the penalty for sin becomes an instrument of virtue (13. 4). But in itself death remains an evil ('malum'), though one that may be used well by the good (13. 5, 7). The separation of body and soul is always harsh and unnatural, always a penalty (13. 6). We must distinguish between the process of dying and its consequences: for the good, death has good consequences (13. 8; cf. 12. 9 on the 'rest' of the dead 'in the secret repositories and dwelling-places of souls').

Chapters 9–11 explore meanings of the expressions 'in death', 'after death', and 'dying'. Is death a state, or simply an event? The process of dying is real enough, and it is true to say that only a living person, one not yet dead, can be a dying one. But what does the phrase 'in death' mean? For after death, the soul is alive, and it is the state of the soul, not the fact of death that determines whether its condition is good or evil. Perhaps the phrase 'in death' refers to the human condition before death, for dying is an ever-closer prospect from the moment of birth. Paradoxically, one is in life and in death

---

[28] On the theme of the 'second death' see below Ch. 10 on 19. 28 with n. 28.

simultaneously, until death occurs. Augustine finds this puzzling: it is rather like saying that one is awake and asleep at the same time. On investigation, the concept of being in death seems to evaporate: the living person is before death, the dead person past death. The moment of 'dying' is as elusive as the instant which we call 'the present' or 'now'. And yet death is a reality, as much as time is. It is as troublesome in fact as it is to define. Augustine suggests that all we can do is follow common usage and scriptural idioms, imprecise as these are. He finds it significant that the Latin verb 'to die' is not conjugated regularly, but has a perfect-tense form ('mortuus') that is without reference to past time.

In chapter 12 Augustine returns to the theme of the Fall. God's threat of death in Genesis 2: 17 includes every kind of death, whether first or second, or of body or soul. But death is not the only consequence of the Fall. Another is the soul's loss of control over the body, where sexual urges are concerned (13. 13).[29] Since all humans were 'in that one man' when Adam sinned, all are affected by the consequences of his sin (13. 14).[30] Adam's sin is a first death of the soul, an act of the will in which he forsook God (13. 15). As for death in the usual sense (the separation of soul from body), Platonists (probably Porphyry is meant) find it hard to credit that this separation is a punishment: on the contrary, it seems to them to be the precondition of bliss. Augustine stresses that it is the corruptible body, and not body as such, which is a burden to the soul. Plato appears to have assumed that the lesser gods created by the demiurge have astral bodies, from which they will never be separated:[31] so Platonists should not repudiate embodiment as such. Augustine is agnostic (13. 16) on the question of whether stars have souls (O'Daly 1987: 68). Platonist objections to the Christian attitude to the body, especially in its resurrected form, are inconsistent with their own attitudes to embodiment. If, for them, the earth is everlasting, a

[29] For the development of Augustine's views on the body see Miles (1979, 1990), Frederiksen (1988).

[30] For the sense in which all humans are 'in Adam' see Rist (1994: 121–9), with proper caution (ibid. 124 n. 93), following S. Lyonnet (*DB* Suppl. 7. 528–9, 540–1), against assuming that Augustine's Latin text of Romans 5: 12 ('in quo omnes peccaverunt', understood as 'in whom all sinned') determined his doctrine of original sin, rather than simply confirming it: cf. 1 Cor. 15: 22 ('For as in Adam all die . . .'), echoed in *Conf.* 10. 20. 29.

[31] *Tim.* 41a–b is meant: Augustine cites (inaccurately) Cicero's translation, *Tim.* 11. 40.

part of the universe that has itself a soul and will persist for ever, in accordance with the demiurge's plan, why cannot God plan the immortality of human bodies (13. 17)? Augustine argues once again against mechanistic application of the principle of the relative weights of elements (cf. 11. 34). The claim that earthly bodies cannot exist in heaven may be countered by familiar apparent infringements of the principle: objects floating in water or flying, for example. Our own bodily weight is experienced differently by ourselves and others, depending on whether we are fit or ill. It is not inconceivable that our bodies could be cleansed of corruption, made weightless, and yet retain their bodily nature and symmetry (13. 18). Augustine promises fuller discussion of this whole question at the end of the work: he will keep this promise in Book 22.

It is not just the lesser gods of the *Timaeus* who provide Augustine with evidence for Platonist views about embodiment. He also finds evidence in the idea of reincarnation, especially in the view (which he assumes to be Platonist) found in Virgil's *Aeneid* 6. 750–1, that the souls even of the just desire reincarnation after a period of disembodied bliss.[32] He finds a similar view in Plato.[33] Augustine finds the notion of the good souls returning to corruptible human or other bodies unacceptable, and once again expresses his understanding for Porphyry's views that human souls cannot enter animal bodies, and that the souls of the wise escape embodiment for ever. He speculates that this view may have been developed by Porphyry to compete with Christianity, just as Porphyry's denial of bodily immortality may be in opposition to Christianity. Augustine suggests that it is inconsistent for the Platonists to accept the embodiment of gods, and yet to deny the possibility of perpetual embodiment of lesser beings, humans. He reiterates the view that, if there had been no Fall, humans would have enjoyed embodied immortality (13. 19).

Chapter 20 draws a distinction between the resurrected body of the saints and the prelapsarian bodies of Adam and Eve. The difference is between a spiritual and an animal body, for Adam and Eve in paradise had animal bodies, and needed to eat and drink (13. 20; cf. 13. 23). The ability to eat and drink will not be taken away from the spiritual bodies of the saints, but they will not need to do so. The

---

[32] See further below, Ch. 11. 1e.

[33] He gives a grossly simplified résumé of *Phaedrus* 248–9, without naming it explicitly. He uses the same résumé in *Ser.* 240 and 241: cf. O'Daly (1987: 70 n. 197), where it is suggested that his source may be Porphyry.

spiritual nature of their bodies does not lessen their physicality, but means that the spirit sustains and controls the body (13. 22; cf. 13. 20). Augustine stresses the historicity of the Genesis account, but this does not preclude symbolic readings: paradise may represent the life of the blessed, its four streams the four cardinal virtues, its trees the disciplines, and so on. Or paradise may symbolize the Church, the streams the four Gospels, the trees the saints (13. 21).[34] The polysemy of Scripture is once again stressed: the tree of life, of which Adam and Eve ate to guard their pre-Fall immortality (13. 20), is also the wisdom that is Christ (13. 21). The resurrected body will undergo, not a change of substance, but a qualitative transformation: Augustine supports his view with several citations of Pauline texts, especially 1 Corinthians 15 (13. 23).

In Chapter 24 Augustine attacks a doctrine, which probably derives from Origen,[35] that the breath of life breathed into man's face in the creation account at Genesis 2: 7 represents the Spirit's activity in the formation of the living human soul. Augustine wants to guard against an interpretation which makes the human soul a part of the divine substance; he also wants to avoid a non-Trinitarian exegesis of the formation of man (the Spirit is the spirit of the Father and the Son as well). His survey of Greek usage in references to 'spirit' establishes that 'pnoē' is not used when the Holy Spirit is meant (and 'pnoē' is the word used in Genesis 2: 7), and that 'pneuma' does not always refer to the Spirit: there is thus no textual warranty for the doctrine (13. 24). Apart from the repetition of his account of animal and spiritual bodies, this effectively closes the book. But Augustine poses one dilemma at the end. If sexual desire is a result of the Fall, how might children have been produced if the Fall had not happened? This and other questions will be answered in Book 14.

Book 14 discusses a variety of related themes: grace; flesh and spirit; will, love, and the passions; Adam's sin and its punishment; desire, shame, and procreation. It is important as an account of central themes in Augustine's psychology and ethics. The theme of the two cities is stressed in the first and last chapters. In chapter 1 the Pauline

---

[34] Cf. n. 12 above.

[35] See further below, Ch. 11. 3c. Augustine criticizes a similar doctrine, which he assumes to be Manichaean, that part of God's substance has been breathed into man, in *Gen. adv. Man.* 2. 8. 11: but he does not refer there to the activity of the Spirit in connection with the Manichees.

flesh–spirit distinction is invoked to define the two categories of humans, and Augustine (anticipating a theme of Book 19) describes them as pursuing their respective kinds of peace: he stresses that there are 'no more than two types of human society' (14. 1).[36] Later in the book, taking up a theme of 14. 13, Augustine defines the two cities in terms of love: 'So two loves formed the two cities: that is, love of self to the point of contempt for God formed the earthly city, and love of God to the point of contempt for self the heavenly city' (14. 28).[37] With the reference to 'lust for domination' ('dominandi libido') in 14. 28 the political dimension, missing since the opening books, is reintroduced (in part at least because of the historical-political surveys to follow in Books 15–19). But the important distinction between the two cities and any historical societies or nations is also stressed (14. 1).

In 14. 2 Augustine makes the fundamental point that 'flesh' ('caro') in scriptural contexts does not refer exclusively to the body. It can refer to human beings in general, to physical pleasure, but also to faults of the mind, such as jealousy and envy. From a Christian point of view both the Epicureans and the Stoics live by the rule of the flesh. The body in itself is not the cause of sin, although our bodily condition, after the Fall, is a punishment for sin. The devil demonstrates that the body is not a cause of the faults of a wicked life. The principal source of evil is the will to live by the rule of self ('secundum se ipsum vivere'): the devil and humans have this in common (14. 3). Thus the flesh–spirit distinction can be expressed in other terms. For humans, living according to the flesh is living by human standards and values, whereas living according to the spirit is living by the standard of truth, according to God. The 'animal' man of 1 Corinthians 2: 14 is the same as the 'man of flesh' of 1 Corinthians 3: 1 (14. 4). Augustine's stress on the soul's or mind's responsibility for sin distinguishes Christian from Manichaean and Platonist positions. The Manichees would make the body an evil substance. The Platonists would make the fact of embodiment play a role in human vulnerability to the passions: again, Augustine's source is Virgil (*Aen.* 6. 719–21). Yet the same *Aeneid* passage seems also to admit that the

---

[36] The tendency to regard the intermingling of the two cities in the present age ('saeculum') as somehow forming a third, neutral entity should be resisted: see the pertinent remarks of van Oort (1991: 151–3).

[37] Augustine's concept of self-love, in its positive as well as its negative aspects, is perceptively analysed by O'Donovan (1980); cf. Rist (1994: 188–91).

soul can generate these passions in itself, even the purified soul in a disembodied state. Augustine finds this a damning admission on the Platonists' part (14. 5).

The important factor determining the individual's moral status is the direction of the will.[38] The passions can be used well, if the will's direction is right. Augustine defines the four passions[39] in terms of willing. Desire or joy is an act of the will in sympathy with what we wish for; fear or grief is an act of the will disagreeing with what we do not want; fear is when we disagree with something which we do not wish to happen; grief is when we disagree with what happens against our will. The link between willing and loving becomes clearer: if willing is crucial, then the person who lives according to God is a 'lover of the good' (14. 6). In 14. 5 the emotions are, in turn, defined in terms of love. These emotions are bad if the love is bad, good if it is good. The various scriptural terms for 'love' ('caritas', 'amor', 'dilectio', and their verbal equivalents) illustrate this. All can be used in a positive sense, and the second and third can also be used in a pejorative sense. Love is defined by its direction or goal, as is the will (14. 7).

The Stoics, who advocate the extirpation of the passions, argue that the sage experiences corresponding 'stable states' ('eupatheiai', 'constantiae').[40] The sage 'wills' rather than desires, feels 'gladness' rather than joy, and 'caution' rather than fear. The Stoics did not identify a stable state corresponding to distress or pain. Augustine does not find the distinction between passions and stable states acceptable (O'Daly 1987: 50–2), and adduces a series of scriptural and secular texts (the latter from Terence, Cicero, and Virgil) to show that linguistic usage does not distinguish between good and bad when describing emotions, but uses the terms for passions and those for stable states indifferently. His conclusion is: 'The good and bad alike desire, fear, and rejoice, but the former in a good way, the latter in a bad manner, according as their will is right or wrong' (14. 8). Christians may feel appropriate emotions. They may fear eternal punishment, desire eternal life, fear to commit sin, and feel pain over sins committed. They may even feel the emotion for which the Stoics

---

[38] Cf. 12. 6 ff. with n. 21 above.

[39] On the passions in Augustine's thought see O'Daly (1987: 46–54).

[40] On the Stoic 'stable states' see Inwood (1985: 173–5). Inwood's whole discussion (pp. 127–81) of the Stoic doctrine of the passions is illuminating; cf. Nussbaum (1994: 359–401) on extirpation of the passions in Stoicism.

identified no stable state, distress or grief, if it is the distress that leads to repentance of which Paul writes (2 Corinthians 7: 8–11). Christ felt emotions, was grieved, angry, understood desire. Above all, Paul's epistles are an extensive record of his feelings: Augustine documents them copiously (14. 9). These emotions cannot be called diseases or evil passions. Their pervasiveness is, however, a feature of our historical condition, and so a sign of weakness (except in Christ, who assumed them voluntarily, as he did his humanity): yet not to experience them would be a worse condition in our present life. Augustine is unimpressed by the Stoic ideal of freedom from passions ('apatheia'). He quotes Crantor from Cicero (*Tusculan Disputations* 3. 12) in calling it mental inhumanity and bodily insensitivity. Augustine also finds it an unattainable ideal in this life. Moreover, in their heavenly state, the good will feel love and gladness. Some emotions are not peculiar to our earthly condition. The saints in heaven will not suffer fear or pain, but the life lived according to the spirit is not a life without feeling (14. 9). Having given such a positive account of emotions, Augustine feels obliged to add a postscript stressing the wrecking potential of emotions misused. The emotions of the denizens of the city of God may be approved, but those of the city of the wicked, even when they pose as moderate, reveal pride, arrogance, and, it may be, inhumanity (14. 9).

In paradise Adam and Eve felt no fear, distress, or pain, but they experienced gladness, resulting from their love for each other and for God. In Eden, as in heaven, love and joy are the feelings of the blessed. Augustine stresses the similarity of the prelapsarian and heavenly conditions, in which, moreover, the body is not subject to pain or decay (14. 10).

God, who foreknows everything, knows that Adam will sin. But the cause of sin is the human will.[41] The capacity for sin exists in humans because they are created from nothing.[42] In the case of Adam and Eve, the devil acts as a deceptive persuader upon Eve, but Eve does not deceive Adam: rather, he complies with her because of their close partnership. She was, after all, his only companion. Perhaps he thought his offence was pardonable; he did not have experience of divine strictness (14. 11). What was so serious about Adam's fault

[41] See further on 12. 6 ff. above, with n. 21.
[42] For this 'ontological weakness' see Bonner (1986: 369), O'Daly (1989a: 87), Rist (1994: 106 with n. 46).

was that it was one of disobedience (14. 12). Pride was at the root of
it, a falling away from the immutable good, self-satisfaction.[43] The
evil will precedes the evil act. This act involves no ontological loss,
but it is a kind of approximation to nothingness. Paradoxically, the
proud attempt at self-exaltation degrades man, whereas humility
exalts him. Thus humility is a characteristic of the city of God,
and pride of the other city: or, as Augustine also puts it, in the one
city love of God has first place, in the other, love of self. The original
sin is internal, in the mind and the will, a turning-away from the true
light (14. 13). The pride it involves is seen in Adam's subsequent
attempt to blame Eve, and Eve's attempt to blame the serpent: their
attempt to excuse themselves compounds their fault (14. 14). In
commanding obedience, God wished to demonstrate his rule, and
the principle that 'free servitude' ('libera servitus') was in man's best
interest.[44] The punishment for disobedience is disobedience itself.
The human body is no longer obedient to the mind: desire, pain,
ageing, and death all demonstrate this. They are not purely physical
phenomena, but involve the soul's power of sentience: Augustine, as
usual, wants to avoid what he takes to be the Platonist implication
that it is the body which is the cause of human ills (14. 15).

The term 'libido' (14. 15) can be given to several passions, like
anger, greed, obstinacy, and vanity (Bonner 1962, 1994). But when
not qualified in any way, it usually refers to sexual desire. Augustine
argues that sexual desire is in a category apart from all other kinds of
desire. What distinguishes it is its relation to the will. It seems to
function independently of willing. Sexual arousal can both occur, and
fail to occur, without the will's bidding (14. 16). It is the prime
instance of a disobedient element in the human make-up. Augustine
attributes the modesty or shame which the genital organs induce to
our sense that arousal is beyond our control (14. 17). The same is
true of the wish for privacy in sexual intercourse, even of the respectable married kind. Augustine feels that the Cynics cannot have been
serious in their advocacy of lawful sexual intercourse in public, and he

[43] On the theme of pride in Augustine see Green (1949), O'Connell (1968: 173–
83), Macqueen (1973, 1977), Rist (1994: 96–7, 102–4, 188–91). Pride in the context
of *City*: Markus (1990b).

[44] The paradox that true freedom is a form of obedient slavery to the will of God is
well brought out by Augustine in *Ench.* 30. Cf. its development in Luther, in his *De
Servo Arbitrio* of 1525, on the 'enslaved will', on which see Kenny (1979: 72–6).
Burnaby (1938: 219–52) is an unsurpassed account of freedom, grace, merit, and
reward in Augustine. See further n. 21 above.

feels his view vindicated by the fact that later Cynics abandoned such attitudes (14. 20).[45] All this indicates to him that there is an element of punishment in the way we function sexually (14. 18). It is quite different with the emotions. If anger leads to violence, this is a consequence of the will's assent to the emotion. The hand raised in anger or the irate word are under the will's command. But in the case of sexual arousal, the desire commands the bodily organs directly (14. 19).[46]

Augustine therefore argues that, had the Fall not occurred, sexual desire would not have been the motor of human self-propagation. He distances himself from the Manichees, who condemn the production of children on the grounds that it invariably involves desire. Nor should the divine command to increase and multiply be understood in a merely symbolic way (14. 21). Augustine believes that the first humans were created as sexual beings, and were anatomically the same as we now are (14. 22). Otherwise, Christians must run the risk of believing that sin is necessary in order to produce the humans who will complete the number of the saints. He envisages a prelapsarian sexuality where desire is obedient to the will. There would be no shame, no guilt, no obscenity (14. 23). Augustine suggests that we would find this easier to imagine, if we consider the phenomenon of people capable of controlling bodily functions in ways that are out of the ordinary: some people can wiggle their ears, or sweat or weep at will. A priest called Restitutus, from Calama, was able to simulate death. His body would be impervious to pain in that condition, although he would remain conscious of human voices. If the body, in our present condition, is capable of such things, why cannot we imagine a state in which its sexual drives are similarly subject to the will (14. 24)? In fact, to live as one wishes is a precondition of happiness. That is not a possibility in our present life. Even the just are subject to compulsion of various kinds. Patience and acceptance of one's lot are not the same as happiness. To wish for

---

[45] Augustine is thinking of the 'soft' Cynicism that developed in the later 4th and 3rd centuries BC, after Diogenes and Crates: see Moles (1996).

[46] Cf. Seneca, *Letter* 11, on involuntary bodily functions. For discussions of Augustine's views on sexual desire see O'Daly (1987: 52–3); Kirwan (1989: 192–6); Rist (1994: 321–7), who contrasts Augustine's views with those of his Pelagian opponent Julian of Eclanum. On the manner in which desire responds to music without the intervention of assent or will see *C. Iul.* 5. 5. 23; cf. Sorabji (1993: 57 with n. 45). On the related question of moral responsibility in dreams see G. Matthews (1992: 90–106).

happiness is to wish it to be eternal (14. 25). In paradise Adam and
Eve lived as they wished as long as they obeyed God's command.
The temperate climate of paradise harmonized with their joy, a
mean between grimness and frivolity, and their relationship
exhibited the same harmony. This is a Golden Age scenario, in
which effortless bliss prevails. Augustine imagines sexual relations
that match this atmosphere, without passion, tranquil, involving no
breach of the woman's maidenhead, and leading to an effortless
giving birth (14. 26). That this was not to happen does not impugn
God's handiwork: the Fall allows God to exhibit both his punishing
power and his grace towards those saved from the 'condemned
mass' ('massa damnata'). The saved are a 'fixed number' of the
predestined (14. 26).[47] God makes good use of evil. Even in
paradise divine grace was necessary to living the good life. Yet it
was in man's power to overcome the devil, and God did not wish to
deprive man of that power, even if it entailed the possibility of
failure. Adam's and Eve's fall demonstrates the pitfalls of self-
assertion, but also the power of divine grace (14. 27).

The themes of obedience and self-assertion point to the polariza-
tion of the two cities, with their defining kinds of love (14. 28). The
polarity is expressed in political terms, in anticipation of the
political themes of later books. The city of God is a community
where consensus and recognition of authority prevail. The earthly
city (here more or less closely identified with real societies) is
dominated by lust for domination and the acquisition of empire;
it is confident in its own strength and its own values: not surprisingly, in this kind of society false religions flourish.[40] In the city of
God, on the other hand, worship of the one true God anticipates
the fellowship of the saints, humans, and angels, 'that God may be
all in all' (1 Corinthians 15: 28).

---

[47] For Augustine's doctrine of predestination see Mozley (1855), TeSelle (1970: 176–82, 319–38), Rist (1969), Bonner (1963: 358–93). The 'fixed number' of the predestined to which 14. 26 refers fills the place and restores the number of the fallen angels: see 22. 1, where Augustine adds that it is not a strict numerical restoration, but that more may be saved than are required to fill the vacancies (cf. *Ench.* 29). See Madec (1986: 307). Elsewhere Augustine emphasizes that the course of human history ('saeculum') is prolonged to the point where the appropriate number of predestined saints is reached (*Bon. Vid.* 23. 28).

[48] See Lepelley (1992: 954–7) on Augustine's dismissive attitude to the values of the Roman city.

9

The History of the Two Cities:
Books 15–18

> But as it is necessary in this world that the citizens of the
> kingdom of heaven should be harassed by temptations among
> those who err and are irreverent, so that they may be exercised
> and tried as gold in the furnace, we ought not before the
> appointed time to desire to live with the saints and righteous
> alone, so that we may deserve to receive this blessedness in its
> own due time.
>
> (Augustine, *Letter* 189. 5[1])

Books 15–18 deal with the course ('excursus', 'procursus') of the two
cities in human history. Augustine's parameters are defined by the
sequence of events in biblical narrative from Genesis 4 onwards. His
selective exegesis continues, in effect, what has begun in *City* 11. His
book shadows the books of the Bible.[2] Augustine makes it clear from
the outset that he is talking about kinds of human individual, and
that the members of the city of God are those who live 'according to
God's plan' ('secundum deum'), whereas the members of the other
city live 'according to human criteria' ('secundum hominem').
Groups are formed of individuals as a word is formed of single letters
(4. 3; cf. 1. 15): the individual Adam contains the potential for the
two cities in himself (12. 28). These groups may be called cities
allegorically ('mystice').[3] Their identity is most clearly defined in
eschatological terms: 'two societies of human beings, of which one
is predestined to reign with God for ever, and the other to suffer
eternal punishment with the devil'. But they have none the less a

---

[1] Tr. J. H. Baxter (LCL), adapted.

[2] This shadowing continues until the end of *City* 18, with the references there to the
last prophets and the books of the Maccabees. Augustine does not, in *City*, apply to the
New Testament the systematic, if selective, scrutiny of the Old Testament. But *City* 20–
2 treats, among other topics, themes of the last book of the New Testament, Revelation. On the topics and structure of Books 15–18 see Bardy, BA 36. 9–24.

[3] i.e. in accordance with the allegorical interpretation of Scripture: see van Oort
(1997: 163). Cf. Lamirande (1992–4: 961–2).

history running throughout the period ('saeculum') of the entire human race after the fall of Adam (15. 1). Cain, the fratricide, is the first founder of an earthly city (15. 1, 5; cf. Genesis 4: 17): his murdered brother Abel belongs to the city of God, but founds no earthly city. Augustine exploits the exegetical possibilities of their relationship. The fact that Cain is the elder brother symbolizes the animal–spiritual sequence to which 1 Corinthians 15: 46 alludes: Cain represents everyone tainted by original sin ('evil and carnal'), Abel the soul reborn in Christ ('good and spiritual'). The former is 'born a citizen of this world' ('saeculum'), the latter is 'an alien in this world . . . predestined by grace, chosen by grace, by grace an alien below, by grace a citizen above'. Using the potter-clay-vessel imagery of Romans 9: 21–3, Augustine stresses that both Cain and Abel— hence all humans—derive from the same clay condemned ('massa . . . damnata')[4] by God at Adam's fall: but from the same clay were made 'one vessel for honour, another for dishonour'. Thus Cain and Abel represent both the same individual who, by grace, aspires to become 'spiritual', and different individuals, evil and good, members of two cities (15. 1). Abel symbolizes, and in a sense is, the temporal beginning of the Church (*En. Ps.* 118. 29. 9, 128. 2; Congar 1986).

In 15. 2–3 Augustine relates the special status of the Jewish people (the holy city, Jerusalem) to the polarity of the two cities. Jerusalem is a part of the earthly city: but it has symbolic significance as a prophetic image of the city of God (Cranz 1950). Augustine uses Paul's exegesis of the scriptural account of the sons of Abraham in Galatians 4: 21–5: 1 to elaborate this. There it is said that Abraham's two women, the slave Hagar and the free-born Sarah, represent two covenants. Hagar's son Ishmael is born in the course of nature ('secundum carnem'), Sarah's son Isaac is born as a result of a promise. Christians, like Isaac, are children of the promise, persecuted by, but ultimately superseding, the children of nature. Like Cain and Abel, Ishmael and Isaac represent the nature–grace distinction. Returning to the imagery of Romans 9, Augustine links the citizens of the earthly and heavenly cities to the vessels of wrath and of mercy of Romans 9: 22–3 (15. 2). Sarah's barrenness highlights the divine gift of grace—a gratuitous intervention in nature's course—that Isaac represents, just as it points towards the barrenness of corrupted, unredeemed nature. In differing but complementary ways

---

[4] On the concept of the 'massa damnata' in Augustine's doctrine of sin and grace see Bonner (1963: 326–7), Rottmanner (1908: 14–18).

Abel and Isaac symbolize the city of God, and Cain and Ishmael its contrary. But, like Cain and Abel, Ishmael and Isaac also represent the individual's fallen and restored nature (15. 3).

Augustine now turns to characterize the earthly city further. It has a fixed temporal span: when condemned to the final punishment it will be a city no longer. It is typically a city in conflict, divided by wars, litigation, the urge to dominate. Yet it seeks its own kind of peace, the end to which wars are often the means; and when the just cause triumphs, the victory and ensuing peace are desirable, and may be considered gifts of God (15. 4).[5] The earthly city's violent nature is illustrated by the violence with which it is established. Cain and Romulus are both fratricides, and the former may be said to be the archetype of which the latter is the image.[6] But both Romulus and Remus were citizens of the earthly city, struggling for power and glory: Remus is no Abel. The two sets of brothers and their differing feuds show how many and various are the conflicts to which humans are exposed: between the good and the bad, between bad and bad, and (adds Augustine, though the examples do not illustrate it) between the good but not yet perfect (15. 5). Such conflicts are for Augustine a consequence of original sin: hence the numerous scriptural injunctions to co-operative behaviour, restraint, forgiveness. But these moral palliatives are ineffective if divine grace does not supervene, mysteriously but (we must suppose) justly, imposing, but also making acceptable to its recipients, the tranquil rule of God (15. 6).

In chapter 7 Augustine returns to the story of Cain in Genesis 4. He offers an exegesis of God's admonition to Cain in Genesis 4: 6–7, one in accordance with what he calls the 'rule of faith'.[7] God's

---

[5] The theme of peace as end anticipates the teleological themes of Book 19. It also reflects a commonplace of just-war theory: see Cicero, *De Officiis* 1. 35. For Augustine's views on war see *City* 1. 21 with Ch. 6 nn. 6 and 15.

[6] Augustine adopts the motif of Rome's foundation based on fratricide: it was a motif that Roman poets used in moralizing contexts, e.g. Horace, *Epodes* 7. 17–20; Lucan 1. 95 (cited by Augustine in 15. 5), and which was taken over by Christian apologists (Min. Fel. *Octav.* 25. 2, with Clarke ad loc.; Tert. *Ad Nat.* 2. 9. 19). For a wide-ranging discussion of the Romulus and Remus myth see Wiseman (1995).

[7] On the 'rule of faith' ('fidei regula') as applied to the interpretation of Scripture, namely the establishment of a meaning of a scriptural text consistent with the principles of Christian doctrine, see Augustine's illustrative discussion in *Doctr. Chr.* 3. 1. 1–3. 6; cf. *Ser.* 186. 2. 2. See Kelly (1972: 76–88) on the early development of the idea, and the formulation of the rule of faith in Christian creeds; Mayer (1974: 298–301) discusses the use of the rule in Augustine, who believes that it does not preclude diversity of doctrinal and exegetical interpretations (cf. e.g. *C. Faust.* 11. 6).

admonition comes in the biblical narrative after God has disregarded Cain's offering, but accepted Abel's, for reasons not given. It comes before the killing of Abel. There are at least two exegetical questions here. Does the admonition offer any explanation of God's rejection of Cain's offering? What is the significance of Cain's killing of Abel, even after the admonition? Augustine addresses these questions. His answer is based on an admission that the text is difficult. In fact, a large part of the difficulties derives from the fact that the Septuagint version, on which the Latin translation available to Augustine is based, diverges appreciably from the Hebrew.[8] This can be best illustrated by citing the two versions, beginning with a translation of the Hebrew:

The Lord said to Cain, 'Why are you angry, and why has your countenance fallen? If you do well, will you not be accepted? And if you do not do well, sin is crouching at the door; its desire is for you, but you must master it.'   (RSV)

Augustine's Latin version yields the following sense:

And the Lord said to Cain, 'Why have you become sullen? Why has your face fallen? If your sacrifice is rightly offered, but not rightly divided, have you not sinned? Calm yourself; for there is to be a return of it to you (*ad te enim conversio eius*), and you will have the mastery over it.'   (tr. Bettenson)

Augustine's text allows him to link the reference to 'sacrifice' in this version to Cain's offering, made but not accepted by God. What does 'not rightly divided' mean? Its ostensible meaning is that the sacrifice is not rightly apportioned between God and humans, or among humans, but Augustine extends its meaning to connote incorrect distinction or discrimination, whether in the place or time, or in the material, of sacrifice, or in its recipient. He can find nothing in the Genesis text to indicate in which way Cain's offering was incorrect. So he uses an explanation of Cain's murder of Abel to cast light on the mystery. This explanation derives from 1 John 3: 12, where it is said that Cain murdered because 'his deeds were evil'. Augustine links the reference to evil deeds to Cain's offering, speculating that his intention there was evil, deriving from self-will, despite the apparent gift made to God. That gift is tantamount to a bribe to God. When Cain (by whatever means) found out that his gift was unacceptable to God, he did not mend his ways, but turned sullen (through envy, Augustine

---

[8] For similar instances of Latin scriptural texts influenced by the Septuagint version see *City* 11. 9, 12. 14 with Ch. 8 nn. 8–9 and 25.

assumes). God's admonition reveals the reasons for Cain's grimness, which might otherwise have been mistaken for repentance. God's exhortation to Cain to 'calm down' is an injunction to control desires and sinful impulses, for they will 'return', i.e. they are due to his own fault, and not to be blamed on anyone else, and can only be mastered if reason prevails. But Augustine suggests that the words may also refer to 'return' ('conversio') in another way, as the need to make sin subject to oneself by repentance, in which case the text prescribes rather than predicts ('there is to be' in the above translation is an attempt to convey the ambivalence). At all events, the mastery of sin is also symbolically alluded to in a neighbouring Genesis text (3: 16), where there is talk of Adam (= reason) having mastery over Eve (= flesh).[9] Cain's implicit rejection of divine admonition is a terrible warning to those who do not admit their sins. Their faults increase, and in Cain's case lead to murder (15. 7).

This detailed reading of a scriptural text shows that its meaning is applicable to everyone. But the text is also historical, and Augustine recognizes that he has an obligation to defend its historicity. What is the significance of the reference to Cain's founding a city (Genesis 4: 17), when the male population of the earth was apparently no more than three? The answer involves a hermeneutical principle.[10] The scriptural author's aim is to highlight the course of sacred history, from Adam and the generations following him to Abraham and to the people of God, to show the distinctiveness of the Jewish nation, and its prophetic role in relation to Christ and the city of God. References to the earthly city are limited to the extent that they serve this prime purpose, and throw the city of God into relief by contrast. This means narrative selectivity. We may infer that numbers of people and cities existed, to which Scripture makes no reference. Most likely Cain's city was well populated. In his long life the population could grow. Yet in the biblical narrative, until the Flood, the two groups or cities are distinguished in the descendants of Cain and Seth (15. 8).

---

[9] On the variety of symbolic senses given by Augustine to sexual differentiation see Børresen (1981, 1990), J. J. O'Meara (1980: 37–87), Rist (1994: 112–21).

[10] The principle of the part representing the whole ('pars pro toto'), or (to use the rhetorical term) synecdoche, underlies Augustine's approach, though in a less precise way than in Tyconius' fifth hermeneutical rule, *Liber Regularum* pp. 55–66, on which cf. Augustine, *Doctr. Chr.* 3. 35. 50–1: for Augustine's use of Tyconius see Pollmann (1996), Chadwick (1989); cf. above, Ch. 4. 1. In *City* 15. 8 Augustine also stresses that, in the biblical narrative, selectivity enhances the rhetorically effective use of contrast ('conparatio'), here the contrast between the two cities.

If historicity is to be an aim, the longevity of the early humans in Genesis poses a problem. Like many writers of antiquity, Augustine has no difficulty in assuming that people in early times were of gigantic size. He himself has seen a huge human molar at Utica. Pliny the Elder provides a theoretical reason for this: the earth, as it ages, produces ever smaller bodies (*Nat. Hist.* 7. 16. 73–5). But longevity is another matter. True, Pliny knows of a tribe where people live to be 200 years old (*Nat. Hist.* 7. 48. 154). And Scripture cannot but be reliable, in this and other matters (15. 9). When Augustine discusses Genesis 6: 3 ('Their days shall be a hundred and twenty years'), he does not use it as evidence that God is imposing a maximum lifespan on humans: he relates the verse to Noah's age at the time of the Flood (15. 24).[11] But difficulties remain. There are discrepancies in the Hebrew and the Septuagint/Latin versions when the ages at which fathers beget sons are given, even though the age-totals of individuals agree (15. 10–11). Given the belief in the inspired nature of the Septuagint version (a belief which Augustine shares; cf. 18. 42–44), some Christians argued that the Jews introduced changes in the Hebrew version to discredit the authority of versions used by Christians (15. 11). Augustine resists the temptation to accept this explanation. Nor is he impressed by the argument that years were shorter in the period to which Genesis refers, for, even if one assumes that a year then is one-tenth of the length of a year now, not all problems are solved: Seth would be a father at 10, Cainan at 7 (15. 12). Nor is the evidence that other peoples have had years shorter than ours (15. 12) helpful, for references in the Bible to months and days make it likely that biblical chronology was the same as ours.[12] Otherwise we shall have to assume that the Flood may have lasted only four days (15. 14). Rather than assume an implausible worldwide Jewish conspiracy to falsify the Hebrew text, or a no less convincing attempt by the Septuagint translators to keep the Gentiles in the dark about dates, Augustine opts for a

[11] Coincidentally, the figure of 120 years as the maximum human lifespan is given in Cicero, *De Senectute* 19. 69 (see Powell ad loc. for variants) and Censorinus, *De Die Natali* 17. 4 (giving Varro's views); cf. Arnob. *Nat.* 2. 71. 25–6; Lactant. *Div. Inst.* 2. 12. 23 and, with a variation, *Epitome* 22. 5. Ogilvie (1978: 51–2) argues against direct use of Varro by Lactantius in *Div. Inst.* 2. 12; cf. Simmons (1995: 61) and n. 12 below.
[12] Augustine's citation in 15. 12 of Pliny, *Nat. Hist.* 7. 48, on the Egyptian computation of months as years is paralleled in Lactant., *Div. Inst.* 2. 12. 21–4, where Varro is cited as the source of the information (see n. 11 above).

scholarly explanation.[13] A single Septuagint codex incorrectly copied from Ptolemy's library may have been the source of the error. This hypothesis is supported by the observation that there seems to be a certain pattern and consistency to the discrepancies: subsequent attempts to correct the text cannot be excluded. Augustine points out that numbers in manuscripts are notoriously prone to scribal errors. In such cases it is usually best to give credence to the source-text from which the translation is made (15. 13). Moreover, it is significant that the tradition has not attempted to correct the Septuagint version from the Hebrew, a sign that the differences are not considered to be textual corruptions: perhaps the Septuagint translators were exercising prophetic creativity (cf. 18. 44). Both the Hebrew and the Septuagint versions are traditionally used as authoritative evidence (15. 14; cf. 18. 42–4).

Chapter 15 deals with a further problem of plausibility in Genesis. Did the aged fathers of children abstain from sex until they produced the offspring referred to in the text? One possible alternative is that they reached maturity later, in proportion to their longevity (a view that Augustine does not explore); another is that all their children are not named, but only those who provide the line of descent to Noah. Cain and Abel must be the first and second children of Adam and Eve, and their symbolic role in relation to the two cities must be maintained. But Adam and Eve may have had other children before the birth of Seth. The genealogy in Matthew 1 is an example of selectivity, to trace a line from Abraham to David, and it is not confined to first-born sons. Augustine cannot credit a century of sexual abstinence in Adam and his successors, and feels he must opt for the view that only select offspring are named (15. 15).

Marriage with close relatives, even between siblings, is a practice that the human race may have had to tolerate in its beginnings. Later such endogamy was forbidden. The reason which Augustine gives for its avoidance is that social harmony is better facilitated if family relationships are not concentrated in too few individuals. Better to acquire a wife and a new set of relatives by marriage than double up as husband and brother in one relationship. Multiple lines of kinship are a cohesive force in society, though there is also a counter-tendency to strengthen clan solidarity by marriage. Augustine observes that

---

[13] Cf. Augustine, *Qu. Hept.* 1. 2; Jerome, *Hebrew Questions on Genesis*, on Gen. 5: 25–7 (see Hayward's edn. ad loc.).

several societies forbid endogamy. Yet the urge to propagate one's
species is universal: sex is the seedbed of the city.[14] Humans, however, need regeneration as much as generation.[15] The Scripture is
silent on whether there was any visible sign of regeneration in early
man, comparable to the circumcision enjoined later upon Abraham:
but the offering of sacrifices is referred to as early as Cain and Abel
(15. 16).

In the chapters which follow, much is made of the purported
etymological meanings of the names of early biblical figures.[16] The
fact that Cain's name means 'possession', and Enoch's 'dedication',
points to features of the earthly city. Seth's name, on the other hand,
means 'resurrection' and the name of his son, Enos, means 'man' (in
the exclusive sense of male): in this way the regeneration of those who
become members of the heavenly city, and the end of physical
generation there, are symbolized. Significantly, no female members
of the line deriving from Seth are named; it is different with the line
of Cain. The earthly city survives through sexual propagation alone
(15. 17).

Biblical figures also symbolize and foreshadow Christ.[17] Abel,
whose name means 'mourning', and Seth ('resurrection') anticipate
the death and resurrection of Christ. The Septuagint/Latin translation of Genesis 4: 26 contains a reference to hope not found in the
Hebrew. Augustine here expands upon the virtue of hope associated
with Seth's son Enos. The three names (Abel, Seth, Enos) contain a
cluster of religious meanings (15. 18). Nor does Augustine's exegetical ingenuity shrink from finding opposite meanings in the same
name. If Enoch, meaning 'dedication', is Cain's son, then that must
refer to the establishment in this life of the earthly city (15. 17). But
the Enoch 'taken up' because he found favour with God (Genesis 5:
24; cf. Hebrews 11: 5) also anticipates the dedication of saved

[14] Augustine echoes Cicero's words, De Officiis 1. 17. 54, that the union ('con-
iugium') of man and wife is the origin of society and the 'seed-bed of the state'
('seminarium rei publicae'). B. D. Shaw (1987: 10–11) rightly stresses that Augustine
reflects both the Stoic tone of this passage and the Roman legal definition of marriage:
it is not the family as such, but the biological joining of man and woman, that is the
fundamental natural unit of society.

[15] On regeneration and 'reform' in Augustine see above all Ladner (1959); cf.
Augustine, Vera Rel. 26. 49 (Pauline 'old' and 'new' natures: see Rom. 6: 6, Eph. 4:
24, etc.); Simpl. 1. 2. 2 (applying the metaphor of conception and birth to baptism, in
an interpretation of John 3: 5).

[16] Augustine uses Jerome's Onomasticon, on which see Kelly (1975: 153–5), Bardy
in BA 36. 702–3. Cf. Doctr. Chr. 2. 16. 23.   [17] Cf. Ch. 8 n. 4.

humans to the true God through Christ, 'who rose, never to die afterwards, but he too was taken up'. Christ is the foundation of the house or temple of God, another association with dedication (15. 19). There may also be numerological symbolism in the details of Genesis. Why is the line of succession from Adam through Cain to the Flood given for eight generations only, whereas Noah belongs to the tenth generation from Adam? Augustine rehearses the selectivity options which he has discussed earlier in the book, but he prefers on this occasion to speculate about numbers.[18] In the eighth generation through Cain there are eleven children of Lamech named: eleven, one more than the ten which, through the decalogue, symbolizes the law, must, by 'transgressing' ten, represent sin. What is more, the eleventh name is a woman's name, and it (Naamah) means 'pleasure'. Augustine feels that he can rest his case, and that he has explained an odd omission in Genesis, especially odd in view of his insistence that the earthly city is all about physical generation (15. 20).

Augustine next tries to account for the fact that the descendants of Cain are listed continuously in Genesis 4: 17–22, whereas Seth's son Enos is first mentioned in Genesis 4: 26, and then his descendants from Genesis 5: 9 onwards, but only after a return in 5: 1–2 to the theme of the creation of Adam and Eve. Why this fresh start from Adam, or, as Augustine calls it more technically, this 'recapitulation'?[19] One reason may be that the earthly city, though included in the account, is thereby somehow excluded from the reckoning of generations. Another is, that by focusing on Cain at the beginning and Lamech at the end of the 'earthly' genealogy, the author starts and concludes his list with a murderer. Likewise, the attention given to Enos by separating him from his descendants in Genesis 4: 26 emphasizes the virtue of hope. The earthly city is actual, the heavenly city exists in hope, in this life. The moral of this juxtaposition of the two cities (Augustine returns to the vessels imagery of Romans 9; cf. *City* 15. 1–2) is that we should hope in God rather than trust our free will, which, because we are created from nothing, may lead to evil, from which only divine grace can save us (15. 21).

Another problem text is Genesis 6: 1–4, which refers to sons of God mating with daughters of men, and children being born to them.

---

[18] Tyconius' fifth hermeneutical rule deals with numerological interpretation: on it see further n. 10 above. Cf. Pollmann (1996: 48, 204–5).
[19] See further 16. 5 with n. 26 below.

Augustine speculates whether angels, who can certainly assume human bodies to communicate with humans, could also have sex with them. He cannot believe that these are the fallen (or falling) angels of which, for example, 2 Peter 2: 4 speaks. He argues that these sons of God must be humans. The fact that in his text they are called angels of God is explained by parallels with other biblical texts where humans are called angels (Mark 1: 2; Malachi 2: 7). He is not concerned about the information that they or their offspring were giants. If giants can exist in his own day (he knows of a giant woman living in Rome shortly before the Gothic sack of the city), then surely they could have existed in the remote past. One does not need to resort to references to giants in apocryphal writings attributed to Enoch: there are references to them in canonical books (15. 22–3).[20] There is also a moral dimension to the story of the sons of God and the daughters of man. It symbolizes the seductions of the earthly city for the citizens of the city of God. The sons of God infringe the virtue that can be defined as 'order in love' ('ordo amoris'), by loving physical beauty wrongly: that is the significance of the God–men antithesis in the Genesis text. Augustine quotes three lines from his own poem in praise of a candle, which talk of the good, order, and love (15. 22).[21]

The next biblical event to which Augustine must turn his attention is the Flood. It is an instance of divine punishment, although, even if good people had perished in it (which was not the case), that would not have harmed them in the afterlife (15. 24). The divine anger which provoked the Flood is not like a human passion ('perturbatio animi'), but is rather a judgement of God: the scriptural narrative suggests anger, using language in that way to create an effect on as wide an audience as it can, whether to terrify, exhort, or stimulate.[22]

---

[20] In *Doctr. Chr.* 2. 8. 13 Augustine gives his list of the canonical books of the Old and New Testaments. It corresponds to the canon prescribed by the Council of Hippo in 393 and adopted by the Council of Carthage in 397 (*Breviarium Hipponense*: CCL 149. 340, c. 47). For discussions of this and other contemporary versions of the canon see Costello (1930), La Bonnardière (1986: 287–301), Wermelinger (1984), Ohlig (1992). Barr (1983) is an informative general account of the establishment of a canon. Bonner (1970) surveys Augustine's biblical scholarship; several of Augustine's biblical texts are analysed in La Bonnardière (1960–75).

[21] For the text of the three lines quoted, and the rest of the fifty-three line poem, entitled *De Anima*, see *Anthologia Latina* i. 2, no. 489.

[22] Cf. O'Daly (1987: 50–1). Lactantius' treatise *De Ira Dei* deals with the topic. Nussbaum (1994: 402–38) discusses the philosophical implications (esp. in Seneca's *De Ira*) of righteous anger.

The magnitude of the Flood is suggested by references to the annihilation of animals, and that too is effective use of language: there is no suggestion that irrational animals could sin (15. 25). The ark is a symbol of the city of God, and hence of the Church.[23] Its measurements and features represent Christ's body and his crucifixion (among other details, both the cross and the ark are of wood), the saints' lives, and so on. Its three storeys symbolize the peoples restored after the Flood from Noah's three sons; or faith, hope, and charity; or the three harvests with ever richer returns of Matthew 13: 8; or wedlock, widowhood, and virginity (15. 26). Once again, Augustine insists that the account of the Flood is both a historical narrative and to be understood figuratively. To become preoccupied with details of the narrative, or to question the size of the ark, or ask whether fish, or creatures which reproduce asexually, were included in those admitted to it, is to be excessively contentious, Augustine argues, placing his trust in the prestige and authority of the Bible (15. 27).

Not all the details of the opening chapters of Genesis are susceptible to Augustine's interpretative treatment. Between the end of the Flood narrative and the chapters devoted to Abraham, that is, from Genesis 9: 18 to 12: 28, there is little more than genealogies, with the exception of the episodes of Noah's vineyard and the tower of Babel. It is not, therefore, surprising that Augustine focuses on these episodes. But he none the less wishes to give the impression of comprehensiveness. Hence, at the start of Book 16, he asks whether at any period after the Flood there were no earthly members of the city of God: between the end of the Flood and Abraham, Genesis does not name anybody whose devotion to the true God is explicitly attested (16. 1). All Augustine can suggest is that it would be implausible to assume that none existed. He appeals once again to the selectivity of the biblical narrative. But there is another reason. The biblical text, even in its historical books, is not exclusively historical; its historical narrative is also prophetic ('prophetica historia').[24] Often the prophetic elements are framed in a narrative that lacks any symbolic significance (16. 2). The implication is that

---

[23] For speculation about the source of Augustine's treatment of Noah's ark see below, Ch. 11. 3b.

[24] Augustine uses the term 'prophetica historia' in 16. 2 (p. 125. 11 Dombart and Kalb). On the close links between his concepts of history and prophecy see Markus (1970: 187–96).

the vineyard episode is one such prophetic element, embedded as it is in a genealogical wilderness. Noah is a figure of Christ, his drunkenness and nakedness a symbol of the Passion, Shem and Japheth represent Jews and Gentiles, but also Christ and the Church, Ham the heretics, and so on. Etymologies feed these symbolic readings (16. 1–2).

In 16. 3 Augustine attempts to wring some meanings from the genealogies descending from Noah's sons in Genesis 10. From Ham's line Nimrod is born, and he establishes the kingdom of Babylon, which symbolizes for Augustine the earthly city, as Jerusalem symbolizes the city of God. The mention of Nineveh and other cities is understood by Augustine to be an anachronism, anticipating the later kingdom of the Assyrians, the great eastern counterpart and antecedent of the Roman empire. Its association here with Ham underlines its role as an earthly city. There is a similar anticipation in the naming of Heber as first among Shem's descendants, although he belongs to a later generation: the Hebrew language, and people, are thereby highlighted. The antithesis of the two cities is read into these lists.

Augustine connects the tower of Babel (Genesis 11: 1–10) with Babylon, which he understands to mean 'confusion'.[25] The foundation of Babylon, archetype of the earthly city as a political reality, is thus linked with the tower, a symbol of Nimrod's pride (16. 4). The Babel narrative allows Augustine to employ an exegetical principle that enables him to explain why Genesis 11: 5 has 'the Lord came down' and 11: 7 the Lord saying 'Come, let us go down' to Babel. The principle, which Augustine takes from Tyconius, is called recapitulation, which accounts for such features by relating them to an earlier point in the narrative: here, 11: 7 alludes to 11: 5, and describes the same phenomenon, but also shows how the action occurred.[26] Augustine stresses that these passages are not to be taken literally,

[25] 'Babylon' was traditionally understood by Akkadian scribes to derive from words meaning 'gate of god'; 'Babel' is linked by the Hebrew text of Gen. 11: 9 to the root 'bil', 'confuse'.
[26] Tyconius' sixth hermeneutical rule, *Liber Regularum* pp. 66–70, deals with 'recapitulation' or discontinuity in narrative sequence; cf. Augustine's extended discussion of the rule in *Doctr. Chr.* 3. 36. 52–4. See Steinhauser (1984); Dorival (1987: 101–8), who outlines the earlier Patristic tradition of the concept; Dulaey (1989); Pollmann (1996: 48–50, 205–11). Augustine modifies the account of recapitulation found in *Reg.*, apparently using material from Tyconius' commentary on Revelation (cf. *In Apoc.* 114–16, 132, 281–2, 407, 422). Cf. further *City* 15. 21; 16. 15; 20. 14, 17.

indicating as they do God's movement and sudden decision: he suggests that they refer to an angelic intervention (16. 5). The attribution to God of language here leads Augustine to consider the divine words of Genesis 1: 26, 'Let us make man'. The plural here is not to be understood to refer to angels, as that would involve them in creation. Rather, it refers to the Trinity, which makes man 'in our image' (ibid.). In Genesis 11: 7, however, the words are more appropriately those of angels: the reason Augustine gives is the artificial one that the exclamation 'Come' there alludes to the angels' approach to God as the source of eternal truth, towards which they move. God's meta-language is soundless, it precedes his action as the unchanging ground ('ratio') of the action itself, communicating itself directly to the angelic minds.[27] Augustine, who has little to say about the multiplicity of human languages other than that it exists, reckons that from Noah's sons after Babel seventy-two languages came into existence, and even more peoples (16. 6).

Augustine's discussion of the implications of the Flood account in Genesis moves from its symbolic to its practical aspects with often bewildering suddenness. In 16. 7 he is perplexed about the means whereby animals that reproduce sexually could spread to islands after the Flood. Some could have got there by swimming, but not all. Perhaps some were brought there by men. Maybe angels transported some there, in a kind of divinely ordained airlift. Or perhaps we should not read Genesis so literally after all. The presence of species in the ark may have to do, not with their survival, but with the representation of the various nations, and hence the Church (16. 7). What about monstrosities, human freaks? Pliny the Elder (*Nat. Hist.* 7. 2) is Augustine's source for a number of types, but he also reveals that he knows of some from mosaics on the esplanade at Carthage. Are they descended from Noah and Adam? If they really exist, and are rational beings, then they must descend from Adam. Some certainly do exist: Augustine knows of a man at Hippo Zaritus who has crescent-shaped feet and hands, and only two toes on each foot. Augustine urges acceptance of authenticated cases as human: it is not for humans to question the purpose of divine creation. The existence of whole races of such freaks may be intended by God to pre-empt criticism of his handiwork in the cases of individual monstrosities, as if he were a craftsman who made the odd mistake.

[27] On God's language see further Ch. 8 n. 3.

Interestingly for post-Darwinians, Augustine observes that if we did not, in fact, know that monkeys, apes, and chimpanzees were animals, natural historians might well have been able to pass them off as human curiosities: we must, therefore, remain sceptical about the truth of such accounts, although some are true (16. 8). As for the antipodes, Augustine is doubtful about the attempts to demonstrate that they must, in logic, exist, whether the earth is spherical or not. He also doubts whether any humans have sailed and settled there (16. 9).

In 16. 10 Augustine returns to the biblical text in search of evidence for the existence of the city of God among humans after the Flood and before Abraham. It should be found, if anywhere, among the descendants of Shem (and, secondarily, of Japheth: cf. Genesis 9: 26–7). But the Bible is not explicit about this, and we should not jump to conclusions. There is no reason why we should not believe that there were good descendants of Ham, and wicked descendants of Shem. The world was certainly never devoid of humans of both kinds (16. 10). The fact that the world had only one language until Babel does not clarify the issue, for that was the case before the Flood, when the wicked certainly existed alongside the few good. Yet the continued transmission of Hebrew in the post-Babel period suggests that it is among its speakers that the people of God are found. Not all of Heber's descendants spoke Hebrew, but only the line descending to Abraham, just as not all of Abraham's descendants did, but only the line descending from Jacob (16. 11). Language, covenant, and sacred history go together, but that is not the same as saying that all Hebrew speakers are members of the city of God.

Throughout the work Augustine makes occasional references to the scheme of six ages ('aetates') of human history which he adopts in other writings.[28] But the scheme is not fully or extensively employed in our work. There is a passing allusion to it at the beginning of 16. 12, where Augustine speaks of the 'division of time' ('articulus temporis') that begins with Abraham: it would, in fact, be the start

---

[28] Cf. esp. *Gen. adv. Man.* 1. 35–41, *Vera Rel.* 48–50. See Kötting and Geerlings (1986), Deane (1963: 71). Horn (1997: 182–4), in a judicious discussion of Augustine's views on history, takes his use of the 'aetates' scheme to be an indicator of his historical awareness, but stresses that the scheme is not used by Augustine to support either a concept of progress in human affairs (although there is progressive education of God's people in the unfolding of scriptural history: see Ch. 7, on 10. 14, with n. 35) or one of decline. On the use of this and other schemes in Augustine's evolving views on society between 386 and 400 see Cranz (1954).

of the third age (after Adam–Noah and Noah–Abraham; cf. 16. 24).
It is only at 16. 43 that the ages are explicitly linked to the periods of
human life, when Augustine talks of the age beginning with David
(the fourth age) as humanity's 'young manhood' ('iuventus'), and to
the earlier periods as, respectively, the 'infancy' ('infantia'), 'childhood' ('pueritia'), and 'adolescence' ('adulescentia') of humankind.
The scheme is introduced again at the very end of the work in 22. 30
by way of elucidating the typology of the Sabbath. It never becomes
an organizing feature of the work's historical books, although the
focal figures of the ages' scheme—Adam, Noah, Abraham, David—
are, of course, central to these books. Book 17 will treat the period
from David to Christ's incarnation as one phase.

From 16. 12 on, Augustine focuses attention exclusively upon the
rich scriptural material concerning Abraham, Isaac, and Jacob (16.
12–42). With Abraham, he observes, our knowledge of the city of
God becomes clearer, and there is more evidence of divine promises
which are fulfilled in Christ (16. 12).[29] He devotes chapters 16–32 to
the promises made to Abraham. Augustine is always on the look-out
for traces of the two cities in the biblical text. When Terah,
Abraham's father, leaves the land of the Chaldeans and settles in
Haran, in Mesopotamia, there is no mention of him taking one of his
sons, Nahor, with him (Genesis 11: 31), although we know from
Genesis 24: 10 that Nahor settled in Mesopotamia also. Had Nahor
abandoned his father's religion, and fallen under the spell of the
Chaldeans? Did he emigrate to Mesopotamia later, because he
repented or was being persecuted? Augustine finds evidence for persecution of the household of Terah in Judith 5: 5–9 (16. 13). Further
scrutiny of the Biblical text leads Augustine to identify another
instance of recapitulation at Genesis 12: 1, where God's command
to Abraham cannot follow, as in the narrative, upon his father's
death, but, for reasons based on details of the ages of Terah and
Abraham, must have been issued while Terah was still alive (16. 14–
15).[30] Another possibility that Augustine mentions here (but clearly
does not favour) as an alternative to recapitulation is that Abraham's
age, 75 years, when he leaves Haran (Genesis 12: 4) is reckoned from
his legendary liberation from the fire of the Chaldeans. The oblique

---

[29] On Abraham as a Christian archetype see Pelagius on Rom. 4: 1–24 and De
Bruyne ad loc. On Abraham in Augustine see Mayer (1986a).
[30] For recapitulation see on 16. 5 with n. 26 above.

and allusive nature of these discussions is in part due to the fact that Augustine had gone over the same ground in his recently written *Questions on the Heptateuch*: what he is now doing is coming down more firmly in favour of one of the three explanations of the problem which he mentions there (the third explanation was that Abraham was born later in Terah's life).

For reasons of clarity it makes sense to extrapolate and discuss together Augustine's review of the promises made by God to Abraham in Genesis 12–17. In his discussion, Augustine is concerned above all to identify universal meanings, which apply to the city of God as whole, and hence to the Christian Church. Thus the promise that 'in you all the tribes of the earth will be blessed' (Genesis 12: 3) is to be understood spiritually, to refer to all who follow in the footsteps of Abraham's faith (16. 16), whereas the promise of the land of Canaan in Genesis 12: 2 and 12: 7 refers specifically to the Israelite nation (16. 16, 18). On the other hand, the promises of Genesis 13: 14–17 are not so easily categorized. They appear to refer to Canaan again, but Augustine has some difficulty with the promise that Abraham's seed will possess the land for ever. The facts of history seem to contradict this, unless, Augustine suggests, somewhat disingenuously, the Romanized Christians who in his day inhabited the land could be considered children of Abraham. Or does the promise refer to the fact that, though excluded from Jerusalem, the Jews inhabit other cities of Canaan, and will be there until the end of history? The words of the same promise, 'I shall make your seed like the sands of the earth', might seem to imply all peoples who follow Abraham's faith, but Augustine points out that this may merely be an instance of the trope known as hyperbole (16. 21). Is it any different when God later promises Abraham that his descendants will be as numerous as the stars of heaven (Genesis 15: 5)? Augustine is inclined to think that this refers to the heavenly bliss of his posterity rather than mere numbers, for grains of sand are surely more numerous than stars: but he hesitates, considering the likely numbers of stars, and the hesitation allows him to include a jibe at astronomers like Eudoxus and astronomer-poets like Aratus, who, he alleges, claim to list the stars comprehensively, 16. 23.[31] The great promises of Genesis 17: 1–21 are read to contain references to the 'calling of the Gentiles', for Isaac, as Augustine has already argued (15. 2–3), is the son of

---

[31] Augustine's source is Cic. *Rep.* 1. 14. 22.

promise and the child of grace, not born in the normal course of nature. Circumcision is the renewal of nature, its universality represents the universal nature of grace, its occurring on the eighth day symbolizes Christ, who rose from the dead after the sabbath. The old covenant (from the Christian perspective) of these verses symbolizes the new covenant (16. 26). The change of Abraham's name—from Abram he now becomes Abraham (Genesis 17: 5)—is also a token of his universal significance: his name now means 'the father of many nations' (16. 28). Genesis 18: 18 refers both to the people of Israel ('according to the flesh', 'secundum carnem') and all peoples ('according to faith', 'secundum fidem'), 16. 29. Finally, the name of Isaac, meaning 'laughter', alludes both to Abraham's laughter when he was promised to him (Genesis 17: 17) and to Sarah's different kind of laughter, prompted by doubt, at the promise (Genesis 18: 12–15), but later made good (Augustine suggests, unconvincingly) by her postnatal comments (Genesis 21: 6). Augustine reminds us of his discussion at 15. 2–3, and the symbolism of the two covenants attending the figures of Sarah and Hagar (16. 31).

Augustine's discussion of the promises made to Abraham is interwoven with other themes. One of these is an anticipation of the history of other kingdoms (Sicyon, Egypt, Assyria) in Book 18, introduced briefly here because of their synchronization in Eusebius' *Chronicle* (which Augustine knows in Jerome's version)[32] with Abraham's purported dates (16. 17). Augustine dwells on Assyria in particular to keep the theme of the two cities in the reader's mind: Assyria is the great Asian kingdom, identified with Babylon under Ninus: Augustine sees it as a forerunner of the 'second Babylon' in the West—Rome (16. 17). Abraham is an idealized figure: his concealment of Sarah's identity in Genesis 12: 11–20 cannot be lies, for the falsehood was perpetrated to preserve his life and her chastity (16. 19). His sexual relations with Hagar do not compromise him either (16. 25). The instructions to Abraham concerning the sacrifice that he must make, in Genesis 15: 8–21, are exploited for their figurative allusions to the history of Israel, and Genesis 15: 17 (the smoking furnace and the burning lamp) is read, with the implicit help of 1 Corinthians 3: 13–15, as a reference to the final judgement, Antichrist, and the end of the world (16. 24), anticipating themes of Books 20–22. Genesis 17: 14 (on the consequences of not circumcis-

---

[32] See below, Ch. 11. 3e.

ing) is related, as so often by Augustine, to original sin, suggesting as
it does infant guilt that is not due to any sinful action and hence does
not entail individual blame, but has to do with the fault of others and
with origins (16. 27).[33] The three men who appeared to Abraham by
the oak of Mamre (Genesis 18) are angels: Augustine here resists the
tendency to identify one of them, whom Abraham addresses, as
Christ (elsewhere he identifies them with the Trinity[34]): his argument
depends upon an examination of the language Lot uses in conversa-
tion with them in Genesis 19 (16. 29). Sodom is punished on account
of its homosexuality (16. 30).[35] The injunction to Lot and his family
not to look back represents the requirement that we should not return
in thought to the old life, once saved from it by grace (16. 30).
Finally, God's command to Abraham to sacrifice his son Isaac tests
and demonstrates Abraham's faith, not least in the resurrection of his
son: Isaac is a Christ-figure, and so subsequently is the ram, who,
caught in the brambles, foreshadows Christ's crown of thorns (which,
Augustine, misrepresenting Scripture, insinuates was put on him by
the Jews). God's promises to Abraham after the aborted sacrifice are
a token of the promises which the real sacrifice of Christ brings
towards fulfilment (16. 32).

Other details of the Abraham sequence in Genesis also anticipate
the incarnation of Christ. It is not always evident why this is so.
When the servant whom Abraham is sending to Mesopotamia to
bring Isaac back a wife is instructed to place his hand under
Abraham's thigh and swear that he will not take a wife for Isaac
from the Canaanites (Genesis 24: 2), Augustine finds that this is an
indication that Christ will be born of a descendant of Abraham
(16. 33). Possibly the reason is that Abraham's instructions stress the

[33] Cf. the interpretation of Gen. 17: 14 in the anti-Pelagian writings, e.g. *Nupt. et
Conc.* 2. 11. 24; *C. Iul.* 2. 6. 18, 3. 18. 34, 5. 11. 45. For further references see the
note in the LCL edn. of *City* ad loc. On Augustine's doctrine of original sin, infant
guilt, and divine grace see TeSelle (1970: 258–66, 278–94, 313–19), Burnaby (1938:
181–252), J. P. Burns (1980), Kelly (1977: 361–9). Kirwan (1989: 129–50) provides
an analytical critique of the doctrine's principles.

[34] Cf. Augustine, *C. Max.* 2. 26. 5–7. See Bardy's note in BA 36. 726–7.

[35] In *Conf.* 3. 8. 15 the behaviour of the Sodomites is the one example given of sins
'against nature' ('contra naturam'): Augustine there follows early Christian exegesis of
the Sodom story (Gen. 19), and Rom. 1: 26–7 in both language and attitude. On Paul's
condemnation of homosexuality see Sanders (1991: 110–13). Christian intolerance of
homosexuals appears to have intensified in the later 4th c.: male prostitutes were
publicly burned in Rome in 390, if an edict of the emperor Theodosius was implemented: *FIRA* 1. 2. 481; Brown (1989: 383). On the question of an autobiographical
allusion to homosexual involvement in *Conf.* 2. 2. 2. see O'Donnell ad loc.

importance of Isaac marrying within the Jewish people, and hence
their role as the chosen people. The same instructions are given by
Isaac about Jacob's choice of wife (Genesis 28: 1–4), and Augustine
appears to place the same interpretation upon this episode (16. 38).
Abraham's marriage to Keturah after Sarah's death is seen as important by Augustine because Keturah, like Hagar, is called 'concubine'
(but, unlike her, also 'wife'), and so symbolically related, like Hagar,
to the earthly city. The fact that Isaac is Abraham's heir, while the
sons of his concubines receive gifts (Genesis 25: 5–6), indicates
symbolically, Augustine thinks, that Jews by physical descent and
heretics do not come to the promised kingdom. The episode may
also be a way of answering those heretics (the Montanists) who claim
that a second marriage is sinful (16. 34).[36]

The prophecy concerning Rebekah's twins (Genesis 25: 23) is taken
by Augustine, following Paul (Romans 9: 1–13), to symbolize the
workings of divine grace, which is not determined by antecedent
merit. Augustine refers to, but does not name, his other treatments
of these texts: the most detailed is Ad Simplicianum 1. 2. There, the
further points made here are stressed: unborn children are equal in
respect of original sin and also of guiltlessness regarding personal sin;
the statement that the elder will serve the younger typifies the
relations of Jews to Christians (16. 35).[37] The contrast between
the monogamous Isaac and the polygamous Abraham is striking,
but Augustine warns against making comparisons favourable to
Isaac.[38] The important thing about Abraham is his obedience to
God (Genesis 26: 5), from which Isaac and his descendants benefit.
One must look at the total context, and particularly for exceptional
qualities in individuals who in other respects are inferior, in making
any moral judgements. Objectively, continence is superior to
marriage, but a married believer is superior to a celibate unbeliever
(16. 36). Isaac's blessing of Jacob prefigures the universal proclama-
tion of Christ, just as Isaac himself represents the law and prophecy:
his unwitting blessing of Jacob symbolizes the ways in which the
Jewish prophetic books, unknown to the Jews themselves, foretell
Christ, the true Messiah: 'the smell of my son is as the smell of a
fruitful field which the Lord hath blessed' (Genesis 27: 27); 'the

[36] Cf. Haer. 26, C. Faust. 32. 17. On Montanism see Frend (1965: 287–94), Trevett
(1996).   [37] See above on 16. 27 with n. 33.
[38] On interpreting scriptural references to polygamous patriarchs see Doctr. Chr. 3.
18. 27–22. 32, Conf. 3. 7. 12–13; cf. further 16. 38 below.

world, like a field, is filled with the fragrance of the name of Christ' (16. 37).

The promises given to Jacob about his posterity, like those given to Abraham and Isaac, point towards the advent of Christ. Jacob's dream about the ladder, and his understanding that he has had a vision of the gate of heaven and the house of God, lead him to anoint the stone on which he slept and call the place of the dream 'house of God' (Genesis 28: 10–19). The association of anointing with the derivation of Christ's name from 'chrisma' is easily made, and together with the link to John 1: 51, where Christ's words allude to Jacob's ladder, intensifies the Christocentric tendency of the interpretation. Perhaps even more striking is the way in which Jacob's action establishes the house of God on earth, although Augustine does not draw our attention to this explicitly. Jacob's polygamy gives him pause for thought, and he rationalizes it by pointing out that it was legal behaviour to improve the birth-rate, and that Jacob was, in any case, only obeying orders (his wives') and was concerned with procreation (16. 38).[39] The angel who wrestles with Jacob (Genesis 32: 24–32) is a type of Christ, apparently but not really defeated, and blesses Jacob with the name 'Israel', which Augustine, following a popular etymology, understands to mean 'seeing God' (cf. Genesis 32: 30). The lameness of Jacob symbolizes the non-believers, his continued blessedness those who believe. We should note how in this passage Augustine is making Jacob, who is so often understood by him in ways that refer to Christ, a symbol of what the Jews do to Christ (16. 39). Yet it is from Jacob that the line of descent to Christ passes through his son Judah, and Jacob's (= Israel's) blessing upon Judah (Genesis 49: 8–12) is a prophecy of Christ's death and resurrection, and of baptism and the Church (16. 41). As with Esau and Jacob, so Manasseh and Ephraim, the sons of Joseph, represent Jews and Christians, with the repeated paradox that the younger is put before the elder brother in Jacob's blessing (Genesis 48: 14–20). Once again, the universality of Christianity is the key to the prophetic sense of Jacob's words (16. 42).

Augustine has concentrated on the figures of Abraham, Isaac, and Jacob. By contrast, Moses and Joshua get only one chapter (16. 43). Aspects of the narrative that clearly point to Christ—the Paschal lamb and the feast of Passover, for example—are seized upon, but

[39] See n. 38 above.

we get the impression that Augustine must move on to other matters, and that he wants to round off this part of his sacred history with a brief survey of developments: the Jews in Egypt, their period in the wilderness under Moses' leadership, the arrival in the land of promise under Joshua, the rule of the judges and of the kings, beginning with Saul and David, who is the start of a new era. Augustine reflects that, whereas Book 15 dealt with one age, this book has been devoted to two, and that in the third age the first beginnings of the earthly kingdom can be identified (cf. 16. 17). But it is also the age in which the yoke of the law is imposed on a sinful, if not entirely sinful, humanity (16. 43).

Although Augustine abandons the scheme of the ages ('aetates') of history after 16. 43, he alludes to it implicitly in the first chapter of Book 17. For the Babylonian captivity to which he refers there is used elsewhere by him to mark the end of the fourth and the beginning of the fifth age.[40] But the division is not of any use to him in this book, which derives its unity from the phenomenon of prophecy, more precisely from the period when Samuel began to prophesy until the return of the Israelites from exile. This does not mean that Noah, Abraham, and others are not prophets. But Augustine is committed to a chronological survey of sacred history, and he finds that the category 'prophetic age' gives both a thematic and a chronological coherence to the book. He stresses once again that he must be selective in his choice of prophetic texts, and reminds the reader that there is much prophecy of the future in the historical biblical narratives (17. 1).

The prophecies given to Abraham about the people of Israel's political greatness were fulfilled only in the age of the kings, David and Solomon (17. 2). Those were prophecies about the earthly Jerusalem. In 17. 3 Augustine distinguishes three kinds of prophetic text. One refers to the earthly Jerusalem only. Another refers only to the heavenly Jerusalem, or to the city of God. A third refers to both the earthly and the heavenly cities. Nathan's warnings to David of coming misfortunes (2 Samuel 12: 1–15) are of the first kind. But Augustine understands Jeremiah 31: 31–3, on the new covenant, to be of the second type, and to refer only to the city of God. Scriptural texts which refer to Jerusalem as the city of God have a double sense,

[40] See 16. 12 and 16. 43 with n. 28 above.

especially when they prophesy the future house of God there: they allude both to Solomon's temple and to the heavenly Jerusalem, and are an instance of the third kind of prophecy. Augustine wishes to run a middle course between mere literalism and excessive symbolism in biblical hermeneutics.[41] But he does not censure those who have made a fully figurative interpretation, provided that they recognize the historicity of biblical narrative. He acknowledges implicitly that we may not be able to discern in each and every case a figurative meaning, even though there may be one. He simply does not think that it is necessary to assume that there must be a figurative meaning every time. He argues the common-sense position (17. 3).

Key events of scriptural history have a symbolic sense. The rejection of Eli the priest and his replacement by Samuel, and the rejection of Saul as king and David's accession, both point to the transition from the old to the new covenant, and to the transformation of both priesthood and monarchy by the new king-priest, Christ (17. 4). But more often than not Augustine comments on the words of prophets. In 17. 4 he offers a long commentary on the prophecy of Samuel's mother Hannah in 1 Samuel 2: 1–10. Since Hannah's name is understood to mean 'God's grace' we expect her words to be found to contain layers of hidden meanings. Augustine uncovers meanings that relate to the city of God, more especially the Church (including the numerological symbolism of the seven in 1 Samuel 2: 5), to the earthly city (and particularly to Israel), to Christ, to the exaltation of the humble and the humbling of the proud, to God the judge, to the soul in its earthly body, to Christ's ascension, and to the final judgement (17. 4). The spirit who speaks to Eli at 1 Samuel 2: 27–36 delivers a mixture of specific prophecies about Eli's descendants, about Israel, and about Christ. But his words are also understood to be about the faith of the predestined, so that Augustine finds in the passage a 'short avowal' ('confessio') of faith (17. 5). These two commentaries are given as examples of exegesis, finding side by side in the same text the three types of prophecy that Augustine has spoken of in 17. 3. References to the non-fulfilment of the earlier prophecy of the eternal survival of the Jewish priesthood, such as

---

[41] In *Doctr. Chr.* 3. 5. 9–29. 40 Augustine discusses distinctions between the literal and figurative senses of Scripture, urging discrimination and advancing various kinds of criterion. He asserts (ibid. 3. 22. 32) that 'all, or nearly all' events in the Old Testament may be interpreted both literally and figuratively. On Augustine's method see further Ch. 8 n. 12.

1 Samuel 2: 30, allude to the temporal nature of that priesthood as a foreshadowing of Christianity, but are also to be read as texts about the eternal survival of what is foreshadowed. Saul, the Lord's anointed, despite his rejection, is a prophetic image of Christ, the anointed one; and the reference in 1 Samuel 13: 13 to the kingdom of Saul which would have lasted for ever, had Saul not offended, rather than being understood literally, should be seen as a reference to what it foreshadows (17. 6). Other prophecies which were not fulfilled point clearly towards later fulfilment in Christ. These include Samuel's prophecies about Solomon at 2 Samuel 7: 8–16. Solomon, like Saul, thus becomes a figure of Christ (17. 8). It is a principle for Augustine that literal non-fulfilment of prophecies is a sign of their symbolic meaning: this is applied to a text like Psalm 89 in 17. 9–12. For the Psalms are a primary prophetic text. Their poetry, with its 'rational and proportional concord of different sounds', is like the unity of a well-ordered city (17. 14).[42] Augustine stresses that any symbolic interpretation of the Psalms depends upon an understanding of the individual context of the whole psalm: otherwise exegesis will come to resemble a selection of individual verses to form a cento (17. 15). His discussion of some psalms in the following chapters (17. 16–19) can hardly be said to put his principle into practice, for he proceeds no differently than in the rest of Book 17, selecting those passages that he can relate to Christ. The Book of Wisdom and Ecclesiasticus, which, despite scholarly doubts, were, as Augustine tells us, regarded by the western Church as works written by Solomon, likewise contain prophecies about Christ's Passion and the future faith of the nations, and these books are no less prophetic than the canonical works attributed to Solomon, namely: Proverbs, Ecclesiastes, and the Song of Songs.[43] This last book is about Christ and his Church. Augustine accounts for its erotic content thus: 'this

[42] Augustine is probably influenced by the comparison of the political concord of the various classes in society to musical harmony ('concentus'), in a passage from Cicero's *Republic* quoted in *City* 2. 21 (= *Rep.* 2. 42. 69). Pöschl (1993: 361–2) refers to Platonic and other antecedents of the comparison, in his discussion of musical metaphors for order in Augustine: see esp. *Mus.* 6. 11. 29, *Vera Rel.* 22. 42–3, *Letter* 138. 1. 5, *Conf.* 11. 28. 38 (with O'Donnell and Meijering ad loc.), *City* 11. 18. Cf. Ch. 12 n. 10.

[43] In *Doctr. Chr.* 2. 8. 13 Augustine reports similar doubts about the deuterocanonical Wisdom and Ecclesiasticus. There he refers to the tradition that Jesus Sirach wrote them, a view repudiated by him in *Retr.* 2. 4. 2. See further n. 20 above; Wermelinger (1984: 179–80).

pleasure [at the "marriage" of Christ and the Church] is wrapped in allegorical clothing, so that it may be more ardently desired, and that the removal of its clothes may give more delight' (17. 20). It is a figurative strip-tease.

The narrative concerning the kings after Solomon contains, in Augustine's opinion, scarcely any prophecy, whether in their words or their deeds. He confines himself accordingly to a brief narrative summary of the division of the Jewish kingdom after Solomon into the kingdoms of Judah and Israel. Jeroboam, Solomon's servant, became king of Israel, and abandoned his faith, chiefly, it is suggested, on political grounds, in order to prevent his people visiting the temple in Jerusalem, in what was then the centre of his rival's kingdom. The division of the kingdom is discovered through prophecy to be an act of divine punishment (1 Kings 12: 24) and so war between the kingdoms, which Rehoboam, Solomon's son and king of Judah, wished to wage, was prevented. In the times which followed, impious rulers of Israel were castigated by prophets. Among the later prophets, Elijah and Elisha are mentioned here in passing by Augustine (17. 21–2). Whereas all the kings of Israel in this period seem to have been bad, in Judah there were both good and bad kings. This was a period of civil and external wars, the time of the Babylonian exile and the restoration of a single state in Israel. The wars and periods of peace reflect alternating divine anger and mercy. But the Jews thereafter never lacked enemies, and eventually they were conquered by the Romans. All this, and the eventual diaspora, Augustine sees as divinely ordained punishment (17. 23; cf. 17. 2, 7).

In the final chapter of Book 17 Augustine passes quickly over the prophets of the post-exile period. He will return to some of them in the next book (18. 27–36), but he wants to conclude this book about prophecies by showing how the last prophets are active at the time of Christ's birth: Zechariah and Elizabeth, the parents of John the Baptist, John himself, and Simeon and Anna. He wishes to suggest the continuity between these prophets of the Gospel texts, not accepted by the Jews, and the earlier Jewish prophets. With these observations and an anticipation of a return to prophecies Augustine concludes the book (17. 24).

In Book 18 the events of non-biblical history are synchronized with biblical events from Abraham's time onwards. Augustine makes extensive use of the synchronization in Eusebius' *Canons*, which had been translated and continued by Jerome (cf. 18. 8).[44] He points out that he has been concentrating on the city of God's course from Abraham to the time of the kings (in 16. 12 to the end of 17): this is because he has wanted to trace the progress of the city of God more clearly. Now the need for both comprehensiveness and contrast means that he will trace the other city's course (18. 1). In fact, there is no attempt in Book 18 to be comprehensive. Augustine's account is, rather, impressionistic. There is indeed chronological juxtaposition of events and persons, but there is also, for example, polemic against myths as fictions about the gods. At times we seem to have re-entered the world of Books 2–7.

Augustine's view of secular history is dominated by the notions of conflict and striving for power in societies where traces of the sense of human fellowship none the less remain. The desire for peace often leads to acceptance by conquered peoples of rule by others. The two great examples of empire are Assyria (which Augustine confuses with Babylon) and Rome: one eastern and one western power, the rise of the latter following immediately upon the decline of the former. All other kingdoms Augustine considers to be like appendages ('velut adpendices') of these two. Ninus was ruling the Assyrian kingdom when Abraham was born. In Greece at this time there was the small kingdom of Sicyon. Its appearance in Augustine's account is due to the fact that its list of early kings is synchronized in Eusebius' *Canons* with events in scriptural history.[45] Moreover, Varro began his work *De Gente Populi Romani*, on which Augustine depends heavily in Book 18, with the Sicyon list (18. 1).[46] Varro's antiquarian interest in the list gives Sicyon a historical status that it does not deserve: for Augustine, as for Eusebius and Jerome, Sicyon provides a Greek counterpart to the Jewish nation and the Assyrian kingdom. The presence of details about Argos (upon which Sicyon was dependent in early times) in the chronicle sources[47] also accounts for its appearance in Augustine. For his view of Athens Augustine is dependent on Sallust, *Catiline* 8. 2–4, which he cites. He thus considers Athens'

[44] See further Ch. 11. 3e.
[45] According to Eusebius' chronology, Abraham was born in 2016 BC, in the twenty-second year of the reign of Europus, the second king of Sicyon (Euseb. *Chron.* p. 20). On the beginnings of Greek chronography see Pfeiffer (1968: 51, 163–4, 255–7), Bickerman (1980: 87–9), T. D. Barnes (1981: 119–20). On Greek and Roman chronography in general see Samuel (1972: 189–276).
[46] See further Ch. 11. 1b. On Varro's *De Gente* see Fox (1996: 236–56).
[47] Cf. Euseb. *Chron.* pp. 27 ff.

renown to be largely due to the city's image, as presented by its
writers, rather than to any great achievement. Certainly nothing in
this early pre-Roman period compares to Assyria/Babylon, the 'first
Rome', just as Rome is the 'second Babylon'. Augustine will therefore
give a place to the Assyrian kings in his chronology, but he points out
that this chronology is Greek/Roman, and that most of the details of
the history which he is about to survey are from Greek and Roman
sources (18. 2).

In his survey an attempt is made to locate developments which are
the basis of civilized life, such as the establishment of a legal system
and a calendar in the Argolid, and the invention of writing in Egypt by
Io, identified by Eusebius, and hence by Augustine, with Isis (18. 3).
Mention of Egypt prompts Augustine to include details of Joseph's
time there (18. 4). The origin of Serapis—a posthumously deified king
Apis of Argos—is explained by means of a false etymology given by
Varro. It suits Augustine that Varro's account is Euhemeristic and
rationalizes the origins of an important Greco-Egyptian cult.[48] At
the same time Augustine adduces the other factor which he elsewhere
uses to account for pagan religious phenomena: demons. They will
have performed the miracles associated with the bull-cult of Apis, by
means of influencing an embryo through working on the imagination
of its mother (18. 5).[49] The same kind of Euhemeristic account is
given of Argus' death and deification, and it is contrasted implicitly
with the pious death of Jacob (18. 6). Even major gods of the Greeks
like Prometheus, Mercury, and Minerva are presented as humans:
Atlas was a great astrologer (18. 8). Varro's account of the foundation
myths of Athens and the Areopagus are exploited for their contradictions.[50] Why did Minerva not defend the women of Athens, whose
champion she had appeared to be? Varro himself does not believe the
derivation of the name 'Areopagus' from the trial of Ares, any more
than he believes in the judgement of Paris. Once more, Augustine is
undermining the status of pagan myths as fictions (18. 9–10).

The synchronization exercise allows Augustine to include in his

[48] For Augustine's and other Christian writers' use of Euhemerism see Ch. 3 with n.
17, Ch. 7 with n. 5.
[49] Cf. O'Daly (1987: 111): the theory of such influences on embryos was advanced
by Porphyry. Russell (1979: 6) discusses an earlier instance, in Dionysius of Halicar-
nassus, *De Imitatione* fr. 6 (= 2. 203 Usener and Radermacher).
[50] In 18. 8 Augustine also exploits the fact that Eusebius(-Jerome) did not follow
Varro's chronology for the pre-regal and early regal periods to expose alleged limitations in Varro's account: see further Simmons (1995: 59).

historical narrative details of sacred history for which there was no
place in earlier books. Thus Moses' career as lawgiver and leader of
the Jews in the desert, as well as his prophetic role, are outlined in
18. 11. The synchronization also leads to odd details. Between
Israel's departure from Egypt and the death of Joshua fall such events
as Dionysus' introduction of the vine to Attica and the kidnapping of
Europa (Augustine prefers the version which has her brought to Crete
by Xanthus the Cretan king, rather than by Jupiter[51]). There are
absurdities in myths about Athens—the birth of Erichthonius is
one—on which Augustine dwells, with by now familiar polemic
against dramatic performances of the myths. Even if they are fictions,
it is wrong to enjoy the invented crimes of the gods (18. 12). Some
myths Augustine exploits for their absurdities (the Centaurs, Bellero-
phon and Pegasus), others for their immoral content (Ganymede,
Danaë), others again for the confusion which they cause (different
myths about Apollo or Hercules, which seem to presuppose not one
but many individuals of those names). Accounts of the vulnerability
of Dionysus and of his death and place of burial undermine the
religious standing of the cults which they have inspired (18. 13).
The so-called theological poets—Orpheus, Musaeus, and Linus—
are really no more respectable than the anonymous inventors of
myths. Although they have a more sophisticated concept of divinity,
and may on occasion sing of the one true God (Augustine seems
aware, by implication, of the exploitation of Orphic poetry in the
philosophical tradition), they are polytheists at heart (18. 14).

In the time when Deborah was a judge in Israel, the Mycenaean
kingdom displaced Argos, and the Laurentine kingdom was established in Italy, under Picus, son of Saturn: Augustine recalls Virgil's
lines (*Aeneid* 8. 321–5) about this time in Latium. But even Virgil
idealizes and is writing fiction. In reality, Picus' father was Sterces, a
farmer and the inventor of the practice of fertilizing the fields with
dung (18. 15). Troy then falls, while Latinus is king in Latium
(18. 16). The story of the transformation of Diomedes' companions
into birds (18. 16) leads Augustine into a digression on metamor-
phosis, with examples drawn from Varro (Circe's transformation of
Odysseus' companions, werewolves, 18. 17). Augustine recalls

---

[51] Augustine probably prefers this variant to the standard version because it
demythologizes the Europa story by making her captor human. The variant is likely
to be related to the tradition that Europa eventually married Asterius, king of Crete. I
have found no other attestations of a Xanthus in this connection.

travellers' tales of Italian landladies who drugged cheese and changed travellers temporarily into pack-animals (O'Daly 1987: 119–20). He remembers the story of Apuleius' *Metamorphoses*, and is here the first ancient source of its popular name, *Asinus Aureus* (René Martin 1970), and the account by a certain Praestantius of how his father, drugged, had experienced becoming a pack-horse in the Roman army. Augustine also recalls the story of a philosopher appearing in a vision to another to expound problems in Plato after he had earlier refused to do so, and dreaming that he was doing so. To account for these phenomena Augustine posits the existence of a 'phantom' ('phantasticum') which, though not bodily, can take on bodily appearances in other locations. As these bodily appearances are not real, there is, we must suppose, a hallucinatory element in the percipient's experience of such phenomena (18. 18). Augustine was interested in these and similar paranormal phenomena and also wrote about them elsewhere (Dodds 1973: 173–6).

The arrival of Aeneas in Italy is based, in Augustine's account, on reminiscences of Virgil. It is synchronized with the rule of Labdon as judge over the Jews. Aeneas' rule coincides with Samson's. Augustine is no less concerned to identify the human origin of Roman gods than he was to do so in the case of the Greek gods. Thus Aeneas and the Sabine king Sancus were deified (18. 19), as was Picus (18. 15). In the time of David Athens abandoned monarchy for the rule of magistrates (18. 20). As Rome rose, so Assyria declined, and power in the East passed to the Medes (18. 21). The miracle of the she-wolf nurturing the twins Romulus and Remus is ridiculed, and rationalizing explanations of the myth are adduced, yet Augustine (as so often, reluctant to dismiss myth out of hand as fiction) backtracks to concede that the event might have taken place to save the children who were to found so great a city (18. 21). Rome's growth as a power was slow, but it was God's will that it should unite the world into a single community and impose peace upon it (18. 22). At this point, Augustine interrupts the narrative to discuss Sibylline prophecies, and he cites a Latin verse translation of one (*Oracula Sibyllina* 8. 217 ff.), an acrostic in which, in the original Greek, the initial letters of each verse together spell IESOUS CHREISTOS THEOU UIOS SOTER, 'Jesus Christ, the Son of God, the Saviour'. He reminds his readers of the by now traditional Christian associations, literal and symbolic, of the initial letters of these words with the fish ('ichthus') symbol. In various numerological and other ways the poem can be read as a prophecy about Christ. Augustine knows of further such poems, part of one of which (*Oracula Sibyllina* 8. 287 ff.) he cites in a prose translation made from its citation in Lactantius (*Divine Institutions* 4. 18. 15), to whom he refers.[52] Thus he can claim that there were prophecies about Christ in the time of Romulus, or even earlier (18. 23). In Romulus' reign Thales was active: after the theological poets come the sages. Thus a minimal Greek cultural history is being constructed. Romulus is duly deified after death (18. 24). Other sages live during the reign of Tarquinius Superbus, to make up the traditional total of seven.[53] The early Greek philosophers, including Pythagoras, also lived about this time (18. 25). The end of the monarchy in Rome coincided with the end of the Jewish captivity. By this time Persia had become a great power, and Darius ruled (18. 26).

At this stage Augustine breaks off the synchronized narrative, and turns his attention again to Jewish matters, and in particular to prophecy, which will concern him from chapters 27 to 36. This is to complement the survey of Book 17, and keep the promise made in 17. 24. It becomes clear from 18. 37 that a further reason for the renewed emphasis on prophecy here is to stress its antiquity in relation to Greek philosophy: the Jews had their wise men long before the Greeks. Augustine's survey in Book 18 extends his account of prophecy to the later prophets from Hosea to the Maccabees. Once again, it is the significance of their references to Christ and the Church that is highlighted. For that reason, it does not seem necessary in the present context to go into much detail, for Augustine's method is the same as that followed in Book 17, and discussed above. Sometimes he himself feels there is no need of detailed exegesis, as when he quotes extensively from Isaiah (18. 29). Jonah is a prophet by virtue of what he suffered as much as by what he wrote: his experience of being swallowed by the sea-monster and regurgitated on the third day prefigures Christ's resurrection (18. 30). Habakkuk 3: 17 is understood as a prophecy of the consequences for the Jews of the killing of Christ (18. 32). Sometimes the synchronization is reintroduced in these chapters, as in the chapter

---

[52] See further Ch. 11. 2e. Like Lactantius (*Div. Inst.* 4. 15. 26), Augustine (*City* 18. 23) erroneously assumes that these Sibylline oracles are texts from a period of early history, considerably older than Christianity.

[53] Other treatments of the seven sages theme in Latin literature of late antiquity: Ausonius, *Lusus Septem Sapientium*, with Green's commentary; Sidonius Apollinaris, *Carmina* 2. 156–63, 15. 42–50, 23. 101–10.

on Jeremiah (18. 33). The books of the Maccabees are considered to
be canonical by the Church (though not by the Jews) because they tell
of martyrs on behalf of the law of God, who anticipate the suffering
of Christ and the Christian martyrs (18. 36).[54]

In antiquity the authority of a text was often reinforced by
demonstrations of its great age. In 18. 37 Augustine, applying the
chronology which he has given, argues that the Jewish prophetic
writings are older, and so more prestigious, than the activities of
the Greek philosophers. Pythagoras, with whom the term 'philosopher' originated, coincides with the end of the Jewish captivity.
Socrates is dated after Esdras in the *Chronicle*. Only the theological
poets antedate the prophets, but Moses, of whom Augustine holds the
common ancient view that he was the author of Genesis and the other
books at the beginning of the biblical canon, antedates these. Egyptian
wisdom is admittedly very old, and Moses was learned in it (Acts 7:
22), but it cannot have been older than Abraham, who may also be
considered a prophet, for it depends on knowledge of writing, which
the Egyptians only acquired in the time of Abraham's grandsons
(18. 37; cf. 18. 3). In any case, Noah and even Enoch can be
considered prophets (18. 38).

In 18. 38 Augustine considers again the question of canonicity.[55]
There are references to prophetic literature that we do not possess in
both the Old and New Testaments (1 Chronicles 29: 29; 2 Chronicles
9: 29; Jude 14). Augustine assumes that such literature was not found
reliable or worthy enough to be included in the canon. He does not
explain what criteria were used to determine this, apart from mentioning that works which contain statements that contradict the testimony
of the canonical books cannot be genuine. He argues that it is
plausible to accept that even inspired writers sometimes write un-
inspired material (18. 38). He assumes that literacy, and not just
the spoken language, was preserved by Heber: written Hebrew did
not begin with the law transmitted by Moses. This makes Hebrew by
far the oldest literature. But even if we confine ourselves to orally
transmitted wisdom, it is unlikely that the Egyptians got very far in a
pre-literate society. The wisdom of the Egyptians, in any case, has to
do with astronomy and other such anthropocentric sciences. As for
philosophy in Egypt, Hermes Trismegistus (Fowden 1986) was the

---

[54] Cf. *C. Gaud.* 1. 38. On the canonicity of Maccabees in Augustine see
Wermelinger (1984: 179–80).   [55] See nn. 20, 43 above.

grandson of Atlas, and he was a contemporary of Moses (18. 39). The great age claimed for Egyptian astronomical discoveries contradicts the known age of human history, not to mention the testimony of Varro that literacy only came to Egypt about two thousand years ago. We should trust his testimony, for it is consistent with biblical chronology. Divergent and opposing views among secular historians can only serve to drive the Christian into the arms of sacred history (18. 40).

Disagreement among historians prompts Augustine to return to the philosophers from whom recent chapters have been a kind of digression, and to observe their widely divergent opinions on such basic questions as the pursuit of happiness. Traditional contrasts—between Epicureans and Stoics, between the Socratics Aristippus and Antisthenes—are paraded, and a range of differing views on the universe, the soul, and ethics is listed. Cities have accepted, or at least tolerated, this bewildering range of views, and given equal privilege to the true and the false among them. We may understand thereby how apt the name Babylon, 'Confusion', is for earthly cities generally. By contrast, true and false prophets were distinguished among the Jews. There was uniformity of doctrine. The authors of the sacred books may be considered the philosophers, the theologians, the wise men ('sapientes') of the Jews, divinely guided: their writings are 'God's utterance' (18. 41).[56]

In 18. 42 Augustine mentions the conquests of Alexander the Great, but he does not consider his rule to rank with the great empires, because it did not last. The mention of Alexander is a prelude to Augustine's account of the Septuagint translation in one of the Hellenistic kingdoms that grew out of Alexander's conquests, the Ptolemaic kingdom of Egypt. The miraculous translation of the seventy-two translators, working independently and yet producing an identical version, down to word-order, is a guarantee of its inspired nature (18. 42). Augustine knows of other translations of the Hebrew Scriptures into Greek, but he stresses the derivation of Latin versions from the Septuagint, with the recent exception of Jerome. Despite expert praise for Jerome's version and scholarly qualms about the absolute accuracy of the Septuagint, Augustine stresses the superiority of the latter. If there is disagreement between the Septuagint

---

[56] Augustine is here alluding to his belief that 'true religion' is also 'true philosophy': see above, Ch. 6 n. 39.

and other versions, then we must at least concede that there is
'prophetic depth' in the former. The very fact that the Septuagint is
not a slavishly literal translation is a sign that it is inspired: the same
Spirit that spoke through the prophets influences the translator,
conveying identical meanings in different ways. The practice of
biblical critics not to correct the Greek version from the Hebrew,
but to add from the Hebrew a translation of what is missing in the
Greek and mark it in the manuscripts by an asterisk (just as a
horizontal stroke marks passages lacking in the Hebrew but found
in the Septuagint), shows their respect for the Septuagint version.
These marks have been carried over into Latin translations.[57] The
same principle of inspiration is applied to explain these divergences.
The Spirit simply wished to communicate some things in one
medium, some in another: the Septuagint translators are the equal
of the prophets, and some of their words carry a unique message
(18. 43). The discrepancy between the Hebrew and Greek versions of
Jonah 3: 4, where the Hebrew has it that Nineveh will be destroyed in
forty days and the Septuagint says three, is a case in point. Jonah
must have said what stands in the Hebrew text. But the alternative
version points symbolically to the three days of Christ's sojourn in
hell before his resurrection, just as do the three days which Jonah
spent in the whale. The number forty has also a symbolic value: it
refers to the number of days Christ spent with his disciples after the
resurrection and before the ascension. These discrepancies complement one another symbolically, and keep readers on their toes, ever
alert for prophetic depths in the text (18. 44).

[57] Augustine refers to these signs (which were used by Origen in his *Hexapla*) in
Letter 28. 2. 2, written in 394–5 to Jerome, with a plea to the latter to use them in his
Latin translation of the Old Testament (as he apparently already had done in his
amended Latin version of Job, ibid.), to distinguish differences between the Septuagint
and the Hebrew, rather than disregard the Septuagint version in favour of a direct
translation from the Hebrew. Augustine's unqualified acceptance of the Septuagint's
divinely inspired authority in this letter is reiterated in *Doctr. Chr.* 2. 15. 22; cf. *City*
15. 10–14. But, whereas in this *Doctr. Chr.* passage Augustine appears to give the
Septuagint precedence over any Hebrew version, in *City* 18. 43 his position has altered
to acknowledgement of the divine inspiration of the Hebrew text, alongside that of the
Septuagint; moreover, even in *Doctr. Chr.* 4. 7. 15–20 he opts for Jerome's Latin
version of Amos 6: 1–6 in favour of one based on the Septuagint. For Augustine's
evolving attitude to the Septuagint see Wermelinger (1984: 180–4), Bonner (1970).
Augustine's revisions of biblical texts are studied by De Bruyne (1931), and La
Bonnardière (1960–75). For Jerome's critical view of the Septuagint version and
championing of what he called the 'Hebrew verity' ('Hebraica veritas') see Kelly
(1975: 153–67).

In 18. 45 Augustine returns to the narrative broken off at the end of 18. 26. The decline of the Jewish nation comes after the end of the prophetic era, and prophecies of future greatness thereafter, such as Haggai 2: 7 and 2: 9, refer to Christ and the new covenant. Conquest by Alexander and subjugation, following the wars recounted in the books of the Maccabees, by the Ptolemies and later by the Seleucids, lie in store for the Jews. The Maccabean rising restores Jewish rule to Jerusalem (Augustine's details are confused). Some details of the beginnings of Hasmonean rule follow, and Roman involvement in Jewish affairs is sketched, with Pompey's conquest of Judaea marking the definitive end of Jewish independence. Later the Idumean Herod becomes their first foreign-born ruler (18. 45). In these circumstances, inauspicious by secular standards, Christ, the harbinger of the new covenant, is born, during the *pax Augusta* (Augustine merely mentions, but does not stress, this latter point).[58] Punishment of the Jews for their disbelief in, and persecution of, Christ leads to the diaspora, which is also the providential means whereby Christianity is disseminated (18. 46).

Just as the Septuagint translators are prophets, so too there are non-Jewish prophets, whom Christians may cite. For even if there was no people of God other than the Jews, there were individuals who were citizens of the heavenly city. Job, presented by Augustine as neither a native of Israel nor a proselyte ('nec indigena nec proselytus'), is one such example.[59] These individuals (Augustine gives no other examples: he may be thinking of Sibylline oracles) are prophets only as the result of a divine revelation. Their faith is one and the same as that of Christian believers (18. 47). Yet in the Christian Church as it is constituted, there are those who are not true members (18. 48; cf. 18. 54). Many unworthy members are mixed with the good, caught in the Gospel's dragnet, and swimming in this world as in a sea (cf. 18. 23),[60] before

[58] Contrast the synchronization of the reign of Augustus and the birth of Christ in the writings of the 2nd-c. bishop Melito of Sardis (cited in Eusebius, *Ecclesiastical History* 4. 26. 7–8), in Origen, *Contra Celsum* 2. 30, and in Eusebius, *Demonstratio Evangelica* 3. 7. 139. There are more general treatments of the theme in Prudent. *Symmach.* 2. 578–768, and Orosius, *Hist.* 6. 22–7. 1. 1. For further texts in Eusebius and a discussion of the topic see—apart from the classic study of Peterson (1935)—Mommsen (1959: 278–84) and Fowden (1993: 86–90). Cf. Ch. 6 n. 24.

[59] Augustine is alluding to the belief, found in both the Rabbinic and Patristic traditions, that Job was not an Israelite: Baskin (1983: 40–1).

[60] For the symbolism of the sea in Augustine see Rondet (1955), Pontet (1944: 450, 576–7). Augustine's sea travels, and his uses of navigation imagery: Perler and Maier

the separation of the evil from the good. This a consequence of the great increase in the numbers of Christians. To these thoughts Augustine appends a further instalment of his historical survey, summarizing events of Christ's life (apostles, preaching, death and resurrection, post-resurrection period with disciples, ascension), the coming of the Holy Spirit, the spread of the Gospel, persecutions and martyrdom of early Christians (18. 49–50). The end of this process is the Christianization of emperors, who succeed those who persecuted Christians and persecute paganism in their turn (18. 50). Christianity is no less free from dissension than are the secular cities with their philosophical schools: heretics abound. Yet they ultimately bring benefits to the Church, testing both its patience and its wisdom. They also give Christians an opportunity to practise neighbourly love, whether this takes the soft form of persuasive teaching or the hard form of stern discipline. The devil, 'the prince (*princeps*) of the impious city' (18. 51), can do the city of God no lasting harm. Providence uses evil to good ends. But heretics and other dissidents are a source of scandal and dismay to Christians, and discourage others from joining the Church. Distress and anguish are therefore a feature of the Church even in a Christianized empire, 'in this wicked world' (18. 49):

The Church proceeds, a pilgrim,[61] in these evil days, not merely since the time of the bodily presence of Christ and his apostles, but since Abel himself, the first righteous man, whom his impious brother killed, and from then on until the end of time, among the persecutions of the world and the consolations of God. (18. 51)

With this sentence Augustine not merely reiterates his concept of the 'Church since Abel' ('ecclesia ab Abel'; Congar 1986), but spans in ring-composition the historical survey of the two cities that began with Cain and Abel in 15. 1. Nor have persecutions ceased once for all: Augustine repudiates the idea of a fixed number—such as ten—of persecutions. More recent history has shown that figures like Julian and Valens the Arian can acquire power and turn it against the Church, just as there have been persecutions in Persia. There may and may not be more to come, before the final persecution in the time

(1969: 57–81). Sea monster imagery, especially Leviathan, in Jewish apocalyptic and the Book of Revelation: Price (1984: 196–7). On the sea as symbol of the material world in the Neoplatonist and Patristic traditions see O'Daly (1991*b*: 108 n. 8).

[61] The sense of 'peregrinando' in this passage, when taken with 'procurrit' ('proceeds'), seems be 'on pilgrimage' rather than 'as an alien', even if the latter is the dominant sense of 'peregrinari' and related words in *City*. See further Ch. 5 n. 4.

of the Antichrist (18. 52). Augustine resists the temptation to be precise about when this will happen. He does not wish to adopt beliefs (millennialist or other) about the specific duration of the Church in history or Christ's second coming (18. 53). He is particularly scathing about the otherwise unknown oracle, linked to Peter, which apparently predicted that Christianity would survive for no more than 365 years (18. 53–4).[62] Thus the glimpse into the future reaches no clear conclusion. Augustine's forward thinking will concentrate on other goals, as the next books of the work will show.

In Books 15–18 a sense of the course of history is given, but the significance of historical events for Augustine is pre-eminently found in the course of scriptural history. He links the chronology of biblical events to those of the histories of other peoples, and thus, in exploiting the Christian chronographical tradition, conveys a sense of the universal scope of history. But he neither provides, nor intends to provide, a global interpretation, or theoretical account, of history.[63] Moral lessons may be read from the histories of peoples and kingdoms, but they are the same kinds of lesson that can be observed in individual lives and actions. What distinguishes the 'privileged strand' (Markus 1970: 9) of history—the biblical narrative and prophecies culminating in the coming of Christ and the establishment of the Church as an institution—is its inspired nature. Because of divine inspiration the scriptural writers enjoy the understanding and judgement that enable them to convey religious truths, literally and symbolically: they reveal God's 'temporal arrangement' in history, and the order and coherence of significant historical events.[64] In the *City of God* Augustine combines the categories of history and prophecy. The authority of 'prophetic history' (16. 2) consists in the insight which it provides into the meaning of one temporal event, some of whose effects paradoxi-

---

[62] J. J. O'Meara (1959: 67–72) argues that Augustine knows this oracle from Porphyry's *Philosophy from Oracles*: he is followed by Simmons (1995: 282–4), who also finds evidence for the influence of Porphyry's attitude to Peter in Arnobius. For a discussion of the chronology of 18. 54 see App. D.

[63] Augustine's views on history, and the question of whether he has a theory of history, have been much discussed: see in particular Markus (1970) and Schmidt (1985: 64–109), who provides a critique of earlier German-language studies. Of these, Scholz (1911: 137–93) and Kamlah (1951) remain of scholarly value. See also Mommsen (1959: 265–98, 325–48), Cochrane (1940: 456–516), Ladner (1959: 153–238), Lettieri (1988), and Müller (1993), reviewed by Pollmann in *Classical Review*, 27 (1997), 341–2. See further n. 28 above.   [64] Cf. Ch. 12 n. 10.

cally precede it in time: the salvation proffered through Christ's incarnation to those predestined to be saved. Yet Augustine's use of historically based argument is none the less innovatory. He may not have a theory of universal history, but the special historical events of Scripture, prophetically mediated, are bearers of more than merely moral meanings.

Final Destinations: Books 19–22

> God is not a God of confusion but of peace.
>
> (1 Corinthians 14: 33)

> For the trumpet shall sound, and the dead shall be raised incorruptible, and we shall be changed.
>
> (1 Corinthians 15: 52)

With the general aim of discussing the 'ends' ('fines') of the two cities, these books deal with four discrete but related topics. Book 19 is, in part at least, a critique of the teleological views of ancient philosophy and the provision of a Christian teleology. Book 20 deals with the last judgement and the final separation of the two cities. In Books 21 and 22 two consequences of God's final judgement are discussed, the punishment of the damned (21), and the eternal bliss of the saved humans, whose predestined salvation will fill the places of the fallen angels in the heavenly city (22). There is, inevitably, some thematic overlap between the books.[1]

The beginning of Book 19[2] marks a transition from authority to reason: Augustine will proffer a critical survey of philosophical opinions about the nature of human happiness and the 'final good'. The latter is defined as 'that on account of which other things are to be desired, but it is itself to be desired for its own sake'. The 'final evil' ('finis mali') is defined in parallel terms: 'that on account of which other things are to be avoided, but it is itself to be avoided for its own sake'. Augustine explains—for philosophical novices, perhaps—that these 'ends' are not the ceasing-to-be of good and evil, but rather their final, inalterable states. Philosophical systems

---

[1] On the themes and structure of Books 19–22 see Bardy, BA 37. 9–20.

[2] Book 19 is probably the most studied part of *City*. Barrow's edn. (see Bibliog. A) provides a running commentary on most of the book; Fuchs (1926), Laufs (1973), and Budzik (1988) study its concept of peace. See further Baynes (1955: 288–306), Markus (1970), Duchrow (1970: 268–98), Brown (1972: 25–45), O'Donovan (1987), Geerlings (1997).

may be classified by their attempts to define these ends, and to explain how the good may be attained and evil avoided. Augustine adopts an attempted complete classification of philosophies which he found in Varro's *De Philosophia*.[3] Since it is an a priori classification it includes possible as well as real systems.

Varro's classification (which Augustine reports in the lengthy 19. 1) begins by observing that there are four things that people naturally and instinctively seek, without the help of teaching or conscious effort, or without acquiring virtue (which he considers to be something which is learned, not natural). These are:

A1. pleasure
A2. repose;
A3. the combination of these;
A4. the 'first things according to nature' ('prima naturae'), which are both bodily (the integrity and health of the body) and mental (natural innate abilities).

These may be sought in the following ways:

B1. because virtue (acquired by teaching) is desirable for their sake;
B2. because they are desirable for the sake of virtue;
B3. because both they and virtue are desirable for their own sake.

Augustine gives examples (possibly Varronian) of these categories. In B1 physical pleasure would be an end, and virtue would be whatever serves that end. In B2 virtue would be the end (for example, living for one's country and producing sons for it), and pleasure (here sexual) the means. In B3 both virtue and pleasure are (presumably compatible) ends in themselves. Varro then introduces a further pair of variables:

C1. when these ends are pursued for the sake of the individual pursuing them;
C2. when they are pursued for others' sake as well as one's own.

---

[3] On this work and its classificatory scheme see Tarver (1997). See further Ch. 11 n. 10. On the 'prima naturae' referred to in *City* 19. 1 see Cicero, *De Finibus* 5. 6. 16 ff. Cicero's discussion, based, like Varro's, on Antiochus of Ascalon's use of Carneades' method of division, parallels Varro's in several respects; cf. J. Barnes (1989: 86–9), Dillon (1977: 69–72), Tarver (1977: 153–5).

A further differentia is introduced, of an epistemological kind:

D1. these views are defended as certain (as the Stoics defend theirs);

D2. they are defended as uncertain or probable (as the sceptical New Academy does).[4]

The next pair of variables have to do with lifestyle:

E1. one may follow one's philosophical inclinations by adopting the lifestyle of the general run of philosophers;

E2. one may adopt the Cynic lifestyle (cf. 14. 20; 19. 19).[5]

Finally, each philosophical position may be followed

F1. by those who prefer the life of leisure;

F2. by those who prefer the life of activity (especially politics);

F3. by those who opt for a life which combines the two.

Since any of these variables in one category may be combined with any one in the others, Varro arrives at the following total of possibilities:

$$4A \times 3B \times 2C \times 2D \times 2E \times 3F = 288.$$

Augustine then reports Varro's own options. Varro argued that what characterizes a philosophical position is its view about the final good, and that entails its views on the nature of human happiness. Every other question is not a question about a philosophical grouping as such. Thus the alternatives under *C–F* do not raise the question of the definition of the final good (19. 1). So only *A* and *B* remain, yielding a possible twelve groups. But Varro reduces further the number of groups, arguing that the 'primary things according to nature' include both pleasure and repose, and proposing that *A* become a single category, consisting generically in the 'primary things'. Thus the only differentiae that count are those in category *B* (19. 2). In deciding upon his options Varro relies on the threefold enumeration, referred to earlier in the chapter, of the location of the highest good: in the soul, in the body, in both. He argues that although the soul is

---

[4] For a survey of the scepticism of the New Academy and its Pyrrhonist background see Long (1974: 75–106), Sharples (1996: 27–32, 113–15). For Augustine's reception of Academic scepticism through Cicero and his riposte in *C. Acad.* see J. J. O'Meara's annotated tr. of the work and Fuhrer's comm. on Books 2–3; cf. O'Daly (1987: 162–71). Rist (1994: 41–91) gives an excellent account of Augustine's views on knowledge and belief.   [5] On the Cynics see Moles (1996).

the better and more excellent part of humans, the human being is a body-soul entity, and the highest good must relate to this fact. So he opts for $B3$, together with $A4$, as redefined by him. There are degrees of happiness: virtue is a necessary condition of it, but one may be happy without possessing all of the bodily goods, and some of the bodily goods are preferable to others. Having made his choice, Varro then gives his preferences among the non-essential categories $C–F$. He opts for $C2$, $D1$, and $F3$, and remains indifferent about E. This position he considers to be true to the Old Academy from Plato to Polemo, citing the authority of Antiochus of Ascalon, his and Cicero's teacher, for it (19. 3).

Varro's schematic classification and his reaction to it are the framework on which Augustine's counter-view is formed. Thus the identification of a supreme or ultimate good in relation to virtue and the life of society ($A–C$ of Varro's differentiae) is the theme of 19. 4–13, and the questions of the attainability of certainty, the proper lifestyle, and the relative value of the lives of action and contemplation (Varro's differentiae $D–F$) are discussed in 19. 18–19. From the outset Augustine is critical of philosophical teleology, but not of the teleology principle as such, which he accepts. The ultimate good for the Christian is eternal life, the ultimate evil eternal death, and living rightly entails living by faith, by divine grace. Thus two principles of philosophical enquiry are rejected: the principle that the good sought, and thus happiness, is to be found in our temporal, earthly existence, and the belief that happiness, and so virtue, can be found by unaided human effort. Augustine, by contrast, stresses the tensions and difficulties of social life. He is, on his own admission, influenced by Cicero's consolation on the death of his daughter (cf. 19. 8), but adds to the catalogue of life's miseries found there. The 'primary things' can be impaired by accidents, ill-health, deformity, amputations, no matter how wise one is. Sensation can be affected by deafness or blindness, and there are forms of mental illness, where reason is impaired. Demonic influences may assail us. Our very impulses may lead to uncoordinated movements and crazed actions. As for the several virtues, in this life they are continuously engaged in a struggle with the vices. Temperance is in conflict with lust, prudence is always on the alert in the avoidance of error and consent in evil, justice labours uninterruptedly at the task of giving to each its due (and that includes God, the soul, and the body), and fortitude is called for in the perpetual endurance of life's ills. The Stoic notion of the serene sage is a myth: one cannot be in any real sense happy while enduring ills, and happiness seems incompatible with the Stoic acceptance of suicide for the sage. Why seek to escape from a happy life? Cato may have lacked fortitude, rather than possessing it. Augustine prefers the Peripatetic and Platonist (= Old Academic) position that life's ills are evils for the sage, but finds it surprising that these philosophers, like Varro, claim that we can none the less be happy in this life. He also finds it contradictory that Varro (surprisingly, if he claims to be following the Old Academic line) appears to allow 'escape', i.e. suicide, if the severity of these ills grows excessive. In particular, it seems inconsistent with the principle of self-preservation which these philosophers adopt.[6] The very evidence of the 'great force in those evils' argues against the attainability of happiness here and now. It is better, Augustine suggests, to be led by hope of happiness in a future life, and he cites Romans 8: 25: 'But if we hope for what we do not see, we wait for it with patience.' The problem with philosophers is that they do not believe in what they cannot see (19. 4).

Augustine has no difficulty in endorsing the philosophers' view that the sage's life should be social. The life of the saints (with God, it should be assumed) is of its very nature social. But social life is also full of anxieties. Even the closest human relationships are fraught with pain. Terence[7] is quoted to list the disorders that love can bring about, and its mutability:

> Wrongs, suspicions, enmities, war, then peace again.

> (*Eunuchus* 59–61)

Deceitfulness in those we trust is particularly painful. And if there are such tensions in the household, which we think of as a refuge from society, how many more and greater are there in the city, with its litigation, its violence, sedition, civil wars (cf. *Ser.* 32). These events, or the threat of them, are never far away (19. 5). The practice of justice is full of risks. It can involve torture of innocent witnesses,

---

[6] By the phrase 'that a person should be attached to himself' ('ut homo concilietur sibi', p. 361. 8 Dombart and Kalb) in 19. 4 Augustine signals that he is referring to the Stoic concept of self-preservation or 'oikeiosis', on which see Pembroke (1971), Sorabji (1993: 122–3). Cicero translates the term by 'sibi conciliari' (*De Finibus* 3. 5. 16) and 'conciliatio' (ibid. 3. 6. 21); the concept is elucidated ibid. 5. 9. 24.–11. 33. For the concept in Augustine see O'Donovan (1980: 48–56); O'Daly (1987: 103). Cf. *City* 11. 27 on the natural 'will to exist' in all animals.   [7] See further Ch. 11. 1a.

persecution of those wrongly accused, miscarriages of justice. Will the wise man dare to become a judge in these circumstances? He will, Augustine avers, and out of a sense of duty to society. He acts out of this sense of duty, but in relative ignorance: mistakes are part and parcel of his task, part of the human condition. We should not expect him to be a happy judge (19. 6).

There is a system in Augustine's survey of human ills. The sequence which he follows is individual–household–city (or state)–world–angelic society. In 19. 7 he reaches the world. Lacking either the talent or the opportunity to learn foreign languages, he finds diversity of languages a major disadvantage, separating humans from one another: 'a man would more readily have his dog for company than a foreigner'. He finds it a great benefit of Roman imperial rule that it has imposed Latin as an international language, but he admits the high costs in war and violence that led to empire. We sense that, for Augustine, 'the world' ('orbis terrae') is, first, the Roman empire and, second, the rest of the world cut off from Roman rule. For among the world's evils he reckons civil wars, and, if he is not thinking in purely historical terms, he must mean wars between emperors and usurpers in recent Roman history. Wars may be just, a necessity imposed by the injustice of others: but they are none the less terrible (19. 7).[8] Friendship may seem to be an antidote to life's miseries.[9] But we feel anxiety for our friends, especially when they are separated from us. We fear that friendship may end, or be distorted into hatred. We grieve at the death of friends, and need consolation, no matter how much moral progress we have made. Among the thoughts which console us is, that a dead friend has escaped life's evils (19. 8). Angels would be more reliable friends, but we do not have the opportunity to associate with them in this life, and demons often masquerade as angels, to tempt us: we may think we have made friends with an angel, but our friend may be the devil himself (19. 9). It will be different in the heavenly city. There nature's gifts will be inalienable and beneficial, to be enjoyed in the resurrected body, the virtues will be stabilized in an eternal peace. Compared with the ultimate bliss, happiness here on earth is utter misery. Here virtue consists in the right use of good and

---

[8] For modern studies of Augustine's views on the just war see Ch. 6 n. 6.

[9] For Augustine's discussions of friendship see MacNamara (1964); E. A. Clark (1986b), on the fatal friendship of Adam and Eve; Lienhart (1990), who emphasizes Augustine's divergence from the philosophical tradition of friendship. On friendship in antiquity (to the 4th c. AD) see Konstan (1997).

evil things; there virtue refers both what it uses and itself to its proper
end of perfect, stable peace (19. 10).

   The word 'peace' ('pax') has occurred a number of times, especially
in 19. 10. Augustine now goes on to posit peace as the final good for
the Christian, inasmuch as it is the condition, in its perfect form, of
eternal life.[10] The name Jerusalem means, according to the interpretation favoured by Augustine, 'vision of peace' (in Midrashic interpretation it was understood to mean 'foundation of peace'). The
image of the heavenly city, therefore, is an image of peace: 'the highest
good . . . whether peace in eternal life, or eternal life in peace' (19.
11). Peace is a universal desire. Wars are waged as a means of arriving
at the end of peace. Seditious allies and conspirators maintain a kind
of peace among themselves in order to achieve their ends by violence.
Robbers keep peace with their comrades, the better to attack the peace
of others. The man of violence seeks to be at peace with his family and
household, even achieving it by cruel and vicious means, if necessary. If
he were offered political power on the terms which he has imposed on
his household, he would accept it, and let his vices be seen in public
(19. 12). Having given this example, Augustine goes on to give an even
more extreme one, a test-case, in fact. He alludes to the monstrous
figure of Cacus in *Aeneid* 8. 190–305. Cacus' name is derived from
the Greek 'kakos' ('bad'), and he is a solitary cave-dweller. Yet in his
cave he craves, as does any being, peace, a calm state untroubled by
violence. Even his savage eating habits are a means to the end of
satisfying, and so pacifying, his appetites. Perhaps Cacus is a fiction,
but he is still an object-lesson in how peace can be identified in the
most unpromising situation. The life of wild creatures (tigers, kites)
exhibits an instinct to preserve their species: Augustine calls this
'peace' as well. Even the human rebellion called pride (routinely
defined by Augustine as 'perverse imitation of God') is the attempt
to impose an unjust peace, infringing the universal hierarchy.[11] A

---

   [10] Augustine's primary motive in choosing 'peace' as the final good is to define a
characteristically Christian good that can both keep company with, and differ from,
pagan teleologies. On his teleological speculation in general see Holte (1962). In *City*,
apart from his use of the symbolism of the name 'Jerusalem', he exploits Christian use
of 'peace' language (see further n. 12 below); and he is likely to have had in mind
Christian modes of greeting, especially the eucharistic liturgical 'kiss of peace'
(*ODCC*[3] s.v.). He may, in addition, be influenced by the iconographical tradition of
personifications and symbols of peace in Roman coinage and monuments, especially of
the Imperial period: on this see Simon (1988: 19–30).
   [11] For discussions of Augustine's concept of pride see Ch. 8 n. 43.

human body hung head downwards is not physically at peace, but in it the soul is at peace with the body, and even the gravitational pull of the body is a tendency towards its proper place of rest in the elemental order. An embalmed body preserves its peace through artificial means. The corruption of the body after death, though repulsive, is a form of coalescence with the elements: the body 'vanishes into their peace'. This happens even when a corpse is devoured by other animals. The creatures which are born spontaneously (Augustine expresses the common ancient view) from a decaying body are seekers after a natural peace, as all creatures are. Augustine finds 'peacemaking laws' in all nature (19. 12).[12]

Having traced this presence of peace in nature, Augustine next provides a classified and hierarchical series (but not listed in strict hierarchical order) of definitions of kinds of peace, ranging from the peace of the body, through the irrational and rational soul, the body-soul conjoint, peace between humans and God and among humans themselves, domestic peace, the peace of the city of God, the peace of all things as a 'tranquillity of order' ('tranquillitas ordinis').[13] It is not coincidental that the series emphasizes the notion of order, which appears in every definition. The concepts of peace and order are complementary.[14] Augustine ends the series with a definition of order itself: 'order is the disposition of things equal and unequal, assigning to each its proper place' (19. 13). This order does not exclude those who are wretched, for, inasmuch as their wretchedness is deserved, they are included in a kind of punitive order. And because they are natural beings, there is in them the order proper to a natural being: if

[12] Augustine's reference to 'leges . . . pacificantes' in 19. 12 (p. 376. 20–1 Dombart and Kalb) echoes the language of the Sermon on the Mount ('blessed are the peace-makers', Matt. 5: 9; 'beati pacifices' in Augustine's version in *Ser. Dom. Mont.* 1. 3. 10, where the Beatitudes are related to a hierarchical series of stages of spiritual progress, the 'peacemakers' representing wisdom, which is contemplation of truth, in which human likeness to God is realized).

[13] See Geerlings (1997: 228–31, here 229), with emphasis on the substantives that characterize each definition.

[14] See Rief (1962) on *Ord.* and other early discussions of order in Augustine; cf. Evans (1982: 91–8). Burnaby (1938: 111–37) discusses the 'order of love' ('ordo amoris') in Augustine; cf. O'Donovan (1980: 13–16), a study which throughout incisively clarifies the relation between love and order in Augustine. See also Holte (1962: 193–300). Brown (1972: 30–45) brings out brilliantly the importance of order in Augustine's political thinking, esp. in *City*: cf. Markus (1970: 66–104). The Neoplatonist elements in Augustine's views on peace and order are discussed by Theiler (1966: 225–30). On the related concepts of hierarchy and order see O'Daly (1989*b* and 1991*a*).

they are in pain, they are alive, and if they are alive there is some
undisturbed core in their being. The concepts of order and good are
also related. There cannot be a nature in which there is no good. Even
the devil's nature is not evil. When we feel pain, that is evidence of
diminution of good, but also of good that is left: 'for he who grieves
at the lost peace of his nature, grieves as a consequence of some
remains of that peace, through which his nature is still friendly with
itself'. The urge to self-preservation and social fellowship is an urge
to maintain or recover temporal peace: using ('uti') the temporal
peace properly is, or should be, a means for humans to eternal
enjoyment ('frui') of the heavenly city (19. 13).[15]

In humans body and soul have their distinct stable states, their
'peace', and they also have a mutual peace. Because humans are
rational, there should be subordination of both the irrational soul
and the body to the mind, and knowledge and action should be in
harmony. But the attainment of knowledge in our human condition is
uncertain and partial, so that faith and divine grace are needed.
Augustine therefore adds to the requirements for human temporal
peace 'ordered obedience in faith, subject to the eternal law'. The
social dimension is essential. The divine commandment includes love
of one's neighbour. This applies even when an individual is in a
position of authority. When authority is exercised, not through desire
to rule, but as a service of those ruled, the demands of rule and peace
can be reconciled (19. 14).[16] Rule and authority over other humans
are consequences of original sin. Slavery is an extreme instance of
those consequences. Slavery is only natural inasmuch as it is a feature
of our sinful, fallen condition. It is, therefore, a form of punishment,
and so should be preserved as part of the order of nature, constituted
in the conditions of society as it now is (19. 15).[17] But rule over
slaves should be exercised with a view to the welfare of all the
members of the household: this ethos Augustine finds enshrined in

[15] On 'use' and 'enjoyment' see Ch. 7 n. 20.
[16] On the origins of political authority in 19. 14–15 see Markus (1970: 197–210).
Augustine's views on authority are not just about principles: he was involved with men
of power, such as Marcellinus, Macedonius (for these see Ch. 2 above), and Boniface,
military commander (*comes*) of Africa (for Augustine's correspondence on political
matters with Boniface see *Letters* 189 and 220).
[17] Corcoran (1985) discusses Augustine's attitude to slavery; cf. Deane (1963: 113–
15). Among the recently discovered letters of Augustine, *Letter* 10* throws remarkable
light on the contemporary slave trade in North Africa: see the notes and bibliog. in BA
46B. 466–79; see also *Letter* 24* and cf. Chadwick (1983: 432–4).

the term 'paterfamilias' for the head of the household. Punishment should be just and restrained, but leniency is no service to the offender.[18] Domestic peace contributes to the peace of the city, and the same laws and rules should govern both, for both are concerned with agreement in the giving and obeying of orders (19. 16).

Augustine stresses the similarities between households that live by Christian faith and others, in so far as temporal goals and practices are concerned. Both use the same means, but for different ends. Christians use the earthly peace: what holds for the household holds for larger groupings as well. The 'alien' part of the heavenly city, which is in captivity (note the 'Babylonian' imagery),[19] does not hesitate to obey the laws of the heavenly city which apply to civic life. Laws of religion[20] are, of course, the exception, and it was Christian dissent in religious matters which led to persecution in the past, until the sheer mass of numbers of Christians led to change. It is interesting that Augustine does not see the conversion of Constantine as a watershed, considering the Roman state to remain even after that event what it always was, but forced by the pressure of Christian success to acknowledge that there are separate religious laws for Christians. In social terms, Christians are essentially conservative, preserving and following the laws and institutions, using the earthly peace to serve heavenly peace (19. 17).

In chapter 18 Augustine returns to Varro's differentiae, and specifically to D. He upholds the attainability of epistemic certainty against the New Academy (the position he had defended in his first extant work, the *Contra Academicos*).[21] At the same time he stresses how little we can know for certain, and the reason he gives sounds quite Neoplatonic: the corruptible body weighs down the spirit. But the Christian can also have beliefs which are not to be doubted, and so are tantamount to knowledge, such as the evidence of the senses and the content of the Scriptures (19. 18).

[18] This argument contains the germ of Augustine's justification of religious coercion, as practised against the Donatist schismatics after the Conference of Carthage in 411: see Willis (1950: 127–43), Frend (1952: 227–99), Brown (1967: 233–43, 330–9; 1972: 260–78), Deane (1963: 172–220).

[19] See further Ch. 4 above. On 'peregrinari' and 'peregrinatio' denoting 'of alien status' (rather than 'pilgrim(age)') here and often in *City* see Ch. 5 n. 4.

[20] By 'laws of religion' in 19. 17 Augustine means the principles of Christian faith and morals: see *Exp. Prop. Rom.* 72; *Mor.* 1. 24. 44–30. 63; *Ser.* 62. 13, 326. 2; *Letters* 105. 7, 185. 8; Combès (1927: 154–6, 306–24), to whom I owe these references.

[21] See further n. 4 above.

Chapter 19 turns to *E* and *F* of Varro's differentiae. Dress and lifestyle do not matter, provided divine instructions (presumably about modesty) are not infringed. Philosophers who become Christians can dress and eat as they did before conversion. As for the kind of life to be led, Augustine, like Varro, favours a mixture of the active and the contemplative, leisurely lives. Activity should not preclude contemplation of the divine; inactivity should not mean lack of concern for, and involvement in, society, nor should it mean a reluctance to investigate and discover the truth. The active life is a contribution to those over whom one has authority. Augustine thinks, quite naturally, of the bishop's role. Whereas it is love of truth that drives contemplation, 'compulsion of love' ('necessitas amoris') leads to the active life: but we should not let ourselves be crushed by compulsion through neglect of the contemplative life (19. 19).

In chapter 20 Augustine returns to the question of the attainability of happiness in this life. We can speak of happiness here and now, although that happiness includes an element of hope in the perfect happiness to come. Otherwise it is not happiness at all, for it is not directed towards the proper end, God's eternal peace (19. 20).[22]

With chapter 20 the complex of themes which has been exercising Augustine since the beginning of the book comes to an end. But, since he has been discussing political themes, he can now appropriately turn to something promised as early as 2. 21, the discussion of Cicero's definition of 'res publica' ('state') in the work *De Re Publica* (*Republic*).[23] The 'res publica' is a 'res populi', and a 'populus', in Cicero's definition, is 'an association of a large number brought together by a common sense of what is right and by shared utility' (*Rep.* 1. 25. 39).[24] In this definition 'common sense of what is right' ('iuris consensus') entails justice, and without justice there cannot be a people in the sense of the term in the definition. More precisely, no justice means no 'common sense of what is right', hence no 'populus', hence no 'res populi', and so no 'res publica'. The state is built on the foundations of justice. At this juncture, Augustine breaks off his report. If, he argues, justice is assigning to each his due, there is no justice in taking a person away from the true God and leaving him at

---

[22] Augustine on happiness: see Holte (1962), Beierwaltes (1981), O'Daly (1987: 5, 163–4, 181–4), Rist (1994: 48–53).

[23] Cf. Ch. 6 above, on 2. 20–1, with nn. 16–17. O'Donovan (1987) analyses Augustine's critique perceptively. For Augustine's use of Cicero in *City* see Ch. 11. 1c.

[24] 'Populus' in Augustine: Adams (1971: 123–35).

the mercy of demons, whether that person is oneself or another. The implication of this argument is that there can be no justice in a state where the true God is not properly worshipped. Augustine then returns to Cicero's *Republic*. There, Scipio's claim that the best regime cannot endure 'without the strictest justice' (*Rep.* 2. 70; cf. *City* 2. 21) is countered by another participant in the dialogue, Philus, who puts the Academic sceptical viewpoint that states cannot function without some injustice, giving the example of imperial rule (19. 21). Laelius replies to this argument with a defence of Roman imperialism as something in the best interests of provincials. The defence uses what Augustine calls the 'striking example' ('nobile exemplum') drawn from nature, that God rules the soul and the soul the body, with reason ruling desires. By this analogy it is argued that servitude is beneficial to some people. In Cicero this analogy was used in connection with the Stoic natural-law theory. Augustine's use of it is different, and he seems to be primarily interested in the implications for justice of serving God properly, that is to say, in the distinction between what should constitute justice for a Christian, and the realities of the Roman state when it worshipped false gods (19. 21). His argument is intended to reinforce Scipio's argument in Cicero about the necessary conditions of justice, by adding the specifically Christian dimension.

At the end of chapter 23 Augustine returns to Scipio's definition of the state, reiterating what he has said earlier. In chapter 24 he puts forward an alternative definition: 'A people is an association of a large number of rational beings brought together by a common agreement about what they love.' This is a value-free definition, or rather, it is one which depends on the objects 'loved' by a community, its perceived interests and goals, which define it as a better or worse community, but do not deprive it of its communal nature. It has been called positivistic.[25] By this definition, the Roman state is indubitably a state, and so are the other historical states of which Augustine spoke in earlier books, especially Book 18 (19. 24).

There can be doubt who the true God is, the one to be worshipped.

[25] By Markus (1970: 65): see his discussion, ibid. 64–71. On Augustine's analysis of the state see also Deane (1963: 116–53). The tendency of Markus (1970) in particular to see in Augustine's concept of the state, however limited its autonomy, the beginnings of the modern theory of a secular, pluralist society is criticized with theoretical acumen by O'Donovan (1987) and Höffe (1997); cf. Duchrow (1970: 289–90).

That there is one true God was intimated by thinkers such as Varro and Porphyry, who spoke of a supreme deity (19. 22). Augustine quotes oracles from Porphyry's work *Philosophy from Oracles* concerning Christ.[26] In one, an oracle of Apollo, Christ is said to have been justly condemned by the Jews, and Porphyry comments that the Jews have a sounder concept of God than the Christians, praising Jewish monotheism, or at least the idea of a supreme deity. In another oracle, of Hecate, Christ is said to have been a man pre-eminent in piety, who shares the posthumous fate of good men, even though he was the occasion of deadly error in his devotees. Specifically, Porphyry argues that Christians are cut off from knowledge of God and from receiving the 'gifts of the gods'. Augustine alleges an agenda behind these oracles. They praise Christ, in order to gain credence for their vituperation of Christianity, which is seen by them as an invention of Christ's disciples. In fact, they are propounding a heretical view of Christ, Photinianism,[27] considering him to be merely human. Christ, according to Porphyry's interpretation, forbade his followers to worship lesser earthly spirits and the demons who control them, but encouraged them to worship the heavenly gods, especially the father god. But in their impiety and because of fate they have rejected the higher gods and worship the very demons against whom they have been warned. What all we humans—so Porphyry—should be doing is worshipping the father god by means of being virtuous, purifying ourselves by seeking to know him, and imitating him and so deifying ourselves. Augustine professes to be shocked at such a travesty of Christian worship. The Hebrew Scriptures are full of the very injunctions to worship the one true God that Porphyry commends, and they forbid what he condemns. Augustine reminds us that the members of the city of God are God's best sacrifice, and that self-offering is the purpose of Christian liturgy. The prophets delivered the true oracles (Augustine uses the term deliberately, in view of the Porphyrian context). Justice is only found where God rules an obedient city though grace, where the souls of individuals rule their bodies and reason rules vice (cf. 19. 21) in a system of law, where there is faith, but also love, of both one's neighbour and God. Where these conditions are met, Scipio's definition is realized (19. 23). The subordina-

---

[26] See J. J. O'Meara (1959), Wilken (1984: 148–56), Simmons (1995: 222–42, 295–8). Cf. Ch. 11. 2b.

[27] For Photinus' beliefs see O'Donnell on *Conf.* 7. 19. 25. Kelly (1977: 223–51) provides the doctrinal context of this and related controversies.

tion of everything else to God is a necessary condition of the realization of virtue: control of the body and its desires is not sufficient. Augustine argues against the self-sufficiency of virtue (19. 25). The peace which the earthly city enjoys is, in the end, a 'Babylonian peace' ('pax Babylonis'), but the members of the city of God profit from it as long as the two cities are intermingled in history (19. 26). In our human earthly condition perfection of the virtues is, after all, impossible to achieve: Augustine reminds us of the struggles and tensions inherent in all human existence, which he conjured up in 19. 4. Perfect as we may seem, there are still faults in us. Justice can only be maintained in this life by means of divine authority and human obedience, by the rule of soul over body, and of reason over the vices. Only in the heavenly state, where there will be no vices, will reason be freed of the obligation to rule them: God will simply rule humans, and souls (who will accept divine rule with delight and ease) will spontaneously rule bodies (19. 27). The wicked, on the other hand, will die the 'second death',[28] and their state, the contrary of peace, will be a kind of war, and will exhibit war's opposition and conflict. In this conflict will and passion, body and pain, are perpetually opposed (19. 28). But this is the subject of a future book, and here, with a reference to the theme of the next book—the final judgement—Augustine ends Book 19.

Book 19 is perhaps the most studied of all books of the *City of God*.[29] It is regularly included in discussions of the history of political theory. It comes as near as any work of Augustine's to propounding his political views. But it is important to realize what it does not do. It is not a discussion of the relations between church and state: rather, it gives an account of how Christians may, and why they must, be good citizens of the empire, by defining the limited but significant area where the aims and interests of the two cities, in their historical form, coincide. The book discusses definitions of the state and accounts of justice, but no details of constitutional practice or

---

[28] The term 'second death' originates in Rev. 2: 11, 20: 6, and 21: 8. Plumpe (1951) sketches its early Christian exegesis in e.g. Hippolytus (?), *De Antichristo* 65; Tertullian, *De Fuga in Persecutione* 7; Lactant., *Div. Inst.* 2. 12. 7–9, 7. 10. 9–11, 7. 26. 6; cf. Prudent., *Cathemerinon* 6. 92. See also Pelagius on Rom. 6: 9 and 6: 22 with De Bruyn ad loc. Influential pre-Christian exegesis: Philo, *Legum Allegoriae* 1. 105. Christian interpretations of the 'second death' usually understood it (as Augustine does) to refer to the eternal punishment of the damned. See further below on 20. 7.
[29] See n. 2 above. A typical discussion in a modern historical survey of political theory is Haddock (1988).

theory: it accepts implicitly the Roman imperial *status quo*. The ideal
of 'concordia' is praised (19. 13), and is an important formative
element in Augustine's elaboration of his concepts of peace and order.
But Augustine offers no programme for the Christianization of
Roman political institutions, and implies that, religious laws apart,
the pre-Christian and the Christianized empire is the same kind of
society. However, no state is an autonomous mechanism. States are
judged by their approximation to, or deviation from, the ideal
embodied in the concept of the city of God. And no state, no matter
how perfect, can exemplify the ideal, for that is eschatological and
other-worldly. All historical states exhibit violence and tensions, their
justice carries a necessary punitive element, and they cannot realize
peace perfectly.

Book 20 deals with the last judgement and final separation of the two
cities.[30] In it Augustine is chiefly concerned to demonstrate that this
judgement of God will take place, and to show of what kind it is, on
the basis of scriptural testimonies from both the Old and New
Testaments. There is in consequence only a brief discussion (confined
to the opening chapters) of the concept of divine judgement as such:
Augustine relies on 'the evidence of Scripture' ('testimonia divina'), in
his assumption that it will happen, or rather that it happens
continually in human history, starting with the expulsion of Adam
and Eve from paradise. Before that event, God judged the angels who
rebelled. Moreover, present punishments—of demons, for example—
are instances of divine judgement (20. 1). It is often difficult to
discern traces of divine judgement in people's lives, especially when
the good suffer and evil-doers prosper. There appears to be no
consistency in God's behaviour: but this is because of our inability
to have more than a partial understanding of his purpose. At the final
judgement this purpose will become evident (20. 2). The evils of this
life are common to good and bad alike: that is the import of
Ecclesiasticus (the common attribution of which to Solomon is
accepted by Augustine[31]), with its talk of the 'vanity' of human
affairs. What is important is to accept, and not resist, the truth,
and to participate in the true religion (20. 3).

In chapter 4 Augustine proceeds to the scriptural evidence

[30] For a survey of early Christian eschatological beliefs see Kelly (1977: 459–89).
[31] Cf. Ch. 9 above on 17. 20 with n. 43.

concerning the final judgement. He deals first with the New Testament material (20. 5–20), then with the evidence in the Old Testament (20. 21–30). The reason which he gives for this order prefers value ('merita') to chronology ('tempora'). The Old Testament heralds what the New Testament reveals: in particular, the New Testament reveals God's justice, to which the law and prophets of the Old Testament bear witness (Romans 3: 20–2 provides the wording of this argument). The legal vocabulary (justice, law) suggests to Augustine Roman legal procedure, in which the case must first be presented, and then the witnesses called: 'things new and old' (Matthew 13: 52), in that order (20.4). Augustine's case is made by citing several passages reporting Christ's words—chiefly from Matthew (chapters 11–13, 19, 25) but also from John 5—which refer to a day of judgement. These passages are to be distinguished from others which are ambiguous, and which may refer to the destruction of the city of Jerusalem, or Christ's continued presence in his Church. Such passages must be verified by reference to related ones in the other Gospels: Augustine directs the reader towards his treatment of the topic in his *Letter* 199 (20. 5). Some passages refer to what Augustine calls the first resurrection, namely the soul's liberation, through baptism, from the death-like state of sin: Augustine finds this referred to in John 5: 22–6 and 2 Corinthians 5: 14–15. The final judgement will be the second one, and will lead, for some, to the second death of eternal damnation (20. 6). A further potent text is Revelation, especially chapter 20. Augustine uses the distinction between the first and second resurrections (Revelation 20: 14 speaks of a 'second death') to counter millennialist interpretations.[32] Thus references to Christ's thousand-year reign with his saints and to a first resurrection (Revelation 20: 4–6) do not allude to a bodily resurrection and a specific period of time. Augustine has in mind a seventh, sabbatical, age after the 6,000 years since the creation, but he rejects this notion. He proposes two alternative explanations. One is, that the 'thousand years' refers to the present, sixth, millennium (or at least that part of it remaining when Revelation was written), to be followed by an

---

[32] The early Christian belief in Christ's return (or second coming) and earthly thousand-year reign ('chiliasm' or 'millennialism') was subject to criticism as early as Clement of Rome (late 1st c.), as Hill (1992) shows. Origen was perhaps the most influential non-millennialist: for his views, esp. his exegesis of Rev. 20, see Hill (1992: 127–41). In *Ser.* 259. 2 (*c.*393) Augustine seems to express the millennialist view to which he later, esp. in *City*, objects; cf. Markus (1970: 19–20).

eternal Sabbath. The other explanation is that the number 'thousand' is used, as 'hundred' sometimes is, to refer to a totality, here the total time remaining of the existence of the world (20. 7). The full significance of these explanations only becomes apparent when Augustine develops his discussion of the rest of the Revelation passage. In the remainder of 20. 7 he demonstrates that what Revelation says about the devil is consistent with the two senses of 'thousand years' that he would admit. The binding of the devil symbolizes the belief that, although the devil may tempt, he cannot undermine the Church. His release, referred to in Revelation 20: 3, does not entail that he can then do serious damage, but is rather intended by God to demonstrate the power of the defeated enemy. The period of the release, forty-two months (Revelation 11: 2, 13: 5), is understood in a literal sense by Augustine, but he does not propose that there will be any great difference in the pattern of those falling away from, or joining, the Church in that period (20. 8).

The two explanations favoured by Augustine of the thousand-year reign relate it firmly to this life, from the first coming of Christ onwards. It is thus coterminous with the existence of the Church on earth. The Church can also be called the kingdom of God, and both Church and kingdom can be understood in two senses, the mixed society of just and unjust as it is now found, and the eschatological state of the Church, purified of evil.[33] But even now the saints reign with God, for even now the Church is the kingdom of heaven. The present state of the Church is that of a kingdom at war, with evil and with its enemies; but the final state of the kingdom of God will be one of peace. Thus references to judgement in Revelation (e.g. 20: 4) are not to the final judgement, but to the historical administration of the Church. This present state of the Church includes the souls of the pious dead, who already reign with God (though not in a bodily condition): that is why they are commemorated in the eucharist liturgy.[34] Revelation 20: 4 refers to martyrs now in heaven, but they are singled out, not because they are an exclusive group, but because they typify pre-eminently the pious dead (20. 9).[35] Augustine smooths over any apparent inconsistency between the thousand-year reign and

[33] For Augustine's parallel terminology of cities, kingdoms, and Church see esp. Cranz (1950).   [34] Cf. 12. 9, *Ser.* 280. 5: see Lamirande (1992–4: 967).
[35] Augustine here reflects the tradition of non-millennialist exegesis of Rev. 20: 4 which, as Hill (1992: 111 ff.) demonstrates, is already found in Hippolytus and Clement of Alexandria.

the three years and six months in which the devil is loosed. It is intolerable that the saints should not reign with God during this latter period. So one must accept that the length of their reign is expressed in approximate language, which includes the period of the devil's release (20. 13).

The first resurrection to which Revelation refers is thus understood by Augustine to be a spiritual one. He must therefore confront those who argue that resurrection can only be bodily. He does so by citing scriptural texts which refer to spiritual resurrection: Colossians 3: 1–2, Romans 6: 4, Ephesians 5: 14. There is also metaphorical talk of souls 'falling': it is not merely bodies who fall and are resurrected (20. 10). Revelation 20: 7–8 alludes to the last persecution of the faithful, which will be universal. Gog and Magog are not some barbarian invaders, alien to Rome, active in a single spot. The 'camp of the saints and the beloved city' (Revelation 20: 9) will be under siege everywhere (*City* 20. 11). The fire which descends from heaven and devours the enemy (Revelation 20: 9) is to be understood symbolically, with reference not to the last judgement, but to the steadfastness of the saints, whose burning zeal prevails. Or it may possibly refer to Christ's defeat of Antichrist (*City* 20. 12).

It is only in the later verses of Revelation 20 that there is talk of the last judgement, which is also the second resurrection, following upon the second death of Revelation 20: 14. The new heaven and earth of Revelation 21: 1 allude to the fact that there will be transformation, rather than annihilation, of the universe. The book of every man's life (Revelation 20: 12) is not to be understood in material terms, but rather to symbolize the divinely realized review, at miraculous mental speed, by each individual of all his or her actions, in a simultaneous judgement of all persons. In this way, we become our own judges, accusing or excusing ourselves. Revelation 20: 13 is an instance of 'recapitulation' (cf. 16. 5, 15), referring to a time before the judgement (20. 14).[36] The dead in the sea of that verse are to be understood in terms of the sea symbolizing this age ('saeculum'), and so the dead are those still living in mortal bodies (20. 15).[37] The reference to the sea being no more in Revelation 21: 1 is again to the metaphorical sea of life: 'for from that time the turbulence and stormy weather of life in this age will cease to exist; and he [the author of

---

[36] On recapitulation see Ch. 9 n. 26.
[37] For sea symbolism in Augustine see further Ch. 9 n. 60.

Revelation] used the sea as an allegory of that' (20. 16). The book of
life (Revelation 20: 15) signifies the predestined and God's foreknowledge of their identity: what is written in this symbolic book is known
beforehand (*City* 20. 15). The renewal of heaven and earth has its
counterpart in the purgation of our corruptible bodily elements and
renewal of our bodies (20. 16). This is the true sense of the new
Jerusalem. A verse like Revelation 21: 4 ('. . . death shall be no more
. . . neither shall there be pain any more') makes a historical
thousand-year reign of the new Jerusalem implausible: Augustine
argues that the state of deathlessness and painlessness evoked there
can refer only to a final, heavenly condition. The book of Revelation
is an obscure work: often it refers to the same phenomena in different
terms. Yet there are also times when its meaning is unambiguous
(20. 17).

Augustine now turns to other New Testament texts about the final
judgement. One is 2 Peter 3: 3–13. This is primarily about the
destruction of the universe. Augustine points out that the range of
the destruction is effectively described by the reference to the Flood as
a kind of historical parallel. But if the destruction is so vast, what
about the saints? They must occupy some bodily place even then.
They will be in the higher regions where the flames cannot reach
them. But presumably their bodies will be immune to fire, like those
of the three men in the burning furnace to which Daniel 3: 13–27
refers (20. 18). A further text is 2 Thessalonians 2: 1–12. Augustine
reads here a reference to the Antichrist (cf. 1 John 2: 18), though the
reference to him sitting in the temple of God (2 Thessalonians 2: 4)
may allude to all who follow him. The obscurity of 2 Thessalonians
2: 6–7 creates difficulties. Augustine's text reads:

et nunc quid detineat scitis ut reveletur in suo tempore. iam enim mysterium
iniquitatis operatur. tantum qui modo tenet teneat, donec de medio fiat.

And now you know what restrains him, that he may be revealed at the right
moment. For the secret power of evil is already at work. Only let him who
now restrains restrain him, until he is taken away from the scene.

Who or what 'restrains' ('tenere', 'detinere')? And who is being
restrained? Augustine dismisses the view that the Roman empire is
referred to here in carefully chosen language ('secret power of evil'),
and that Nero in particular is the Antichrist (cf. *ODCC*[3] s.v.
'Number of the Beast'; Jenks 1991), still living in concealment, to
be revealed in due time. On the other hand, the intransitive reference

to 'restrains' in 'qui modo tenet', may plausibly refer to the Roman empire, with 'restrains' used in the sense of 'reigns'. With the end of the empire, the Antichrist comes. Or the words may refer to evil forces within the Church, and the verbs 'tenere' and 'detinere' may be used in the sense of the faithful 'holding on' or persevering, until 'it' (the power of evil) is removed from the scene. In fact, the text cannot bear the sense of 'holding faith', but must allude to restraining evil. Augustine does not, however, opt for a meaning here, stressing that the crucial feature of the passage is its insistence on the antecedent role of the Antichrist in the final judgement, and that the delusive power of the Antichrist is part of God's secret purpose in his judgement of the wicked (20. 19). The final New Testament passage that Augustine cites is 1 Thessalonians 4: 13–17. He resists the tendency to read this passage as an assertion that those alive at the final judgement will not die at all. Their death and immortalization can be instantaneous, and other Pauline texts seem to insist on the universality of death, a view with which Augustine concurs (20. 20).

In chapter 21 Augustine turns to the evidence in the Old Testament for a resurrection and last judgement. Some passages in Isaiah (26: 19, 66: 12–16, 65: 17–19) are adduced. These typically combine figurative and literal expressions: Augustine argues that the 'Jerusalem' to which Isaiah refers is the spiritual city. The divine vengeance and violence of which these texts speak are symbols of punitive judgement (20. 21). There is a more distinctive prophetic vision in Daniel 7. Augustine is familiar with the interpretation of the four beasts and kingdoms that makes these symbolize the kingdoms of the Assyrians, Persians, Macedonians, and Romans.[38] He refers to Jerome's work on Daniel. He does not pronounce on this view, but suggests that the important feature of the text is its evocation of the Antichrist as a prelude to the everlasting reign of God and the saints (20. 23). There are passages about the end of the world in the Psalms, for example 102: 25–7. This seems unambiguous, and Porphyry, who condemns Christians for believing that the world will perish but praises the Jewish concept of God (*City* 19. 23), would have found much to

---

[38] Cf. Mommsen (1959: 267–70); for Orosius' views see ibid. 338–43. On Daniel see above all Bickerman (1967); cf. Momigliano (1975: 109–12) and Lane Fox (1991: 331–7), a stimulating section of an illuminating book to which, not least because of its well-judged bibliographical notices, I owe much. For Jerome's commentary on Daniel see Kelly (1975: 298–302): Jerome's prologue summarizes Porphyry's critique of Daniel, on which see Wilken (1984: 137–43).

criticize in the Jewish tradition which the Psalmist represents. Psalm 50: 3–5 refers to the last judgement. Augustine elucidates its language by reference to passages from the Old and New Testaments, putting forward an audacious and unconvincing interpretation of 'who put his covenant above sacrifices' ('qui disponunt testamentum eius super sacrificia') as a reference to the replacement of sacrificial traditions by the new covenant (20. 24). Malachi 3: 1–6 appears to refer to purgatorial punishments: Augustine postpones discussion of this topic. References to the sons of Levi, Judah, and Jerusalem in the Malachi passage are understood to allude to the Church. The whole passages enriches the metaphors for judgement: refining, purifying. Augustine adds the image of winnowing (20. 25). The reference in Malachi 3: 3 to the sons of Levi making 'an offering in righteousness' is taken by Augustine to mean that they will not offer the traditional kind of 'carnal' Jewish sacrifice, and so this text becomes a justification of the discontinuation of sacrifice. In the phrase 'days of old' (Malachi 3: 4) Augustine sees a reference to man's paradise state, before sacrifice, or when humans themselves were the purest sacrifice to God. But the phrase may also be comparing the unblemished victims of traditional sacrifice with the purity of the saints of God (20. 26). Augustine quotes a further passage from Malachi 3: 17–4: 3 (cf. 18. 35), which refers to rewards and punishments, separation and the 'sun of righteousness' (20. 27). References to the law of Moses in a text like Malachi 4: 4 draw attention to the need to obey moral precepts, and thus to 'law' in a spiritual sense: this interpretation is the answer to those who, in Malachi 3: 14–15, complained about the wretchedness of the good and well-being of the unjust. In the last judgement, such apparent wrongs will be righted (20. 28). In Malachi 4: 5–6 the allusion to Elijah's advent before the final judgement may not be so much a direct reference to the conversion of the Jews, as a reference to the Father's eternal conversion, in love, towards the Son. That in turn will, Augustine asserts, lead Jews, who assume that God cannot approve of Jesus, to accept him (20. 29).

Old Testament passages which refer to the last judgement do not distinguish explicitly between God and Christ as judge, whereas in the New Testament it is clear that Christ is to be the judge. Augustine thus tries to establish that there are Old Testament passages where the language used indicates that Christ is meant when God is spoken of. One such passage is Isaiah 48: 12–16, where the words of the final verse ('And now the Lord God has sent me and his Spirit') signal the application of the passage to Christ. Zechariah 2: 8–9 is a similar case ('the Lord almighty has sent me'). In Zechariah 12: 9–10 references to insults and to sorrow as for an only-begotten son point in the same direction. This passage also prophesies the repentance and conversion of the Jews. Augustine knows that the Septuagint-Latin version, with 'insulted' ('insultaverunt'), differs from the Hebrew 'pierced'; but he, as elsewhere, combines divergent versions which he considers divinely inspired in order to enrich the meaning of a passage (here because both verbs apply to aspects of Christ's passion).[39] There is a special appropriateness in the phenomenon of Christ, who was judged as a man, being the judge of men, in the persecuted one becoming the minister of punishment. Christ suffered, but was not broken by suffering, a symbol of the Church's power to survive adversity. 'And in his name the peoples will hope' (Isaiah 42: 4, following the Septuagint version): the paradox of the vulnerable, executed Christ, of the death that gives life, is well caught in the role of Christ as the one in whom people hope, and who will be the judge of all. Augustine now feels that he can set out in summary form what is to be believed will 'come' at the final judgement: 'Elijah the Tishbite, the belief of the Jews, Christ in judgement, the resurrection of the dead, the separation of good and evil, the conflagration of the universe and its renewal.' But how, or in what order, or when, we cannot know, although Augustine inclines to the sequence he has just given. The chapter, and the book, end with Augustine's anticipation of the themes of the two following books, and a reassertion of the truthfulness of Scriptures, if properly understood (20. 30).

At the beginning of Book 21 Augustine refers to the cities of God and of the devil: the latter title—one of a number used to designate the second city—is particularly appropriate in this part of the work, where the final separation of the two cities is being discussed. Augustine will deal with eternal punishment before eternal bliss, and he justifies this sequence by observing that it is harder to believe in the concept of eternal torment than in that of painless eternal happiness. He finds support in those scriptural texts (Matthew 13: 41–3, 25: 46) which refer to punishment before reward (21. 1). His chief task is

---

[39] Cf. Augustine's argument in 18. 43–4 that there can be complementary acceptable meanings in different versions of biblical texts.

to make credible the idea that a human body can both endure and not
be destroyed by eternal pain. The precedent of animals like the
salamander who apparently survive in fire is of limited value in
controversy with opponents of the concept of eternal punishment,
for these animals are not immortal, and fire is their natural environment: above all, they do not suffer pain in it. Augustine, for his part,
finds the fact that animals can survive in fire without suffering even
more incredible than survival with suffering (21. 2). The common-
sense objection that there is no body that can endure unending pain
without dying may be countered by speculating that demonic bodies
do so, and that one can envisage an afterlife human body that is so
united to the soul that the shock of extreme pain does not cause body
and soul to separate, as is now the case. This afterlife state will be a
totally different condition to that which now obtains. Whereas here
pain is a sign of life, there pain will co-exist with death, the 'second
death', and so death will never supervene as a release from it.
Furthermore, it is wrong to consider pain as a bodily phenomenon:
the soul experiences pain, just as it experiences all sensation, even if
pain's origin is bodily. Augustine recalls Virgil, *Aeneid* 6. 719–21,
730–4, which he has discussed in 14. 3 and 14. 5 (he mistakenly
refers to the twelfth book of *City* here). Those Virgilian passages,
which he takes to represent a Platonist position, suggest that, although
bodies are the source of the passions, even disembodied and purified
souls desire to return to bodies.[40] Desire entails the possibility of
experiencing pain. The soul is an instance of an immortal entity
experiencing pain and not being annihilated by it. Pain is not a proof
of future death (21. 3).

Augustine now adduces the example of natural phenomena to
support his argument that things can survive fire, and bodies may
be immune to decay: the salamander, volcanoes, the flesh of the
peacock (Augustine attests this phenomenon from his own observation that roast peacock meat remains fresh indefinitely). Fire itself is
something full of contradictory powers. It both destroys and preserves (charcoal), it burns most things black, but some white (stones).
It can be stored in lime, and then activated by the addition of water,
which normally extinguishes fire: but it is not activated by oil, which
normally is a fuel for fire. This final example is a transitional one. For
it is Augustine's purpose in this argument, not merely to discourse on

[40] See further Ch. 11. 1e.

the qualities of fire, but to turn our attention to natural wonders that, through familiarity, we take for granted. Thus he goes on to remind the reader of the qualities of diamonds and, in particular, of the magnet, and then of the neutralizing power of the diamond in proximity to magnets. Pliny (*Nat. Hist.* 20. 1, 28. 9) is a source for much of this passage (21. 4), just as, with Solinus, he is for the material adduced in 21. 5: salt of Agrigentum (possibly a kind of lime), which melts in fire, but crackles in water; springs that are cold by day but hot by night, or that can rekindle an extinguished torch; asbestos; wood that sinks in water and then resurfaces; 'apples' that appear to be ripe, but dissolve into dust and ashes when opened; mares impregnated by the wind, and so on. The argument which Augustine adopts is: if such things occur, contrary to the normal course of nature and in some scientifically inexplicable way, why cannot there be living human bodies which will burn and suffer for ever, but never die? To believe in wonders of nature without being able to give an explanation for them, and at the same time to deny the possibility of everlasting punishment after death, seems inconsistent. A modern objector will, of course, say that the difference is that properly attested wonders of nature have in fact occurred, while posthumous punishments must remain a matter for speculation, or, in Augustine's case, for religious belief (21. 5). Augustine adds that we should not be shy of attributing some miracles to demonic agency, such as the unquenchable lamp in the shrine of Venus (Pliny, *Nat. Hist.* 2. 96 speaks of an altar of Venus at Paphos on which the rain never falls). Individual demons are attracted to specific tokens— stones, herbs, wood, and so on.[41] They inhabit and act through these. It is better to admit their power, if the alternative is to deny the possibility of miracles. Their magical effectiveness is easily out-done by God's wonders (21. 6).

One reason given by critics of Christian views of afterlife punish-ment for the wonders of nature is that the latter are simply expres-sions of the nature of the phenomena concerned. Augustine does not really counter this argument, preferring to fall back on the assump-tion of God's power to will apparent exceptions to the norms of nature. Augustine finds it reasonable to believe the securely attested wonders. As for the scope of what God will or will not do, Augustine argues that if some scriptural prophecies have been fulfilled, that is a

---

[41] On Augustine's use of Pliny and other related sources see Ch. 11. 1j.

sufficient reason for believing that others, including the afterlife punishments, will be (21. 7). In 21. 8 Augustine returns to the question of whether and how a being can come to be different from its determined nature. He proffers the example of the prelapsarian nature of humans, whose bodies were immortal. But he realizes that this example cuts no ice with non-believers. Varro, however, can be cited on the phenomenon of a portent which changed its colour, size, shape, and course. Yet such portents are not really contrary to nature, so much as contrary to what we know of nature. God's intervention can upset the apparent laws of nature, making exceptions 'natural'. Augustine here endeavours to turn the table on critics by accepting a modified form of their argument (21. 7) that natural wonders are simply the nature of the entities in question: he does so by stressing the distinctive element of the will of an almighty God. Even within species such as the human race, dissimilarities abound: why not in the case of astral and other phenomena? God is not circumscribed by the laws of nature which humans identify (21. 8).

In 21. 9 Augustine argues against those who would interpret the fires of hell in a purely mental or psychological way. His argument, that bodily images refer more plausibly to the body, or at least include the body, is not a good one, given the freedom with which he interprets bodily images in a metaphorical sense elsewhere. He has to fall back on the outcome of the preceding chapters, that bodies can survive fire, and that God's power over nature is unlimited (21. 9). But how can immaterial demonic spirits be punished by fire? Well, perhaps they have a kind of airy body. Or it may be that they have some kind of contact with material fire, analogous to the conjoint of soul and body in humans, that enables them to suffer without animating the fire in any way. They may burn as the rich man does in hell (Luke 16: 24), without bodily existence, imagining both the flames and the water craved for. But in the hell of the final punishment fire will be material, and will torture human bodies, as well as the demons in whatever form, unknown to us, they may exist (21. 10).

Augustine next turns to consider the question of whether eternal punishment is a just punishment. Discrepancy between the time taken to commit a crime and the duration of punishment awarded is a feature of penal systems. The death penalty is a matter of a moment, and the justification lies in the gravity of the offence, meriting the supreme penalty. One matches evil with evil, but not in the sense of strict retaliation. Another kind of equivalence has to be found

(21. 11). The real reason for eternal punishment lies in the gravity of original sin, which led to the condemnation of all humanity. Those—the minority—who are not eternally condemned have to thank divine grace (21. 12). Augustine argues against the view that afterlife punishment is purificatory. This is a Platonist position. Augustine again cites Virgil as his source (*Aeneid* 6. 733–42). Augustine accepts temporary penalties, both in this life and in the next, and those in this life may be, and those in the next life must be, purgatorial: but these are not to be confused with the eternal punishments (21. 13). A human life lived without punishment of some kind is rare: every schoolchild knows how grim education is. Who would not prefer to die than to experience infancy again? Zarathustra is the only human who is said to have laughed rather than wailed at birth (Pliny, *Nat. Hist.* 7. 16. 72): much good it did him (21. 14). The 'heavy yoke laid on Adam's sons', to which Ecclesiasticus 40: 1 refers, can, of course be a teacher. It can teach us to behave with sobriety, to accept the lot of post-lapsarian man, to live by faith, to appreciate the saving incarnation of Christ: 'for just as we have descended to such great evil as this through one man who sinned, so through one man, who is at the same time God, who justifies us we will come to that good, high as it is.' Until we reach that final stable state, life is a struggle, a kind of warfare with evil (21. 15). Augustine returns to the 'ages' ('aetates') scheme to elaborate this point. The first two stages of human life, infancy and childhood, are not subject to the control of reason. Yet if an infant or child is baptized and then dies, it is saved from all punishment, including purgatory, after death. A mixture of reason and faith sustains the individual in the struggle against evil: faith is necessary, for some vices are otherwise only overcome by others. A man may be virtuous through pride, for example. To escape eternal punishment one who has reached the age of reason must not merely be baptized but also justified in Christ by faith. It may be that eternal punishment will be of different degrees, depending on the crimes being punished. The fires of hell may be thermostatically controlled, or simply experienced in unequal ways (21. 16).

Augustine devotes the remainder of Book 21 to dealing with a variety of compassionate views about afterlife punishments held by Christians whom he considers to be 'wet'. It will be best to deal with these views and his answers to them in succession.

1. Some believe that punishment after death will not be eternal. Origen is an extreme and distinct case, arguing that even the devil and his fellow-demons will be released.[42] Augustine reminds us that Origen's views on cycles of existence and rebirth have already been rejected by him. But even if this view is restricted to humans on grounds of mercy, it is not cogent. If mercy is the criterion, then why not extend it to the devil and his fellows? (21. 17). In any case, scriptural texts seem to make it clear that punishment is eternal for the devil and fallen angels (Matthew 25: 41; Revelation 20: 10). Similarly, humans seem to be given eternal punishments in this and other Matthew passages (e.g. 25: 46). Matthew 25: 41, moreover, cannot be true when it refers to the devil, but false when it refers to humans (21. 23).

2. Others[43] maintain that divine mercy will prevail, but because of the intercession of the saints on behalf of those facing judgement. Yet this view is, for the most part, concealed in the Scriptures, so that the fear of punishment may be an incentive to be good. Once again, this compassionate view is confined to humans (21. 18). Why should the saints not pray for the fallen angels also? The fact that the Church does not do so, despite the general injunction to pray for one's enemies, is because of the realization that in the afterlife repentance is no longer possible. Christians pray for living enemies because they may yet be saved. Some of those who were born again in Christ and who have lived a life that was not perfect but none the less worthy of mercy will be purgatorially punished in the next life: that is another matter.[44] The divine combination of anger and mercy (Psalm 77:

---

[42] Cf. Origen, *De Principiis* I. 6.

[43] As Bardy, BA 37. 806–9, points out, Augustine's account does not refer to distinctive groups or individuals, Origen apart: he identifies laxist tendencies of those he calls 'compassionate' ('misericordes') in 21. 17, classifying them primarily according to the scriptural texts invoked, and incidentally bringing out the difference between Origen's and other views. Cf. the briefer references to such tendencies in *Ench.* 18. 67, 19. 70, 20. 75, and 29. 112. Bardy compares the method adopted in *City* 21. 17–27 with that of 22. 12–20, where Augustine responds to pagan objections to bodily resurrection, explaining his method at the beginning of 22. 13. Given Augustine's method, it is superfluous to attempt to identify the individual 'compassionate' groups, although remarks of Jerome in his *Letter* 119. 7 and *Dialogue against the Pelagians* 1. 28 on salvation through faith, despite persistent sinfulness, could be identified with group 5: see Bardy, BA 37. 808–9.

[44] Cf. the tentative account in 21. 26: see also 20. 25 and *Ench.* 68–9. Bardy's note on Augustine's cautious attitude to the idea of posthumous purgatorial fire (BA 37. 812–16) is helpful. Hill (1992: 121 n. 199, 148–9) is commendably sceptical about attempts to foist a doctrine of purgatory on Clement of Alexandria or Cyprian.

9–10) is focused upon the living: if it applies to the punished dead (Augustine is not certain that it does), then it does not mean that their punishment will have a term, but that it will be milder in degree than they strictly deserve. Divine predictions of eternal punishment are no mere threats. The case of Nineveh is not a counter-example: the Ninevites repented (Jonah 3: 5–10). Faith that is founded on hope, rather than fear, is a precondition of salvation. A text like Romans 11: 32 is not to be read as an assertion that nobody will be condemned: Paul is speaking about the Jews to converted believers, and is referring to all those—Jews and Gentiles—who are pre-destined to be saved, not to all humanity (21. 24).

3. Others argue that baptism saves humans from eternal punish-ment, irrespective of how they have lived, whether they have been heretics or irreligious (21. 19). Augustine finds clear evidence in Scripture that good moral conduct is a prerequisite to salvation: this seems to be the unequivocal message of Galatians 5: 19–21. Those who hold this view of the efficacy of baptism cite John 6: 50–2 in support of it, but so do the proponents of view 5, regarding the taking of the eucharist as the precondition and sign of membership of the Church (21. 25).[45]

4. Others hold the same view about baptism, but argue that only those who are both baptized and members of the universal ('catho-lica') Church will be saved, even if they lapse into heresy or idolatry (21. 20). Augustine finds it preposterous that heretics and heresiarchs should be exempt from eternal punishment, whereas those who have not fallen into their snares would not be, if they have not become 'catholici'. Those who lapse jeopardize their salvation, because they do not persevere in the faith. Participation in the sacrament of the eucharist must be participation not merely in its form ('sacramento tenus'), but in its reality ('re vera'), and that entails a will to avoid sin (21. 25).[46]

5. Others again make perseverance in the universal Church, irrespective of moral wickedness, a precondition of being freed from eternal punishment (21. 21). But will faith alone save? James

---

[45] Augustine alludes in 21. 25 to the practice of administering the eucharist to neophytes at the same time as baptism: see the vivid account of the rite in van der Meer (1961: 361–79).

[46] Underlying Augustine's comments on the eucharist here is his distinction between the sacramental rite and its efficacy ('virtus sacramenti'), which depends on the recipient's disposition: see Bardy, BA 37. 811–12, citing *Io. Ev. Tr.* 26–7.

2: 14 seems to imply that works are also necessary. Augustine defends this viewpoint with an extended exegesis of 1 Corinthians 3: 10–15. Christ is the foundation, but lives may be variously built upon this foundation, and sinful behaviour, in effect, undermines it: to place temporal things (Augustine's example is love of other humans) before Christ is to have a foundation other than Christ. The value and durability of what is built will be tested by fire. The fire which tests is not, however, the eternal fire of punishment, but one that tests all, and as a result of which some will be blessed. Augustine is again inclined to see in this fire an allusion to purgatory, that is, to a testing after the death of the body and before the final judgement. But persecutions of martyrs are also a form of testing in this life, as will be the persecutions perpetrated by the Antichrist (21. 26).

6. A further group believe that only those who perform works of mercy in atonement for their sins will be freed, even if they live wickedly. The important thing is their attitude, especially that of forgiveness of those who have harmed them (21. 22). But failure to turn from sin or to attempt to change one's life for the better remains reprehensible, even if one gives alms and is forgiving. One cannot buy oneself out of sin. One has to begin with one's own moral condition. A Christian is not merely one who is baptized, but one who is justified ('iustificatur').[47] Matthew 5: 20–4 shows that acts of charity and even worship are futile if one's inner disposition is not in order. Matthew 6: 12 ('forgive us our debts, as we forgive our debtors') does not entail that forgiving others leads in itself to forgiveness for us, just as its gloss in Matthew 6: 14 ('if you forgive men their trespasses, your Father will also forgive you your trespasses') is a reminder that, even if one is behaving appropriately, one is not free from sin. Behaving mercifully is indeed a prerequisite of being good (James 2: 13), but it is not the sum total of goodness. Obtaining the friendship and goodwill of the saints is not inappropriate. It remains none the less difficult to know what effect their intercession may have on alleviating the punishments due to humans: this very uncertainty should put us on our guard, and make us depend for salvation more on our own moral progress than on favours done to, or by, us (21. 27).

With these observations Augustine brings the book to a close. He reiterates at the end that his appeal against these different views

---

[47] On the Pauline doctrine of justification or righteousness see Sanders (1991: 44–64).

about afterlife punishments is to the authority of Scripture. By implication, the views rebutted are based on a partial and partisan reading
of the sacred texts.

In Book 22 Augustine deals with the other consequence of the final
judgement, the eternal bliss of the saved humans whose predestined
salvation will fill the places of the fallen angels in the heavenly city.
'Eternal' in this context means 'without end', not merely 'of long
duration'. Augustine does not make it clear here whether eternal bliss
is endlessly durational, unlike divine eternity, though what he
suggests elsewhere implies that it is.[48] Eternal life for humans is a
stable state, free from significant change, but not from all change.
Being subject to change does not entail being evil: had Adam not
chosen to sin, human nature would have remained free of evil.
Adam's fall is proof of the natural goodness of human nature, and
the high degree of its goodness, given the ruinous consequences of
original sin. Similarly, the freely willed fall of the angels is justly
punished by the penalty of eternal unhappiness (22. 1). God's will is
unchangeable.[49] Talk of God changing his will is a way of expressing
changes which humans, as temporal beings, experience. Likewise,
God's righteousness can be the realization of righteousness in a
human. When God is said to come to know something, the meaning
may be that he causes it to become known by others. Augustine refers
to earlier discussions of these locutions (11. 8, 21; 16. 5, 32). To say
that something will happen when God wills, means that something
eternally foreknown in God's unchanging will is going to take place
at some future time (22. 2). This is the case with the future happiness
of the saints, as prophesied in several scriptural texts: Augustine gives
a selection in 22. 3 (cf. 20. 21).

That this future state will be a bodily one, albeit with a special
body, is unacceptable to philosophers.[50] Cicero in *Republic* 3. 40
argues that the deification of Hercules and Romulus does not involve
a transfer of their earthly bodies to the sky ('caelum'). Augustine's

---

[48]   The created human soul is mutable, and if it is immortal, it is not eternal: *Div.
Qu.* 19, *Trin.* 4. 24, 14. 6. In the resurrected body, though it is perfect and incorruptible, the blessed will have affections and memories, and be capable of motion, so that
their bliss appears to entail duration: *City* 10. 31, 11. 12, 14. 9, 19. 27–8, 21. 3, 23.
See further O'Daly (1986: 163–4).

[49]   Cf. *City* 11. 4–6, 21; 12. 15, 18; *Conf.* 11. 8, 15, etc. See Gunnersdorf von Jess
(1975: 82–8), Sorabji (1983: 240–1), O'Daly (1986: 162–3).

[50]   Cf. Augustine's earlier confrontation of philosophers' objections to bodily resurrection in *F. et Symb.* 6. 13, 10. 24.

counter-argument is that, if God wills it, it can happen. It would be
no stranger than the animation of an earthly body by an incorporeal
soul, something that, because of its familiarity, we take for granted
(22. 4). Furthermore, there is now widespread belief in Christ's
bodily resurrection: it will be a repeated theme of this book that
Christian beliefs have found assent among educated and uneducated
alike (cf. 22. 25). In fact, Christianity seems to be a crystallization of
'unbelievable things' ('incredibilia'): that Christ has risen from the
dead; that the world believes this; and that humble and uneducated
men, the apostles, should have been able to persuade the world of
it.[51] Augustine points out that the philosophical adversaries of bodily
resurrection must at least accept the second and third of these 'incredibilia'. The low social status of the apostles made what they
preached persuasive, for they did not have the prestige of learning
on which to fall back. Miracles lent support to their mission, but the
great and more recent spread of Christianity has been accomplished
without any miracles (22. 5). Augustine contrasts this with the
deification of Romulus. Cicero (*Rep.* 2. 18–19) remarks that it is
significant that this miracle occurred at a late date (i.e. in the eighth
century BC), and in a time, he claims, of relatively high culture.
Augustine argues that it was the belief of a small group of founding
fathers, and later accepted, for fear of offending Rome, by Rome's
subjects. Belief in Romulus' deification is a case of misguided love for
the city's founder. It is essentially retrospective, whereas Christian
faith in God is future-oriented, anticipating the city of God. Belief
that leads to and motivates love is superior to love that determines
what is believed. Moreover, Christ's divinity is anticipated by prophecies and supported by miracles: in the case of Romulus, there is only
the she-wolf, and that myth may mean that he was nursed by a
prostitute ('lupa'). The fear which led to worship of Romulus under
Roman rule stands in sharp contrast to the fearlessness of the martyrs.

   Augustine establishes a further contrast between the two cities, by
alluding to the reasons which the best kind of state, according to
Cicero, should have for entering into war.[52] In *Republic* 3 it is argued

---

[51] The emphasis on the 'incredible' nature of Christianity is reminiscent of Tert. *De
Carne Christi* 5; cf. Wolfson (1970: 103).
[52] For Augustine's views on the just war see further 1. 21 and 19. 7; for modern
studies see Ch. 6 n. 6. The passage from *Rep.* 3 (= 3. 23. 34) is known only from this
citation by Augustine. On the uses of *Rep.* in *City* see Ch. 11. 1c. Hagendahl (1967:
549) believes that the Saguntine episode (also adduced in 3. 20) may derive from the
same Cicero passage, but Augustine could have known it from Livy, 21. 5–15 or the
Livian tradition (for his use of which see Ch. 11. 1f).

that only 'fides' and 'salus' are sufficient grounds for engaging in war. A state may make war to defend its security ('salus'), or to adhere to treaties and contractual obligations, and the kind of binding guarantees which these involve ('fides'). The security of the state is vital to Cicero's thinking, and he proposes the view that the state should be so established that it lasts for ever: the death of the state, unlike human death, is not natural. It is as if the universe should perish. Now Saguntum, a Spanish ally of Rome, was destroyed by the Carthaginians under Hannibal at the start of the Second Punic War in 218 BC, because of its 'fides' towards Rome. Yet this action led to the undermining of its 'salus'. The Saguntum affair is presented by Augustine as a test-case: what is to be preferred, when loyalty and safety are in conflict? There is, Augustine implies, no answer in Cicero to this. By contrast, the martyr preserves 'fides' and realizes the 'salus' of the city of God: Augustine shifts the meanings of the terms, so that 'fides' now refers to the martyr's belief (but it may still include the traditional Roman connotations of 'fides' in a Christian context), and 'salus' means the salvation of the members of the city of God, while, again, including the traditional meanings, especially the notion of the state's survival (22. 6). Augustine feels that he can turn Cicero's argument about the relatively late date of Romulus' deification to polemical advantage by pointing out that Christ lived later than Romulus, and in a still more culturally advanced period: yet his resurrection was accepted by many, with the support of prophecy and martyrs, whose blood made fruitful the seed of faith (22. 7).[53]

The miracles which lent credibility to Christ's claim to be God have not entirely ceased to happen, but they are local events, less widely known than those which are included in the canonical Scriptures. Augustine assembles in 22. 8 a series of individual instances, twenty in all, which he documents with care.[54] All but the first occurred in North Africa, many in the Hippo region. A common element is the link with a martyr's shrine and its relics (especially the relics of the first martyr Stephen, which had been found in Gaza in 415), but not

---

[53] Cf. Tert. *Apol.* 50. 13: 'the blood of Christians is seed'. Augustine's image is more complex, but may betray the influence of Tertullian; cf. Ch. 3 n. 5. For speculation on further use of the *Apol.* in 22. 6–7 see Bardy, BA 37. 823–4.

[54] See the discussion in van der Meer (1961: 527–57). Augustine's attitude to miracles evolved from a belief that they had occurred at an early period of Christianity in order to bolster faith, but did so no longer (*Vera Rel.* 25. 47, *Vtil. Cred.* 16. 34), to mature acceptance, as a bishop, both of their continuing reality and value. Miles (1979: 35–9) relates this development to Augustine's changed evaluation of the body.

all the miracles involve martyrs: a virgin is cured of possession by a demon by anointing herself with oil into which the tears of the priest praying for her have fallen. In the case of Paulus and Palladia, Augustine was himself directly involved, and a number of his sermons, as he makes clear here, dealt with it (*Ser.* 320–4: *Ser.* 322 is the official report or 'libellus' of the miracle).[55] He also tells us that he was concerned to preserve the written reports of miracles and have them read publicly (22. 8). Martyrs are witnesses to the faith in Christ's resurrection and ascension. Miracles performed through their intercession, or by angelic intervention, are a further strengthening of the claims of that faith (22. 9).[56] If pagan gods appear to have performed miracles also, these are due to demonic agency. But Christians, unlike pagans, do not deify those who, like martyrs, seem to be the means whereby miracles are performed. And the naming of martyrs in the liturgy does not mean that they are invoked as gods in the sacrificial rite (22. 10).

In 22. 11 Augustine returns to the Platonist objections to bodily resurrection. The chief objection is the perceived sequence and relative weight of elements: sky (fire)–air–water–earth.[57] There can, the argument runs, be no earthly body in the sky, which is the proper place of the element of fire. Augustine counters this argument by pointing to apparent infringements of the alleged rule: birds in the air, terrestrial animals who need air to live (cf. 13. 18). And what about the soul-substance, which some place above the four elements, and which Aristotle (according to Cicero, *Tusculan Disputations* 1. 65) calls a fifth body (in Cicero a fifth 'nature')? Pagans who accept miracles cannot object to the belief that a supreme God could make an earthly body subsist in whatever element he chooses. Nor is the order of the elements in itself convincing. Clouds, made of water, are above air. Air fills the space between earth and sky, with no water necessarily in between. Fire is found on and even in the earth. If philosophers object that the sky-element fire is different from our

---

[55] These 'public' readings were most likely in church, and may be compared with readings of martyrdom accounts, permitted in Africa alongside readings from the canonical Scriptures by the Council of Carthage in 393 and confirmed by the Council of Hippo in 397 (*Breviarium Hipponense*, canon 47; CCL 149. 340); cf. Palmer (1989: 230–2). Augustine's presentation of miracles in 22. 8 demonstrates the close links between miracles and martyrs' shrines. Cf. Delehaye (1933).

[56] Markus (1990a: 139–55) writes perceptively on the role of martyrs' shrines in the increasingly Christianized urban world of the 5th c.; cf. van der Meer (1961: 527–57).   [57] Cf. O'Daly (1991a: 146–7).

destructive fire, which is adapted for the earth, then why cannot they accept that the substance of resurrected bodies may be adapted for heaven (22. 11)? Augustine's argument in this chapter is *ad hominem*. There is thus an ambiguity in his references to 'caelum'. In countering the Platonists on the relative weight and position of elements, 'caelum' refers to the sky. But for Augustine the sky can never be the location of resurrected bodies: they can be imagined to exist only in some incorruptible 'place', i.e. 'heaven' ('in caelo').

A further kind of objection to resurrection asks awkward questions about the form of resurrected bodies. Will aborted foetuses be resurrected and what shape and size will they have? What about the bodies of those who die in infancy? What about fat people? And hair? And horribly deformed bodies? What of those who were victims of cannibalism (22. 12)? Augustine inclines to the view that foetuses will be resurrected (22. 13).[58] All human beings have a limit of perfection ('perfectionis modus') in size and stature, but they have it as a potentiality ('in ratione'), in the same way that all parts of the body are potentially in the seed, although some (teeth, for example) are lacking at birth. So infants will be resurrected with this bodily potentiality realized (22. 14). If Ephesians 4: 13 refers to the resurrection of bodies (as well as to Christ as the head of a body of which Christians are the members), then we may speculate that all resurrected bodies, of young and old, will have the age and physique of Christ at his death: and that happens to coincide with a widely held belief that the age of 30 is the prime of life (22. 15).[59] But Augustine feels that it is idle to dispute with those who do not believe in resurrected bodies of equal size and 'age'. The matter must remain unresolved (22. 16). Will there be female bodies in heaven? 'A woman's sex is not a defect, but a natural state': so women will be

---

[58] In *Ench.* 85–6 he was more confident in asserting that formed foetuses would be resurrected. His hesitation has to do with his uncertainty about the point at which the embryo begins to live: see Wermelinger (1986), O'Daly (1987: 19–20). Augustine's developing account of bodily resurrection is discussed in Miles (1979: 99–125). For the progress of Christian doctrine on the topic see Kelly (1977: 459–89).

[59] In 22. 15 Augustine, following a traditional scheme (cf. Censorinus, *De Die Natali* 14. 2, where Varro's demarcations are reported), refers to the age of 30 as the beginning of 'iuventus': cf. *Conf.* 7. 1. 1, where he describes himself, aged about 30, as proceeding from 'adulescentia' to 'iuventus'. For these schemes see O'Donnell on *Conf.* 1. 8. 13. But there was variety in the perception of the stages of life: B. D. Shaw (1987: 40–1) suggests social and economic reasons for this. For Christ as 'iuvenis' see also *Ser.* 88. 10. 9.

there, but there will be no lust, sex, or childbirth (22. 17).[60]
Ephesians 4: 10–16 and other texts evoke the body that is the
Church, with Christ as its head: and it is to maturity in truth, and
growing out of error, that Ephesians points. Augustine is anxious to
stress this point in the debate about physical details of the individual
resurrected body. The whole (the city) should be the focus of attention (22. 18). In the individual bodies an aesthetic principle governs
the inclusion or exclusion of features like hair or nails. An artist
works on a statue, creating something beautiful without using less (or
more) material. By analogy, God, the supreme artist, can reshape our
bodies into something pleasing, redistributing parts of excessive size
(cf. 22. 20). The very thin and the obese need not fear. They will get a
perfect body, which will exemplify a standard definition of beauty:
'all bodily beauty is a harmony of the parts, together with a certain
attractiveness of complexion'.[61] But will martyrs bear their honourable wounds? Perhaps, but they will not lack limbs lost in martyrdom, though it may be that scars will be visible where they were
severed; for their visible proofs of valour are no defects (22. 19).
Victims of cannibalism must surely have their flesh restored to them:
it was only on loan, so to speak, to those who, for whatever reason,
ate them (22. 20). The spiritual body will be a thing of perfect
beauty, but it will still be a body (22. 21).

To sharpen the contrast between this life and the next, and to stress
the goodness of God, Augustine now paints an uncompromisingly
grim picture of the human condition. There are vices, but even the
correction of faults in childhood and youth is itself painful. We are
vulnerable beings, susceptible to accidents and natural disasters, to
illnesses. Nothing is safe: Eli the priest fell from his chair and died
(1 Samuel 4: 18). Then there are the demons. Drugs are painful
remedies. Sleep, instead of being rest, is often the occasion of night-
mares, and there are terrifying hallucinations at other times. Religion
is not proof against the ills of this life: its purpose is to seek the best

---

[60] Dean-Jones (1994) discusses Greek scientific views of women's bodies. For
modern studies of the theological dimension of Augustine's views on sexual differentiation see Ch. 9 n. 9.

[61] Cf. Cic., *Tusc. Disp.* 4. 13. 30–1; Plotinus, 1. 6. 1. 20–3. The definition is Stoic:
cf. also *SVF* 3. 278 (Stobaeus), 3. 472 (Galen). It is often given by Augustine: e.g.
Letter 3. 4; *Ord.* 2. 11. 33. On Augustine's first (not extant) work *On the Beautiful and
the Fitting* (*De Pulchro et Apto*) see *Conf.* 4. 13. 20–16. 31 with the commentaries of
O'Donnell and G. Clark; Harrison (1992: 3–5). On the terms 'pulchrum' and 'aptum'
see Augustine, *Letter* 138. 1. 5.

in the life to come. Philosophy is considered by pagans to be the greatest gift, yet even they admit that true philosophy is found by only a few, or, as Cicero says, given by the gods to a few (*Acad. Post.* 1. 7). Augustine sees this as an admission of the need for divine grace (22. 22). The righteous also suffer evils of their own, in addition to those common to the good and the bad. They may be deceived by error, provoked into retaliation, seduced into unfounded suspicion of others, tempted by desire, and so on. Life is an unceasing war with evil (22. 23).

Yet this life also has its good things. One is the power of propagation. Another is conformation to type, which preserves the several species according to formal and numerical principles.[62] Then there is the gift of reason, and there are the virtues, the various 'artes' (which include such skills as agriculture and navigation, but also drama, painting, sculpture), language, music, philosophy, the organization and functioning of the human body, its utility as well as its beauty, the natural world. All these are given to those predestined to damnation[63] as well as to those who will be saved: imagine the goods in store for the blessed in heaven (22. 24)!

There are contradictions between Platonists on the relation of soul and body. Augustine has discussed this point in 13. 16. He now reminds the reader that Plato, in the *Timaeus*, gives the created gods eternal bodies, whereas it is a cardinal theme of Porphyry's *De Regressu Animae* that 'one must escape from every kind of body' ('corpus . . . omne fugiendum').[64] Moreover, Plato's God gives the created gods immortality because he so wills, even if, for Plato, that which has an origin in time cannot be immortal (*Tim.* 41b). Why then cannot the true God make human bodies incorruptible and

---

[62] On Augustine's concept of 'conformatio' in creation see *Gen. ad Litt.* 2. 8. 16, 19; cf. 'forma/formabile' in *Lib. Arb.* 2. 17. 45–6, 2. 18. 49. On 'reasons' ('rationes causales/seminales') in creation see *Gen. ad Litt.* 5–7, *Trin.* 3. 13. 16; cf. TeSelle (1970: 216–18). Forms as numbers: *Lib. Arb.* 2. 16. 42. Augustine uses the 'conformatio' concept and the doctrine of seminal reasons to establish his argument that God's creative activity continues to the present day, here (22. 24) citing 1 Cor. 3: 7, and emphasizing that God, not the parents, creates and forms the child; cf. Sorabji (1983: 302–5).

[63] From texts like this (see also *Ench.* 100. 26) Calvin concluded that Augustine had a doctrine of double predestination, of the saved and of the damned: Mozley (1855: 393–409) understands Augustine in a Calvinist sense; Bonner (1963: 380–9) argues against such an interpretation. A key text like *Persev.* 13. 35 reserves talk of predestination for the saints. See in general the balanced discussion of TeSelle (1970: 319–32); cf. Rist (1994: 269–70 with n. 38).

[64] See Ch. 7, on 10. 29; cf. Ch. 11. 2b.

immortal (22. 26)? Yet both Plato and Porphyry had some true insights which, if combined, would yield the truth about souls and bodies. For Plato's belief that souls will naturally return to bodies is true, though the view that the souls of the good will return to mortal bodies is not true. And it is true, as Porphyry says, that purified souls will not return to earthly bodies, although untrue that all bodies are to be shunned by the soul (22. 27). If to the true beliefs of Plato and Porphyry one were to add the theory that Varro reports, of reincarnation in the same body, omitting its untenable aspects (such as the subsequent separation once more of body and soul, and the mortality of the body), one would arrive at the elements of the Christian truth (22. 28).[65]

The final state of the blessed will be one of perfect peace and rest: we cannot now comprehend what this will entail. It will involve some kind of vision of God, as several scriptural texts attest. But will they see with the eyes of their resurrected bodies, as we now see our surroundings? If they close their eyes, will they cease to see God as long as their eyes remain closed? It is perhaps better to think of their vision as like the ecstatic visions of prophets, who can see things even when they are not present to them. Perhaps spiritual eyes can see the incorporeal. Against the standard philosophical view that the mind perceives intelligible objects and the senses bodily objects, Augustine proposes the interesting counter-thesis that the spiritual senses will see intelligible objects in a corporeal way:

Therefore it is possible, and in fact most probable, that we shall then see the corporeal bodies of the new heaven and the new earth in such a way that we shall see God present everywhere and ruling all things, even physical things, seeing with perfect clarity wherever we turn our gaze, through the bodies that we shall inhabit and the bodies we shall see. (22. 29)[66]

---

[65] On the use of Cicero's *Republic* in 22. 28 see Doignon (1993). On Labeo see Ch. 11. 1l. Varro's report on incarnation theory comes from his *De Gente Populi Romani*: see further Ch. 11. 1b. In these late chapters of the work (22. 26–8) Plato and Porphyry, Varro, Cicero, and Virgil are all adduced, in a final parade of the secular authors, who, with Sallust, are at the heart of Augustine's apologetic confrontation with his classical heritage.

[66] For the idea of 'senses of the soul', which is implied here (with the reference to 'eyes of the spirit' in the same chapter), see *Sol.* 1. 6. 12, *An. et Or.* 2. 2. 3. Gannon (1956: 173–5) suggests Ambrose's influence on Augustine. There are Platonic parallels (e.g. *Republic* 533d2); cf. also Plotinus on acts of intellection as 'clear sense-perceptions' (6. 7. 7. 29–31). On the vision of God in *City* 22. 29 see Bardy, BA 37. 853–6.

It may be like seeing living bodies now. We see that a body is alive, and so see something invisible, its life. Seeing God may be like seeing life in a body: we may see God in ourselves, in others, in everything (22. 29). One will certainly see the rational numerical structures of all things. There will also be bodily movements, but of what kind, one cannot say. There will be glory and honour there, in a graded hierarchy, but there will be no jealousy of others. The will's freedom will be undiminished, but it will consist of the incapacity to sin, that is, it will be freedom from even the possibility of sinning (whereas Adam had the freedom not to sin).[67] This will be one and the same in all, though also individually possessed: there will be no fusing of wills. There will be knowledge of past evils, but they will not be felt, and so will cause no distress. The saints will also know of the eternal punishment of the damned, so that they may appreciate all the more the quality of divine mercy. This will be an eternal sabbath: indeed, 'we ourselves too will be that seventh day, when we shall be filled and restored by his blessing and sanctifying power' (22. 30). We shall rest and be at peace in God's eternal rest and peace. Augustine adds the conceit that the end of this sabbath will not be an evening, but the eighth eternal Lord's Day ('dominicus dies velut octavus aeternus'). This conceit leads to talk of an 'end' without end. For the 'finis' of which Augustine speaks is the eschatological end, the theme towards which the argument of the entire work has been moving.[68] The conclusion of the *City of God* is thus about the end of all ends:

> ibi vacabimus et videbimus,
> videbimus et amabimus,
> amabimus et laudabimus

> There we shall be at rest and see,
> we shall see and love,
> we shall love and praise.

(22. 30)

[67] In *Corrept.* 34 Augustine stresses that Adam in paradise had the capacity not to sin ('posse non peccare') with the help of divine grace: that entails Adam's capacity to sin ('posse peccare', cf. *City* 22. 30). The elect will be unable to sin ('non posse peccare', 22. 30; cf. *Corrept.* 16). Cf. Rist (1994: 129–35).

[68] The theme of the 'end' or 'finis' was that of the first book (19) of this final part of *City*. Earlier in this chapter (22. 30) Augustine echoes the theme of Book 19, where 'peace' is the final good, by asserting that there will be true glory, honour, and peace (all Roman virtues, transformed into Christian terms) in the final and perfect state of the city of God. Now, at the end of his book, Augustine hyperbolically deconstructs the concept of teleology, by proposing that the final state is an endless end.

I I

Influences and Sources

In the *City of God* Augustine uses a large variety of literary sources, and in a variety of ways. Some are cited in passing, others are repeatedly used; some are referred to by name, others may be inferred; in some cases, a specific use or influence is disputed by modern interpreters. In the preceding chapters (6–10) several such instances have been discussed. This chapter brings together and develops observations scattered throughout those chapters, cites the specific influences, and considers the nature and scope of Augustine's readings in earlier and contemporary authors. But for a discussion of two special kinds of material the reader is referred to earlier parts of this book: Chapter 3 deals with Augustine's debt to the apologetic tradition, and Chapter 4 with the other possible influences (including Tyconius) upon his elaboration of the theme of the two cities.

One may distinguish between different categories of literary influence on the author of the *City of God*. There is the pervasive presence of Latin secular authors, from Terence to Claudian, whether these be poets, historians, philosophers, or antiquarians. There is a more closely defined, but none the less highly influential group of Greek, mainly philosophical writers, most, if not all, of whom were read by Augustine in Latin translation. Finally, there are Jewish and Christian writers who certainly or probably influenced him. Each of these categories will be discussed in turn in this chapter.[1]

1. Secular Latin Writers

a. Terence

Of pre-Classical authors Terence alone is used in any significant way. This is not surprising, for Terence's comedies, together with Cicero,

---

[1] Although all the major influences upon Augustine in *City*, and most of the minor ones, are discussed here, the chapter does not refer to every attributable or possible influence. For general accounts of Augustine's sources in specific areas see Altaner (1967), Bartelink (1987), Bastiaensen (1987), Hagendahl (1967: with *testimonia* in vol. i), O'Donnell (1980), Testard (1958, 1992). Angus (1906) discusses the sources of *City* 1–10; Frick (1886) the sources of Book 18.

Sallust, and Virgil, had formed the staple Roman educational diet for
a considerable time prior to Augustine's schooldays, and continued to
do so.[2] Terence is cited in the *City of God* in short, sententious
extracts, usually to lend rhetorical colour and force in moralizing
contexts: this is the reason for which he is generally quoted by
Augustine.[3] One such instance is 14. 25, where *Andria* 305–6:

> . . . quoniam non potest id fieri quod vis,
> id velis quod possis

. . . since you can't have what you want, want what you can have

is made to represent a philosophical ethical ideal (will what you can
achieve) whose limitations Augustine is criticizing (similar use is
made of the lines in *De Beata Vita* 25). Augustine may have been
attracted to the passage because of its use of the verbs 'velle' and
'posse'. But at 14. 8 *Andria* 306–8 is adduced as part of an
investigation of the vocabulary of the passions, and Terence's own
text is used to demonstrate that 'volo' in *Andria* 306 is equivalent to
'libido' in 308:

I don't want anything (*nihil volo*) but Philumena.

It would be much better for you to try to rid your heart of this passion,
instead of saying things that only inflame your desire (*libido*), pointlessly.

This untechnical and indiscriminate use of literary language (Cicero
and Virgil are similarly indicted in the same chapter) is evidence for
Augustine that discretion has to be used in interpreting scriptural
references to the emotions, and in deciding whether a particular
passage is using terms in a precise and technical way. The passage
is a good illustration of the way in which citation of a poet can be
part of Augustine's hermeneutical strategy. In 19. 5 passages from
two other plays of Terence, *Adelphoe* 867–8 and *Eunuchus* 59–61,
are quoted to illustrate the point that the human condition is full of
distress. Augustine may have recalled the *Eunuchus* passage because it
uses the key terms of Book 19, 'war' and 'peace'. Finally, parts of
Eunuchus 584–91 are adduced in 2. 7 as an example of the way in

---

[2] In the late 4th c., the senator Arusianus Messius compiled a book of grammatical
and rhetorical examples from these four authors (cf. H. Keil, *Grammatici Latini*, vii.
449–514), which Cassiodorus (*Institutiones* 1. 15. 7) calls the 'quadriga Messii'; cf.
O'Donnell on *Conf.* 1. 16. 26; Alan Cameron (1977: 7).

[3] Cf. Hagendahl (1967: 378–81).

which the immoral example of the gods' behaviour (here the myth of Jupiter and Danaë) may be used to justify human misbehaviour.[4]

b. Varro

Varro is Augustine's chief source of information on the details of Roman religion criticized in Books 4, 6, and 7. The principal Varronian work used here is the *Antiquitates Rerum Divinarum* (for the fragments of which Augustine is the principal source); to a lesser extent, the *Logistoricus* entitled *Curio De Cultu Deorum* is also adduced.[5] There has been detailed discussion of Augustine's critique of Varro in Chapters 6 and 7 above. The following remarks are intended in part as a summary of the general conclusions reached in those chapters, and in part to put Augustine's use of a source like Varro into its historical context.

In 4. 8 ff. Augustine engages in detailed, piecemeal polemic against Varro's lists of minor 'certain gods' ('di certi') in the *Antiquitates*, which are ridiculed on the assumption that Varro himself believed monotheism to be the rational norm.[6] Varro's account of the internal functioning of the Roman polytheistic system is criticized on grounds of inconsistency (4. 17–25). But Augustine also finds fault with monotheistic pantheism (4. 12–13). The distinction attributed to Scaevola in the *De Cultu Deorum* between the three kinds of gods (of poets, philosophers, and political leaders) is introduced (4. 27), but Augustine argues that the evaluation of the various categories by Scaevola is out of tune with the actual or possible influence of the views of philosophers and poets on popular religious beliefs (for further use of the *De Cultu Deorum* see 7. 9 and 34).

Books 6 and 7 offer a comprehensive critique of Varro, whose views are now dealt with more systematically. The structure of the *Antiquitates* is summarized in 6. 3. One reason why Varro is treated so seriously by Augustine is that he was read and invoked by educated pagan contemporaries (7. 22); another is that Augustine found in his

---

[4] Cf. 2. 12. See *Letter* 91. 4, where the lines are also cited, in a discreetly polemical context: cf. the discussion in Ch. 1. 3 above. See further *Conf.* 1. 16. 26 and O'Donnell ad loc., who points out that Augustine's moralizing reading of the Terence passage resembles that of Donatus in his Terence commentary ad loc.

[5] For modern editions of Varro's works see Bibliog. C. For the title *Logistoricus* see Dahlmann and Heisterhagen (1957); cf. Tarver (1997: 145–50). Varro in Augustine: Hagendahl (1967: 589–630), O'Daly (1994*b*).

[6] For the term 'di certi' see *City* 7. 17 (= fr. 204) and Cardauns' edn. of *Antiquitates*, ii. 183.

writings elements of a system of natural theology that could be pinpointed and confronted (6. 5, 7. 5–6, 17, 28).[7] Varro's disbelief in traditional religion allows Augustine to engage with him on the level of general theory. The tripartite distinction reported in 4. 27 is further exploited as a threefold discourse about the gods ('theologia', 6. 5): but Augustine's strategy is to apply a reductionist critique to what Varro says, critically, about mythical and civil 'theologia', and so argue that Varro's remarks about either of these two kinds of discourse undermine both of them (6. 5–9). Augustine suggests that this was, in fact, Varro's concealed intention, though vitiated by his attempt, at one and the same time, to give a descriptive account of Roman religion and naturalistic explanations of religious phenomena (6. 4, 7. 23, 28). This latter attempt is criticized in detail in Book 7, with reference to Varro's twenty principal or 'select gods' ('di selecti'), in a manner reminiscent of the polemic of Book 4 against the 'certain gods'.[8]

Varro's historical work *De Gente Populi Romani* is used in Book 18, and is the principal, if not exclusive, source of Augustine's views on Greek history. It is also a source on the earliest phases of Roman history, and will have interested Augustine, as it propounds a Euhemeristic theory of the deification of kings and other humans.[9] It is also the source of a view attributed by Varro to astrologers, that rebirth in which the soul is brought into conjunction with the same body with which it was formerly united takes place after 440 years (22. 28). Varro's *De Philosophia* is exploited in Book 19 (which is our sole source of information about the work), especially chapters 1–3, where Varro's classification of philosophies by reference to their concept of the final Good is adduced, and becomes the organizational principle of the book.[10]

Augustine refers to these four works of Varro by name: *De Cultu Deorum* at 7. 9 and 34; *De Philosophia* at 19. 1; *De Gente Populi*

---

[7] See also Dihle (1996): cf. Ch. 7 n. 2.

[8] For the term 'di selecti' and a list of the gods see *City* 7. 1–2. Varro treated them in Book 16 of the *Antiquitates*.

[9] For Euhemerism in apologetic contexts generally see Ch. 3 above, with n. 17; cf. in relation to Varro *City* 6. 7–8 and 7. 18, with Ch. 7 n. 5. On Varro's *De Gente* see Fox (1996: 236–56).

[10] Tarver (1997: 145–61) is a general discussion of the *De Philosophia*, with comment on Varro's use in it, following his teacher Antiochus of Ascalon, of Carneades' method of division ('Carneadea divisio', cf. Cic. *De Finibus* 5. 6. 16), as reported in the classification of *City* 19. 1–3. Antiochus is named ibid. 19. 3 as Varro's authority.

Romani at 18. 2 and 13, 21. 8, and 22. 28; and the *Antiquitates* at 6.
3 (cf. 7. 35 for the dedication of the work to Julius Caesar;[11] for the
title see also 4. 1, 6. 4, 7). This display of documentary care is
unusual in antiquity. Does it reflect the apologetic nature of much
of the anti-Varronian argument, with evidence mustered and cited in
legalistic fashion? The reason has probably to do with generic conventions: although Augustine probably made some use of Varro's
Disciplinarum Libri in his early writings (cf. *De Ordine* 2. 12. 35),
he never refers to the work, and the conventions of the dialogue form
of those early writings would have discouraged him from doing so.
There can be no doubt that Augustine is citing Varro at first hand,
something that cannot be claimed with confidence about, for example,
Lactantius (see Chapter 3 above). Sometimes he says that he is citing
Varro verbatim (21. 8 and 22. 28, both with reference to the *De Gente
Populi Romani*). At other times he follows a widespread ancient
convention of giving the substance of Varro's views 'in my own words'
(3. 4, 19. 1). He combines admiration of Varro's scholarship with
criticism of his style, which he finds 'not especially attractive' ('minus
. . . suavis eloquio', 6. 2): but this criticism would not necessarily have
been a reason for not citing Varro directly. Augustine's admiration for
Varro did not begin with his use of him in the *City of God*: there is
similar praise for him in *De Doctrina Christiana* 2. 17. 27. Although
Augustine could have made up his own mind about Varro's scholarly
abilities, it is likely that he was influenced in this respect, as in so many
others, by Cicero, whose eulogy of Varro (= *Acad. Post.* 1. 3. 9) he
cites in 6. 2.[12]

c. Cicero

Cicero's *Republic* (*De Re Publica*), for the lost parts of which the *City
of God* provides important summaries and fragments,[13] is exploited
by Augustine for its critique of political and moral decline in the late

[11] Jocelyn (1982: 164–77, 203–5) and Tarver (1994) have differing views on the
date and dedication of the *Antiquitates*.
[12] Cf. Tarver (1997: 136–7). The practice of eulogizing model writers may have
been a feature of rhetoric treatises: see Quintilian on Varro (*Institutio Oratoria* 10. 1.
95), Sallust (ibid. 10. 1. 101), and Cicero (ibid. 10. 1. 110). Thus Augustine the rhetor
practises professional praise in the cases of Cicero as well as Varro, Virgil as well as
Sallust: cf. Hagendahl (1967: 728), and, for Sallust, Sect. 1 d below.
[13] See esp. Testard (1958: i. 194–6, 237–43; ii. 36–71), Hagendahl (1967: 540–
53), Heck (1966: 111–42).

Roman Republic.[14] Inasmuch as the *City of God* is a work of political theory, the *Republic* is the work that inspires and defines Augustine's elaboration of that theory. But Augustine is not concerned with Cicero's analysis of constitutions or forms of government in *Rep.* 1. The discussion in *Rep.* 1. 25. 39 and in *Rep.* 3 of the definition of 'res publica' provokes in Augustine an important critique of the realization of justice in any state (2. 21, 19. 21, 24).[15] In Book 3 of his work, Cicero allows the possibility of an immortal state, opposing the view that there is an inevitable decline of every state: Augustine counters this position at 22. 6 (= *Rep.* 3. 23. 34). Augustine also uses the account of Roman history given in *Rep.* 2: Tullius Hostilius' death by thunderbolt and the fact that he was not deified are reported at 3. 15 (= *Rep.* 2. 17. 32). A reference at *City* 5. 12 to the Roman decision to have two chief magistrates and call them consuls rather than kings may come from *Rep.* 2, but the attribution is not certain (= *Rep.* 2. 31. 53; cf. Zetzel ad loc.; see Sallust, *Catiline* 6. 7). The text of *Rep.* 2. 10. 18–19, on the deification of Romulus, is supplemented by Augustine's citation, also in 22. 6. Likewise, *Rep.* 2. 42. 69 is supplemented by a citation in Augustine (2. 21), and in the same chapter, Augustine reports on the conclusion of *Rep.* 2 (= *Rep.* 2. 43. 69), and alludes to Scipio's view there that the best state cannot endure 'without strictest justice' (*Rep.* 2. 44. 70), before giving his summary of the argument of *Rep.* 3. The same chapter (2. 21) provides an extensive citation from the beginning of *Rep.* 5 on the decline of the Roman Republic (= *Rep.* 5. 1. 1–2). The *Republic*'s discussion of whether imperial rule is just or unjust is reported in 19. 21, as part of Augustine's attempt to specify the necessary conditions of justice (= *Rep.* 3. 24. 36). The passage is supplemented by Augustine, *Contra Iulianum* 4. 12. 61 (cf. *City* 14. 23). In *City* 2. 8–13 Cicero's criticism of the theatre (one of many features of the *Republic* which echo Plato's *Republic*) in *Rep.* 4 is used (= *Rep.* 4. 9. 9 at 2. 14; *Rep.* 4. 10. 10–12 at 2. 13 and 2. 9; *Rep.* 4. 11. 13 at 2. 11; cf. 2. 12). Cicero can, therefore, be used as an important pagan critic of his own society and religion, and at the same time exploited as a reformer whose views are, Augustine believes, inevitably misplaced.

Other writings of Cicero are also used in the *City of God*. The discussion of the emotions in *Tusculan Disputations* 3–4 is influential

---

[14] For a possible earlier use of *Rep.* 3. 9. 14 ff. in *De Doctr. Christ.* 3. 14. 22 see Green ad loc.

[15] See Augustine's report of the argument of *Rep.* 3 in 2. 21 (= Ziegler, p. 81).

in 9. 4–5 and 14. 3–9. *Tusc. Disp.* 5. 8–10, on the origin of the term 'philosophus', is reflected in the doxographical 8. 2, and *Tusc. Disp.* 5. 119–20 in 9. 4. There are several further influences of *Tusc. Disp.* on points of detail: the work is an important source of Augustine's knowledge of Greek philosophy (Hagendahl 1967: 510–16). Cicero's *De Fato* and *De Divinatione* are exploited in the discussion of astrology and fate in *City* 5. 1–10. There are discernible influences of *Fat.* 9, 31, 34, and 40–1 in *City* 5. 3, 9–10: in addition, fragments 3 and 4 (Müller) of Cicero's work are generated from *City* 5. 2, 5, 8.[16] Cicero's position in *De Divinatione* 2 is countered by Augustine in *City* 5. 9. Because he relied chiefly on Varro for details of Roman religion, Augustine did not exploit Cicero's *De Natura Deorum* to the extent that might have been expected. Apart from some borrowing on points of detail, the Academic attack on anthropomorphic conceptions of the gods in *Nat. Deor.* 2. 70–2 is cited at *City* 4. 30, but with critical observations by Augustine, who sees there, as he does in Varro, cryptic support for, or, at most, only private criticism of, traditional religion. Augustine's extended account of the 'beauty and utility' of the universe in 22. 24 is indebted to *Nat. Deor.* 2. 133–62 (Testard 1955). The otherwise influential *Hortensius* is apparently not used in the *City of God*, with one exception (3. 15 = fr. 54 Müller).[17]

d. Sallust

Augustine will have been familiar with Sallust's historical writings since his schooldays, and Sallust is for him 'most exquisite weigher of words' (*De Beata Vita* 31), 'most skilled in the Roman language' (*Letter* 167. 6), and 'a historian most renowned for his veracity' (*City* 1. 5)—phrases which stress both the rhetor's admiration for a master of eloquence and, especially in the *City of God*, the apologist's anxiety to emphasize the status of the source which he will use as Roman evidence of Rome's long-standing political corruption.[18]

Augustine's citations of Sallust are, for the most part, a direct consequence of his planning of, and work on, the *City of God*. Most occur in the work itself, and the remainder are found chiefly

[16] Cf. Sharples' edn. of *Fat.*, pp. 162–3. On *Fat.* and *Div.* in *City* see Hagendahl (1967: 525–35). Cf. Ch. 6 n. 38.

[17] For its importance for Augustine see *Conf.* 3. 4. 7–8 and O'Donnell ad loc., Testard (1958: i. 11–39), Hagendahl (1967: 486–97).

[18] See further n. 12 above. Sallust in Augustine: Hagendahl (1967: 631–49).

in thematically related letters written immediately before, or in the early stages of, its composition (*Letters* 137, 138, 143), or in other writings of the period 413–26 (Hagendahl 1967: 631–3). Sallust is the historian most frequently cited in the *City of God*, but Augustine uses him less as a source for details of Roman history (in that respect Livy and his epitomists, and Varro, are of greater importance) than as a theorist of moral decline in Roman political and social life.[19] For that reason, the generalizing prologues of the *Catiline*, *Iugurtha*, and *Histories* are the passages most often cited, together with the speeches and comparison of Caesar and Cato in *Cat.* 51–4. Most citations and paraphrases of Sallust are found in Books 1–5 of the *City of God*.[20] Sallust's idealized account in the *Catiline* of early Roman history down to the destruction of Carthage in 146 BC is a foil to Augustine's counter-polemic in *City* 2. 17–22, of which the starting-point is *Cat.* 9.1: 'the principles of justice and morality (*ius bonumque*) prevailed among them as much by nature as by laws' (cited three times—and contested—in *City* 2. 17–18).[21] But Augustine also exploits Sallust's account of the decline of the Roman Republic in these chapters, making the words of *Cat.* 5. 9 ('[the state] changing little by little from the finest and the best, and becoming the worst and most disgraceful') a leitmotif, cited in whole or in part eight times, in 2. 18–22.[22]

In 2. 18 Augustine highlights the differences in Sallust's accounts of early Roman history in the *Catiline* and *Histories*, juxtaposing passages from the two works.[23] *Cat.* 9. 1 is cited first ('the principles of justice and morality prevailed'), followed by an allusion to *Cat.* 7. 3 in Augustine's words: '[Sallust was] praising the period in which, after the expulsion of the kings, the state (*civitas*) expanded considerably in

[19] On dissent as a motive for Sallust's adoption of the theme of Rome's decline, and its influence on his style, see Woodman (1988: 117–28). For the influence of 2nd-c. historiography on Sallust see Badian (1966).

[20] On Augustine's text of Sallust see Hagendahl (1967: 634–6). Sallust's historiography is excellently surveyed, with copious references to modern studies, in Kraus and Woodman (1997: 10–50).

[21] For the significance of Sallust's deviation in his account of early Roman history in *Cat.* from annalistic and earlier historiographical traditions see Earl (1961: 41–59). Augustine seems not to have used the parallel account in *Iugurtha* 41–2.

[22] On the vocabulary of Sallust's theory of decline and its debt to Roman thought see Earl (1961: 5–40). On the theme of order and disorder see Scanlon (1987).

[23] On these differences in Sallust see Earl (1961: 41–2), who regards the version in *Hist.* as 'nothing more than a response to criticism of his [Sallust's] earlier idealised view' (p. 42). In general, Earl (pp. 104–10) stresses the continuity of views maintained between *Hist.* and the two monographs. Cf. McGushin's comm. on *Hist.* 1. 8–15.

an incredibly short space of time.' This is the optimistic viewpoint;
but *Histories* gives another picture. Augustine first alludes to a
passage of *Hist.* 1. 11 that he will cite later in the chapter, attributing
social tensions in the early Republic to 'the injustice of the powerful
and, because of that, the separation between plebeians and patricians
and other disagreements in the city'. In this account, the high moral
standards and 'concordia' that prevailed in Rome between the Second
and Third Punic Wars were due to fear of Carthage rather than love
of justice: Augustine alludes briefly to the debate between Scipio
Nasica and the elder Cato (though without mentioning Cato here)
on whether it was better to destroy Carthage, with Nasica arguing
that the preservation of the enemy was a means of restraining faults
in Rome through fear.[24] From Augustine's allusion Maurenbrecher
reconstructed Sallust's words as follows: 'and the cause . . . was not
love of justice, but fear of an undependable peace, so long as
Carthage still stood' ('causaque . . . non amor iustitiae, sed stante
Carthagine metus pacis infidae fuit'). Scholars have not always
accepted this as Sallustian phraseology.[25] But references to 'fear of
the enemy' ('metus hostilis') and 'fear of Carthage' ('metus Punicus')
are found elsewhere in Sallust (*Iug.* 41. 2; *Hist.* 1. 12), and the
general idea is commonplace (Earl 1961: 47–8). In the account in
Histories, Sallust presents the period after the expulsion of the kings
as one of the rule of justice only through fear of another 'external'
enemy, Tarquin and the Etruscans. Oppression by the powerful and
social discord were endemic in Rome: only gradually, through seces-
sion, the tribunate, and acquisition of rights was the Roman *plebs*
free from such treatment, and it was only in the time of the Second
Punic War (under the pressure of 'fear of the enemy', it is implied) that
there was an end to dissension ('discordiae', 'certamen'). Augustine
cites these views directly in three successive quotes from *Hist.* 1. 11.
He then reverts ironically to the quote from *Cat.* 9. 1 at the beginning
of the chapter ('the principles of justice and morality prevailed'). To
this he adds the other much-cited phrase from the *Catiline* ('changing
little by little', 5. 9), also in a critical and ironical sense. The *Histories*
agree with Sallust's other works that, in the words cited by Augustine
in this chapter, 'discord, greed, ambition, and the rest of the evils that

[24] On the tradition of the debate see Earl (1961: 47–9).
[25] Klingner (1928: 173–6); cf. Hagendahl (1967: 639–41). Reynolds (edn. ad loc.)
doubts that 'amor iustitiae' is a Sallustian phrase.

commonly spring up in a time of prosperity increased enormously
after the destruction of Carthage'. But Augustine questions the
validity of the judgement of *Cat.* 5. 9 that after the destruction of
Carthage, Rome became 'little by little changed from the finest and
best [state] to the worst and most disgraceful'. It is precisely the vision
of the 'finest and best' state that the account in *Histories* appears to
undermine. Augustine concludes this review of Sallustian texts with a
further citation from the beginning of *Histories*, in which 'traditional
morality' ('maiorum mores') is, in the Republic after Carthage's
destruction, swept away, as society is corrupted by luxury and greed
(*Hist.* 1. 16), 'not little by little, as hitherto, but in a torrential
fashion'. Augustine does not comment on the possible contrast
between the 'little by little' of *Cat.* 5. 9 and 'not little by little' in
Hist. 1. 16: perhaps he did not perceive it as a contrast. In any case, his
polemical point has been made, by playing off one set of Sallustian
views against another, and so undermining, he believes, a benevolent
image of early Roman society and its morals.

   In other sections of the work Augustine interweaves Sallustian
quotations and allusions with those from, and to, other authors. In
2. 21 Sallust and Cicero are combined in this way. Augustine alludes
first to the leitmotif of *Cat.* 5. 9, then to a passage in Cicero's
Republic (3. 43), where Scipio says 'so, where there is a tyrant, one
must say, not, as I said yesterday, that the state is corrupt, but that . . .
there is no state at all.' Then follows the chronological reference to
the death of Tiberius Gracchus, made precise by an allusion to Sallust
('the discussion [in Cicero] is set at the time when one of the Gracchi
had been killed, from when, Sallust writes, serious political strife
began' = *Hist.* 1. 17). Augustine then cites from the end of Book 2 of
the *Republic* Scipio's views on harmony in the state and the need for
justice as the basis of concord (*Rep.* 2. 69), and the questioning of
those views by Philus (*Rep.* 2. 70), before going on to provide a
summary of the argument of Book 3 of Cicero's work. Cicero's
argument is used to undermine Sallust's account of the Roman state
as 'the worst and most disgraceful' (*Cat.* 5. 9 again): the Republic
'did not exist at all' (*Rep.* 3. 43 again). Then follows an extended
quotation from the *Republic* (5. 1–2) on the fading of old Republican
traditions, and the loss of the substance of the Republic. The state,
according to Scipio's definition of it (*Rep.* 1. 39 is alluded to briefly),
never really existed, because it never exemplified true justice. Again,
as in *City* 2. 18, the argument has been advanced almost exclusively

with reference to other writers' texts. Sallust's account of Rome's
moral decline is trumped by Cicero's more radical questioning of the
value of the Roman state, even in its purportedly better periods.

Sallust is not merely a witness ('testis', *City* 2. 18) to the evils of
Roman society. When Augustine praises Roman virtues, he bases
himself on Sallust's historical synopsis of the rise of Rome. At *City*
3. 10, *Cat.* 6. 3–5 is cited in this connection, and Augustine
comments that 'Rome grew honourably great through these qualities'
('his artibus'), alluding to Sallust's talk at *Cat.* 11. 2 of Rome's 'good
qualities' ('bonae artes'). In 5. 12 Sallust and Virgil together are
sources of Augustine's account of Rome's virtues, and once again
Augustine's method is to interweave citations of both authors, like
'an expert mosaic artist' (Hagendahl 1967: 632). Passages on
'passion for glory' ('cupido gloriae') and 'freedom' ('libertas') from
the *Catiline* (6. 7, 7. 3, 7. 6) lead to a brief allusion to the comparison of Cato and Caesar in *Cat.* 53–4. Then in one phrase a Virgilian
line and a Sallustian phrase are combined: 'So it came about that men
of considerable excellence desired that Bellona should rouse wretched
peoples to war and goad them with her bloody whip' (*Aen.* 8. 703:
'[Discord] which Bellona follows with bloody whip'), 'that there
might be an opportunity for their ability to shine' (*Cat.* 54. 4:
'[Caesar] hankered after a new war, where his ability might shine').
Sallustian concepts and phrases ('greed for praise and passion for
glory'; 'through love of domination and desire for praise and glory')
are illustrated by a Virgilian reference to Roman defence of 'freedom'
('libertas') against Porsenna and Tarquin (*Aen.* 8. 646–8, but the
episode is also one highlighted by Sallust, *Hist.* 1. 11). The chapter's
argument is advanced by further reference to Sallustian analysis: 'but
when freedom had been won, such a great passion for glory had come
over them that freedom alone was insufficient unless domination was
also sought'. With this one may compare *Cat.* 7. 3: 'but it is amazing
to relate how much the state, once freedom had been won, expanded
in a short space of time: such a great passion for glory had come over
it'.[26] Again, the general, abstract point in Sallust is illustrated by two
Virgilian passages, *Aen.* 1. 279–85 and 6. 847–53. The latter
passage talks of the 'qualities/skills' ('artes', 6. 852) that are the
means of Roman rule: this allows Augustine to align it with Sallustian

---

[26] For 'dominatio' as a form of slavery ('servitium') contrasted with freedom
('libertas') see *Hist.* 1. 55. 2, 6, 8–10, 26; on 'dominatio' see Earl (1961: 106–8).

talk of 'good qualities' ('bonae artes') and leads to the citation of *Cat.*
11. 1–2, with its contrasts of ambition and greed, the good and the
base, the virtues and treachery and deceit. The rest of the chapter is
citation and elaboration of Sallustian themes, with the comparison of
Cato and Caesar the dominant motif. But Augustine continues to
combine passages that are separate in Sallust. The true glory attaching
to Cato was unsought: *Cat.* 54. 6 is cited. The theme of *Cat.* 11. 2, a
passage previously quoted, is reiterated in close paraphrase: 'therefore
glory and honour and power, which the good hankered after and strove
to attain by fair means, should not be the goal of virtue, but should
rather be its consequences'. What is added to Sallust in the preceding
words—the notion of virtue based on conscience, not on others'
judgement—has been introduced through two quotations from Paul
on glory (2 Corinthians 1: 12 and Galatians 6: 4). The theme of
'virtus' has been broached: Augustine alludes to the fact that Sallust
had spoken of the 'virtus' of Caesar and Cato (*Cat.* 53. 6: 'but in my
time there were two men of great excellence, but opposed characters';
City 5. 12: 'but since there were two Romans of great excellence at
that time').[27] Cato's speech is cited in part (*Cat.* 52. 19–23): it
represents a Roman ideal, and also an idealized view of history, as
Augustine goes on to point out. For Cato argues that it was not force
of arms, but rather 'industry at home, just rule abroad, a mind that is
free in making political decisions' that brought about Rome's greatness. In their place extravagance, avarice, and other faults have
supervened. Augustine suggests that Sallust's readers (and he stresses
that these words are Sallust's as much as Cato's) take this speech at
face value, as an accurate view of early Roman history. But he
challenges its accuracy, again citing the more pessimistic view of a
history characterized by social and political strife given by Sallust at
Hist. 1. 11. The reflections of this chapter end with ideas taken over
from the *Catiline*. Rome's achievements were due to a few good men:
Augustine paraphrases *Cat.* 53. 2–4 and concludes by quoting *Cat.*
53. 5, where this theme is developed. The chapter ends with allusions
to passages already used in it: *Cat.* 11. 2 and 52. 21–2. Throughout
it, Sallust has been employed to put Roman achievements into a
critical perspective: the Virgilian quotations lend colour and emphasis
to the argument.

[27] On 'virtus' in Sallust see Earl (1961: 28–40). Augustine never engages with the
specifics of Sallust's concept, but understands 'virtus' in an exclusively philosophical
sense.

If Augustine's Caesar and Cato are Sallustian, so is his Sulla at 3. 7, where *Cat.* 11. 4 is alluded to, and at 2. 18 and 2. 22, where *Hist.* 1. 16 is cited in the first passage and echoed in the second. In other writings of Augustine (e.g. *Confessions* 2. 5. 11) the influence of Sallust's portrayal of Catiline is no less evident (Hagendahl 1967: 646–7).

e. Virgil

Virgil's *Aeneid* is the poetic text most often cited by Augustine in the *City of God*.[28] In the early books of the work it is an integral part of the argument. Virgil is perceived by Augustine to be a repository and representative of the pagan Roman culture which he is combating. *Aeneid* 6. 853 ('to spare the conquered and subdue the proud'), cited in the preface to Book 1, epitomizes the earthly city's urge to dominate others, just as Jupiter's promise to the future Romans in *Aeneid* 1. 278–9:

> to these I set no bounds of place or time,
> but have granted an empire without end

expresses the illusory nature of the imperialistic 'Roma aeterna' myth (2. 29). But Virgil also gives expression to the perceived paradox of pagan religion that gods may at one time protect, and at another abandon, their worshippers, whether these be individuals or states. In Books 2–3 the lines:

> the gods, through whom this empire had stood fast,
> all left the shrines and the abandoned altars

from *Aen.* 2. 351–2 appear repeatedly (2. 22, 24–5; 3. 3, 7, 14–15) as a leitmotif to underline this point. In Book 1 Augustine exploits the irony that Troy's ineffectual gods became the very gods whom pagan critics of Christianity allege might have protected Rome against Alaric. In 5. 12, however, both *Aen.* 1. 279–85 and 6. 847–53 are quoted, with 8. 646–8, this time in a positive context: Augustine is accounting for Roman imperial achievements by seeing them as a divine reward for Roman virtues. Virgil thus serves both a documentary and a rhetorical purpose. His poetry is a repertoire of pagan Roman attitudes and assumptions, and at the same time an

---

[28] Virgil in Augustine: Hagendahl (1967: 384–463), Schelkle (1939). Virgil in *Conf.*: Bennett (1988). Courcelle (1984) surveys the reception of the *Aeneid* in late antiquity generally.

eloquent, challenging expression of these. Even when he is citing Virgil with polemical intent, Augustine seems to be aware that the citation embellishes his own text. The extended paraphrase of the description of Cacus (*Aen.* 8. 193–267) in 19. 12 serves a different purpose: Augustine uses it to conjure up the vivid and extreme image of a monster, exemplifying disorder, and then to argue, against all odds, that even Cacus is an instance of inner coherence and order.

Virgil's poetry is not Augustine's primary source for Roman religion, but Augustine uses it to illustrate Roman attitudes to magic (8. 18–19, 18. 16–18, and 21. 6, 8, passages in which, besides *Aen.* 4. 487–93, *Eclogue* 8. 70 and 99 are used) and to the allegorical understanding of the gods (4. 9–11, using *Ecl.* 3. 60 and *Georgics* 3. 325–6 and 4. 221–2), just as it is used to explore pagan views of the afterlife and such special doctrines as metempsychosis (14. 3–9, 21. 13, using passages from *Aen.* 6). Augustine assumes that *Aen.* 6. 713–51 (on afterlife punishments, purification, and rebirth) expounds Platonic doctrine (10. 30, 14. 3, 21. 13, 22. 26).[29] It is possible that he is using a Neoplatonist commentary on the *Aeneid* here: the citation of *Aen.* 6. 750–1 at 13. 19, followed by the words 'which Virgil is praised for having formulated from Plato's teaching', suggests 'an explanatory source' of the remark.[30] Thus Virgil is cited to give substance to a Platonic view which Augustine contrasts unfavourably with Porphyry's more nuanced views on reincarnation.

When Augustine cites *Aen.* 1. 278–9 at 2. 29 he adapts Jupiter's words in an *interpretatio Christiana* of the prophecy: recast, they can be made to refer to Christian appropriation of their heavenly country: the one true God

> sets neither bounds of place or time,
> he will grant an empire without end.

In the same chapter of Augustine's work, *Aen.* 11. 24–5, referring to the 'outstanding souls' of heroes fallen in battle, is applied to the Christian martyrs. But this Christianization of Virgil is isolated in the *City of God*, and is not characteristic of Augustine (Hagendahl 1967: 437–44).

[29] For a similar assumption that in *Georgics* 2. 325–6 (on the sexual image of Heaven and Earth as a divine couple) Virgil is using 'books of the philosophers', see *City* 4. 10.
[30] Cf. Hagendahl (1967: 406). See Courcelle (1955, 1957, 1984). P. Hadot (1971: 215–31) discusses the question of whether Marius Victorinus wrote a Neoplatonizing Virgil commentary.

In 10. 27, quoting *Eclogue* 4. 4 and 13–14, Augustine seems to accept the view that these lines about the child who will free the world from crime and fear represent a Sibylline prophecy about Christ. Augustine's view is that Virgil does not speak 'on his own' ('a se ipso') here, but rather conveys the prophecy 'in a poetical manner . . . but nevertheless truthfully': its truth-content is that Christ is the one who will heal men's sins. But neither here nor elsewhere does Augustine explicitly identify the birth of the child of *Ecl.* 4 with Christ's birth: the lines are rather about Christ as saviour (Hagendahl 1967: 442–4).

f. Livy, Florus, Justinus, Eutropius, and other historians

Sallust is the only Roman historian whose ideas are reported and discussed by Augustine. Historiography other than Sallust's is for him a source of historical facts, anecdotes, and examples (Hagendahl 1967: 650–66). Apart from Sallust, the only historians whom Augustine mentions by name (if we exclude Varro's historiography) are Livy (2. 24, 3. 7), and Pompeius Trogus and his epitomist (or, more accurately, excerptor) Justinus (4. 6). Livy and his epitomists are the most important of these sources. Sometimes their use is concentrated in clusters, as in 3. 17, where Augustine, asking polemically where the Roman gods were when Rome suffered disasters, collects thirteen examples (each prefaced by the question 'where were [those gods]?') of such disasters. It can be argued that all but three of these come from Livy, and, moreover, from Books 3–12 of his work, with the Livian order preserved, with one exception, by Augustine (Hagendahl 1967: 650–4). Augustine does not cite Livy verbatim, although he transfers certain Livian phrases to his account. Sometimes he summarizes and generalizes the Livian account (Hagendahl 1967: 652 no. 8). Given the nature of his use of his source, it is not always possible to determine whether Augustine is working from the Livian text, the summaries known as *Periochae*, or the Livian tradition.[31] The series of *exempla* of Roman contributions to the glory of the state in 5. 18 probably derives from a number of sources, which certainly include Virgil and the fourth-century *Breviarium* of Eutropius, used for details of the stories of Cincinnatus, Regulus, and Valerius Publicola. Livy is also used in this chapter (Hagendahl 1967: 654–6). The Regulus story (almost the only detail of the First

---

[31] On the *Periochae* see Begbie (1967); Budé edn. (1984) by P. Jal.

Punic War that interests Augustine: 1. 15, 24, 5. 18) is an episode where, typically, it is difficult, if not impossible, to decide whether Livy or the Livian tradition is being used. Moreover, other sources, for example, Cicero's *De Officiis*, may have played a role.[32] Livy is the predominant source for events of the Second Punic War (1. 6, 3. 21, 31). Interestingly, it is only in relation to events from the Sullan period that Livy is named expressly: in 2. 24 a fragment of Livy 77 is preserved, and Augustine's account (3. 7) of Fimbria's destruction of Ilium probably derives from Livy 83 (Hagendahl 1967: 660). In 2. 17 and 3. 21 Augustine replies to Sallust's optimistic account of early Rome by counter-examples taken from Livy or the Livian tradition (Hagendahl 1967: 639, 660).

Augustine appears to use Eutropius on occasion, as in the account of the violent death of several of Rome's kings (3. 15), which may be influenced by *Breviarium* 1. 2–7. He also uses the second-century epitomist Florus, most clearly in 3. 19, where he seems to adapt a rhetorically charged phrase from Florus 1. 22. 1 ('the nation which was victorious was more like the one that had been defeated') about the Second Punic War.[33] Although Florus is not mentioned by name here, Augustine's judgement on him, which also explains his rhetorical attraction, is given: 'he is one of those who set about, not so much narrating Rome's wars, as praising the Roman Empire'. In the same chapter a further passage from the same section of Florus on desperate Roman measures after defeat at Cannae (1. 22. 23–4: 'There were no arms; they were taken down from the temples. There were no men; slaves were liberated and took the military oath') is imitated by Augustine: 'they granted freedom to slaves . . . there were no arms: they were taken down from the temples'. Vivid details of the horrors of the struggle between Marius and Sulla in 3. 27–8 owe much, but not everything, to Florus 2. 9 (Hagendahl 1967: 664). Augustine is capable of combining Florus with other sources, most notably in 3. 15 on the death and apotheosis of Romulus, where some of the details derive from Florus 1. 1. 17–18, others from Cicero's *Republic* 2. 17 and 2. 20 (Hagendahl 1967: 665–6).

As for other historians of the Imperial period, Augustine's use of them is minimal (Eusebius apart: see Sect. 3e below), as are his references to, and exploitation of, the Empire as a theme. The unimportance of the history of the Imperial period in the *City of*

---

[32] See above, Ch. 6 n. 10.   [33] Cf. however similar phrasing in Livy, 21. 1.

God is probably to be attributed to the work's apologetic purpose: Augustine wants to demonstrate that, before the coming of Christ, Rome and other peoples experienced violence and catastrophes from which their gods could not save them. Augustine, as can be seen from his use of Eutropius, whose survey extends to 364, could have incorporated Imperial subject-matter in his account, had he so wished. He does so, notably, in the reference in 4. 29 to Hadrian's relinquishing of three eastern provinces, which may derive from Eutropius (*Breviarium* 8. 6). Moreover, Orosius devoted Book 7 of his *Histories* to the Imperial period, and we must assume that Augustine would have had access to the same sources as his protégé. Yet the one Imperial historiographer referred to by name in the *City of God* (4. 6) is Justinus, the beginning of whose epitome or excerpting of the Augustan writer Pompeius Trogus is cited verbatim in the same chapter, on the topic of the rise of the Assyrian kingdom: Augustine will have found there a fuller treatment of the topic than that given by Eusebius. In 4. 6 Augustine appears to question the truthfulness of Trogus–Justinus by comparison with the chronographers (he must mean Eusebius and Jerome). But in a number of chapters of Book 18 (2, 19, 22) he appears to use Justinus again.[34]

g. Seneca

Augustine scarcely refers to, or uses, Seneca, with the exception of the extensive use made of his *De Superstitione* in *City* 6. 10–11. These chapters provide most of the fragments of that lost work (Lausberg 1970: 201–25; Hagendahl 1967: 676–80), with extensive citations. The work was familiar to Christian apologists like Tertullian (*Apologeticum* 12. 6), although it may not have been known to Lactantius (Lausberg 1970: 197–201). Augustine uses the *De Superstitione* chiefly as a complement to, and as part of his critique of, Varro's attitude to Roman religion. He finds in Seneca polemic against philosophically unacceptable concepts of the gods: their theriomorphic form (fr. 31), gods like Cluacina, Pavor, and Pallor (fr. 33), and rites (Isis, Magna Mater, Bellona) which incite to irrational, violent, and self-mutilatory practices (frr. 34–5). Augustine argues that Seneca, with greater freedom than Varro, undermines the credibility of state religion. Seneca, writing as a philosopher,

[34] For speculation on Augustine's attitude to the Imperial period of Roman history see Schindler (1987). On the possible source of an anecdote in 2. 25 see Ch. 6 n. 19.

accepts that popular religious cult is a matter of laws and custom, not of truth (frr. 38–9). Through Augustine we also learn that Seneca criticized Jewish religious practices in the *De Superstitione* (*City* 6. 11). But he also acknowledged the self-awareness of Jewish religion, its insight into the origin and meaning of its rites (fr. 43), by contrast with Roman ignorance of the reason for Roman religious practices.[35]

h. Lucan

Writers of the Imperial period are less frequently used by Augustine in the *City of God* than those of the Republican or Augustan periods, with the exception of Seneca and Apuleius. Among the later Latin poets, Lucan's rhetoric attracted Augustine, who called him Rome's 'great poetic declaimer' at *De Consensu Evangelistarum* 1. 30. 46. Citations of Lucan are rarely found in works prior to the *City of God* (Hagendahl 1967: 470–2). Here they embellish and highlight Augustine's polemic against the violence of Roman history, whether in the fratricide with which Rome's history begins (15. 5, citing *Bellum Civile* 1. 95), or in Sulla's purge of Marius' supporters (3. 27, citing *Bell. Civ.* 2. 142–4: the chapter amalgamates the views and language of Cicero, Florus, and Lucan), or in the civil war between Caesar and Pompey (3. 13, citing the striking opening lines, *Bell. Civ.* 1. 1–2). A line of Lucan's may be quoted for its epigrammatic force: when Augustine is answering Christian disquiet about the fact that many of Alaric's victims were unburied, he uses (1. 12) the phrase 'he who does not have an urn is covered by the sky' from *Bell. Civ.* 7. 819. Lucan's estimation of Cicero ('Tullius, supreme author of Roman eloquence', *Bell. Civ.* 7. 62–3) is often used by Augustine as a prelude to citations from Cicero (e.g. *City* 14. 18), and is adapted once to refer to Virgil (10. 1). But these uses are occasional and fragmentary. They reveal a knowledge of Lucan that is probably more than mere familiarity with excerpts of his work, but whose profundity we cannot gauge, any more than we can assess, on similar evidence, Jerome's knowledge of Lucan.[36]

---

[35] For this interpretation of 'maior pars populi' ('the greater part of the [Roman] people') in fr. 43 see Lausberg (1970: 205–6).
[36] For Lucan in Jerome see Hagendahl (1958: 229–30, 284). On the difficulty of evaluating late antique citations of earlier authors see Ogilvie (1978: 14–16).

i. Persius

Persius is cited by Augustine at 2. 6 in an extended quotation of *Satire* 3. 66–72.[37] The context is polemical, and Persius' invocation of what philosophy can teach is exploited by Augustine to underline the moral vacuity of traditional Roman religion, by contrast with Christian teaching. Part of another verse from the same *Satire* (3. 37) is cited in the next chapter of the *City of God* (2. 7). These citations do not exploit Persius' vivid and novel style, but there is limited use of some of his striking phrasing in other writings of Augustine, where citations from *Satires* 1, 3, and 5 are found (Hagendahl 1967: 472–4). However, the only extended citation is that found in *City* 2. 6, and it fulfils a characteristic polemical function: a pagan source critical of its society's attitudes and behaviour is invoked as a witness on the apologist's behalf. There is a similar purpose to Augustine's one long quotation from Juvenal (*Satire* 6. 287–95) in *Letter* 138. 16 to Marcellinus (one of the letters of 411–12 that anticipate themes of the *City of God*). Although Persius is the satirist most often cited by both Augustine and Jerome, Augustine does not share Jerome's penchant for satire, or his tendency to recall Persius' most outrageous language.[38]

j. Pliny the Elder, Solinus, Aulus Gellius, and others

Pliny the Elder is named in the *City of God* (15. 9, 12), and is the source of Augustine's examples of long-living people (15. 12), of the view that human stature is continually in decline (15. 9), and of the catalogue of deformities in 16. 8. All of this information comes from the seventh book of the *Naturalis Historia* (Hagendahl 1967: 670–3). An additional source of the examples of natural wonders in 21. 4–5 and in a passage in 21. 8 may be the *Collectanea Rerum Memorabilium* of the (probably third-century) compiler Solinus.[39] Aulus Gellius' anecdote (*Noctes Atticae* 19. 1) about the Stoic philosopher in the sea-storm is paraphrased by Augustine at 9. 4. A passage in Valerius Maximus' collection of *exempla* (1. 8. 4) has been held to be the source of what Augustine says in 4. 19 about the talking statue of Fortuna Muliebris, but it is likely that the anecdote derives from Varro (= *Antiquitates* fr. 192), as does the rest of what is said about

---

[37] For Augustine's text of Persius see Hagendahl (1967: 217 n. 1).

[38] Cf. Jerome, *Letter* 22. 29, using Persius, *Sat.* 1. 104–5. Wiesen (1964) studies Jerome as satirist.

[39] Cf. Mommsen's edn. pp. xxxi–xxxii, 255; cf. Hagendahl (1967: 671–3).

Fortuna and Felicitas in 4. 18–23 (Hagendahl 1967: 667–8). It is by
no means certain that the work of the Tiberian encyclopaedist
Cornelius Celsus is alluded to in 8. 1, even if *Opiniones omnium
philosophorum* is the title of that work.[40]

k. *Apuleius*

Augustine's fellow North African Apuleius ('the Platonist from
Madauros', *City* 8. 14; 'an African, better known to us Africans',
Letter 138. 19) is the source of the catalogue of natural catastrophes
in *City* 4. 2, where he and his work *De Mundo* are named (Augustine's
information comes from *Mund.* 34). In 18. 18 the theme of Apuleius'
Metamorphoses (Augustine is here the first to refer to the work by its
popular title, *Asinus Aureus*[41]) is adumbrated, in a discussion of
accounts of human transformation into animal forms and other paranormal phenomena.[42] Augustine refers to the alleged role of demons in
such matters, and it is in relation to demonology that he makes his most
extensive use of Apuleius' writings, in Books 8–9, from 8. 14 on, where
his Apuleian source, *De Deo Socratis*, is named. Although Augustine
used doxographical accounts of Platonism and other philosophical
doctrines, there is no evidence that he used Apuleius' *De Platone*.
Apuleius' *Apologia* is alluded to in 8. 19 (cf. *Letter* 138. 19).

Augustine's critique of Apuleius' demonology in Books 8 and 9 has
been discussed in detail in Chapter 7. In 8. 23–7 Augustine also
makes use of a work found among Apuleius' writings in the manuscript tradition, the Hermetic treatise *Asclepius*, which is almost
certainly not by Apuleius, and which is not attributed to him by
Augustine, who regards the work as a translation (8. 23). Augustine
is attracted to the *Asclepius* because it offers an account of demons
different from that of Apuleius with which he can, in part,
sympathize. But in general Augustine opposes the false mediation
of demons with the true mediator, Christ, just as he sees the magic of
Apuleius and Apollonius of Tyana as being in sharp contrast to
Christ's miracles (*Letters* 102. 32, 137. 13, 138. 18–19).[43]

[40] See further below, Sect. 2c.
[41] Apuleius in Augustine: Hagendahl (1967: 680–9), O'Donnell (1980: 149–50).
The title *Asinus Aureus*: René Martin (1970).
[42] Cf. Moine (1975). See Courcelle (1963: 101–9) on the possible influence of
Apuleius' *Metamorphoses* on the structure and themes, esp. the motif of 'curiosity'
('curiositas') in *Conf.* On the theme of curiosity in Augustine see further Ch. 6 n. 42.
[43] On Apuleius' demonology see Beaujeu's Budé edn.; cf. Bernard (1994). See
further Ch. 7 n. 24.

l. Cornelius Labeo

Cornelius Labeo, who provided antiquarian and philosophical interpretations of Roman religion, writing probably in the third century, is
referred to by Augustine on a number of occasions in the *City of
God*.[44] All the references are to Labeo's lost work *De Diis Animalibus*,
for which Augustine is the principal source.[45] Apart from the intri-
guing reference in 22. 28 to an anecdote about two men dying and
subsequently returning to their bodies (Mastandrea 1979: 105–7), all
of Augustine's allusions to Labeo deal with the related themes of good
and evil 'divinities' ('numina'), demons, and the deification of
humans. Labeo's dualist doctrine of good and evil 'numina' (*City* 2.
11), though philosophically founded,[46] exploited the phenomenon of
contrary deities in Roman religion (e.g. Febris and Salus: *City* 2. 25).
In 2. 11 and 8. 13 Labeo is reported to have claimed that evil divine
beings are propitiated by blood-sacrifice and grim supplications,
whereas good ones are propitiated by cheerful rites ('ludi', 'convivia',
'lectisternia'), again building on traditional religious thinking (some
gods are worshipped that they may not do harm, others that they may
do good).[47] Augustine's polemic against Labeo is piecemeal. In 2. 11
he is using him as an expert witness whose claim that good 'numina'
are favourably influenced by stage shows contradicts Roman contempt
for actors: Greeks are more consistent than the confused Romans in
this respect. In 8. 13 (cf. 2. 14), alluding to Labeo's inclusion of Plato
among the 'demi-gods' ('semidei'), like Hercules and Romulus,
Augustine draws attention to Plato's rejection of poetic fictions,
including stage shows, and highlights the alleged contradiction
between Plato's views (which he takes to be endorsed implicitly by
Labeo) and Labeo's account (which Augustine assumes to be approv-
ing) of the place of stage shows in the rites of good 'numina'. In 9. 19
terminological debates about the terms 'demon' and 'angel' are
reflected: this was a staple of pagan–Christian polemic.[48] Implicit,
though not expressed, in Augustine's allusions to Labeo's evil

---

[44] Mastandrea (1979) is the standard study: here pp. 49–50 on Labeo's date. Labeo
is cited as an authority by writers like Macrobius and John Lydus.

[45] See Mastandrea (1979: 236–9). Augustine does not name the work: for its title
see Servius on *Aen.* 3. 168.

[46] For the doctrine's origin in beliefs about good and evil demons, and its appropriation by Neoplatonists and others, see Mastandrea (1979: 148–58); cf. Porphyry,
De Abstinentia 2. 36–43.

[47] Cf. Servius Danielis on *Aen.* 4. 58; see Mastandrea (1979: 146–8).

[48] Cf. Origen, *Contra Celsum* 5. 5; see Mastandrea (1979: 139–44).

divinities is the rejection of a concept of deity that includes malignant powers, a theme of the *City of God* and of Christian apologetic in general.[49] Augustine's references to Labeo need not presuppose that he knew his work directly: there are no compelling indications that Augustine is quoting Labeo, as opposed to reporting his views.

m. Claudian

Augustine's limited use of later Latin poetry in the *City of God* reflects a similar tendency in his writings generally (Hagendahl 1967: 470–8). It is, therefore, exceptional when he cites Claudian's panegyric on the third consulship of Honorius (*III Cons*. 96–8) at *City* 5. 26, making the lines into praise of Theodosius' victory over the usurper Eugenius at the Frigidus in 394 (although they refer to Honorius rather than Theodosius), and omitting the mythical allusion to Aeolus in verses 96–7.[50] In the same passage of the *City of God* the motif of *III Cons*. 93–5 (to which the cited verses 96–8 summarily refer), that the wind miraculously turned the enemy spears back on themselves, is employed by Augustine in the lines immediately before the citation, suggesting familiarity with the Claudian passage generally. Augustine, believing Claudian not to be a Christian,[51] stresses his praise of a Christian emperor, glossing Claudian's account of the Frigidus battle by asserting that Theodosius 'fought more by prayer than by armed force'. Augustine rarely refers in the work to recent or contemporary events: this makes the citation of Claudian all the more remarkable.

2. Greek, Mainly Philosophical, Writers in Latin Translation

a. Plato

The one extended portion of Plato's writings that Augustine read is the section of the *Timaeus* (27d–47b) translated by Cicero.[52] Augustine

[49] See Wissowa (1912: 246 n. 1). For the topic's philosophical origins see Cic., *De Legibus* 2. 11. 28, *De Natura Deorum* 3. 25. 63–4.
[50] The same telescoping of the lines, and the same application to Theodosius, are found in Orosius, *Histories* 7. 35. 21, who probably copies Augustine: see Alan Cameron (1970: 191).
[51] On the question of Claudian's Christianity see Alan Cameron (1970: 189–227).
[52] See Powell (1995: 273–300) on Cicero's translations from the Greek, here pp. 280–1 on his *Timaeus* translation. Cf. Hagendahl (1967: 535–40), whose account omits a number of specific influences of *Tim.* on Augustine (details below); Courcelle (1969: 169–70), who argues against earlier scholarly views that Augustine used

acknowledges his source at 13. 16, where the longest citation, of Cicero, *Tim.* 40 (= Plato, *Tim.* 41a–b), is found, preceded by 'these are Plato's words, as translated by Cicero into Latin'. On two occasions where there are lacunae in our text of Cicero's translation, Augustine provides some evidence for what that translation must have been (Cicero, *Tim.* 28 = Plato, 37c, in 11. 21; Cicero, *Tim.* 48 = Plato, 45b, in 13. 18). Augustine approves of some of Plato's views, and disapproves of others. From Plato he derives the argument that the universe is good, and gives its good creator joy (11. 21: Cicero, *Tim.* 4 (not in Hagendahl), 9–10, 28 = Plato, 28a, 29e–30a, 37c). He believes that the *Timaeus* claims that God's mind contains the Forms of the whole universe and all ensouled beings (12. 27: Cicero, *Tim.* 11–12 = Plato, 30c–d (not in Hagendahl), understood in a Middle Platonist sense). He takes issue with Plato's assertion that lesser gods, created by the supreme God, have a part in the formation of humans and other animals (12. 25, 27: Cicero, *Tim.* 41 = Plato, 41c–d). He uses the view that the lesser gods are mortal by nature, but immortal because of God's will, to argue polemically against Porphyrian attitudes to embodiment (13. 16; cf. 22. 26: Cicero, *Tim.* 40 = Plato, 41a–b). He observes that Plato maintained that the universe was a living, ensouled, everlasting being (13. 17; cf. 10. 29: Cicero, *Tim.* 10, 16, 28 = Plato, 30b, 32c–d, 37c–d), exploiting this view to argue, against Porphyry and other Platonists, that a body can be immortal, if God so wills. The harmony in the world-soul, as well as the role of the elements in perception and the proportions established between the elements, demonstrate that, for Plato, the union of body and soul was unproblematic: by implication, Plato should not object to bodily resurrection (13. 17–19: cf. 8. 11, 15, 22. 11: Cicero, *Tim.* 13, 15, 22–6 (not in Hagendahl), 45, 48 = Plato, 31b, 32b–c, 35c–36e, 42c, 45b). Plato's views on metempsychosis are reported, but this time Augustine finds more to approve in Porphyry (10. 30, 12. 27: Cicero, *Tim.* 45 = Plato, 42b–c). Augustine sees similarities between the account of the formation of the universe in the *Timaeus* and the Genesis account of its creation: in *De Doctrina Christiana* 2. 28. 43 he believed, with Ambrose (accepting Philo of Alexandria's view that Plato was influenced by the Hebrew Bible), that this derived from Plato's encounter with Jeremiah in Egypt. But by the time he came to write the *City of*

Calcidius; Waszink (1972: 243) agrees with Courcelle. Augustine refers to *Tim.* in *Ser.* 241. 8. 8 and 242. 5. 7.

God Augustine, having become familiar with Eusebius' *Chronicle*, dismissed an encounter of Plato with Jeremiah, or even his familiarity with the Septuagint, on chronological grounds: Plato's knowledge, he now believed, must have been derived from an oral tradition (8. 11; cf. 11. 21).[53]

b. Plotinus and Porphyry

When Augustine refers to the 'moderns' ('recentiores') who have followed Plato's doctrine and call themselves 'Platonists' ('Platonici'), he names Plotinus, Porphyry, and Iamblichus, along with Apuleius (8. 12). Augustine probably derived all that he knew of the Neoplatonists from Marius Victorinus' translations. It is uncertain which Neoplatonist writings Victorinus translated, but works of both Plotinus and Porphyry are likely to have been among them.[54] In the *City of God* a number of treatises of Plotinus are referred to in the discussion of Platonism in Books 9 and 10. At 9. 10 a short citation of *Ennead* 4. 3. 12. 8–9 is found, on the theme of human mortality. In 9. 17 we appear to have an amalgam of two Plotinian passages, 1. 6. 8. 16–22 and 1. 2. 3. 5–6 (cf. also 1. 6. 9. 32–4), with evocations of the return to the divine and becoming godlike. *Ennead* 5. 6 is used in 10. 2, where the theme is illumination (*Enn.* 5. 6. 4. 14–22). In the same chapter Augustine attributes to Plotinus a view not explicitly attested in the *Enneads*, that the source of the world-soul's and individual soul's happiness is the same (Theiler 1966: 162 n. 5). Plotinus' views on providence are referred to in 10. 14, where 3. 2. 13. 18 27 in particular is influential *Enn.* 1. 6. 7. 32–4, on happiness and the vision of beauty, is echoed in 10. 16. In 10. 23 the title

---

[53] Cf. Ch. 7 on 8. 11, with n. 22.

[54] 'Certain books of the Platonists' are referred to in *Conf.* 7. 9. 13, and are said to have been translated by Victorinus (*Conf.* 8. 2. 3). On these 'libri Platonicorum' see P. Hadot (1971: 201–10). O'Donnell on *Conf.* 7. 9. 13 summarizes earlier views on whether they contained writings by Plotinus or Porphyry or both, and notes the tendency towards Porphyry in recent scholarship, reinforcing the position of Theiler (1966: 160–251 (first pub. 1933)) against that of Henry (1934); cf. the fundamental discussion in Courcelle (1969: 173–89). TeSelle (1970: 43–5, 49–54; 1974) provides a balanced account of the question. Beatrice (1989) is an extreme—and unconvincing—version of the view that Augustine is indebted solely to Porphyry, arguing that he knows only one work of Porphyry's, and that this was the *De Regressu Animae* (Beatrice agrees with J. J. O'Meara (1959) in identifying this work with the *Philosophy from Oracles*, but he also wants to argue that it is identical with *Against the Christians*). P. Hadot (1960b), a lengthy review of J. J. O'Meara (1959), has often been cited as if it were a refutation of O'Meara's argument: in retrospect, that argument remains plausible.

of *Enn.* 5. 1 is given ('On the Three Principal Substances'), and the
relation between intellect and soul adumbrated in 5. 1. 3 is mentioned by Augustine in the same chapter. In 10. 30 Plotinus' views on
transmigration, in agreement with those of Plato, are alluded to:
passages like *Enn.* 3. 4. 2 and 4. 3. 12 may have been influential
here. Finally, towards the end of the work, a definition of beauty given
in *Enn.* 1. 6. 1. 21–2, and subsequently criticized by Plotinus, is
paraphrased (22. 19). Despite these allusions to, and echoes of,
Plotinus, Augustine never engages with the broader issues of Plotinus'
philosophy. There is no sustained discussion of a Plotinian text. The
very brevity of the Plotinian passages alluded to, as well as the fact
that some of them are eminently quotable and become famous
quotations, like 1. 6. 8. 16–22 and 4. 3. 12. 8–9 (Theiler 1966:
161–2), make it uncertain that Augustine read Plotinus extensively:
we cannot exclude the possibility that what he knew of the great
Neoplatonist derived from Porphyrian commentaries on the *Enneads*
or summaries or citations of his doctrines. In his early writings
Augustine stresses how little he read of Plotinus and the 'certain
books' prior to his conversion in 386 ('having read a very small
number of Plotinus' books', *De Beata Vita* 1. 4; cf. 'very few drops',
Contra Academicos 2. 2. 5). It is impossible to quantify the extent of
these readings. Authorial modesty may play a role in the choice of
language in *De Beata Vita* and *Contra Academicos*: both passages in
question come from proems, where such modesty is conventional
(Janson 1964). Augustine may also want to emphasize the enormous
effect that even a limited reading of the books of the Platonists had
on him ('when they had let a very few drops of most precious unguent
fall upon that meagre flame, they stirred up an incredible conflagration', *Contra Academicos* 2. 2. 5, tr. J. J. O'Meara).[55] Even if we
conclude that Augustine's Platonist readings were restricted in 386,
that would be no reason for excluding further reading of Plotinus
later: but there is no evidence for this either.

It is quite different with Porphyry. Augustine refers to the work
which he calls *De Regressu Animae* at 10. 29, and this work has been
used extensively from 10. 9 onwards to the end of the book: it is also
used in 22. 26–8. What we know of it comes exclusively from this
part of the *City of God*.[56] Augustine engages with Porphyry's views

---

[55] On the stylistic effect here see O'Connell (1963: 3 n. 14), Du Roy (1966: 69 n. 5).
[56] The testimonia are in Bidez (1913: 27*–44*); cf. Courcelle (1969: 181–8).

on metaphysical principles, theurgy, purification and salvation (especially the notion of a 'universal way' of liberation), mediation, demonology, reincarnation, and the body–soul relation (see Chapters 7 and 10 above). A key phrase from the *De Regressu Animae*, 'one must escape from every kind of body' ('omne corpus fugiendum'), is repeatedly cited by Augustine in his polemic (10. 29, 22. 26, etc.).[57] In 10. 11 another work of Porphyry's, the so-called *Letter to Anebo*, is the source of views on magic and demonology.[58] In 19. 23 Porphyry's work on divine worship and human religious beliefs, the *Philosophy from Oracles*, is adduced, and oracles related to Judaism and Christ are cited and discussed.[59] Porphyry's work on images may be the source of the symbolic explanation of Attis at 7. 25 and of heroes and Hera at 10. 21.[60] Augustine appears not to have known Porphyry's work *Against the Christians*, although he, of course, knows of Porphyry's anti-Christian polemic, which was not confined to one work.[61] In general, Porphyry is an essential source for Augustine's views on higher, philosophically influenced attitudes to the afterlife and preparation for it, the themes both of the last book of the first part of the work (10) and of the last book of the second part (22).

c. Doxographies

Augustine undoubtedly also used handbooks of philosophical doctrines.[62] One such handbook is behind the historical survey of 8. 2–4 and later doxographical chapters of Book 8, though Augustine does not name its author. In the prologue to his late work *De Haeresibus* he refers to 'Opinions of all the Philosophers' (the phrase

[57] Cf. the citation of key phrases from Sallust and Virgil (see Sect. 1d–e above). Cf. 'the divinities shudder' ('numina perhorrescunt') from the oracle cited from Porphyry in 19. 23: the phrase recurs in 20. 24, 22. 3, and 22. 25: see Courcelle (1969: 183–4 n. 152).

[58] Cf. Courcelle (1969: 185–6). The work is also known from Eusebius, *Praeparatio Evangelica* 3. 4 and 5. 10, as well as Iamblichus' *De Mysteriis*.

[59] See further Ch. 10, on 19. 22–3. On *Philosophy from Oracles* see Wolff's edn. of the frr.; Courcelle (1969: 183–4); Meredith (1980), on Porphyry and Julian; Wilken (1984: 148–56), part of a wider discussion (pp. 126–63) on Porphyry and Christianity; den Boer (1974), who discusses historical arguments in Porphyry's polemic; T. D. Barnes (1981: 175–6).   [60] Cf. Bidez (1913: 7*, 10*), Courcelle (1969: 185).

[61] Cf. Augustine, *Retr.* 2. 31, *Letter* 102. 28, 30; Courcelle (1969: 188 n. 176, 210 n. 14). On the question of this work's existence and its contents see Harnack's edn. of the frr.; Wilken (1984: 135–47); cf. T. D. Barnes (1973), Beatrice (1989 (see n. 54 above)). On later 4th-c. debates about Dan. 9 see Wilken (1980).

[62] Cf. Solignac (1958). Dillon (1993) provides an introduction to, and commentary on, a handbook of Platonist doctrine.

is found also in *City* 8. 1) in six substantial volumes by 'a certain Celsus'. This may or may not be the early first-century encylopaedist Cornelius Celsus, to whom Augustine alludes in *Soliloquia* 1. 12. 21, on the question of the highest good. In *Contra Academicos* 2. 2. 5 he names a Celsinus, whose view of the Neoplatonists' books was that they were 'full to the brim'. It has been suggested that this may be Celsinus of Castabala, the author of a compendium of philosophical doctrines.[63] Celsinus' dates are unknown, but if he is the Celsinus of *Contra Academicos* 2. 2. 5 his work must have included Neoplatonic doctrines. It is possible that he is the 'certain Celsus' mentioned in *De Haeresibus*, who wrote about philosophers 'up till his own day' (*Haer.* pref.). Augustine may simply have confused the names. The unnamed source of the doxography in Book 8 may also be Celsinus (and the names of the three Neoplatonists listed in 8. 12 may indicate that they were included in his handbook), but we cannot be certain (Courcelle 1969: 192–4).

d. Hippocratic writings

The reference to Hippocratic writings in 5. 2 derives from Cicero's *De Fato* (= fr. 4), although it is not explicitly attributed to it.[64]

e. Sibylline oracles

Augustine had access to an anonymous Latin verse translation of Sibylline verses forming a single acrostic, which he cites, commenting on the impossibility of preserving the acrostic in the Latin version (18. 23).[65] It is unlikely that he made his own prose translation of the other Sibylline verses, quoted in Greek by Lactantius, which he cites, also in 18. 23.[66]

---

[63] Cf. *Suda*, s.v. Kelsinos; Stephen of Byzantium, s.v. Kastabala. See further above, Ch. 7 n. 13.   [64] See Sharples's edn. of *Fat.*, p. 162.

[65] Courcelle (1969: 190) speculates that he may have found them in Porphyry's *Philosophy from Oracles*.

[66] See Lactant. *Div. Inst.* 4. 18. 15; cf. Ogilvie (1978: 28–33) on Lactantius' use of the Sibylline oracles. For the latter and other oracles and prophecy in the Roman empire see Potter (1994). On the prose translation in *City* 18. 23 see Courcelle (1969: 190–2), whose argument that the translation is Augustine's own is not persuasive. Augustine's use of Lactantius: Bastiaensen (1987: 44–5). Augustine and Sibylline oracles: Altaner (1967: 204–15).

3. Jewish and Christian Writers

a. Josephus

It has been suggested that in 18. 45 Augustine may have used an
epitome of Books 11–14 of Josephus' *Antiquities of the Jews* in his
resumé of the history of Israel from the building of the Temple to the
birth of Christ (Courcelle 1969: 198 n. 9), adding only the synchron-
ism with Rome's history ('By then Rome had already subjugated
Africa'). There is no known Latin translation of the *Antiquities*
that Augustine could have used, whereas he may have had access to
one of the *Jewish War*.[67]

b. Philo of Alexandria

The question of Augustine's direct access to Philo of Alexandria is
disputed.[68] If Augustine used Philo's *Quaestiones et Solutiones in
Genesin* (as with Josephus, a Latin translation must be posited) in
his *Contra Faustum* in 398, then that work may have been the
source of the treatment of Noah's ark in *City* 15. 26. But Ambrose
may have been the intermediary of Philo to Augustine, in his *De
Noe et Arca* 7. 16.

c. Origen

The influence of Origen's writings in the Latin West was widespread
and complex, as their role in the confrontation between Jerome and
Rufinus and in the Priscillianist movement in Spain demonstrates.[69]
Augustine responded to Orosius' request to counter Origenist
theology by writing in 415, at a time when he was also engaged in
the composition of the *City of God*, the treatise *Contra Priscillianis-
tas et Origenistas*, in which he attacked Origen's views on the life of
the stars, the punishment of the fallen angels, the pre-existence of

---

[67] A Latin translation of the *Jewish War* was made by a Hegesippus (identity
unknown) at the end of the 4th c.: Altaner and Stuiber (1966: 385). The earliest
attested Latin version of the *Antiquities* is that of Cassiodorus in the mid-6th c. Cf.
Courcelle (1969: 198 with n. 8), who cites *Letter* 199. 9. 30, where Josephus is
named.

[68] For the contrary positions see Altaner (1967: 181–93 (first pub. 1941)) and
Courcelle (1961; 1969: 197 with n. 7); cf. Bartelink (1987: 13).

[69] Origen in the dispute between Jerome and Rufinus: Kelly (1975: 195–209, 227–
58). Origen and Priscillian's teaching: Chadwick (1976: 71–2, 77, 190–208 (on
Orosius' *Commonitorium* and Augustine's *C. Prisc.*)). On the 4th-c. Origenist controversy: E. A. Clark (1992), here 227–43 on Origen's role in Augustine's treatment of
Origenist themes, before and during the Pelagian controversy.

souls, and the world as a place of punishment.[70] These topics are also
found in the *City of God*, where Origen's major theological treatise *De
Principiis* is cited with both its Greek and Latin titles at 11. 23. The *De
Principiis* is used there and elsewhere throughout the work.[71] Augustine
may have known both Rufinus' doctrinally edited translation of
Origen's treatise and Jerome's more literal one, and the latter would
have exposed, more clearly than the former, the contentious elements in
Origen's thought. In 11. 23 the view that the universe was created as a
place of gradated punishment for different categories of sinful souls
(*Princ.* 1. 4. 1, 1. 5. 5) is attacked. In 12. 14 Origen's interpretation of
Ecclesiastes 1: 9–10 (cited *Princ.* 1. 4. 5 and 3. 5. 3; cf. 2. 3. 1) in terms
of historical cycles and periodic repetitions is countered, as is, in 13. 20,
his understanding of the nature of the Pauline spiritual body (cf. *Princ.*
2. 10. 1). Augustine's polemic against cyclical theories of history in 12.
11–28 embraces Origen's views. Origen is not named in 12. 14 or 13.
20, but he is in 21. 17, where Augustine alludes to his belief that the
devil and fallen angels would be ultimately delivered from their punishment (*Princ.* 1. 6. 3, 3. 6. 5), and points out that he has been
condemned by the Church for these and other views: Origen's position
is formally countered by Augustine in 21. 23. The interpretation of
Genesis 2: 7 to mean that the Spirit brings the human soul to life,
criticized by Augustine in 13. 24, may be known to him from Origen, to
whom 'some have maintained' at the beginning of the chapter probably
refers (for the interpretation of Genesis 2: 7 see *Princ.* 1. 3. 6; *Contra
Celsum* 4. 37).[72] The polemic of 12. 4 may be directed against *Princ.* 1.
4. 3 and 3. 5. 5.

As for Augustine's use of other works of Origen, *Homilies on
Genesis* 2. 2 influences 15. 27,[73] though there seems to be no
compelling reason to assume that the *Contra Celsum*, rather than
the *De Principiis*, is influential in 12. 14–15.[74]

---

[70] Origen on the stars: Scott (1991). On Augustine's *C. Prisc.* see O'Connell (1984).
[71] Origen in Augustine: Altaner (1967: 224–52), Courcelle (1969: 198–200),
Bartelink (1987: 14–18), E. A. Clark (1992: 227–43).
[72] Cf. Theiler (1970: 562–3), who cites further Origen texts.
[73] Cf. Augustine, *Qu. Hept.* 1. 4; Courcelle (1969: 199 with n. 13).
[74] Salin (1926: 203, 244) adduced *C. Cels.* 4. 67 and 5. 20–1; Altaner (1967: 231
n. 4) suggested *Princ.* 2. 3. 4 as a source. If Altaner is right, then Augustine was
surprisingly unimpressed by Origen's use of biblical examples here in place of the
commonplace instances—Socrates, Phalaris, Alexander of Pherae—given at *C. Cels.* 4.
67–8 and 5. 20–1 (for parallels see Chadwick's tr. at 4. 67 n. 5). Augustine himself
gives the conventional instance of Plato at *City* 12. 14.

d. Epiphanius

It has been suggested that the *De Mensuris et Ponderibus* of Epiphanius of Salamis, in a Latin translation, is the source of the story about the Greek translation of the Hebrew Bible in 18. 42, but Augustine could have got the story from Jerome or other sources more accessible than Epiphanius.[75]

e. Eusebius and Jerome

The *Chronicle* of Eusebius is the basis for Augustine's synchronization of biblical and non-biblical events in Book 18 of the *City of God* (cf. also 4. 6).[76] Augustine knows it in Jerome's translation and continuation (Eusebius' second edition of the *Chronicle* extended as far as 325/6; Jerome continued it until 378), and follows this version faithfully. Sometimes he refers to it as Eusebius' work (16. 16, 18. 25), sometimes as that of Eusebius and Jerome (18. 8, 10, 31). What Jerome translated and Augustine used was the second part of the *Chronicle*, the so-called *Canons*, or chronological tables, with columns giving, as appropriate, Assyrian, Median, Persian, Sicyonian, Argive, Egyptian, and other regnal years, Olympiads, and events of Jewish history (T. D. Barnes 1981: 116–18; Mosshammer 1979). Augustine did not know the first part of the *Chronicle*, the *Chronography*, which provided the source material for the *Canons* (this first part survives in the original Greek in fragmentary form, and in an Armenian translation, possibly dating from the sixth century, of the entire *Chronicle*). Eusebius made use of the *Chronographiae* of the third-century Christian writer Julius Africanus, but his debt to Africanus must not be overestimated (Mosshammer 1979: 146–57): it is unlikely that Augustine made any direct use of Africanus (Altaner 1967: 218–23; Bartelink 1987: 18 n. 40). As for other works of Eusebius, it remains debatable whether Augustine had access to the polemical *Praeparatio Evangelica*.[77] Augustine knows Rufinus' translation of 402/3 of Eusebius' *Ecclesiastical History*, referring to it in late works, *De Cura pro Mortuis Gerenda* 6. 8, and *De Haeresibus* 10, 22, and 83. But it is questionable whether the praise of Theodosius in *City* 5. 26 is influenced by Rufinus' supplement to

---

[75] Altaner (1967: 290–5), following Draeseke, suggested Epiphanius as source; cf. Courcelle (1969: 207 n. 52).

[76] On the *Chronicle* see Mosshammer (1979), T. D. Barnes (1981: 111–20). On Augustine's use of it see Courcelle (1969: 200–1), Bartelink (1987: 18–19).

[77] J. J. O'Meara (1969) argues that he had, against Altaner (1967: 258 n. 46).

Eusebius' work: part at least of Augustine's information on the Thessalonica massacre may have come from Paulinus of Milan's *Vita Ambrosii* 24. 1.[78]

Jerome's *Onomasticon* or *Interpretation of Hebrew Names* is the source of Augustine's biblical etymologies in *City* 15–17.[79]

f. Orosius

In repudiating the scheme of ten persecutions in 18. 52 Augustine is opposing what Orosius (*Histories* 7. 27) proposes. If Augustine is directing his argument against Orosius here, he does not mention him by name: nor is there any evidence elsewhere in the *City of God* that he is influenced by Orosius' work, which he, in a sense, commissioned (Orosius, *Histories* 1. prol. 8–9).[80]

---

[78] Duval (1966: 144–68) argued for the influence of Rufinus' supplement. On the chronological difficulty of making Paulinus' *Vita* a source for *City* see Bastiaensen (1987: 47–8).

[79] On the *Onomasticon* see Kelly (1975: 153–5); for its use in *City* see Ch. 9.

[80] See in general Mommsen (1959: 325–48), here 346–7 on *City* 18. 52.

12

The Place of the *City of God* in Augustine's Writings

The *City of God*, like other major works of Augustine—such as the *De Trinitate* (begun in 399 and concluded in the years 422–6) and *De Genesi ad Litteram* (written between 401 and 414)—took shape over several years. In common with the other works just mentioned, it explores central themes of Augustine's thought. Thus Books 11–14 of the *City of God* give Augustine's culminating account of the opening chapters of Genesis: it is not as broad an exegesis as that found in *De Genesi ad Litteram* (itself the continuation of two earlier Genesis commentaries by Augustine[1]), but it demonstrates, because of his repeated concentration on certain thematic clusters, that Augustine's ideas continued to develop. For example, the discussion of the emotions in *City of God* 14 extends beyond anything found in the Genesis commentaries proper. Conversely, some discussions in *City* are less full than those found elsewhere: for an account of the question of whether time has a beginning and of the relation of creation to God's eternity we would have to supplement what is said in Book 11 by reading Book 11 of the *Confessions*.[2] What is true of thematically related parts of Augustine's major works is also true of the relationship between the *City of God* and other works of Augustine. To name one instance, his views on the just war cannot be understood unless his somewhat oblique statements in *City* are related to more comprehensive discussions elsewhere—in an anti-Manichaean treatise, a work of biblical exegesis, and some letters written at considerable intervals.[3] For Augustine does not, for the most part, write works on self-contained topics. As has been seen in Chapter 4, even the two cities' theme is adumbrated in other, earlier works, most notably the

---

[1] For Augustine's sequence of Genesis commentaries see Pelland (1972). For studies of their themes see Ch. 8 n. 2.

[2] Time, eternity, and related topics in Augustine: Meijering (1979), O'Daly (1987: 152–61), Kirwan (1989: 151–86), Rist (1994: 73–85).

[3] *Contra Faustum* 22. 75, *Quaestiones in Heptateuchum* 6. 10, *Letters* 47. 5, 153. 16, 189. 6. For modern studies of Augustine's attitude to war see Ch. 6 n. 6.

De Vera Religione, the *De Catechizandis Rudibus*, and the *De Genesi ad Litteram*, as well as in a number of sermons. Yet the full scope of the theme only becomes apparent in the *City of God*.

Inevitably, in a major work like the *City of God*, Augustine exploits his earlier treatments of certain topics. Thus the discussion of difficulties relating to bodily resurrection in *Enchiridion* 84–92 is the background to *City* 22. 12–19. The account of biblical history from Cain and Abel to Jacob given in *City* 15–16 makes use of *Quaestiones in Heptateuchum*. In *City* 15. 26, on Noah's ark, Augustine cites his own allegorical interpretation of the ark in *Contra Faustum* 12. 14. Throughout *City*, refutation of Manichaeism remains a concern of Augustine's (1. 20, 6. 11, 11. 13, 22, 14. 5, etc.), and arguments developed in earlier works are rehearsed.[4] Yet two earlier works above all anticipate linked themes of *City*: the *De Vera Religione*, written in 390 or 391, and the *De Catechizandis Rudibus*, of about 400 or 404–5.[5] It is revealing to observe how their pre-occupations form the positions adopted by Augustine in the later, and larger, *City of God*.

The phrase 'true religion' ('vera religio') and its variants occur several times throughout the *City of God*, particularly in the first half of the work, where it is used to contrast Christianity with pagan religions (4. 1, 7. 33, 35, 8. 17, 10. 3; 'vera pietas' is found in 5. 14, 19, 20). This 'true religion' is monotheistic (10. 1, 3, etc.): the one God is the 'true God' (10. 19, 26), of whom the Platonists have an intimation, even if they also condone polytheism (8. 12, 10. 1, etc.). This nexus of themes, with their apologetic connotations, opens the *De Vera Religione*:

Since the complete way of the good and blessed life is established in the true religion, wherein the one God is worshipped and recognized with purest piety as the principle of all things, by whom the universe is begun and completed and contained: the error of those peoples is, in consequence, all the more clearly detected who have preferred to worship many gods rather than the one true God and Lord of all; for their wise men, whom they call philosophers, used to have squabbling schools, but shared temples.   (1. 1)

---

[4] On Manichaeism's enduring popularity in late 4th and early 5th c. Rome, and Christian reaction to it, see Pietri (1976: ii. 913–14), Lieu (1985: 165). Cf. *Liber Pontificalis* 50. 3, 51. 2.

[5] For the question of its date see van Oort (1991: 177 n. 72).

The common aims of philosophy and true religion—the realization of
happiness and the appropriation of truth—are stressed in *Vera Rel.* 3.
3, as they will be in the *City of God*. For Augustine, philosophy and
religion should share in the search for wisdom:

> For so it is believed and taught as the essential element in human salvation
> that philosophy, that is, the pursuit of wisdom, is not different from religion,
> for they whose doctrines we do not commend do not share in our rites
> (*sacramenta*).   (*Vera Rel.* 5. 8)

The implication of this argument—that in the establishment of truth
in religious doctrine philosophers must be confronted, not avoided—
is crucial to Augustine's extended polemic against Varro's philosophical account of religion, as well as against Platonist doctrines,
in the *City of God*.

   Although the theme of the two cities is not formulated expressly in
De Vera Religione, the passage cited above from 1. 1 is typical in that
it sets out a thematic range that corresponds to that of the *City of
God*. Thus we find in *Vera Rel.* (1. 1–4. 7) the qualified praise of
Platonism and the argument that Christianity achieves what Platonism
aims at, together with repudiation of Platonist demonology, that is
characteristic of *City* 8–10.[6] The polarity of types of 'men' that under-
pins the contrast of the two cities is also developed there. Augustine
works with a series of opposites that reveals the basis of the contrast.
His terminology is Pauline: old–new, earthly–heavenly, carnal–spiritual, inward–exterior. These antitheses run throughout the work, but
in *Vera Rel.* 26. 48–28. 51 they are expounded in a particularly
revealing way. There Augustine begins by contrasting the natural
sequence of phases ('aetates') of human life from infancy to old age
with a scheme of spiritual stages, progressing from learning by precept
and historical example to eternal blessedness (26. 48–9).[7] But even
the natural sequence of life-phases has a symbolic relevance: it represents life in the body and in the temporal dimension. In this respect it
finds political expression in the state, and distinctions of value can be
made between various kinds of state:

> This is called 'the old man' and the 'exterior and earthly man', even though
> he gains what people call felicity in a well-ordered earthly city, whether under

---

[6] Cf. *City* 2. 19 with *Vera Rel.* 4. 6, and *City* 18. 50 with *Vera Rel.* 3. 4: these
parallels were noted by Madec (1991: 16–17), in a perceptive study of *City*'s debt to
the earlier work.
[7] For the 'aetates' theme see *City* 16. 12, 43, 22. 30; cf. Ch. 9 n. 28.

kings or emperors (*principibus*) or laws or all of these. For no people can be well ordered in any other way, not even one which pursues earthly things: for even such a people has some measure of a beauty of its own.   (26. 48)

Augustine's broad indifference in the *City of God* to types of constitution,[8] and his insistence on the order or peace appropriate to the state (*City* 19), are anticipated here. In *Vera Rel.* 27. 50 the necessary association between the old and the new man in earthly life is stressed, anticipating the theme of the mingling of the two cities; and Augustine talks of 'two kinds' ('duo genera') of people throughout history, the impious and the people of God. The antitheses which shape Augustine's thinking are further enriched here by the linking of old/earthly and new/heavenly both to peoples and to Scripture: the 'history' ('historia')[9] of the Jews is the Old Testament, with its promise of an earthly kingdom, whereas the New Testament has the promise of the heavenly kingdom. The life of the new people of God extends from Christ's incarnation until the final judgement, which will bring about a definitive separation of the pious and the impious. The various themes rapidly suggested here—polar groupings, history, Scripture, eschatology—demonstrate how long and seriously Augustine reflected on the subject-matter of *City of God*.

Other chapters of *Vera Rel.* develop the theme of history's special importance for the Christian:

What is of prime importance in following this religion is the history and prophecy of the temporal arrangement (*dispensatio temporalis*) of divine providence for the salvation of the human race—its reform and restoration to eternal life.   (7. 13)

The role of historical events is understood Platonically. They are reminders of eternal truths for fallen souls:

For in cleaving to the eternal creator we must, of necessity, be affected by eternity. But because the soul, overwhelmed by and entangled in its sins, cannot by itself see and hold on to this—there being no level interposed in human affairs by which the divine might be appropriated, and by means of which man might strive towards likeness to God from out of earthly life—God in his ineffable mercy comes to the help of individual humans and indeed

---

[8] But see *City* 4. 15, although it is more about the size of states than their constitutions. For Augustine's indifference, echoing Cicero's *Republic*, to types of constitution see *City* 2. 21.

[9] For the senses in which Augustine uses 'historia' see n. 10 below; cf. the concluding para. of Ch. 9, with n. 63 (modern studies). See also Ch. 7 nn. 35, 45, Ch. 9 n. 28.

of the human race, in a temporal arrangement by means of his changeable creation, which is nevertheless subject to his eternal laws, to make the soul recall its original and perfect nature.   (10. 19)

Scripture is the means of revealing the 'temporal arrangement' ('dispensatio temporalis').[10] It is a moral guide (3. 5), and, particularly in its account of Christ's life, it provides 'moral instruction' ('disciplina morum') (16. 32). Its teaching is partly literal, partly it uses figurative means (17. 33). History forms opinion, appeals to belief (9. 16). But, especially when understood allegorically, it also conveys unchanging truth; and Augustine poses questions, which he does not answer in *De Vera Religione*, on the scope and nature of allegorical interpretation, on the understanding of scripture in translation, and on the anthropomorphism of the Bible (50. 99). Although the development of these themes is not peculiar to the *City of God* (several are pursued in the *De Doctrina Christiana*, on which Augustine probably began work in 396[11] Augustine's reflections in *Vera Rel.* influence the role that the interpretation of history has in Books 15–18 of the later work, and in the persistent preoccupation with scriptural exegesis in its second half, from Genesis in Books 11–14 to Revelation in Books 20–2.

In *Vera Rel.* these themes are linked to other dominant concerns of Augustine that are also crucial to the *City of God*. Among these are: appropriate and other loves (46. 86–48. 93), pride and its correction (45. 84, 48. 93), the concept of order (39. 72–44. 82). The

---

[10] In *Vera Rel.* 55. 110 the 'temporal arrangement' is said to include Christ's incarnation for the salvation of humanity. In *Div. Qu.* 53. 1 Augustine talks of 'arrangements of the two Testaments', which he explains as the revelation through Scripture of the role of divine providence in history 'from Adam until the end of time' (ibid.); cf. ibid. 57. 2 on the place of the Church and of faith in the 'temporal arrangement'. The importance of faith/belief in the 'temporal arrangement' is also stressed in *F. et Symb.* 4. 6, 8. In *Doctr. Chr.* 2. 28. 44 Augustine, classifying 'historia' among 'divine institutions', says that the past is 'part of the history of time, whose creator and controller is God'. In *City* 10. 32, playing upon Porphyry's phrase, 'the universal way of the soul's liberation', Augustine identifies this 'way' with scriptural revelation of the purifying Christian truth, validated by prophecies which have been fulfilled, culminating in Christ's human birth and resurrection. See TeSelle (1970: 130–1). The 'temporal arrangement' presupposes an order and coherence in significant historical events (*Lib. Arb.* 3. 21. 60). Augustine uses metaphors to convey this idea: the beauty of a poem or song (*Letter* 138. 1. 5) or the continuously self-renewing foliage of trees (*En. Ps.* 101, *Ser.* 2. 10); cf. Horn (1997: 185–6). For further musical metaphors for order in Augustine see Ch. 9 on 17. 14 with n. 42.
[11] On the scriptural hermeneutics of *Doctr. Chr.* see Pollmann (1996); cf. Young (1997: 270–7).

significance of these subjects for *City* lies in their interconnection, demonstrating the way in which Augustine constructs thematic complexes. Thus, although there is no structural affinity between the short, one-book treatise *Vera Rel.* and *City*, the earlier work has long, and rightly, been seen as a forerunner of the later one, and it has even been suggested, not implausibly, that *City* can be read as a treatise 'on true and false religion' ('de falsa et vera religione').[12]

Augustine's *De Catechizandis Rudibus* discusses the theoretical basis of instruction to be given to those who aspire to become Christians, as well as providing two model catecheses. It served as a model of catechetical instruction from Cassiodorus' time onwards (van Oort 1991: 177). I shall examine it selectively here, to bring out the connections with the *City of God* (cf. van Oort 1991: 175–98).

Augustine begins the theoretical section of the work with a general discussion of the place of 'narratio' in instruction. By this he means biblical narrative. He argues for a summary exposition of the contents of the Old and New Testaments, emphasizing the periodization ('articuli') of scriptural history. He suggests that some exemplary and especially remarkable ('mirabiliora') episodes be examined in detail (*Cat. Rud.* 5). God's love for humanity, culminating in Christ's incarnation, is to be the central theme of this exposition (6–8). But understanding of divine mercy should be tempered by a sense of the fear of God, and the individual's motives for seeking instruction should be uncovered (9–10). Historical exposition is to be followed by familiarizing the catechete with the doctrines of the resurrection of the body and the last judgement, with the temptations and dangers that evildoers, Christian and non-Christian (including heretics and Jews), present, and with the principles of Christian behaviour (11). Educated and uneducated postulants are to be treated differently (12–13). What Augustine has to say about the educated catechete (12) shows an awareness of means of communication with the literate and sophisticated that is reflected in practice in the *City of God*.

When, later in *De Catechizandis Rudibus*, Augustine gives his model catecheses, he again stresses a flexible approach, adapted to the needs of the instructed (23). The catecheses are samples, no more. Each is prefaced by reflections on what constitutes true happiness: not

---

[12] Madec (1991: 12). For earlier studies that stress the link between *Vera Rel.* and *City* see Theiler (1966: 171), Trapé (1986: 464).

longevity, nor honours, nor pleasure, but being with God in his eternal kingdom, enjoying the repose of the eternal sabbath (24–8, 52). This is revealed in Scripture (28). Then follows, in the longer catechesis, the exposition of the six periods of biblical history: from the creation of the universe to Noah; from Noah to Abraham; from Abraham to David; from David to the Babylonian captivity; from the departure from Babylon to Christ's coming; from Christ's coming to his second coming at the end of the universe (29–44).[13] Throughout the historical account of the first five phases the allegorical, prophetic references to Christ and the Church are stressed (32–8): the New Testament is to be seen as the fulfilment of the prophetic nature of the Old Testament. The new covenant enables humans to live a new, spiritual life (40). In two chapters (31 and 37; cf. 45) Augustine sketches his theory of the two 'civitates' mingled in history, but to be separated on the day of judgement, and links them to Jerusalem and Babylon.[14] The spread of Christianity, reinforced by persecution, as well as its divisions through schism and heresy, are evoked in 42–4. In the shorter catechesis, the emphasis is again on the prophetic aspect of Biblical history (53).

The thematic similarities between *De Catechizandis Rudibus* and the *City of God* are evident. The most obvious is the use of historical exposition in the service of Christian doctrine, and the related extension of the historical horizon to the end of history and the last judgement. Books 11–22 of *City* can be understood as a massive expansion of the catechetical 'narratio' of *Cat. Rud.*[15] But this does not make *City* a catechesis, except in the broadest sense. Its function may be to present Christianity in a manner accessible to Christians as well as pagans, but it is no more exclusively aimed at those awaiting Christian instruction ('rudes') than it is at pagans hostile to, or suspicious of, Christian beliefs and practices. Rather than separate the apologetic and catechetical aspects of *City*,[16] we should understand its catechetical themes to be subsumed into the apologetic whole. What Augustine (perhaps depending on traditional methods of catechesis) does is exploit the practice of instruction in the service of a wider concern: the full exposition and defence of Christianity.

---

[13] See above on *Vera Rel.* 26. 48–9 with n. 7.

[14] The passages are quoted in Ch. 4. 2 above.

[15] The relation of *City* 1–10 to catechesis proper is less obvious: for an attempt to argue it see van Oort (1991: 188, 197).

[16] This is the tendency of van Oort (1991: 164–98), but see his qualifying remarks (p. 176).

Augustine's *City of God* reflects themes and preoccupations of his
earlier and contemporary writings. As this chapter has shown, it is
above all a development of ideas found in two earlier works. But it
would be a mistake to see Augustine's development as a purely
literary one, reworking and elaborating topics from one work to
another. His synthesis of themes in *City* develops out of specific
practical concerns. Augustine, bishop, ally, and counsellor of statesmen and officials, preoccupied with the implications of the prescrip-
tion of Donatism and attempts to coerce Donatists into orthodoxy,
increasingly concerned with the theological (and perhaps also
political) questions raised by Pelagianism, writes *City*, as he wrote
so many of his works, in response to the stimulus and pressures of his
environment. What began as a reaction to the repercussions of the
sack of Rome extended into a vast polemic against the pagan tradition in its related political and religious aspects. But it was always
potentially more. The bulk of this work reflects Augustine's mature,
and maturing, thought on grace and predestination, history and
eschatology, the role of philosophy in systems of belief, the nature
of civic justice, and of political and ecclesiastical authority. Despite
the long time of gestation, Augustine's fundamental views on certain
issues did not change radically in this period, and that fact, as much
as the work's structure, gives the *City of God* its underlying unity.
This coherence of thematic content, and the sense that the work may
be read as an exploration and summation of Augustine's most deeply
held convictions on the human condition, help to account for the
extraordinary influence of the *City of God* in Western culture.[17]

[17] To trace the influence of *City* is beyond the scope of this book. Among general
works of reference see J. H. Burns (1988) for Augustine's presence in medieval political
thought; H. Liebeschütz in Armstrong (1967: 538–639) for philosophy from Boethius
to Anselm; Kretzmann, Kenny, and Pinborg (1982) for later medieval philosophy; *TRE*
iv. 699–723 for Augustinian influence from the early medieval period to the end of the
19th c. Horn (1995: 154–66) is an excellent brief survey of Augustine's influence from
Gregory the Great to Hannah Arendt (bibliog. of modern studies: ibid. 179). De Lubac
(1959–64) traces his influence on medieval biblical exegesis. Thraede (1983) surveys
the concept of the city of God in antiquity before and after Augustine. There are classic
studies of Augustine's role in the formation of medieval political theory by Troeltsch
(1915) and Arquillière (1955). Abercrombie (1938) examines Augustine in classical
French thought (esp. Descartes and Montaigne). On Descartes and Augustine see
G. Matthews (1992) and Menn (1998). There are essays on the later reception of *City*
in Cavalcanti (1996) and Donnelly (1995). For early anthologies of, and commentaries
on, *City* see App. B below.

Appendix A

The Title *De Civitate Dei*

In *Retractations* 2. 43 Augustine gives the title 'de civitate dei' three times, adding that, although the work treats of both cities, it is named after the 'better' city.[1] The title given in Possidius' catalogue of Augustine's works ('De civitate dei libri viginti duo', *Indiculum* 1. 23)) concurs with *Retr*. The same title is used by Augustine when he refers to the work in letters (*Letters* 169. 1, 184A. 5, 1A*. 1–2, 2*. 1) and other writings (*C. Adv. Leg.* 1. 18; *Trin.* 13. 12). The phrase 'contra paganos' appended to titles of printed editions of the work is derived from the 'explicit'–'incipit' of the earliest manuscripts: it is also found in the subscriptions of some manuscripts.[2] Given the evidence of Augustine's own references to the work, the phrase cannot be attributed to him. It may derive from the title ('Contra paganos') of the first group of Augustine's works listed in Possidius' *Indiculum*, where *De Civitate Dei* is the last work of the group.[3] But it would also be an understandable addition to the title, given the subject-matter of Books 1–10 of the work.

By his choice of title Augustine signals the thematic affinities between the work and his earlier treatments of the theme of the two cities (see Ch. 4). In *City* he refers explicitly to the scriptural source of the term 'civitas dei'. *City* 11. 1 cites Psalms 46: 4, 48: 1, 8, and 87: 3 (Septuagint and Vulgate: 45: 5, 47: 2, and 86: 3). The Latin Bible versions used by Augustine translate the Septuagint's *polis tou theou* by 'civitas dei', and this, rather than any specific Roman connotations of the word 'civitas' (see below), is the primary reason

---

[1] Augustine is probably influenced here by the tradition of naming something by its better/best or dominant/ruling part: cf. Aristotle, *Nicomachean Ethics* 10. 7. 1178ᵃ 2–7; Plotinus, 3. 4. 2. 6–11.

[2] On the 'explicit'–'incipit' evidence see Dombart and Kalb's edn., e.g. i. 599; Marrou (1976: 258–9). On the subscriptions see Dombart and Kalb, ii, pp. xviii–xix.

[3] See Thraede (1977: 112 with n. 78). For Augustine and his contemporaries the word 'paganus' meaning 'non-Christian' is common usage (an 'usitatum nomen', *Retr.* 2. 43. 1). A number of the recently discovered sermons of Augustine published by Dolbeau contain important evidence for contemporary attitudes to pagans: see *Ser. Dolbeau* 4, 25, and esp. 26 (= *Ser.* 198, augmented).

for Augustine's choice of term. The use of Jerusalem and Babylon as symbols of the two opposing cities reflects typological elements in the New Testament, where Jerusalem is the *polis (tou) theou* (Hebrews 12: 22, cf. 11: 10, 16; Revelation 3: 12, cf. 21: 2, 10). The linking of Jerusalem, the city of God, with the Christian Church is found in Greek and Latin Christian texts before and contemporary with Augustine.[4] Tyconius posited a duality within the Church itself, linking it to the 'civitas' theme and the Jerusalem–Babylon contrast (cf. Ch. 4 n. 10), but without, it appears, talking of two 'civitates'.

Apart from these scriptural and typological antecedents, Augustine may also have been attracted to the title *De Civitate Dei* by the fact that the word 'civitas' has a range of meanings extending beyond those of a specific physical city or geographical territory to 'citizen body' and 'citizenship'.[5] The group membership implied by these last two meanings is essential to Augustine's understanding of 'civitas' in the work.

[4] Cf. Scholz (1911: 76–8), van Oort (1991: 274–351). See Ch. 4 above for details.
[5] See Stark (1967: 80–3), Duchrow (1970: 235–6 with n. 236), Schmidt (1985: 77–8 with n. 39). For the theme that the city is its citizens see *Exc. Vrb.* 6.

Appendix B
Manuscripts and Editions

The *City of God* is among the most (and is probably the most) copied of early Latin Christian texts. Wilmart (1931) identified 376 MSS, to which the CCL 1955 edition of the work added a further eighteen. Recent research has led to further discoveries.[1] The oldest known MS, Veronensis 28 (V), dates from the early fifth century (*CLA* iv. 491, xii, p. ix). It is of North African origin, and contains *City* 11–16: it is one of the earliest MSS of any work of Augustine's. There are two sixth-century MSS, one being the north Italian Lugdunensis 607 (L), containing *City* 1–5 (*CLA* vi. 784). The other, the Italian Corbeiensis (C), so-called because it was at Corbie until the early seventeenth century, was divided at the time of the French Revolution: its text of *City* 1–9 is Parisiensis lat. 12214, and its version of *City* 10 is Leningradensis (= Petropolitanus) Q. v. I. 4 (*CLA* v. 635, xi. *635). Codex Frisingensis (F) = Monacensis lat. 6267 contains an eighth- or ninth-century version of *City* 12–17, and an early ninth-century text of *City* 1–11 and 18 (*CLA* ix. 1257). Bruxellensis 9641, a northern French MS from the eighth or ninth century (*CLA* x. 1545), appears to be the oldest version of the complete work: it was not known to the modern editors, Dombart and Kalb. Dombart posited two recensions of *City*, represented by L and C, and constructed a stemma based on his examination of *City* 1–2. In the absence of further research it must remain hypothetical.[2] Eugippius' *Excerpta ex Operibus Sancti Augustini*, made in the early sixth century (ed. P. Knöll, CSEL 9. 1, Vienna 1885), included extracts from *City* 9 and 11–22.

---

[1] See Wilmart (1931: 279–94); cf. Dombart and Kalb, i, pp. ii–xxxiv, ii, pp. iii–xxii and 1–2. Additional MSS listed in the CCL edn., v* n. 2, viii*. Gorman (1982) includes the MSS already listed or at the time forthcoming in the Vienna catalogue of Augustine MSS (*Die handschriftliche Überlieferung der Werke des heiligen Augustinus*, i–vi (1969–93)) that are not in Wilmart's list or the CCL supplement. See also Stoclet (1984). Cf. Bardy, BA 33. 135–7. Illuminated MSS of *City*: de Laborde (1909).

[2] See Dombart and Kalb, i, pp. xiii–xxiii, ii, p. xix. Cf. Lambot (1939: 116–17), Gorman (1982: 409 n. 3).

The earliest printed edition[3] of the work is the 1467 Subiaco incunabulum by C. Sweynheim and A. Pannartz (whose edition of Lactantius' principal works in 1465 is the first dated book printed in Italy). The 1468 Strasbourg edition by Mentelin incorporates commentaries by the English Dominicans Nicholas Trevet (or Trivet) and Thomas Walleys, written in the late thirteenth or early fourteenth century. Of other early editions the following deserve mention: Amerbach (Basle 1489), Froben (Basle 1522, with a commentary by the Spanish humanist Ludovicus Vives (Juan Luis Vivès), subsequently included by Erasmus in his edition (Basle 1529) of Augustine's works), and that by the Louvain theologians (Antwerp 1576). In the great edition of Augustine's works by the Benedictines of the congregation of St Maur in Paris, *City* appeared in vol. vii (Paris 1685): this is the text reprinted in 1841 by Migne (*PL* 41). The Maurists consulted thirty-four MSS, but knew only ten of the seventy-six oldest ones, and only C (but not the St Petersburg (Leningrad) part) of the earliest five MSS (Gorman 1981: 253–68). Of modern editions, that of Dombart and Kalb, first published by Dombart in 1863, provides, in its fourth edition of 1928–9, the best available text and critical apparatus, though Dombart consulted only twenty-three of the oldest MSS.[4] In 1899–1900 E. Hoffmann published his edition in the CSEL series (40. 1–2).

[3] On the text of the earliest editions see Dombart (1908); cf. Bardy, BA 33. 137–40.
[4] See Gorman (1982: 399–400). The CCL edn. reproduces that of Dombart and Kalb, with some modifications and many misprints (see Alexanderson 1997).

Appendix C

'Breviculus', 'Capitula', and 'Canon'

At the end of *Letter* 1A* Augustine refers to a summary ('breviculus')
of the whole of the *City of God* which he is sending with the letter to
Firmus. This 'breviculus' is intended to give an indication of the
scope of the work ('the enclosed summary will show what has been
brought together in the composition of the twenty-two books', *Letter*
1A*. 3). This summary has been identified with the chapter headings
('capitula') found grouped together at the beginning of MSS of *City*
and often placed confusingly before the individual chapters to which
they refer in printed editions (beginning with Mentelin's 1468
edition: see Appendix B) and modern translations.[1] But this identification is not sound. The 'capitula' are found in only one of the three
earliest MSS (C), which divides the text into numbered chapters,
unlike V and L (though in the latter there is some indication of
chapter divisions). Moreover, the chapter divisions in C often differ
from those of later MSS, and variant chapter-headings have also been
transmitted. Finally, there is no manuscript authority for the desig-
nation of the chapter-headings as 'breviculus': C refers to them as
'canon', presumably in the sense of 'list' or 'table'.[2]

A division of the text into paragraphs, for which Augustine uses the
term 'capitulum' (*Conf.* 8. 12. 29), appears to have been a regular
feature of the codex, and, as with books ('libri'), such 'capitula' could
have titles ('tituli'), like those prefixed to individual Psalms in the Bibles
used by Augustine (*En. Ps.* 93. 3, 139. 3).[3] Sometimes he summarizes
his own work: a striking example is found at *Trin.* 15. 4. 4–5,

---

[1] For the identification see Marrou (1976: 253–65 (first pub. 1951)); cf. Petitmengin
(1990: 136). For the practice of providing summaries see Pliny the Elder, *Naturalis
Historia*, pref. 33.

[2] See Dombart and Kalb, i, p. xii, ii, pp. xiii–xviii, Lambot (1939: 117 with n. 3),
Marrou (1976: 260), Gorman (1982: 408).

[3] For details see Petitmengin (1994: 1033–5). Biblical texts had 'capitula', marking
the 'verses' (*Adnotationes in Iob* 39) of the text by a projecting letter: the text of
Romans which Augustine seizes in *Conf.* 8. 12. 29 had such an initial letter ('caput',
OLD 16b), directing his eyes to Rom. 13: 13. Augustine refers in *City* 18. 23 to the use
of 'capita' as a means of demarcating sections of a continuous citation.

where the contents of the first fourteen books of the work are presented in compressed form. In the prologue to *Qu. Ev.*, Augustine provides chapter-headings or 'tituli' designed, as he there explains, to help the reader identify the subject-matter of the individual 'quaestiones'. The 'breviculus' sent to Firmus must have been of this kind. Even if it cannot be identified with the 'breviculus', the 'canon' appears to fulfil the same function as 'capitula' or 'tituli' elsewhere. It is not so much a summary of contents as a list of topics treated in the work, to enable readers (in this instance, it will make more sense to those already familiar with its contents) to refer to specific chapters (Marrou 1976: 263–4).

Augustine cannot, with confidence, be identified as the author of the 'canon' of MS C. It is possible that it derives from a recension by Eugippius, who certainly used it in compiling his *Excerpta*: if this is the case, the recension would resemble the one which he made, with numbered chapters and headings, for *Gen. ad Litt.*, while assembling the extracts from that work (Gorman 1982: 408–10).

The suggestion that the 'capitula' represent the 'breviculus', not as written by Augustine himself, but as authorized by him on completion of *City* and not scrutinized by him (Lambot 1939: 118 n. 3; cf. Marrou 1976: 255–6), while it might explain the inept nature of some of the headings, is open to the same general objections made above.

Appendix D

The Chronology in *City* 18. 54

The precise nature of the chronological references in this chapter creates a problem. To begin with, Augustine, following traditional western practice, dates the death of Christ to 25 March 29, the year of the consulship of C. Fufius Geminus and L. Rubellius Geminus (Tertullian, *Adversus Iudaeos* 8; *Calendar of* AD *354* (*MGH AA* 9. 1); Lactantius, *Div. Inst.* 4. 10. 18 has the same year, but a date of 23 March, which would place the resurrection on 25 March); cf. Bardy, BA 36. 773. But in adding the 365 years mentioned in an otherwise unknown oracle (see Ch. 9 n. 62) Augustine arrives, not at the correct date (29 + 365 =) 394, but at 398, the year of the consulship of the emperor Honorius and Flavius Eutychianus. He also refers to the consulship of Manlius Theodorus (399), and adds that 'roughly ('ferme') thirty years' have elapsed between then and 'the present time', i.e. of composition of *City* 18. But *c.* 429 is an unacceptably late date for this stage of the work: in fact, *City* appears to have been completed by 426–7, when Augustine wrote the *Retractations*. There are four possible explanations of the passage:

1. Augustine gets the fourth-century consular dates right, but assumes Christ's death to have been in the year 33 (i.e. he names the wrong consuls, or—more plausibly—assumes a wrong year for the consulship of the two Gemini). He might make this assumption as a result of combining the information from Luke 3: 23, that Christ began his ministry when he was about 30, with an estimate of the number of years from then until his death. But this explanation is open to the objections just mentioned, for it assumes a date of composition of *City c.* 428–9. Nor is Augustine likely to have got the consular year of Christ's death wrong: in *Doctr. Chr.* 2. 28. 42 he criticizes the chronological ignorance of those who make mistakes about the consulships in which Christ was born and died. Moreover (see above), he is following standard western practice in his dating of Christ's death.

2. Augustine gets the fourth-century dates wrong, assuming, for example, Manlius Theodorus to have been consul in 395. Against this is the fact that Augustine recalls the destruction of pagan temples and statues by Gaudentius and Jovius in March 399 (enacting the imperial edict of 29 January 399, *CTh* 16. 10. 15). Augustine is unlikely to have been mistaken about the date of such a significant event, particularly as he was in Carthage for a church council in April 399 (Perler and Maier 1969: 222–7), and there were further anti-pagan incidents in Carthage in the same year (ibid. 391–5).

3. Augustine gets the arithmetic wrong, so that 29 + 365 gives 398 rather than 394, but he then silently corrects this. This gives a date of *c.* 424 for the composition of *City* 18, which is plausible.

4. Perhaps we have to assume that Augustine is using the phrase 'roughly thirty years' in a loose sense, i.e. that it can refer to a period of twenty-six or twenty-seven years. This is not impossible. Even in a work that has several accurate chronological markers, the *Confessions*, Augustine refers to a period of some fourteen years (from the time he first read Cicero's *Hortensius* in 372–3 to his conversion in 386) as 'possibly twelve years' (*Conf.* 8. 7. 17), perhaps led, as O'Donnell ad loc. suggests, by 'the lure of the significant number twelve'. A similar influence may be at work in *City* 18. 54 (for 'about 30' as the perfect age, based on Christ's age at his death and received wisdom, see *City* 22. 15).

Bibliography

A. The City of God: editions, commentaries, and translations
(See further Appendix B above.)

S. Aurelii Augustini Hipponensis Episcopi ad Marcellinum De Civitate Dei contra Paganos Libri XXII, PL 41. 13–804 (reprints Maurist edn. of 1685).

Sancti Aurelii Augustini Episcopi De Civitate Dei Libri XXII, ed. B. Dombart and A. Kalb (4th edn.; Leipzig, 1928–9; repr. Stuttgart, 1981). The standard critical edition. Its text is reprinted in CCL 47–8.

S. Aurelii Augustini De Civitate Dei contra Paganos Libri XXII, ed. J. E. C. Weldon (London, 1924). With brief but occasionally still useful notes.

La Cité de Dieu. Œuvres de Saint Augustin: BA 33–7. Reprints the Dombart and Kalb text, with introduction and notes by G. Bardy, and a French translation by G. Combès (Paris, 1959–60). The excellent notes are the closest that there is to a modern commentary in any language.

St Augustine: City of God, tr. H. Bettenson, with an introduction by J. J. O'Meara (Penguin Classics; Harmondsworth, 1984). The best available English translation.

Saint Augustine: The City of God against the Pagans, 7 vols., Loeb Classical Library, tr. G. E. McCracken (i), W. M. Green (ii; v; vii, with index), D. S. Wiesen (iii), P. Levine (iv), E. M. Sanford (v), W. C. Greene (vi) (London and Cambridge, Mass., 1957–72).

Introduction to St Augustine, The City of God (selections from *City* 19 and other books, with translation and commentary), by R. H. Barrow. (London, 1950).

B. Other works of Augustine: editions, commentaries, and translations

PL provides the only complete modern edition of Augustine's works. Several works, and all of the most important ones, are edited in the CCL and CSEL series, and (with notes in French) in BA. For sermons edited since PL see MA, PL Suppl. 2, and Dolbeau's edition of the Mainz sermons (details below). Wide selections of works in English translations are to be found in *The Works of Aurelius Augustine, Bishop of Hippo*, ed. M. Dods, 15 vols. (Edinburgh, 1871–6) and *A Select Library of the Nicene and Post-Nicene Fathers of the Christian Church* (New York, 1887–1902; repr. Grand Rapids, Mich.,

1979), of which vols. i–viii are devoted to Augustine. There are several volumes of English translation of Augustine's writings in the two series ACW and Fathers of the Church. The following list is confined chiefly to those writings of Augustine, apart from *City*, which are referred to most frequently in this book.

Augustin: Contra Academicos (vel De Academicis) Bücher 2 und 3, introduction and commentary T. Fuhrer (Patristische Texte und Studien, 46; Berlin and New York, 1997). *St. Augustine: Against the Academics*, tr. with notes J. J. O'Meara, ACW 12 (New York and Ramsey, NJ, 1951).

Augustine: Confessions, ed. with commentary J. J. O'Donnell, 3 vols. (Oxford, 1992). *Confessions, Books I–IV*, ed. with commentary G. Clark (Cambridge, 1995). Eng. tr. H. Chadwick (Oxford, 1991).

Augustin d'Hippone: Vingt-six sermons au peuple d'Afrique, ed. F. Dolbeau (Paris, 1996).

Augustine: De Doctrina Christiana, ed. and tr. R. P. H. Green (Oxford Early Christian Texts; Oxford, 1995). Translation reprinted, with introduction and notes, in *Saint Augustine: On Christian Teaching*. (World's Classics; Oxford, 1997).

Augustine: De Excidio Vrbis Romae Sermo, ed. M. V. O'Reilly (Washington, 1955).

De Catechizandis Rudibus, in *Aurelius Augustinus: Vom ersten katechetischen Unterrricht*, New German tr. W. Steinmann; ed. with notes O. Wermelinger (Schriften der Kirchenväter, 7; Munich, 1985).

Retractationes, ed. A. Mutzenbecher, CCL lvii (1984); Eng tr. M. I. Bogan, Fathers of the Church, lx (Washington, 1968).

C. Other authors: editions, commentaries, and translations

Apuleius, *De Deo Socratis*, in *Apuleius: De Philosophia Libri*, ed. P. Thomas, with addenda by W. Schaub (Stuttgart, 1970); *Apulée: Opuscules philosophiques*, ed. J. Beaujeu (Budé edn.; Paris, 1973).

Arnobius, *Adversus Nationes*, ed. A. Reifferscheid, CSEL (Vienna, 1875); ed. C. Marchiesi, (3rd edn.; Turin, 1953); Eng. tr. G. E. McCracken, 2 vols, ACW (Westminster, Md., 1949).

Beatus of Liebana, *Beati in Apocalypsin libri XII*, ed. H. A. Sanders (American Academy; Rome, 1930).

Callinicus, *Vita Sancti Hypatii*, in *Callinicos: Vie d'Hypatios*, ed. G. J. M. Bartelink (Sources chrétiennes; Paris, 1971).

Cicero, *De Re Publica*, ed. K. Ziegler (7th edn.; Leipzig, 1969). Commentary K. Büchner (Heidelberg, 1984). *Selections*, ed. J. E. G. Zetzel (Cambridge, 1995). Eng. tr. G. H. Sabine and S. B. Smith, *Marcus Tullius Cicero: On the Commonwealth* (Columbus, Oh., 1929; often repr.); tr. N. Rudd, introd. and nn. J. Powell and N. Rudd, *Cicero: The Republic and The Laws* (World's Classics; Oxford, 1998).

—— *De Fato*, ed. R. W. Sharples (with tr. and commentary), *Cicero: On Fate (De Fato) and Boethius: The Consolation of Philosophy IV. 5–7, V (Philosophiae Consolatio)* (Warminster, 1991).

Claudian, *Carmina*, ed. J. B. Hall (Teubner edn.; Leipzig, 1985). Eng. tr. M. Platnauer (LCL; Cambridge, Mass., and London, 1922).

—— *Panegyricus Dictus Olybrio et Probino Consulibus*, ed. W. Taegert (Zetemata, 85; Munich, 1988).

Codex Theodosianus, ed. T. Mommsen and P. M. Meyer (Berlin, 1905); 12th edn. P. Krüger (1954). Eng. tr. C. Pharr, *The Theodosian Code and Novels* (Princeton, 1952).

Corpus Hermeticum, *Hermetica*, ed. W. Scott, 4 vols. (Oxford, 1924–36). *Hermès Trismégiste*, ed. A. D. Nock and A.-J. Festugière, 4 vols. (Budé edn.; Paris, 1945–54). Eng. tr. with notes, B. P. Copenhaver, *Hermetica* (Cambridge, 1992).

Eusebius, *Chronicle*, in *Eusebius: Werke 7. Die Chronik des Hieronymus*, ed. R. Helm (2nd edn., GCS; Berlin, 1956).

Eutropius, *Breviarium*, tr. with introduction and commentary by H. W. Bird (Translated Texts for Historians, 14; Liverpool, 1993).

Florus, *Epitome of Roman History*, with an Eng. tr. by E. S. Forster (LCL; Cambridge, Mass., and London, 1929; repr. with additional bibliography, 1984).

Jerome, *Chronicle*. See under Eusebius above.

—— *[Onomasticon] Liber Interpretationis Hebraicorum Nominum*, ed. P. de Lagarde, CCL 72 (Turnhout, 1959).

—— *Hebrew Questions on Genesis*, tr. with an introduction and commentary by C. T. R. Hayward (Oxford Early Christian Studies; Oxford, 1995).

Justin(us), *Epitoma Historiarum Philippicarum Pompei Trogi*, ed. O. Seel (2nd edn.; Stuttgart, 1972). *Epitome of the Philippic History of Pompeius Trogus*, Eng. tr. J. C. Yardley, introduction and notes R. Develin (Atlanta, Ga., 1994).

Lactantius, *Divinae Institutiones*, ed. S. Brandt and G. Laubmann, CSEL (Vienna, 1890; rep. New York, 1965). Eng. tr. W. Fletcher (Edinburgh, 1871). *Epitome*, ed. E. Heck and A. Wlosok (Teubner edn.; Stuttgart and Leipzig, 1994).

—— *De Mortibus Persecutorum*, ed. and tr. J. L. Creed (Oxford 1984).

Life of Melania the Younger: Vie de Sainte Mélanie, ed. D. Gorce (Sources chrétiennes; Paris, 1962). Eng. tr. E. A. Clark (Lewiston, NY, 1984).

Mani-Codex. *P. Colon. inv.* 4780, ed. A. Henrichs and L. Koenen, *Zeitschrift für Papyrologie und Epigraphik*, 5 (1970), 27–216; 19 (1975), 1–85; 32 (1978), 87–199; 44 (1981), 201–318; 48 (1982), 319–77 (with commentary and German tr.). Eng. tr. of part of text by R. Cameron and A. J. Dewey, *The Cologne Mani Codex 'Concerning the Origin of His Body'* (Missoula, Mont., 1979).

Minucius Felix, *Octavius*, ed. B. Kytzler (Teubner edn.; Leipzig, 1982). Eng. tr. G. W. Clarke, with notes, ACW 39 (New York, 1974).

Origen, *Contra Celsum*, ed. P. Koetschau, GCS, 2 vols. (Leipzig, 1899). Eng. tr. H. Chadwick, with notes (Cambridge, 1953).

—— *De Principiis*, ed. P. Koetschau, GCS (Leipzig, 1913). Eng. tr. G. W. Butterworth, *Origen on First Principles*, (London, 1936).

—— *De Principiis*, in *Origines: Vier Bücher von den Prinzipien*, ed. with German tr. H. Görgemanns and H. Karpp (Darmstadt, 1976).

Orosius, *Histories*, in *Pauli Orosii Historiarum Adversus Paganos Libri VII*, ed. K. Zangemeister, CSEL (Vienna, 1882). *Orose: Histoires*, ed. M.-P. Arnaud-Lindet, 3 vols. (Budé edn.; Paris, 1990–1).

Pacatus, *Panegyricus . . . Dictus Theodosio*, in *XII Panegyrici Latini*, ed. R. A. B. Mynors (Oxford, 1964), 82–120. Eng. tr. C. E. V. Nixon, *Pacatus: Panegyric to the Emperor Theodosius* (Translated Texts for Historians, 3; Liverpool, 1987).

Pelagius, *Expositiones XIII Epistularum Pauli. Pelagius's Expositions of Thirteen Epistles of St Paul*, ed. A. Souter (Texts and Studies, 9), 3 vols. (Cambridge, 1922, 1926, and 1931).

—— *Pelagius' Commentary on St Paul's Epistle to the Romans*, tr. with introduction and notes T. De Bruyn (Oxford Early Christian Studies; Oxford, 1993).

Porphyry, *Philosophy from Oracles*, in *De Philosophia ex Oraculis Haurienda Librorum Reliquiae*, ed. G. Wolff (Berlin, 1856; repr. Hildesheim, 1962).

—— *De Regressu Animae*, Fragments in Bidez (1913); see Bibliography E below.

—— *Against the Christians*, Fragments in *Porphyrius, 'Gegen die Christen', 15 Bücher*, ed. A. von Harnack (Berlin, 1916) (repr. in Harnack, *Kleine Schriften zur alten Kirche* (Leipzig, 1980), ii. 362–474).

Possidius, *Indiculum*, ed. A. Wilmart, MA ii. 149–233.

—— *Vita Augustini*, ed. A. A. R. Bastiaensen, *Vita di Cipriano. Vita di Ambrogio. Vita di Agostino* (Verona, 1975) (text in *PL* 32. 33–66).

Prudentius, *Carmina*, ed. M. P. Cunningham, CCL (Turnhout, 1966). Eng. tr. H. J. Thomson, 2 vols. (LCL; Cambridge, Mass., and London, 1949–53).

Sallust, *C. Sallustii Crispi Catilina, Iugurtha, Historiarum Fragmenta Selecta. Appendix Sallustiana*, ed. L. D. Reynolds (Oxford 1991).

—— *C. Sallustius Crispus. Bellum Catilinae*, a commentary by P. McGushin (Leiden, 1977; student edition, Bristol, 1987).

—— *Sallust. The Histories*. tr. with commentary by P. McGushin, 2 vols. (Oxford, 1992, 1994).

Seneca, Fragments in *L. Annaei Senecae Opera*, ed. F. Haase (Leipzig, 1853) iii. 418–45 (See also Lausberg (1970)).

Solinus, *Collectanea Rerum Memorabilium*, ed. T. Mommsen (2nd edn.; Berlin, 1895).

Symmachus, *Prefect and Emperor: The Relationes of Symmachus*, A.D. 384, ed. and tr. R. H. Barrow (Oxford, 1973).

Tertullian, *Apologeticum. Tertullien: Apologétique*, ed. J.-P. Waltzing and A. Severyns (Budé, 2nd edn.; Paris, 1961). Commentary J.-P. Waltzing (revised edn.; Paris, 1931). Eng. tr. T. R. Glover (LCL; Cambridge, Mass., and London, 1931). Annotated edn. J. E. B. Mayor, tr. A. Souter (Cambridge, 1917).

Theophrastus of Eresus, *Sources for his Life, Writings, Thought and Influence*, ed. W. W. Fortenbaugh, P. M. Huby, R. W. Sharples, and D. Gutas, 2 vols. (Philosophia Antiqua, 54. 1–2; Leiden, 1992).

Tyconius, *In Apocalypsin. The Turin Fragments of Tyconius' Commentary on Revelation*, ed. F. Lo Bue (Texts and Studies NS 7, prepared for the press by G. G. Willis; Cambridge, 1963).

—— *Liber Regularum. The Book of Rules of Tyconius*, ed. F. C. Burkitt (Texts and Studies 3, 1; Cambridge, 1894). Eng. tr. W. S. Babcock (Texts and Translations, 31; Atlanta, Ga., 1989).

Varro, M. *Terentius Varro: Antiquitates Rerum Divinarum*, ed. B. Cardauns. Akademie der Wissenschaften und der Literatur, Mainz. Abhandlungen der Geistes- und Sozialwissenschaftlichen Klasse, 2 vols. (Wiesbaden, 1976).

—— *Curio De Cultu Deorum*, in *Varros Logistoricus über die Göttervereh- rung*, ed. B. Cardauns (Würzburg, 1960).

—— *De Philosophia*, in M. *Terenti Varronis Liber de philosophia*, ed. G. Langenberg (Cologne, 1959).

—— *De Gente Populi Romani*, in *Historicorum Romanorum Reliquiae*, ii, ed. H. Peter (Leipzig, 1906).

D. Bibliographies; concordance

Donnelly, D. F., and Sherman, M. A., *Augustine's De Civitate Dei: An Annotated Bibliography of Modern Criticism, 1960–1990* (New York, 1991).

del Estal, J.-M., 'Historiografia de la "Ciudad de Dios". De 1928 a 1954', *Ciudad de Dios*, 167/2 (1954): 647–774.

Mayer, C., *Corpus Augustinianum Gissense*. Computerized concordance of all of Augustine's writings and bibliography on CD-ROM (Basle, 1996).

Vigna, G. S., *A Bibliography of St. Augustine's De Civitate Dei* (Evanston, Ill., 1978).

See further the annual bibliographical bulletins in *REAug*.

E. Secondary studies

Abercrombie, N. (1938), *Saint Augustine and French Classical Thought* (Oxford).

Ackroyd, P. R., and Evans, C. F. (1970) (eds.), *The Cambridge History of the Bible*, i (Cambridge).

Adams, J. duQ. (1971), *The Populus of Augustine and Jerome: A Study in the Patristic Sense of Community* (New Haven and London).

Alexanderson, B. (1997), 'Adnotationes Criticae in Libros Augustini "De Civitate Dei"', *Electronic Antiquity*, 3/7.

Altaner, B. (1967), *Kleine patristische Schriften* (Berlin).

—— and Stuiber, A. (1966), *Patrologie* (7th edn; Freiburg).

Angus, S. (1906), *The Sources of the First Ten Books of Augustine's De Civitate Dei* (Princeton).

Arbesmann, R. (1954), 'The Idea of Rome in the Sermons of St. Augustine', *Augustiniana*, 4: 305–24.

Armstrong, A. H. (1967) (ed.), *The Cambridge History of Later Greek and Early Medieval Philosophy* (Cambridge).

Arnold, D. W. H., and Bright, P. (1995) (eds.), *De Doctrina Christiana: A Classic of Western Culture* (Notre Dame, Ind).

Arquillière, H.-X. (1955), *L'Augustinisme politique: Essai sur la formation des théories politiques du Moyen-âge* (2nd edn.; Paris).

Avi-Jonah, M. (1984), *The Jews under Roman and Byzantine Rule: A Political History of Palestine from the Bar Kokhba War to the Arab Conquest* (New York).

Axelson, B. (1941), *Das Prioritätsproblem Tertullian–Minucius Felix* (Lund).

Babcock, W. S. (1988), 'Augustine on Sin and Moral Agency', *Journal of Religious Ethics*, 16: 28–55.

Badian, E. (1966), 'The Early Historians', in T. A. Dorey (ed.), *Latin Historians* (London), 1–38.

Bardy, G. (1923), *Recherches sur l'histoire du texte et des versions latines du De Principiis d'Origène* (Paris).

Barnes, J. (1982), 'The Just War', in Kretzmann, Kenny and Pinborg: (1982), 771–84.

—— (1989), 'Antiochus of Ascalon', in M. Griffin and J. Barnes (eds.), *Philosophia Togata I* (Oxford), 51–96.

Barnes, T. D. (1971), *Tertullian: A Historical and Literary Study* (Oxford; reissued with a postscript, 1985).

—— (1981), *Constantine and Eusebius* (Cambridge, Mass.).

—— (1982), 'Aspects of the Background of the *City of God*,' *Revue de l'Université d'Ottawa*, 52: 64–80 (repr. in T. D. Barnes (1994), no. XXIV).

—— (1992), 'Augustine, Symmachus and Ambrose', in J. McWilliam (ed.),

Augustine: From Rhetor to Theologian (Waterloo, Ontario), 7–13 (repr. in T. D. Barnes (1994), no. XXII).

—— (1994), *From Eusebius to Augustine* (Variorum Collected Studies Series, 438; London).

Barr, J. (1966), *Old and New: A Study of the Two Testaments* (London).

—— (1983), *Holy Scripture: Canon, Authority, Criticism* (Oxford).

Bartelink, G. (1987), 'Die Beeinflussung Augustins durch die griechischen Patres', in den Boeft and van Oort (1987), 9–24.

Baskin, J. R. (1983), *Pharaoh's Counsellors: Job, Jethro, and Balaam in Rabbinic and Patristic Tradition* (Chico, Calif.).

Bastiaensen, A. (1987), 'Augustin et ses prédécesseurs latins chrétiens', in den Boeft and van Oort (1987), 25–57.

Bauer, J. B. (1965), 'Zu Augustin, De civitate Dei I, praef.', *Hermes*, 93: 133–4.

Baynes, N. H. (1955), *Byzantine Studies and Other Essays* (London).

Beard, M., and North, J. (1990) (eds.), *Pagan Priests* (London).

Beare, W. (1964), *The Roman Stage* (3rd edn., London).

Beatrice, P. F. (1989), 'Quosdam Platonicorum Libros', *Vigiliae Christianae*, 43: 248–81.

Begbie, C. M. (1967), 'The Epitome of Livy', *Classical Quarterly*, 17: 332–8.

Beierwaltes, W. (1981), *Regio Beatitudinis: Augustine's Concept of Happiness* (Villanova, Pa.).

Bennett, C. (1988), 'The Conversion of Vergil: The *Aeneid* in Augustine's *Confessions*', *REAug* 34: 47–69.

Bernard, W. (1994), 'Zur Dämonologie des Apuleius von Madaura', *Rheinisches Museum*, 137: 358–73.

Bickerman, E. J. (1967), *Four Strange Books of the Bible: Jonah, David, Koheleth, Esther* (New York).

—— (1980), *Chronology of the Ancient World* (revised edn.; London).

Bidez, J. (1913), *Vie de Porphyre, le philosophe néo-platonicien* (Ghent and Leipzig; repr. Hildesheim, 1980).

Bingham, J. (1708–22), *The Antiquities of the Christian Church (Origines Ecclesiasticae)*, 10 vols. (London).

Blumenberg, H. (1983), *The Legitimacy of the Modern Age* (Cambridge, Mass.), Eng. tr. of *Die Legitimität der Neuzeit* (Frankfurt, 1966).

Bochet, I. (1983), *Saint Augustin et le désir de Dieu* (Paris).

den Boeft, J. (1979), 'Some Etymologies in Augustine, *De Civitate Dei* X', *Vigiliae Christianae*, 33: 242–59.

—— and van Oort, J. (1987) (eds.), *Augustiniana Traiectina*, Communications présentées au Colloque International d'Utrecht, 13–14 novembre 1986 (Paris).

den Boer, V. (1974), 'A Pagan Historian and his Enemies: Porphyry against the Christians', *Classical Philology*, 69: 198–208.

Bonner, G. (1962), '*Libido* and *Concupiscentia* in St. Augustine', *StudPatr* 6

(= TU 81), 303–14; repr. in id., *God's Decree and Man's Destiny: Studies on the Thought of Augustine of Hippo* (Variorum Collected Studies Series, 255; London, 1987), no. IX.

—— (1963), *St. Augustine of Hippo: Life and Controversies* (revised edn. with new preface; Norwich, 1986).

—— (1970) 'Augustine as Biblical Scholar', in Ackroyd and Evans (1970), 541–63.

—— (1986), 'Adam', *AL* 1/1–2: 63–87.

—— (1994), 'Concupiscentia', *AL* 1/7–8: 1113–22.

Børresen, K. E. (1981), *Subordination and Equivalence: The Nature and Role of Women in Augustine and Aquinas* (Washington).

—— (1990), 'In Defence of Augustine: How *Femina* is *Homo*', *Collectanea Augustiniana: Mélanges T. J. van Bavel* (Louvain), 411–28.

Bourke, V. J. (1979), *Joy in Augustine's Ethics* (Villanova, Pa).

Bowersock, G. W. (1994), *Fiction as History: Nero to Julian* (Sather Classical Lectures, 58; Berkeley, Los Angeles, and London).

—— (1995), *Martyrdom and Rome* (Cambridge).

Bright, P. (1988), *The Book of Rules of Tyconius: Its Purpose and Inner Logic* (Notre Dame, Ind.).

Brown, P. (1967), *Augustine of Hippo: A Biography* (London).

—— (1972), *Religion and Society in the Age of Saint Augustine* (London).

—— (1981), *The Cult of the Saints: Its Rise and Function in Latin Christianity* (Chicago and London).

—— (1989), *The Body and Society: Men, Women and Sexual Renunciation in Early Christianity* (London).

—— (1992), *Power and Persuasion in Late Antiquity: Towards a Christian Empire* (Madison).

—— (1995), *Authority and the Sacred: Aspects of the Christianisation of the Roman World* (Cambridge).

Brunt, P. A. (1989), 'Philosophy and Religion in the Late Republic', in M. Griffin and J. Barnes (eds.), *Philosophia Togata I: Essays on Philosophy and Roman Society* (Oxford), 174–98.

Buchheit, V. (1966), 'Christliche Romideologie im Laurentius-Hymnus des Prudentius', in *Polychronion. Festschrift Franz Dölger zum 75. Geburtstag* (Heidelberg), 121–44.

Budzik, S. (1988), *Doctor Pacis: Theologie des Friedens bei Augustinus* (Innsbruck).

Burleigh, J. H. S. (1949), *The City of God: A Study of St. Augustine's Philosophy* (London).

Burnaby, J. (1938), *Amor Dei: A Study of the Religion of St. Augustine* (London; repr. Norwich, 1991).

Burns, J. H. (1988) (ed.), *The Cambridge History of Medieval Political Thought* (Cambridge).

Burns, J. P. (1980), *The Development of Augustine's Doctrine of Operative Grace* (Paris).

Cameron, Alan (1966), 'The Date and Identity of Macrobius', *Journal of Roman Studies*, 56: 25–38.

—— (1967), 'Rutilius Namatianus, St Augustine, and the Date of the *De Reditu*', *Journal of Roman Studies*, 57: 31–9.

—— (1970), *Claudian: Poetry and Propaganda at the Court of Honorius* (Oxford).

—— (1977), 'Paganism and Literature in Late Fourth Century Rome', in Fuhrmann (1977), 1–40.

Cameron, Averil (1991), *Christianity and the Rhetoric of Empire: The Development of Christian Discourse* (Sather Classical Lectures, 55; Berkeley, Los Angeles, and London).

—— (1993*a*), *The Later Roman Empire* AD 284–430 (London).

—— (1993*b*), *The Mediterranean World in Late Antiquity* AD 395–600 (London and New York).

Cavalcanti, E. (1996) (ed.), *Il De civitate Dei: L'opera, le interpretazione, l'influsso* (Rome, Freiburg, and Vienna).

Chadwick, H. (1966), *Early Christian Thought and the Classical Tradition: Studies in Justin, Clement, and Origen* (Oxford).

—— (1976), *Priscillian of Avila: The Occult and the Charismatic in the Early Church* (Oxford).

—— (1983), 'New Letters of St. Augustine', *JTS* NS 34: 425–52.

—— (1986), *Augustine* (Oxford).

—— (1989), 'Tyconius and Augustine', in Kannengiesser and Bright (1989), 49–55.

—— (1996), 'New Sermons of St Augustine', *JTS* NS 47: 69–91.

Charlet, J.-L. (1993), 'Les Poèmes de Prudence en distiques élégiaques', in *La poesia cristiana latina in distici elegiaci*, Atti del Convegno Internazionale, Assisi, 20–22 marzo 1992 (Assisi), 135–66.

Chuvin, P. (1991), *Chronique des derniers païens* (2nd edn.; Paris). (*Chronicle of the Last Pagans* (Cambridge, Mass., 1990) is an Eng. tr. of chs. 1–10 of the 1st edn. (Paris 1990).)

Clark, E. A. (1986*a*), *Ascetic Piety and Women's Faith* (New York).

—— (1986*b*), 'Adam's Only Companion: Augustine and the Early Christian Debate on Marriage', *RechAug* 21: 139–62.

—— (1992), *The Origenist Controversy: The Construction of an Early Christian Debate* (Princeton, NJ).

Clark, G. (1993), *Women in Late Antiquity: Pagan and Christian Lifestyles* (Oxford).

Clark, M. T. (1958), *Augustine: Philosopher of Freedom* (New York and Tournai).

Cochrane, C. N. (1940), *Christianity and Classical Culture: A Study of Thought and Action from Augustus to Augustine* (Oxford).

Combès, G. (1927), *La Doctrine politique de saint Augustin* (Paris).

Congar, Y. M.-J. (1957), '"Civitas Dei" et "Ecclesia" chez saint Augustin', *REAug* 3: 1–14.

—— (1968), *L'Ecclésiologie du haut moyen âge* (Paris).

—— (1986), 'Abel', *AL* 1/1–2: 2–4.

Corcoran, G. (1985), *Saint Augustine on Slavery* (Studia Ephemeridis 'Augustinianum'; Rome).

Cornell, T. J. (1995), *The Beginnings of Rome: Italy and Rome from the Bronze Age to the Punic Wars (c. 1000–264 BC)* (London).

Costello, C. J. (1930), *St. Augustine's Doctrine on the Inspiration and Canonicity of Scripture* (Washington).

Courcelle, P. (1955), 'Les Pères de l'Église devant les Enfers virgiliens', *Archives d'histoire doctrinale et littéraire du Moyen-Age*, 22: 5–74.

—— (1957. 'Interprétations néo-platonisantes du livre VI de l'Enéide', in *Recherches sur la tradition platonicienne* (Entreteins Fondation Hardt, 3; Geneva), 95– 136.

—— (1961), 'Saint Augustin a-t-il lu Philon d'Alexandrie?', *Revue des études anciennes*, 63: 78–85.

—— (1963), *Les Confessions de saint Augustin dans la tradition littéraire: Antécédents et postérité* (Paris).

—— (1964), *Histoire littéraire des grands invasions germaniques* (3rd edn.; Paris).

—— (1968), *Recherches sur les Confessions de S. Augustin* (2nd edn.; Paris).

—— (1969), *Late Latin Writers and their Greek Sources* (Cambridge, Mass.). (Eng. tr. of *Les Lettres grecques en Occident de Macrobe à Cassiodore* (2nd edn.; Paris, 1948).)

—— (1984), *Lecteurs païens et lecteurs chrétiens de l'Enéide*, 2 vols. (Paris).

Cranz, F. E. (1950), '*De Civitate Dei*, XV, 2, and Augustine's Idea of the Christian Society', *Speculum*, 25: 215–25 = Markus (1972), 404–21.

—— (1954), 'The Development of Augustine's Ideas on Society before the Donatist Controversy', *Harvard Theological Review*, 47: 255–316 = Markus (1972), 336–403.

Croke, B., and Harries, J. (1982), *Religious Conflict in Fourth-Century Rome: A Documentary Study* (Sydney).

Dahlmann, H., and Heisterhagen, R. (1957), *Varronische Studien I: Zu den Logistorici* (Wiesbaden).

Daniélou, J. (1950), *Sacramentum Futuri: Études sur les origines de la typologie biblique* (Paris).

Dawson, D. (1992), *Allegorical Readers and Cultural Revision in Ancient Alexandria* (Berkeley).

Deane, H. A. (1963), *The Political and Social Ideas of St. Augustine* (New York and London).

Dean-Jones, L. A. (1994), *Women's Bodies in Classical Greek Science* (Oxford).

De Bruyne, D. (1931), 'Saint Augustin reviseur de la Bible', in *Miscellanea Agostiniana* (Rome), ii. 521–606.

Delehaye, H. (1933), *Les Origines du culte des martyrs* (Brussels).

Demandt, A. (1989), *Die Spätantike: Römische Geschichte von Diocletian bis Justinian, 284–565 n. Chr.*, Handbuch der Altertumswissenschaft, III. 6 (Munich).

Deuse, W. (1983), *Untersuchungen zur mittelplatonischen und neuplatonischen Seelenlehre*. Akademie der Wissenschaften und der Literatur, Mainz. Abhandlungen der Geistes- und Sozialwissenschaftlichen Klasse. Einzelveröffentlichung, 3 (Wiesbaden).

Dihle, A. (1973), 'Der Streit um den Altar der Viktoria', in *Romanitas et Christianitas*, Studia Iano Henrico Waszink a.d. VI Kal. Nov. A. MCMLXXIII oblata (Amsterdam and London), 81– 97.

—— (1982), *The Theory of Will in Classical Antiquity* (Sather Classical Lectures, 48; Berkeley, Los Angeles, and London and New York).

—— (1994), *Greek and Latin Literature of the Roman Empire* (London). (Eng. tr. of *Die griechische und lateinische Literatur der Kaiserzeit* (Munich, 1989).)

—— (1996), 'Die Theologia tripertita bei Augustin', in H. Cancik, H. Lichtenberger, and P. Schäfer (eds.), *Geschichte-Tradition-Reflexion, Festschrift für Martin Hengel zum 70. Geburtstag, ii. Griechische und Römische Religion* (Tübingen), 183–202.

Dillon, J. (1977), *The Middle Platonists: A Study of Platonism, 80 B.C. to A.D. 220* (London).

—— (1993), *Alcinous: The Handbook of Platonism*, tr. with an introduction and commentary (Oxford).

Divjak, J. (1977), 'Augustins erster Brief an Firmus und die revidierte Ausgabe der Civitas Dei', in *Latinität und Alte Kirche. Festschrift für R. Hanslik* (Vienna and Cologne), 56– 70.

Dodds, E. R. (1951), *The Greeks and the Irrational* (Sather Classical Lectures, 25; Berkeley and Los Angeles).

—— (1965), *Pagan and Christian in an Age of Anxiety: Some Aspects of Religious Experience from Marcus Aurelius to Constantine* (Cambridge).

—— (1973), *The Ancient Concept of Progress and Other Essays on Greek Literature and Belief* (Oxford).

Doignon, J. (1990), 'Oracles, prophéties, "on-dit" sur la chute de Rome (395–410). Les réactions de Jérôme et d'Augustin', *REAug* 36: 120–46.

—— (1993), 'Le Libellé du jugement de Cicéron sur le mythe d'Er selon le témoignage d'Augustin', *Rivista di Filologia*, 121: 419–26.

Dombart, B. (1908), *Zur Textgeschichte der Civitas Dei Augustins seit dem Entstehen der ersten Drucke*, TU 32. 2a (Leipzig).

Donaldson, I. (1982), *The Rapes of Lucretia: A Myth and its Transformation* (Oxford).

Donnelly, D. F. (1995) (ed.), *The City of God: A Collection of Critical Essays* (New York).

Döpp, S. (1988), 'Die Blütezeit lateinischer Literatur in der Spätantike (350–430 n. Chr.)', *Philologus*, 132: 19–52.

Dorival, G. (1987), 'Nouvelles remarques sur la forme du Traité des Principes d'Origène', *RechAug* 22: 67–108.

Duchrow, U. (1970), *Christenheit und Weltverantwortung: Traditionsgeschichte und systematische Struktur der Zweireichelehre* (Stuttgart).

Dufourcq, A. (1905), 'Rutilius Namatianus contre saint Augustin', *Revue d'histoire et de littérature religieuses*, 10: 488–92.

Dulaey, M. (1989), 'Le Sixième Règle de Tyconius et son résumé dans le De Doctrina Christiana', *REAug* 35: 83–103.

Du Roy, O. (1966), *L'Intelligence de la foi en la Trinité selon saint Augustin: Genèse de sa théologie trinitaire jusqu'en 391* (Paris).

Duval, Y.-M. (1966), 'L'Éloge de Théodose dans la *Cité de Dieu* (V, 26, 1): Sa place, son sens et ses sources', *RechAug* 4: 135–79.

Dzielska, M. (1995), *Hypatia of Alexandria* (Cambridge, Mass., and London and New York).

Earl, D. C. (1961), *The Political Thought of Sallust* (Cambridge).

Edwards, C. (1996), *Writing Rome: Textual Approaches to the City* (Cambridge).

Evans, G. R. (1982), *Augustine on Evil* (Cambridge).

Feeney, D. (1998), *Literature and Religion at Rome: Cultures, Contexts, and Beliefs* (Cambridge).

Figgis, J. N. (1921), *The Political Aspects of S. Augustine's 'City of God'* (London; repr. Gloucester, Mass., 1963).

Fortin, E. L. (1980), 'Augustine and Roman Civil Religion: Some Critical Reflections', *REAug* 26: 238–56.

Fowden, G. (1986), *The Egyptian Hermes: A Historical Approach to the Late Pagan Mind* (Cambridge).

—— (1993), *Empire to Commonwealth: Consequences of Monotheism in Late Antiquity* (Princeton).

Fox, M. (1996), *Roman Historical Myths: The Regal Period in Augustan Literature* (Oxford).

Fredriksen. P. (1988), 'Beyond the Body/Soul Dichotomy: Augustine on Paul against the Manichees and Pelagians', *RechAug* 23: 87–114.

—— (1995), '*Excaecati occulta iustitia dei*: Augustine on Jews and Judaism', *JECS* 3: 299–324.

Frend, W. H. C. (1952), *The Donatist Church: A Movement of Protest in Roman North Africa* (Oxford; 3rd impression 1985, with additional bibliography).

—— (1965), *Martyrdom and Persecution in the Early Church* (Oxford).

Frick, C. (1886), *Die Quellen Augustins im XVIII. Buche seiner Schrift de Civitate Dei* (Progr. Höxter).

Fuchs, H. (1926), *Augustin und der antike Friedensgedanke: Untersuchungen zum neunzehnten Buch der Civitas Dei* (Berlin; repr. Berlin and Zurich, 1965).

Fuhrer, T. (1997), 'Die Platoniker und die *civitas dei* (Buch VIII–X)', in Horn (1997), 87–108.

Fuhrmann, M. (1977) (ed.), *Christianisme et formes littéraires de l'antiquité tardive en Occident* (Entretiens Fondation Hardt, 23; Geneva).

—— (1994), *Rom in der Spätantike: Porträt einer Epoche* (Munich and Zurich).

Gannon, M. A. I. (1956), 'The Active Theory of Sensation in St. Augustine', *The New Scholasticism*, 30: 154–80.

Gaudemet, J. (1990), 'Asylum', *AL* 1/4: 490–3.

Geerlings, W. (1997) '*De civitate dei* XIX als Buch der Augustinischen Friedenslehre', in Horn (1997), 211–33.

Geffcken, J. (1907), *Zwei griechische Apologeten* (Leipzig and Berlin).

Gnilka, C. (1984), ΧΡΗΣΙΣ. *Die Methode der Kirchenväter im Umgang mit der antiken Kultur*, i. *Der Begriff des "rechten Gebrauchs"* (Basle and Stuttgart).

—— (1993), ΧΡΗΣΙΣ. *Die Methode der Kirchenväter im Umgang mit der antiken Kultur*, ii. *Kultur und Conversion* (Basle).

Gorman, M. M. (1981), 'The Maurists' Manuscripts of Four Major Works of Saint Augustine: With Some Remarks on their Editorial Techniques', *RB* 91: 238–79.

—— (1982), 'A Survey of the Oldest Manuscripts of St. Augustine's *De Civitate Dei*', *JTS* NS 33: 398–410.

Grant, R. M. (1957), *The Letter and the Spirit* (London).

—— (1988), *Greek Apologists of the Second Century* (Philadelphia).

Green, W. M. (1949), '*Initium omnis peccati superbia*: Augustine on Pride as the First Sin', *California Publications in Classical Philology*, 13: 407–31.

Griffin, M. T. (1976), *Seneca: A Philosopher in Politics* (Oxford).

Gunnersdorf von Jess, W. (1975), 'Divine Eternity in the Doctrine of St. Augustine', *AugStud* 6: 75–96.

Guy, J. C. (1961), *Unité et structure logique de la 'Cité de Dieu'* (Paris).

Haddock, B. (1988), 'Saint Augustine: *The City of God*', in M. Forsyth and M. Keens-Soper (eds.), *A Guide to the Political Classics: Plato to Rousseau* (Oxford), 69–95.

Hadot, I. (1984), *Arts libéraux et philosophie dans la pensée antique* (Paris).

Hadot, P. (1960*a*), 'Etre, vie, pensée chez Plotin et avant Plotin', in *Les Sources de Plotin* (Entretiens Fondation Hardt, 5; Geneva), 105–57.

—— (1960*b*), 'Citations de Porphyre chez Augustin', *REAug* 6: 205–44.

—— (1968), *Porphyre et Victorinus*, 2 vols. (Paris).

Hadot, P. (1971), *Marius Victorinus: Recherches sur sa vie et ses œuvres* (Paris).

—— (1972), 'Fürstenspiegel', *RAC* 8: 555–632.

—— (1979), 'La Présentation du platonisme par Augustin', in A. M. Ritter (ed.), *Kerygma und Logos: Beiträge zu den geistesgeschichtlichen Beziehungen zwischen Antike und Christentum, Festschrift C. Andresen* (Göttingen), 272–9.

Hagendahl, H. (1958), *Latin Fathers and the Classics: A Study on the Apologists, Jerome and Other Christian Writers* (Göteborg).

—— (1967), *Augustine and the Latin Classics*, 2 vols. (Göteborg).

Hahn, T. (1900), *Tyconius-Studien: Ein Beitrag zur Kirchen- und Dogmengeschichte des vierten Jahrhunderts* (Leipzig; repr. Aalen, 1971).

Hanson, R. P. C. (1959), *Allegory and Event: A Study of the Sources and Significance of Origen's Interpretation of Scripture* (London).

von Harnack, A. (1981), *Militia Christi: The Christian Religion and the Military in the First Three Centuries* (Philadelphia). (Eng. tr. of *Militia Christi: Die christliche Religion und der Soldatenstand in den ersten drei Jahrhunderten* (Tübingen 1905).)

Harrison, C. (1992), *Beauty and Revelation in the Thought of Saint Augustine* (Oxford).

Heather, P. (1991), *Goths and Romans 332–489* (Oxford).

Heck, E. (1966), *Die Bezeugung von Ciceros Schrift De re publica* (Spudasmata, 4; Hildesheim).

—— (1972), *Die dualistischen Zusätze und die Kaiseranreden bei Lactantius* (Heidelberg, 1972).

Henrichs, A. (1982), 'Changing Dionysiac Identities', in B. F. Meyer and E. P. Sanders (eds.), *Self-Definition in the Graeco-Roman World* (London), 137–60, 213–36.

Henry, P. (1934), *Plotin et l'Occident. Firmicus Maternus, Marius Victorinus, Saint Augustin et Macrobe* (Louvain).

Herrin, J. (1987), *The Formation of Christendom* (Princeton).

Herzog, R. (1966), *Die allegorische Dichtkunst des Prudentius* (Zetemata, 42; Munich).

—— (1989) (ed.), *Restauration und Erneuerung: Die lateinische Literatur von 284 bis 374 n. Chr.* (= R. Herzog and P. L. Schmidt (eds.), *Handbuch der lateinischen Literatur der Antike*, 5). Handbuch der Altertumswissenschaft, VIII. 5 (Munich).

Hill, C. E. (1992), *Regnum Caelorum: Patterns of Future Hope in Early Christianity* (Oxford).

Höffe, O. (1997), 'Positivismus plus Moralismus: Zu Augustinus' eschatologischer Staatstheorie', in Horn (1997), 259–87.

Hoffmann, A. (1991), *Augustins Schrift De utilitate credendi*, Diss. (Münster).

Holte, R. (1962), *Béatitude et sagesse: Saint Augustin et le problème de la fin de l'homme dans la philosophie ancienne* (Paris and Worcester, Mass.).

Homes Dudden, F. (1935), *The Life and Times of St. Ambrose*, 2 vols. (Oxford).

van Hooff, A. (1990), *From Autothanasia to Suicide: Self-Killing in Classical Antiquity* (London).

Horn, C. (1994), 'Augustins Philosophie der Zahlen', *REAug* 40: 389–415.

—— (1995), *Augustinus* (Munich).

—— (1997) (ed.), *Augustinus, De civitate dei* (Klassiker Auslegen, 11; Berlin). Horn contributes the introduction (pp. 1– 24), 'Welche Bedeutung hat das Augustinische Cogito? (Buch XI 26)' (pp. 109–29), and 'Geschichtsdarstellung, Geschichtsphilosophie und Geschichtsbewußtsein (Buch XII 10–XVIII)' (pp. 171–93).

Inwood, B. (1985), *Ethics and Human Action in Early Stoicism* (Oxford).

Janson, T. (1964), *Latin Prose Prefaces: Studies in Literary Conventions* (Stockholm).

Jenks, G. C. (1991), *The Origins and Early Development of the Antichrist Myth* (Beihefte zur Zeitschrift für die neutestamentliche Wissenschaft, 59; Berlin).

Jocelyn, H. D. (1982), 'Varro's *Antiquitates Rerum Diuinarum* and Religious Affairs in the Late Roman Republic', *Bulletin of the John Rylands University Library of Manchester*, 65/1: 148–205.

Jones, A. H. M. (1948), *Constantine and the Conversion of Europe* (London).

—— (1964), *The Later Roman Empire, 284–602: A Social, Economic and Administrative Survey*, 3 vols. (Oxford).

—— (1966), *The Decline of the Ancient World* (London and New York).

Kamlah, W. (1951), *Christentum und Geschichtlichkeit. Untersuchungen zur Entstehung des Christentums und zu Augustins 'Bürgerschaft Gottes'* (2nd edn. Stuttgart and Cologne).

Kannengiesser, C., and Bright, P. (1989) (eds.), *A Conflict of Christian Hermeneutics in Roman Africa: Tyconius and Augustine*, Center for Hermeneutical Studies: Colloquy of 16 October 1988 (Berkeley).

Kaster, R. (1988), *Guardians of Language: The Grammarian and Society in Late Antiquity* (Berkeley and Los Angeles).

Kelly, J. N. D. (1972), *Early Christian Creeds* (3rd edn.; London).

—— (1975), *Jerome: His Life, Writings, and Controversies* (London).

—— (1977), *Early Christian Doctrines* (5th edn.; London).

—— (1995), *Golden Mouth: The Story of John Chrysostom—Ascetic, Preacher, Bishop* (London).

Kenny, A. (1979), *The God of the Philosophers* (Oxford).

Kirwan, C. (1989), *Augustine* (London and New York).

Klingner, F. (1928), 'Über die Entstehung der Historien Sallusts', *Hermes*, 63: 165–92.

Koester, H. (1982), *History and Literature of Early Christianity* (New York and Berlin). (Eng. tr. of *Einführung in das Neue Testament*, chs. 7–12 (Berlin and New York, 1980).

Kötting, B. and Geerlings, W. (1986), 'Aetas', *AL* 1/1–2: 150–8.

Konstan, D. (1997), *Friendship in the Classical World* (Cambridge).

Kraus, C. S., and Woodman, A. J. (1997), *Latin Historians* (*Greece &; Rome*: New Surveys in the Classics, 27; Oxford).

Krautheimer, R. (1980), *Rome: Profile of a City 312–1308* (Princeton).

Kretzmann, N., Kenny, A., and Pinborg, J. (1982) (eds.), *The Cambridge History of Later Medieval Philosophy* (Cambridge).

La Bonnardière, A.-M. (1960–75), *Biblia Augustiniana*, 7 vols. (Paris).

—— (1965), *Recherches de chronologie augustinienne* (Paris).

—— (1986) (ed.), *Saint Augustin et la Bible* (= Bible de tous les temps, 3) (Paris).

Labhardt, A. (1960), 'Curiositas: Notes sur l'histoire d'un mot et d'une notion', *Museum Helveticum*, 17: 206–24.

de Laborde, A. (1909), *Les Manuscrits à peintures de la Cité de Dieu de saint Augustin*, 3 vols. (Paris).

Ladner, G. B. (1959), *The Idea of Reform: Its Impact on Christian Thought and Action in the Age of the Fathers* (Cambridge, Mass.).

Lambot, C. (1939), 'Lettre inédite de s. Augustin relative au "De Civitate Dei"', *RB* 51: 109–21.

Lamirande, E. (1992–4), 'Civitas dei', *AL* 1/5–6 and 7–8: 958–69.

Landes, P. F. (1982), 'Tyconius and the End of the World', *REAug* 28: 59–75.

Lane Fox, R. (1986), *Pagans and Christians* (London).

—— (1991), *The Unauthorized Version: Truth and Fiction in the Bible* (London).

Latte, K. (1960), *Römische Religionsgeschichte*, Handbuch der Altertumswissenschaft, V. 4 (Munich).

Laufs, J. (1973), *Der Friedensgedanke bei Augustinus. Untersuchungen zum XIX. Buch des Werkes De Civitate Dei* (Wiesbaden).

Lauras, A., and Rondet, H. (1953), 'Le Thème des deux cités dans l'œuvre de saint Augustin', in H. Rondet, M. Le Landais, A. Lauras, and C. Couturier (eds.), *Études augustiniennes* (Paris), 97–160.

Lausberg, M. (1970), *Untersuchungen zu Senecas Fragmenten* (Untersuchungen zur antiken Literatur und Geschichte, 7; Berlin).

Lepelley, C. (1979), *Les Cités de l'Afrique romaine au Bas-Empire*, i. *La Permanence d'une civilisation municipale* (Paris).

—— (1981). *Les Cités de l'Afrique romaine au Bas-Empire*, ii. *Notices d'histoire municipale* (Paris).

—— (1992), 'Civis, civitas', *AL* 1/5–6: 942–57.

Lettieri, G. (1988), *Il senso della storia in Agostino d'Ippona: Il 'saeculum' e la gloria nel 'De Civitate Dei'* (Rome).

Lewy, H. (1978), *Chaldaean Oracles and Theurgy: Mysticism, Magic and Platonism in the Later Roman Empire*, 2nd edn., ed. M. Tardieu (Paris).

Lieberg, G. (1973), 'Die "theologia tripertita" in Forschung und Bezeugung', *ANRW* 1. 4: 63–115.

Liebeschuetz, J. H. W. G. (1979), *Continuity and Change in Roman Religion* (Oxford).

—— (1990), *Barbarians and Bishops: Army, Church, and State in the Age of Arcadius and Chrysostom* (Oxford).

Lienhart, J. (1990), 'Friendship in Paulinus of Nola and Augustine', *Collectanea Augustiniana: Mélanges T. J. van Bavel* (Louvain), 279–96.

Lieu, S. N. C. (1985), *Manichaeism in the Later Roman Empire and Medieval China* (Manchester).

Litchfield, H. W. (1914), 'National *exempla virtutis* in Roman Literature', *Harvard Studies in Classical Philology*, 25: 1–71.

Lizzi, R. (1990), 'Ambrose's Contemporaries and the Christianisation of Northern Italy', *Journal of Roman Studies*, 80: 156–73.

Loi, V. (1970), *Lattanzio nella storia del linguaggio e del pensiero teologico pre-niceno* (Zurich).

—— (1977), 'La polemica antiromana nelle opere di sant'Agostino', *Augustinianum*, 17: 307–31.

Long, A. A. (1974), *Hellenistic Philosophy: Stoics, Epicureans, Sceptics* (London).

de Lubac, H. (1950), *Histoire et esprit: L'Intelligence de l'Écriture chez Origène* (Paris).

—— (1959–64), *Exégèse médiévale: Les Quatre Sens de l'Écriture*, i–iv (Paris).

MacCormack, S. (1976), 'Latin Prose Panegyrics: Tradition and Discontinuity in the Later Roman Empire', *REAug* 22: 29–77.

—— (1981), *Art and Ceremony in Late Antiquity* (Berkeley, Los Angeles, and London).

Macleod, C. (1971), 'Allegory and Mysticism in Origen and Gregory of Nyssa', *JTS* NS 22: 362–79 (repr. in id., *Collected Essays* (Oxford, 1983), 309–26, with addenda, 345–6).

McLynn, N. (1994), *Ambrose of Milan: Church and Court in a Christian Capital* (Berkeley and Los Angeles).

MacNamara, M. A. (1964), *Friends and Friendship for St. Augustine* (Staten Island, NY).

Macqueen, D. J. (1973), '*Contemptus Dei*: St Augustine on the Disorder of Pride in Society, and its Remedies', *RechAug* 9: 227–93.

—— (1977), 'Augustine on *Superbia*: The Historical Background and Sources of his Doctrine', *Mélanges de science religieuse*, 34: 193–211.

Madec, G. (1986), 'Angelus', *AL* 1/1–2: 303–15.

—— (1991), 'Le *De civitate Dei* comme *De vera religione*', in *Interiorità e intenzionalità nel 'De civitate Dei' di Sant'Agostino*. Atti del III°

Seminario Internazionale del Centro di Studi Agostiniani di Perugia. Studia Ephemeridis «Augustinianum», 35 (Rome), 7–33.

—— (1996), *Introduction aux 'Révisions' et à la lecture des œuvres de saint Augustin* (Paris).

Maier, F. G. (1955), *Augustin und das antike Rom* (Tübinger Beiträge zur Altertumswissenschaft, 39; Stuttgart).

Mandouze, A. (1958), 'Saint Augustin et la religion romaine', *RechAug* 1: 187–223.

—— (1982), *Prosopographie chrétienne du Bas-Empire* i. *Prosopographie de l'Afrique chrétienne (303–533)* (Paris).

Mansfeld, J. (1988), 'Philosophy in the Service of Scripture: Philo's Exegetical Strategies', in J. M. Dillon and A. A. Long (eds.), *The Question of 'Eclecticism': Studies in Later Greek Philosophy* (Berkeley, Los Angeles, and London), 70–102.

Markus, R. A. (1957), 'St. Augustine on Signs', *Phronesis*, 2: 60–83 = Markus (1972), 61–91 = Markus (1996), 71–104.

—— (1967), 'Marius Victorinus and Augustine', in Armstrong (1967), 327–419.

—— (1970), *Saeculum: History and Society in the Theology of St Augustine* (Cambridge; repr. with new introduction, Cambridge, 1988).

—— (1972) (ed.), *Augustine: A Collection of Critical Essays* (New York).

—— (1974), 'Paganism, Christianity and the Latin Classics in the Fourth Century', in J. W. Binns (ed.), *Latin Literature of the Fourth Century* (London), 1–21.

—— (1983), 'Saint Augustine's Views on the "Just War"', in W. J. Shells (ed.), *The Church and War* (Studies in Church History, 20; Oxford), 1–13 (repr. in Markus (1994), no. V).

—— (1990a), *The End of Ancient Christianity* (Cambridge).

—— (1990b), '*De Civitate Dei*: Pride and the Common Good', in J. C. Schnaubelt and F. van Fleteren (eds.), *Collectanea Augustiniana: Augustine, 'Second Founder of the Faith'* (New York, 245–59; repr. in Markus (1994), no. III).

—— (1994), *Sacred and Secular: Studies on Augustine and Latin Christianity* (Variorum Collected Studies Series, 465; Aldershot).

—— (1996), *Signs and Meanings: World and Text in Ancient Christianity* (Liverpool).

Marrou, H.-I. (1950), *L'Ambivalence du temps de l'histoire chez saint Augustin* (Montreal and Paris).

—— (1958), *Saint Augustin et la fin de la culture antique* (4th edn.; Paris).

—— (1976), *Patristique et humanisme: Mélanges* (Paris).

Martin, J. (1974), *Antike Rhetorik: Technik und Methode*, Handbuch der Altertumswissenschaft, II. 3 (Munich).

Martin, René (1970), 'Le Sens de l'expression "asinus aureus" et la signification du roman apuléien', *Revue des études latines*, 48: 332–54.

Martin, Rex (1972), 'The Two Cities in Augustine's Political Philosophy', *Journal of the History of Ideas*, 33: 195–216.

Mastandrea, P. (1979), *Un neoplatonico latino: Cornelio Labeone, Testimonianze e frammenti*, EPRO 77 (Leiden).

Matthews, G. (1967), 'The Inner Man', *American Philosophical Quarterly*, 4: 1–7 = Markus (1972), 176–90.

—— (1972), '*Si fallor, sum*', in Markus (1972), 154–67.

—— (1992), *Thought's Ego in Augustine and Descartes* (Ithaca, NY, and London).

Matthews, J. (1975), *Western Aristocracies and Imperial Court* A.D. 364–425 (Oxford).

—— (1989), *The Roman Empire of Ammianus* (London).

Mayer, C. P. (1969), *Die Zeichen in der geistigen Entwicklung und in der Theologie des jungen Augustins* (Cassiciacum, 24; Würzburg).

—— (1974), *Die Zeichen in der geistigen Entwicklung und in der Theologie Augustins*, ii. *Die antimanichäische Epoche* (Cassiciacum, 24/2; Würzburg).

—— (1986a), 'Abraham', *AL* 1/1–2: 10–33.

—— (1986b), 'Allegoria', *AL* 1/1–2: 233–9.

van der Meer, F. (1961), *Augustine the Bishop: The Life and Work of a Father of the Church* (London). (Eng. tr. of *Augustinus de zielzorger: Een studie over de praktijk van een kerkvader* (Utrecht and Brussels, 1947).)

Meijering, E. P. (1979), *Augustin über Schöpfung, Ewigkeit und Zeit: Das elfte Buch der Bekenntnisse* (Philosophia Patrum, 4; Leiden).

Mellor, R. (1981), 'The Goddess Roma', *ANRW* ii. 17. 2: 950–1030.

Menn, S. (1998), *Descartes and Augustine* (Cambridge).

Meredith, A. (1980), 'Porphyry and Julian against the Christians', *ANRW* ii. 23. 2: 1119–49.

Miles, M. R. (1979), *Augustine on the Body* (Missoula, Mont.).

—— (1990), 'The Body and Human Values in Augustine of Hippo', in H. Meynell (ed.), *Grace, Politics and Desire: Essays on Augustine* (Calgary), 55–67.

Moine, N. (1975), 'Augustin et Apulée sur la magie des femmes d'auberge', *Latomus*, 34: 350–61.

Moles, J. L. (1996), 'Cynics', *OCD*[3]: 418–19.

Momigliano, A. D. (1963) (ed.), *The Conflict between Paganism and Christianity in the Fourth Century* (Oxford).

—— (1975), *Alien Wisdom: The Limits of Hellenization* (Cambridge).

Mommsen, T. E. (1959), *Medieval and Renaissance Studies* (Ithaca, NY).

Moreau, M. (1973), 'Le Dossier Marcellinus dans la correspondance de saint Augustin', *RechAug* 9: 3–181.

Mosshammer, A. A. (1979), *The Chronicle of Eusebius and Greek Chrono-graphic Tradition* (Lewisburg, Pa.).

Mozley, J. B. (1855), *A Treatise on the Augustinian Doctrine of Predestination* (London).

Müller, C. (1993), *Geschichtsbewußtsein bei Augustinus* (Cassiciacum, 39/2; Würzburg).

Nock, A. D. (1933), *Conversion: The Old and the New in Religion from Alexander the Great to Augustine of Hippo* (Oxford).

Nussbaum, M. C. (1994), *The Therapy of Desire: Theory and Practice in Hellenstic Ethics* (Princeton).

O'Brien, D. (1985), '"Pondus meum amor meus" (*Conf.* xiii. 9. 10): saint Augustin et Jamblique', *StudPatr* 16 (= TU 129): 524–7.

O'Connell, R. J. (1963), '*Ennead* VI. 4 and 5 in the Works of Saint Augustine', *REAug* 9: 1–39.

—— (1968), *St. Augustine's Early Theory of Man*, A.D. *386–391* (Cambridge, Mass.).

—— (1984), 'St. Augustine's Criticism of Origen in the *Ad Orosium*', *REAug* 30: 84–99.

—— (1987), *The Origin of the Soul in St. Augustine's Later Works* (New York).

O'Connor, W. (1985), 'The "uti/frui" Distinction in Augustine's Ethics', *Augustinian Studies*, 14: 45–62.

O'Daly, G. (1986), 'Aeternitas', *AL* 1/1–2: 159–64.

—— (1987), *Augustine's Philosophy of Mind* (London and Berkeley).

—— (1989*a*), 'Predestination and Freedom in Augustine's Ethics', in G. Vesey (ed.), *The Philosophy in Christianity* (Cambridge), 85–97.

—— (1989*b*), 'Hierarchie', *RAC* 15: 41–73.

—— (1991*a*), 'Hierarchies in Augustine's Thought', in F. X. Martin and J. A. Richmond (eds.), *From Augustine to Eriugena: Essays on Neoplatonism and Christianity in Honor of John O'Meara* (Washington), 143–54.

—— (1991*b*), *The Poetry of Boethius* (London and Chapel Hill, NC).

—— (1994*a*), 'Civitate dei (De-)', *AL* 1: 969–1010.

—— (1994*b*), 'Augustine's Critique of Varro on Roman Religion', in A. H. Sommerstein (ed.), *Religion and Superstition in Latin Literature* (Nottingham Classical Literature Studies, 3; Bari), 65–75 (with response by R. A. Markus, ibid. 77–80). The volume was published in 1996.

O'Donnell, J. J. (1979), 'The Inspiration for Augustine's *De Civitate Dei*', *AugStud* 10: 75–9.

—— (1980), 'Augustine's Classical Readings', *RechAug* 15: 144–75.

—— (1985), *Augustine* (Boston).

O'Donovan, O. (1980), *The Problem of Self-Love in St. Augustine* (New Haven and London).

—— (1987), 'Augustine's *City of God* XIX and Western Political Thought', *Dionysius*, 11: 89–110.

Ogilvie, R. M. (1978), *The Library of Lactantius* (Oxford).

Ohlig, K.-H. (1992), 'Canon scripturarum', *AL* 1/5–6: 713–24.

O'Meara, D. J. (1989), *Pythagoras Revisited: Mathematics and Philosophy in Late Antiquity* (Oxford).

O'Meara, J. J. (1954), *The Young Augustine: The Growth of St. Augustine's Mind up to his Conversion* (London).

—— (1959), *Porphyry's Philosophy from Oracles in Augustine* (Paris).

—— (1961), *Charter of Christendom: The Significance of the City of God* (New York).

—— (1969), *Porphyry's Philosophy from Oracles in Eusebius' Praeparatio Evangelica and Augustine's Dialogues of Cassiciacum* (Paris).

—— (1980), *The Creation of Man in St. Augustine's De Genesi ad Litteram* (Villanova, Pa.).

van Oort, J. (1991), *Jerusalem and Babylon: A Study into Augustine's City of God and the Sources of his Doctrine of the Two Cities* (Leiden).

—— (1997), '*Civitas dei—terrena civitas*: The Concept of the Two Antithetical Cities and its Sources (Books XI–XIV)', in Horn (1997), 157–69.

Opelt, I. (1980), *Die Polemik in der christlichen lateinischen Literatur von Tertullian bis Augustin* (Heidelberg).

Orlandi, T. (1965), 'Origine e composizione del I libro del *De civitate Dei* di Agostino', *Studi classici e orientali*, 14: 120–33.

Osborn, E. (1997), *Tertullian, First Theologian of the West* (Cambridge).

Osborne, C. (1994), *Eros Unveiled: Plato and the God of Love* (Oxford).

Pagels, E. (1988), *Adam, Eve and the Serpent* (London).

Palanque, J.-R. (1952), 'St. Jerome and the Barbarians', in F. X. Murphy (ed.), *A Monument to Saint Jerome* (New York), 173–99.

Palmer, A. M. (1989), *Prudentius on the Martyrs* (Oxford).

Paschoud, F. (1967), *Roma aeterna: Études sur le patriotisme romain dans l'Occident à l'époque des grandes invasions* (Rome).

—— (1983), 'Le Rôle du providentialisme dans le conflit de 384 sur l'autel de la Victoire', *Museum Helveticum*, 40: 197–206.

Paul, G. M. (1984), *A Historical Commentary on Sallust's Bellum Iugurthinum* (Liverpool).

Pelland, G. (1972), *Cinq études d'Augustin sur le début de la Genèse* (Recherches, 8; Tournai and Montreal).

Pembroke, S. G. (1971), 'Oikeiōsis', in A. A. Long (ed.), *Problems in Stoicism* (London), 114–49 (repr. London and Atlantic Highlands, NJ, 1996).

Pépin, J. (1958), *Mythe et allégorie* (Paris).

Perler, O. and Maier, J.-L. (1969), *Les Voyages de saint Augustin* (Paris).

Peterson, E. (1935), *Der Monotheismus als politisches Problem* (Leipzig) (repr. in id., *Theologische Traktate* (Munich, 1951), 45–147).

Petitmengin, P. (1990), 'La Division en chapitres de la *Cité de Dieu* de saint Augustin', in H.-J. Martin and J. Vezin (eds.), *Mise en page et mise en texte du livre manuscrit* (Paris), 133–6.

—— (1994), 'Codex', *AL* 1/7–8: 1022–37.

Pfeiffer, R. (1968), *History of Classical Scholarship from the Beginnings to the End of the Hellenistic Age* (Oxford).

—— (1976), *History of Classical Scholarship from 1300 to 1850* (Oxford).

Piccolomini, R. (1971), 'Platone nel libro VIII del "De Civitate Dei"', *Augustinianum*, 11: 233–61.

Pietri, C. (1976), *Roma Christiana: Recherches sur l'église de Rome, son organisation, sa politique, son idéologie de Miltiade à Sixte III (311–440)*, 2 vols. (BEFAR 224; Rome).

Pingree, D. (1990), 'Astrologia, astronomia', *AL* 1/4: 482–90.

Piret, P. (1991), *La Destinée de l'homme: La Cité de Dieu. Un commentaire du 'De Civitate Dei' d'Augustin* (Brussels).

Plumpe, J. C. (1951), 'Mors secunda', in *Mélanges J. de Ghellinck, SJ*, i (Gembloux), 387–403.

Pollmann, K. (1996), *Doctrina Christiana: Untersuchungen zu den Anfängen der christlichen Hermeneutik unter besonderer Berücksichtigung von Augustinus, De doctrina christiana* (Paradosis, 41; Freiburg, Switzerland).

—— (1997), 'Augustins Transformation der traditionellen römischen Staats- und Geschichtsauffassung (Buch I-V)', in Horn (1997), 25–40.

Pontet, M. (1944), *L'Exégèse de saint Augustin prédicateur* (Paris).

Poque, S. (1984), *Le Langage symbolique dans la prédication de saint Augustin*, 2 vols. (Paris).

Pöschl, V. (1993), 'Lieder als Modelle für göttliche Ordnung bei Augustin', in G. W. Most, H. Petersmann, and A. M. Ritter (eds.), *Philanthropia kai Eusebeia. Festschrift für Albrecht Dihle zum 70. Geburtstag* (Göttingen), 355–62.

Potter, D. S. (1994), *Prophets and Emperors: Human and Divine Authority from Augustus to Theodosius* (Cambridge, Mass., and London).

Powell, J. G. F. (1995) (ed.), *Cicero the Philosopher* (Oxford).

Price, S. R. F. (1984), *Rituals and Power: The Roman Imperial Cult in Asia Minor* (Cambridge).

Ramsay, B. (1997), *Ambrose* (London).

Rand, E. K. (1943), *The Building of Eternal Rome* (Cambridge, Mass.).

Raveaux, T. (1986), 'Adversarium legis et prophetarum (Contra-)', *AL* 1/1–2: 107–12.

Rawson, E. (1985), *Intellectual Life in the Late Roman Republic* (London).

Rebillard, É. (1994), *In Hora Mortis: Évolution de la pastorale chrétienne de la mort aux IVe et Ve siècles dans l'Occident latin* (BEFAR 283; Rome).

Regen, F. (1983), 'Zu Augustins Darstellung des Platonismus am Anfang des

8. Buches der Civitas Dei', in *Platonismus und Christentum: Festschrift für H. Dörrie, JbAC* Suppl. 10, 208–27.

Rief, J. (1962), *Der Ordobegriff des jungen Augustinus* (Abhandlungen zur Moraltheologie, 2; Paderborn).

Ries, J. (1961–4), 'Le Bible chez saint Augustin et chez les manichéens', *REAug* 7: 231–43, 9: 201–15, 10: 309–29.

Rist, J. M. (1969), 'Augustine on Free Will and Predestination', *JTS* NS 20: 420–47 = Markus (1972),: 218–52.

—— (1994), *Augustine: Ancient Thought Baptized* (Cambridge).

Rives, J. B. (1995), *Religion and Authority in Roman Carthage from Augustus to Constantine* (Oxford).

Roberts, C. H., and Skeat, T. C. (1983), *The Birth of the Codex* (London).

Roberts, M. (1993), *Poetry and the Cult of the Martyrs: The Liber Peristephanon of Prudentius* (Ann Arbor).

Rondet, H. (1955), 'Le Symbolisme de la mer chez saint Augustin', in *AM* ii. 691–711.

Rottmanner, O. (1908), 'Der Augustinismus', in R. Jud (ed.), *Geistesfrüchte aus der Klosterzelle: Gesammelte Aufsätze* (Munich), 11–32.

Russell, D. A. (1979), 'De Imitatione', in D. West and A. J. Woodman (eds.), *Creative Imagination and Latin Literature* (Cambridge), 1–16.

de Sainte-Croix, G. E. M. (1954), 'Aspects of the "Great" Persecution', *Harvard Theological Review*, 47: 75–109.

—— (1963), 'Why Were the Early Christians Persecuted?', *Past and Present*, 26: 6–38.

Salin, E. (1926), *Civitas Dei* (Tübingen).

Samuel, A. E. (1972), *Greek and Roman Chronology: Calendars and Years in Classical Antiquity*, Handbuch der Altertumswissenschaft, I. 7 (Munich).

Sanders, E. P. (1991), *Paul* (Oxford).

Scanlon, T. F. (1987), *Spes Frustrata. A Reading of Sallust* (Heidelberg).

Schäublin, C. (1977), 'Homerum ex Homero', *Museum Helveticum*, 34: 221–7.

Schelkle, K. H. (1939), *Virgil in der Deutung Augustins* (Stuttgart and Berlin).

Schindler, A. (1987), 'Augustin und die römischen Historiker', in den Boeft and van Oort (1987), 153–68.

Schmidt, E. A. (1985), *Zeit und Geschichte bei Augustin*, Sitzungsberichte der Heidelberger Akademie der Wissenschaften, Philosophisch-historische Klasse, 1985/3 (Heidelberg).

Schofield, M. (1991), *The Stoic Idea of the City* (Cambridge).

—— (1995), 'Cicero's Definition of *Res Publica*', in Powell (1995), 63–83.

Scholz, H. (1911), *Glaube und Unglaube in der Weltgeschichte: Ein Kommentar zu Augustins De Civitate Dei* (Leipzig).

Scott, A. B. (1991), *Origen and the Life of the Stars: A History of an Idea* (Oxford).

Scourfield, J. H. D. (1992), *Consoling Heliodorus: A Commentary on Jerome, Letter 60* (Oxford).

Sedley, D. N. (1997), 'Plato's *Auctoritas* and the Rebirth of the Commentary Tradition', in J. Barnes and M. Griffin (eds.), *Philosophia Togata II: Plato and Aristotle at Rome* (Oxford), 110–29.

Shanzer, D. (1989), 'The Date and Composition of Prudentius's *Contra Orationem Symmachi Libri*', *Rivista di Filologia*, 117: 442–62.

—— (1991), 'Licentius' Verse Epistle to Augustine', *REAug* 37: 110–43.

Sharples, R. W. (1995), 'Counting Plato's Principles', in L. Ayres (ed.), *The Passionate Intellect: Essays on the Transformation of Classical Traditions presented to I. G. Kidd* (Rutgers University Studies in Classical Humanities, 7; New Brunswick and London), 67–82.

—— (1996), *Stoics, Epicureans and Sceptics: An Introduction to Hellenistic Philosophy* (London and New York).

Shaw, B. D. (1987), 'The Family in Late Antiquity: The Experience of Augustine', *Past and Present*, 115: 3–51.

Shaw, G. (1985), 'Theurgy: Rituals of Unification in the Neoplatonism of Iamblichus', *Traditio*, 41: 1–28.

Sherwin-White, A. N. (1973), *The Roman Citizenship* (2nd edn.; Oxford).

Simmons, M. B. (1995), *Arnobius of Sicca: Religious Conflict and Competition in the Age of Diocletian* (Oxford).

Simon, E. (1988), *Eirene und Pax: Friedensgöttinen in der Antike* (Wiesbaden).

Simonetti, M. (1994), *Biblical Interpretation in the Early Church: An Historical Introduction to Patristic Exegesis* (Edinburgh). (Eng. tr. of *Profilo storico dell'esegesi patristica* (Rome, 1981).)

Smith, A. (1974), *Porphyry's Place in the Neoplatonic Tradition* (The Hague).

Smith, R. R. R. (1997), 'The Public Image of Licinius I: Portrait Sculpture and Imperial Ideology in the Early Fourth Century', *Journal of Roman Studies*, 87: 170–202, with plates 1–12.

Solignac, A. (1958), 'Doxographies et manuels dans la formation philosophique de saint Augustin', *RechAug* 1: 113–48.

Sorabji, R. (1983), *Time, Creation and the Continuum: Theories in Antiquity and the Early Middle Ages* (London).

—— (1993), *Animal Minds and Human Morals: The Origins of the Western Debate* (London).

Stark, R. (1967), 'Res publica', in H. Oppermann (ed.), *Römische Wertbegriffe* (Wege der Forschung, 34; Darmstadt), 42–110, Diss. (Göttingen, 1937).

Stead, C. (1994), *Philosophy in Christian Antiquity* (Cambridge).

Steinhauser, K. B. (1984), '*Recapitulatio* in Tyconius and Augustine', *Augustinian Studies*, 4: 1–5.

—— (1987), *The Apocalypse Commentary of Tyconius: A History of his*

Reception and Influence (European University Studies; Frankfurt and Berne).

Stock, B. (1996), *Augustine the Reader: Meditation, Self-Knowledge, and the Ethics of Interpretation* (Cambridge, Mass., and London).

Stoclet, A. J. (1984), 'Le 'De civitate Dei' de saint Augustin: Sa diffusion avant 900 d'après les caractères externes des manuscrits antérieurs à cette date et les catalogues contemporains', *RechAug* 19: 185–209.

Straub, J. (1954), 'Augustins Sorge um die regeneratio imperii: Das Imperium Romanum als *civitas terrena*', *Historisches Jahrbuch*, 73: 36–60.

Studer, B. (1991), 'Zum Aufbau von Augustins *De Civitate dei*', *Augustiniana*, 41: 937–51.

—— (1996), 'La cognitio historialis di Porfirio nel *De civitate Dei* di Agostino', in Cavalcanti (1996), 51–65.

Suerbaum, W. (1977), *Vom antiken zum frühmittelalterlichen Staatsbegriff. Über Verwendung und Bedeutung von res publica, regnum, imperium und status von Cicero bis Jordanis* (3rd edn.; Münster).

Swift, L. J. (1973), 'Augustine on War and Killing: Another View', *Harvard Theological Review*, 66: 369–83.

Tarver, T. (1994), 'Varro, Caesar, and the Roman Calendar: A Study in Late Republican Religion', in A. H. Sommerstein (ed.), *Religion and Superstition in Latin Literature* (Nottingham Classical Literature Studies, 3; Bari), 39–57 (with response by J. G. F. Powell, ibid. 59–64). The volume was published in 1996.

—— (1997), 'Varro and the Antiquarianism of Philosophy', in J. Barnes and M. Griffin (eds.), *Philosophia Togata II: Plato and Aristotle at Rome* (Oxford), 130–64.

TeSelle, E. (1970), *Augustine the Theologian* (London).

—— (1974a), *Augustine's Strategy as an Apologist* (Villanova, Pa.).

—— (1974b), 'Porphyry and Augustine', *Augustinian Studies*, 5: 113–47.

Testard, M. (1955), 'Note sur *De civitate Dei*, XXII. xxiv', in *AM* i. 193–200.

—— (1958), *Saint Augustin et Cicéron*, 2 vols. (Paris).

—— (1992), 'Cicero', *AL* 1/5–6: 913–30.

Theiler, W. (1966), *Forschungen zum Neuplatonismus* (Berlin).

—— (1970), *Untersuchungen zur antiken Literatur* (Berlin).

—— (1982), *Poseidonios: Die Fragmente*, 2 vols. (Texte und Kommentare, 10, 1–2; Berlin and New York).

Thraede, K. (1977), 'Das antike Rom in Augustins De civitate Dei: Recht und Grenzen eines verjährten Themas', *JbAC* 20: 90–148.

—— (1983), 'Gottesstaat (Civitas Dei)', *RAC* 12: 58–81.

Toutain, J. (1917–18), *Les Cultes païens dans l'Empire romain*, i. 3 (Paris; repr. Rome, 1967).

Trapé, A. (1986), *Initiation aux Pères de l'Église*, iv. (Paris).

Trevett, C. (1996), *Montanism: Gender, Authority and the New Prophecy* (Cambridge).

Troeltsch, E. (1915), *Augustin, die christliche Antike und das Mittelalter: Im Anschluß an die Schrift "De Civitate Dei"* (Munich and Berlin; repr. Aalen, 1963).

Trout, D. (1994), 'Re-textualising Lucretia: Cultural Subversion in the *City of God*', *JECS* 2: 53–70.

Versfeld, M. (1958), *A Guide to the City of God* (New York).

Warde Fowler, W. (1911), *The Religious Experience of the Roman People: From the Earliest Times to the Age of Augustus*, Gifford Lectures, 1909–10 (London).

Waszink, J. H. (1948), 'Varro, Livy and Tertullian on the History of Roman Dramatic Art', *Vigiliae Christianae*, 2: 224–42.

—— (1972), 'Calcidius' (*RAC*-Nachtrag), *JbAC* 15: 236–44.

—— (1976), 'Varrone nella letteratura cristiana dei primi secoli', *Atti del Congresso internazionale di studi Varroniani* (Rieti), 209–23 (repr. in id., *Opuscula Selecta* (Leiden, 1979), 386–400).

Watson, G. (1988), 'St. Augustine and the Inner Man: The Philosophical Background', *Irish Theological Quarterly*, 54: 81–92.

Weismann, W. (1972), *Kirche und Schauspiele: Die Schauspiele im Urteil der lateinischen Kirchenväter unter besonderer Berücksichtigung von Augustin* (Cassiciacum, 27; Würzburg).

Wermelinger, O. (1984), 'Le Canon des latins au temps de Jérôme et d'Augustin', in J.-D. Kaestli and O. Wermelinger (eds.), *Le Canon de l'Ancien Testament: sa formation et son histoire* (Geneva), 153–210.

—— (1986), 'Abortus', *AL* 1/1–2: 6–10.

Wetzel, J. (1992), *Augustine and the Limits of Virtue* (Cambridge).

Wiesen, D. S. (1964), *Jerome as a Satirist: A Study in Christian Latin Thought and Letters* (Ithaca).

Wilken, R. L. (1979), 'Pagan Criticism of Christianity: Greek Religion and Christian Faith', in W. R. Schoedel and R. L. Wilken (eds.), *Early Christian Literature and the Classical Intellectual Tradition* (Théologie Historique, 53; Paris), 117–34.

—— (1980), 'The Jews and Christian Apologetics after Theodosius I *Cunctos Populos*', *Harvard Theological Review*, 73: 451–71.

—— (1983), *John Chrysostom and the Jews: Rhetoric and Reality in the Late 4th Century* (Berkeley and Los Angeles).

—— (1984), *The Christians as the Romans Saw Them* (New Haven and London).

Willis, G. G. (1950), *Saint Augustine and the Donatist Controversy* (London).

Wilmart, A. (1931), 'La Tradition des grands ouvrages de saint Augustin', *MA* 2: 257–315.

Wiseman, T. P. (1995), *Remus: A Roman Myth* (Cambridge).

Wissowa, G. (1904), *Gesammelte Abhandlungen zur römischen Religions- und Stadtsgeschichte* (Munich).

—— (1912), *Religion und Kultus der Römer*, 2nd edn., Handbuch der klassischen Altertumswissenschaft IV. 5 (Munich, repr. 1971).

Wlosok, A. (1960), *Laktanz und die philosophische Gnosis* (Heidelberg).

Wolfson, H. A. (1970), *The Philosophy of the Church Fathers*, i. *Faith, Trinity, Incarnation* (3rd edn.; Cambridge, Mass.).

Woodman, A. J. (1988), *Rhetoric in Classical Historiography* (London and Sydney).

Young, F. M. (1997), *Biblical Exegesis and the Formation of Christian Culture* (Cambridge).

Zarb, S. M. (1934), *Chronologia Operum S. Augustini secundum ordinem Retractationum digesta* (Rome).

Zwierlein, O. (1978), 'Der Fall Roms im Spiegel der Kirchenväter', *Zeitschrift für Papyrologie und Epigraphik*, 32: 45–80.

F. Addenda to Bibliography

The following were published, or came to my attention, too late to be taken into account in this book:

Augustine: The City of God Against the Pagans, tr. R. W. Dyson (Cambridge Texts in the History of Political Thought; Cambridge, 1998).

Beard, M., North, J., and Price, S. R. F., *Religions of Rome*, 2 vols. (Cambridge, 1998).

Cameron, Averil and Garnsey, P. (eds.), *The Cambridge Ancient History*, xiii: *The Late Empire*, AD 337–425 (Cambridge, 1997).

Dunn, J. and Harris, I. (eds.), *Augustine*, 2 vols. (Great Political Thinkers, 2; Chelrenham and Lynne, 1997).

Elsner, J., *Imperial Rome and Christian Triumph: The Art of the Roman Empire* AD 100–450 (Oxford History of Art; Oxford, 1998).

Inglebert, H., *Les Romains chrétiens face à l'histoire de Rome: Histoire, christianisme et romanités en Occident dans l'antiquité tardive* (Paris, 1996).

MacCormack, S., *The Shadows of Poetry: Vergil in the Mind of Augustine* (Berkeley, Los Angeles, and London, 1998).

Index of Selected Passages Cited

This index includes references to all passages quoted and discussed, except where they are discussed in their proper place in Chapters 6–10. It generally omits passages that are merely cited as examples or parallels in the text and footnotes. For references to citations of Porphyry and Varro see the General Index.

General Index

This index is selective, especially in its inclusion of material from the footnotes and references to proper names. It omits names of modern scholars.